Worldwide Praise for the Erotica of John Patrick!

"This writing is what being brave is all about. It brings up the kinds of things that are usually kept so private that you think you're the only one who experiences them."

"Angel: The Complete Quintet"
International Edition Chosen Book of the Month
by *The Gay Times*, London:
"John Patrick is a prolific and prize-winning novelist whose ability to crank out wide-ranging homoerotica is as deft and sure as that of a dairy maid churning butter.
"In 'Angel' there is enough graphic sex of just about every description to perk up even the most jaded imaginations. Patrick knows how to mix 'n' match spicy combinations and his enormous cast of characters includes porno stars, sleazy producers, cute young studs with insatiable appetites (there's a bathhouse scene that takes some beating) with sadism, degradation and - improbably - love and affection."

"Tantalizing tales of porn stars, hustlers, and other lost boys...John Patrick set the pace with 'Angel!'"
- *The Weekly News, Miami*

"...Some readers may find some of the scenes too explicit; others will enjoy the sudden, graphic sensations each page brings. Each of these romans á clef is written with sustained intensity. 'Angel' offers a strange, often poetic vision of sexual obsession. I recommend it to you."
- *Nouveau Midwest*

"Self-absorbed, sexually-addicted bombshell Stacy flounced onto the scene in 'Angel' and here he is again, engaged in further, distinctly 'non-literary' adventures...lots of action!"
- *Prinz Eisenherz Book Review, Germany*

"'Angel' is mouthwatering and enticing..."
- *Rouge Magazine, London*

" 'Superstars' is a fast read...if you'd like a nice round of fireworks before the Fourth, read this aloud at your next church picnic..."
- *Welcomat, Philadelphia*

"For those who share Mr. Patrick's appreciation for cute young men, 'Legends' is a delightfully readable book...I am a fan of John Patrick's...His writing is clear and straight-forward and should be better known in the gay community."
- Ian Young, Torso Magazine

"'BOY TOY' is splendid..."
- J.C., Illinois

"...'Billy & David' is frank, intelligent, disarming. Few books approach the government's failure to respond to crisis in such a realistic, powerful manner."
- RG Magazine, Montreal, Canada

"...Touching and gallant in its concern for the sexually addicted, 'Angel' becomes a wonderfully seductive investigation of the mysterious disparity between lust and passion, obsession and desire."
-Lambda Book Report

"Each page of John Patrick's 'Angel' was like a sponge and I was slowly sucked into the works. 'The Kid' had the same effect on me and now 'What Went Wrong?' has blown me away!"
-P. K. New York

"John Patrick has one of the best jobs a gay male writer could have. In his fiction, he tells tales of rampant sexuality. His non-fiction involves first person explorations of adult male video stars. Talk about choice assignments!"
-Southern Exposure

"The title for 'Boys of Spring' is taken from a poem by Dylan Thomas, so you can count on high caliber imagery throughout."
- Walter Vatter, Editor, A Different Light Review

"'Boys of Spring' is Patrick's latest piece of erotic imagination in overdrive!"
- Zipperstore, London

*Book of the Month Selections in Europe and the U.K.
And Featured By A Different Light,
Lambda Rising and GR, Australia
And Available at Fine Booksellers Everywhere*

HEART THROBS

An Anthology of Erotic Tales
And Star Essays By

JOHN PATRICK

STARbooks Press
Sarasota, FL

Books by John Patrick

Non-Fiction
A Charmed Life:
Vince Cobretti
Lowe Down: Tim Lowe
The Best of the Superstars 1990
The Best of the Superstars 1991
The Best of the Superstars 1992
The Best of the Superstars 1993
The Best of the Superstars 1994
What Went Wrong?
When Boys Are Bad
& Sex Goes Wrong
Legends: The World's Sexiest
Men, Vols. 1 & 2
Tarnished Angels (Ed.)

Fiction
Billy & David: A Deadly Minuet
The Bigger They Are...
The Younger They Are...
The Harder They Are...
Angel: The Complete Trilogy
Angel II: Stacy's Story
Angel: The Complete Quintet
Angel: The Complete Quintet
(Expanded International Ed.)
A Natural Beauty (Editor)
The Kid
HUGE (Editor)
Strip: He Danced Alone
The Boys of Spring
Big Boys/Little Lies (Editor)
Boy Toy
Seduced (Editor)
Unforgettable (Editor)
WANTED: The Lusty Boys
Heartthrobs (including
The Boy from El Dorado)
Runaways/Kid Stuff (Editor)
Dangerous Boys (Editor)

Entire Contents Copyrighted © 1994 by John Patrick, Sarasota, FL.

All rights reserved. No part of this book may be reproduced or transmitted in any form by any means, electronic or mechanical, including photocopying, recording, or any information storage and retrieval system, without expressed written consent from the publisher.

Every effort has been made to credit copyrighted material. The author and the publisher regret any omissions and will correct them in future editions. This work is about persons who are at least 18 years of age, unless as revelations about past sexual experience and noted in text within the context of the story.

Library of Congress Card Catalogue No. 92-062453
ISBN No. 1-877978-47-7

Contents

BOOK I.
*On Location in Texas, the Young Hollywood Hunk
Knew the Sex Would Be Hot
But He Never Counted on Falling in Love with*
THE BOY FROM EL DORADO

BOOK II.
Everybody Wanted A Piece of the Action
TEEN IDOL

BOOK III.
HOORAY FOR HOLLYWOOD
Erotic Short Fiction
THE DREAM PALACE
AT A PARTY IN HOLLYWOOD
AT A PARTY IN MIAMI BEACH
THE COVERBOY
THE STALLION

BOOK IV.
*Beefcake, Chickencake:
The Heartthrobs*
LOVING LEONARDO (DICAPRIO)
MADONNA'S MEN
(Rodrigo, Rocky, Tony, Joey, Nick the Dick, et. al.)
GOING DOWN WITH MARKY MARK
THE SHAME OF COREY HAIM
FRESH IDOLS: BILLY IDOL AND RYAN IDOL
STRIKING OUT WITH JEFF STRYKER
ADAM HART & HIS HART-THROBBERS
FOR THE LOVE OF LOWE: TIM LOWE

BOOK V.
The Complete Best-Selling Documentary Novel
WHAT WENT WRONG?
When Boys Are Bad & Sex Goes Wrong

AUTHOR'S NOTE

These tales are works of fiction. Although inspired by real persons, the characters and dialogue are products of the author's imagination and, except for brief appearances by some public figures, actual persons are not portrayed.

"In truth, all movie stars have their scandals. And if they fail to supply one themselves, the public assigns them a rumor. We like to say they're addicted to heroin; we love to say they're gay."
– Hollywood Reporter Jess Cagle

*"Here's the recipe: a pair of deep blue eyes,
a wholesome but inviting pair of lips,
strands of sun-drenched hair, swiveling hips,
a satin jacket subtly revealing a smooth, hairless chest,
and finally a pinch - just a pinch - of androgyny.
As long as what you've created isn't too overwhelming
in the talent department, you've got it.
A teen dream, that is."*
- Broadway Gossip Columnist Michael Musto, 1979

THE BOY FROM EL DORADO

El Dorado: "Any fabulously wealthy place."
  – Webster's Dictionary

Prologue

It was pure heaven, lying in bed with nothing to do, Kyle thought. He yawned and rolled over. Maybe he wouldn't get out of bed until noon. Then he looked at the muscular figure snoring beside him. Kyle lay there, feasting on the sight, remembering. His brother Kale had come to bed nude, with a raging hard-on and, for the first time, he let Kyle suck his cock to orgasm and swallow the cum.

Just remembering it now gave Kyle a hard-on. He leaned back, closed his eyes and began stroking it. Slowly at first, then fast, faster. Soon he was gasping with relief. As he lay back, catching his breath, his hand sticky with the cum, a delicious aroma crept into the bedroom from the kitchen. He sniffed. His mother was frying sourdough pancakes. He leaned over and shook his brother hard.

Kale knuckled his eyes and stared foggily at Kyle. "What's the matter?"

"Smell."

Kale sniffed. "Oh, yeah. But you just hang on. I get the first plate. You'd eat 'em all before Ma could start another batch." He looked at Kyle's hard, flat stomach. "Damned if I know where you put it all, boy."

"And I'm hungrier this mornin' than I've ever been in my life. And you know why."

"Oh, why's that?" Kale chuckled, flipping the sheet off his body. He made his own morning hard-on flop against his belly. Kyle crouched over him, drawing Kale's hips up into his face. He kissed the cock, nibbled on the head, then pulled back to admire it again. To Kyle, his older brother's penis was a majestic sight, longer than his and thicker, so thick he had to use both hands to hold it steady.

"Hmmm," Kyle smiled. "I don't know what I like better any

more, Ma's pancakes or this."

Kale tried wriggling away. "Hey, no more of that."

Kyle caught him and began sucking. Kale sighed and held his brother's head, letting him finish.

. . .

Ma Cartwright set a stack of cakes before Kale first, then Kyle. Both boys poured thick maple syrup on the cakes and watched it flow slowly over the edges. The aroma pleased Kyle and he could feel the juices flow into his mouth, mixing with what was left of Kale's heavy load. He was in heaven once more.

Ma quickly began making more. "How many more can you eat?"

"Oh 'bout fifty," Kyle said, his mouth full.

"That's 'bout right," Kale said, chewing. "He could eat a horse if you'd let 'im."

"Horse cock, ya mean," Kyle chuckled under his breath, punching his knee into his brother's.

Kale shook his head in mock disgust and went on eating. "Just you wait'll you're my age. Just you wait."

Kyle, grinning, took another fork full of cakes into his mouth and some of the syrup slid down his chin. His brother reached over and dabbed the sticky liquid with a napkin. "Yeah, just you wait," Kale repeated with a wink.

. . .

Kyle twisted in the front seat of his brother's old Jeep to look back at the little ranch house.

"Hey, you ain't scared of runnin' away from home are ya?" Kale asked.

"No, but I'm sure gonna miss Ma's cookin'."

"Yeah, but not Pa's whippin's. Remember, in this life ya gotta give up somethin' to get somethin'. You always remember that."

"Guess so," he said, sliding down into the seat, resting his head on his brother's thigh. With this finger he slowly traced the bulge in Kale's jeans. "And this sure is somethin'."

"Yeah, but just you wait, little brother, just you wait."

ONE

Vincent Lawrence had been a feverish young man. It was said he climbed the Hollywood ladder two rungs at a time. His agility and eagerness were electrifying. He was always inventing new camera angles, improving the lighting, speeding up the tempo. He was at one time the highest paid cinematographer in the business.

But to Vinnie life was a grab bag and he reached into it to his elbows; every day there was a new conquest: a young starlet here, an aspiring actor there; gender never mattered to Vinnie, he was just looking for a good time. But, truth be known, the bourbon bottle was his only real companion. Eventually, drink obscured his vision completely.

Now the shock of thick brown hair that had given him a wild, careless look was gone and his hair was thinning. He had the lean, hungry look of a recovering alcoholic, which is what he was, and he was desperate. He had made the rounds of the studios but nobody was hiring. Not even in television.

So it astonished him when he received a mysterious phone call from Joe Bergen's secretary, telling him that the head of Monarch Studios wanted to see him in his office the next day.

His car broken down, and having no money to repair it, Vinnie had to take a bus to the studio. It wasn't until quarter past eleven that he arrived at the two-story, earth-colored adobe building with a red tile roof and bird of paradise plants out front. He was ushered into Bergen's office immediately.

"...I've always admired your work," Bergen told Vinnie, after greeting him and offering him a cup of coffee and a fresh bagel.

"Thanks," Vinnie said, sitting in an armchair across from the free-form, burled wood desk Bergen had created for him by a craftsman in Sonoma County, which at this angle looked like a giant tree stump.

"I've been in Europe, just got back."

"I know where you've been. That's why you're here."

Vinnie gulped. "I don't understand."

"We're starting another Kyle Cartwright western, 'El Dorado,' and I need your help."

"What's Kyle Cartwright got to do with me?"

"You were friendly with him once."

"I was friendly with a lot of people," he said with a gesture of futility. "Once."

"You travelled in the same circle for a while - " Bergen pressed on, nervously rubbing his nose.

The secretary buzzed. Bergen took a call. "Very important."

As Bergen talked on the phone, Vinnie glanced about the room. Joe Bergen's office was larger and more impressive than any he could remember. A full wall of mirrors, combined with leather sofas in the same shade of brown as the thick carpeting made the room seem to go on forever. Several Oscars were lined up like little soldiers on the wall behind Bergen, amid ornately framed pictures of Monarch's biggest stars and a large portrait of the mogul's wife and family. Bergen's children resembled him in that they had no physical features that marked them, that said they might be tough, smart, wily or corrupt.

As the mogul was hanging up the phone, Vinnie scanned his face for some kind of clue that would tell him if the man was intelligent or trustworthy, but there was no ruddiness, no silver hair, no square jawline, no angled nose. He appeared to be what he was, a transplanted New York lawyer with brownish-gray hair cut short to keep it from curling and a sad, round face with dark eyes made murky under horn-rimmed glasses. Vinnie was fascinated by the man's total absence of character. He was a blank, a void, a man so unlike the studio chiefs he had worked for in years past. Clearly, to Vinnie, Bergen appeared to be a man out of his element entirely, that the board of directors of Monarch in New York had chosen him for the job by process of elimination, by finding nothing against him.

"Look," Bergen said, "what I need is an assistant cameraman and someone who can keep an eye on Kyle. With you, I have both." Having made his proposition, Bergen now was able to grin. "You can keep the little bugger occupied, can't you?"

"I guess I could try," Vinnie said softly. He had heard the rumors. He hadn't seen Kyle in three years. First he had been working in Europe, a couple of experimental films never released in the U.S., then he was in recovery. Now, rumor had it, it was Kyle who was careening out of control. Not only was Kyle drinking to excess, he was also doing drugs.

"Good," Bergen went on, "You see, I have some feeling for him. I'd hate to see him destroy himself. And we've got a lot invested in the kid. Girls pay to see this kid. What can I say?"

"You've said it all."

". . . I'm glad you're with us," Bergen said, shaking Vinnie's hand as he left the office. "We start shooting in Texas in two weeks."

"Texas?"

"Hey, you know, in cowboy movies the scenery is the star of the show. You can't have westerns without the West."

"Yeah, I know." Vinnie nodded. He had shot many a western. And he had fucked Kyle Cartwright many a time. He smiled as he pumped Bergen's hand one last time. "I'll be fine."

. . .

"Vinnie!" Kyle shouted as he crossed the parking lot after sliding out of his white Corvette roadster with red leather upholstery. His handsome face was deeply tanned and his long blond hair was brushed off his forehead. He was dressed casually in a light gray Giorgio Armani suit and a white shirt, open at the neck. Sunlight glimmered off his gold neck chain.

Vinnie was leaving the main office building after his meeting with Bergen and waved at the young star, who was now rushing toward him, his hand outstretched.

"Vinnie!" Kyle gushed, vigorously shaking Vinnie's hand. "When Bergen told me you were going to be on this picture, I couldn't believe it."

Vinnie turned and looked back at the office building, then grinned at Kyle. "Shit, news sure travels fast around here. I just left his office."

"Oh, I knew you'd accept." He put his hand on Vinnie's arm. "Where've you been anyway?"

"Away."

Kyle smiled. He knew where Vinnie had been. Kyle had contacts who discreetly kept track of all of his old friends.

"Well, you're back and better than ever. God, look at you! Sleek! That's the only word I can use. You must've lost twenty pounds."

"Thirty." He was quiet in a resistant, impatient way as they began to walk across the parking lot, towards Kyle's trailer.

"Off the sauce, eh?" Kyle asked.

"Two years now."

"Amazing!"

"Yeah, it is. I can't believe it myself but it's true."

When they got to the trailer, Kyle said he was thirsty and he pranced up the steps like a mad bull; he felt like celebrating. He swung the door open for Vinnie.

Once they were both inside, Kyle bolted the door, then went to the bar. "You don't mind if I - ?" he asked, holding up a bottle of vodka.

"Hell, no," Vinnie said, easing his body into the armchair next to a window. "Makes me feel stronger to know I don't need to."

"Thatta boy. But what can I get you?"

"Coke's fine."

"Liquid or powder?"

"You're not into that too?"

Kyle opened a bottle of cola. "Hey, I'm into everything, just like you."

"That's what I've heard."

"Hey, you had your fun. More fun than anybody! Girls, boys, pigs, horses."

"Mostly pigs."

"So how's it hangin'?" Kyle asked, his eyes blazing. He handed Vinnie a bottle of cola.

"Very well, now."

Kyle pulled the drapes, then slid down on the arm of Vinnie's chair. He brought his drink to his lips with one hand while the other slid across Vinnie's shoulder. "It's gonna be great having you along on this shoot. We're going to Texas, you know. Ah, six whole weeks with Vinnie." He took a long swallow of his drink.

Vinnie sipped his cola in silence.

"We had some great parties, didn't we?" Kyle asked.

Vinnie nodded and stared into his drink.

Finishing his vodka and setting the empty glass on the floor, Kyle brought both of his hands to Vinnie's shoulders. Gently massaging, he asked, "Let's see, when was the last time?" He looked up to the ceiling. "Oh, yeah, at Steve Sommers' party for me, when I finished 'Silver City.' Yeah, that was it! God, you had everybody that day. I'll never forget it."

Kyle kneaded Vinnie's shoulder blades.

Vinnie looked up. "I don't think we should start something we can't finish."

"You never had any trouble finishing," Kyle chuckled.

"Don't you have to be on the set?"

"No, I just came in to see you."

"All the way from Malibu?"

"Hey, I remembered it was worth it."

Vinnie's reputation had always preceded him. And when his admirers finally got his cock exposed, they were never disappointed. In Hollywood, there were few cocks as long and thick. When Vinnie belonged to the Beverly Hills Country Club and would be dozing on the table in the locker room after his massage, men would sneak in and lift the towel to show guests the phallic wonder, which in repose was said to measure nine inches. "Now you've got something to tell the folks back home," they would joke. "Fuck Old Faithful, that's the real Old Faithful." And Kyle and the other members of Steve Sommers' gay set knew the truth of it: Vinnie's cock was nine inches soft and grew to eleven inches when hard. But the best part was, it really was "Old Faithful;" he could fuck for hours and he loved buggering gay boys. Indeed, Vinnie said he preferred an ass to a cunt. "You don't have to buy 'em dinner first," he said. What's more, Vinnie loved having a couple of gay boys giving him head at once. "Plenty to go around," he would laugh, shaking it lewdly.

But now there was only Kyle in the darkened star trailer on the Monarch lot; no party, no crowd, and Vinnie felt uncomfortable. It was too intimate a setting for him; he was, at heart, a performer when it came to sex. There was safety in numbers. Still, what Kyle began doing felt good.

Kyle had no trouble living up to his reputation either. Studio executives, heads of talent agencies, producers and directors could attest that the kid gave the best head in Hollywood, especially when he wanted a favor or to be part of a project.

But now Kyle was kissing Vinnie's cock through the fabric of his trousers, eager to suck it simply because he wanted to, and those were the best blowjobs Kyle could give. He would take his time, enjoying every minute, driving the man crazy with desire, with his need to orgasm. But Kyle knew how to prolong it, how to build to an intense orgasm, and then how to get his partner back up and going again. While Vinnie could fuck for hours, Kyle could suck for hours. They seemed made for each other.

"Kyle, don't - " Vinnie said, lifting the silky blond head away from his abundant crotch.

"Please. Just a quickie. It's been so long."

"Yeah, three years is a long time to be away from a Kyle Cartwright special," Vinnie chuckled.

Kyle stroked his chin. "Why didn't you ever go home with me?"

"That might have made it seem something more than it was. I just like 'em quick and easy."

"Okay, I'll make it quick today."

But Vinnie knew quick to Kyle could easily mean hours. Still, Vinnie felt good. He had finally found work, at Monarch no less, and he felt like throwing a good fuck into someone. He decided to agree with Kyle, and they'd work out the reality later.

As they undressed, Vinnie was reminded of how beautifully made Kyle was. The muscles of his long arms were well defined, as was each strong vein. His chest was wide and lightly dusted with hair. The swirling pattern of hair tapered at his narrow waist, then flared again, light and abundant, around his full sex, now jutting out from his body at a rakish angle as he walked toward Vinnie. Seeing the boy like this, Vinnie thought, if he were ever to take a male lover, it would be Kyle.

Kyle lowered his head over Vinnie's enormous cock and flicked the head of it with his tongue. As Vinnie watched his cock being adored with exquisite finesse, he clutched Kyle's head, raking his fingers through the silken hair.

After a few preliminary sucks, Kyle withdrew the prick all the way and kissed the velvety smooth tip. "Oh, God, it's just as big as I remembered. I'm so hot for it today I could scream," he said, saliva trickling from his lips and running down the meaty prick. "Fuck me, Vinnie. Fuck me."

"In a minute," Vinnie said, shoving the cock back into Kyle's mouth. Kyle began rotating his tongue-strokes, taking more and more of the giant penis into his mouth. In spite of himself, Vinnie began moaning, squirming. He had missed Kyle more than he thought.

"Okay, now," Vinnie said after a few minutes of blissful torture.

Kyle went to the little bathroom and got some grease. He handed it to Vinnie and bent over at the waist, his hands clasped on the top of the couch. As it was displayed before him, Vinnie was reminded that Kyle's ass was as lovely as the rest of him. The mounds were soft and hairless, perfectly rounded. He greased his cock and slowly began inching it into Kyle's asshole. The buttocks were taut and Vinnie's hands kneaded the supple muscles of the young star's back as he began fucking him. Kyle's hips lifted and ground against Vinnie in a circular pattern as he watched their images in the mirror above his dressing table. The double shot of vodka had made him light-headed and he felt as if he would pass out when the long cock was all the way in him. He clenched his ass with each of Vinnie's savage stabs until he could feel his own urgency, his toes tingling, his legs beginning to tremble. He grunted and stroked himself to orgasm. A few more ferocious strokes and Vinnie too was coming.

"Oh, fuck me, fuck me harder."

"Hold still," Vinnie ordered, seizing the firm buttocks as he drove his penis as deep as it could go.

"Oh, oh," Kyle kept moaning, his cum streaming from the cockhead onto the cushion of the couch.

Kyle turned and became captivated by Vinnie's image in the mirror, convulsed in his orgasm, grasping, clawing at Kyle's naked skin, his hot load flying into him.

"Oh, yeah, you love it, you really do."

"Always have, kid. Always have."

. . .

When Kyle found Vinnie had taken a bus to get to the studio he insisted on taking him home. On the way, Vinnie explained his car was in the shop in need of $500 worth of repairs. When they arrived at Vinnie's apartment building, Kyle asked, "May I come in?"

"Sorry, I got stuff I gotta do."

"Okay, I'll call you," Kyle said, reaching into his pocket. He counted out five hundred dollar bills.

"No," Vinnie said, shaking his head vehemently.

"A loan," he said.

"Okay. Thanks."

"Thank you," Kyle said, grinning. "You sure I can't come in?"

Vinnie shook his head. "I'll see you in Texas."

For a few moments, Kyle watched Vinnie stride confidently into the old stucco building in a run-down section of West Hollywood. When Vinnie reached the front gate, he turned and waved to Kyle. Kyle smiled and said, "Goodbye." Since he lost his brother ten years before, Kyle always made it a point to say goodbye.

. . .

The money ran out early. The Cartwright brothers would check into a motel before dark and Kale would leave Kyle watching TV while he went to the nearest bar. Sometimes, he didn't return till dawn, or even later. Occasionally, he would bring a girl back to the room and fuck her while Kyle lay in the other bed, pretending he was asleep.

The morning after those occasions, Kyle would beg to suck Kale's dick but his brother would say, "Hey, I just fucked a cunt. You don't want to catch somethin', do ya?"

It was near Spokane that things began to totally unravel. Kale had gotten a job as a ranch hand and the owner had a teenage daughter. The two of them would go for rides in a power boat on a lake on the property. Kale told Kyle they would anchor at the far end of the lake and drink and have intercourse. One night, Kale didn't come back to the bunkhouse. Towards morning, the ranch owner woke Kyle saying, "There's been an accident."

In slow, measured words, he told Kyle that when Kale was bringing the boat into the dock in the dark, the throttle had jammed and the boat crashed into the pilings. Kale had been decapitated. The thought of it gave Kyle nightmares for weeks.

Young Kyle was turned over to a friend of the ranch owner, an Episcopal priest, Reverend Williams, and his housekeeper, Mrs. Jenkins.

It was the Reverend who discovered Kyle had the voice of an angel and the mouth of a whore.

TWO

Film director Grant King had happy memories of Brackettville, Texas, near the banks of the Rio Grande River where the San Felipe Springs water supply makes the land a green spot in the desert. In 1959, King was part of the crew that filmed "The Alamo" there for John Wayne. The Alamo replica, built by adobe craftsmen from Mexico, overlooks a complete frontier village of the 1800s and Grant recalled the townspeople turned the movie set into a tourist attraction. Getting officials to agree to film another western there was an easy matter, provided they did not film in the summer when the park was busiest. Grant promised the owners the company would be gone by the time of the city's Frontier Fair in June.

What wasn't so easy for Grant was resigning himself to the fact that Kyle Cartwright was going to be in the cast. Bergen told him, "You had to put up with Laurence Harvey on 'The Alamo,' for chrissakes. You can certainly put up with someone even younger, even cuter." Bergen winked. "Besides, I hear you've always wanted to get one of his blowjobs."

"You really know how to hurt a guy, don't you!" Grant laughed. "But I don't know, how are they anyway? They must be fabulous, you keep putting him in movie after movie."

"Can I control all the teenage girls who want to see him?"

"If they only knew!"

"That's Mac's department."

Kyle Cartwright, it was widely acknowledged, was Macaulay Kinton's creation. "Hollywood is a dream factory," Mac was fond of saying, "with the emphasis on dreams. And Kyle

Cartwright is every teenage girl's dream lover. He's the kind of non-threatening guy they could take home to meet mother."

When Kyle first appeared on screen in 1969 in "Silver City," one columnist heralded him as "the new Montgomery Clift," but only because he was making his movie debut in a western starring John Wayne, as Clift did in "Red River." While Wayne called Clift "a little shit," and "an arrogant little bastard," he had high praise for Kyle after they finished "Silver City:" "The kid can carry a tune and he looks good on a horse," he told a reporter. Being raised on a ranch, Kyle was indeed at home in the saddle and westerns were to become his favorite kind of film. He and Wayne got along famously; some even wondered, knowing Kyle's reputation for giving head, what really went on in Wayne's trailer when the he-man actor would take the boy there to "coach him on his line readings."

Kyle and Clift differed in other ways. While Clift himself admitted he was "snobbish" and disdained the press, going to great lengths to avoid doing publicity or being cooperative, Kyle Cartwright was the soul of cooperation. And while Clift was an actor in the truest sense, having studied The Method, appeared on the Broadway stage, and was intensely serious about his craft, Kyle was given a role in John Wayne's film only to add marquee lure, and to sing his hit song of that year, "A Lotta Lovin'." Kyle admitted he had a modest voice but he was charming and his picture on the sleeve of the 45 sent sales soaring and led to a three-album contract with Capitol.

While Clift's sexual ambiguity was a private torture for him, Kyle appeared to delight in being able to have sex with anyone he chose and "fool everybody." And, unlike Clift, who was classically handsome, and so hirsute that he looked like a gorilla in a swim suit, Kyle was a boyish, clean-cut, smooth-chested blond with pouty lips and filled out a swim suit as few before him. In fact, at photo sessions, Mac would insist there always be several shots of the boy in retreat, in the tightest trunks imaginable because, he joked, "Kyle Cartwright's ass is the eighth wonder of the world."

"Mac should know," one of the crewmen suggested, "he's spent enough time there."

As one of Hollywood's most ambitious press agents, Mac Kinton had seen what could be done in Hollywood with a boy who was cooperative. He'd watched agents he considered less talented than himself make stars of Tab Hunter, whom Kyle vaguely resembled, Rock Hudson, and Fabian. He longed to meet a boy whom he could mold into the hottest young thing in movies. That longing led him down many a dark alleys and into several agonizingly frustrating relationships.

It was in January 1967, on a day very warm for Los Angeles, when Mac was shopping he noticed a young blond shoplifting. He was especially excited by the fact even though the kid wore next to nothing, he was able to conceal an astonishing amount of merchandise on his person. Mac trailed the kid from store to store and finally, when the boy was leaving one rather prestigious department store, he collared him, pretending to be an undercover member of the security force. If the boy would agree to return what he had stolen - and go home with Mac - everything would be fine. And it was, for four years. They would often joke about how they met. After Kyle became a star making a million dollars a year, Mac would still discover things missing from his house and find them later at Kyle's. Kyle would joke, "Just trying to keep my hand in." Invariably, it was a gift that Kyle had given the older man and all Mac would ever say was, "Indian giver."

Mac was a wiry, intense, birdlike man, yet Kyle found him surprisingly handsome behind rimless glasses and a studious expression. Best of all, Mac had a long, lean cock that bent enticingly to the left and when it entered his ass, Kyle would at first cry out in pain. Once it was in him, however, with Mac doing his thing, Kyle relaxed and enjoyed it. And, Mac had to concede, no one enjoyed get fucked by him as much as Kyle did. He had always considered himself a bottom but Kyle had made him enjoy being a top.

Although they remained on good terms, Mac refused to travel with Kyle after they went to Europe in 1973. Along with many other American stars, Kyle played a cameo role in "The Crusades." By this time, Kyle had tired of their relationship and was eager for new adventures. In Prague, he would sneak out of their hotel and walk the streets alone at night, picking up rough trade and bringing them back to the hotel. In Paris, after Mac took him to the Louvre and then to the Left Bank for lunch, Kyle was feeling contrite about what had gone on in

Prague and it was, for an afternoon, just like it was in the beginning.

After lunch, they returned to the Ritz, the hotel that Mac preferred, and made love for the rest of the afternoon, unhurriedly, passionately. As the shadows deepened, they lay in each other's arms in the huge bed in the elegant gray room and Mac said, "It's those columns outside in the Place Vendome that does it. They just look like big cocks."

"Mine *is* big enough, isn't it?" Kyle asked, stroking it.

"Yes, Kyle. Plenty big enough," Mac said, lowering his mouth over it again.

That evening, Mac took him to the ballet and Kyle insisted they stop at a bistro on their way home. Eventually Mac became disgusted and left, only to spend the next day looking for Kyle, who had gone home with three stars of the ballet they had just seen.

"Did *they* think it was big enough, Kyle?"

"*Oui. Oui,*" Kyle laughed.

It was all Mac would ask about the adventure. He wanted to know more but then he didn't. He preferred to simply imagine what went on.

Kyle loved Rome, where most of the filming was done, more than any other city they visited. "Everywhere church bells sing to you," he gushed. He was enchanted with the fountains, the cobbled streets, the strange "pink over pink" color of the sky. And if any of the men he would pick up in bars said he looked like Kyle Cartwright he'd joke, "I resemble a lot of people."

When really pressed, Kyle told them he was, in fact, a stuntman with the movie company and often had to stand in for the young star. Invariably, the guy would ask Kyle to perform a few *stunts* for him.

Now, a few minutes after Grant left Bergen's office, Mac was keeping his appointment with the mogul. Bergen wanted to inform the agent that the deal with Vinnie, which Mac himself had suggested, had been finalized.

"Vinnie will set a good example for Kyle," Mac contended.

"But do you think he can keep him occupied?"

"Yes, a long time. A very long time."

Bergen arched his brows.

"Hey, Joe," Mac chuckled. "You know what they say, the longer it is the longer it takes."

THREE

As his hand fell to the denim-clad thigh of Kevin Casey, his latest "discovery," Mac reminded himself that the biggest mistake he made in life was falling in love with his creations but, try as he might, this boy, like all the others, had captivated him.

They were in Mac's robin's egg blue 1955 Thunderbird, on their way to Kyle's house to join him in his celebration of going on the wagon for the duration of the making of "El Dorado."

"I intend to get seriously drunk," Kyle told Mac over the phone when he was inviting him.

"I think I'll leave before that happens."

"Hey, you'll miss all the fun," Kyle laughed.

"That's the idea."

Mac was already grooming Kevin Casey to become the "new Kyle Cartwright." Having Kevin around would, Mac reasoned, keep Kyle in line, demonstrating how quickly a "flavor of the month" can be replaced in Hollywood.

Kyle sneered when Mac told him what name he was giving the farmboy from Iowa. "Kevin Casey? Be serious! Mac, you're so terribly obvious it's pitiful. Kevin Casey my ass."

Mac chuckled, "Your ass is right, Kyle. I'm sure he'll find a warm welcome there, whatever his name is."

Kevin was an earnest young man from Iowa State, where an injury while playing football had caused him to seek out theater as an activity, and a place to meet interesting people. He told Mac he hadn't decided whether he was gay or straight: "Maybe a bit of both."

"We all start out that way," Mac had assured him.

Tonight Kevin looked ready to come out. Indeed, he had dressed in pastels. It was the way he thought gay people dressed and Mac told him he would look gayer than anyone else at the party and had him change into blue jeans and a yellow pullover shirt. Now he appeared to be what Mac wanted him to be, a brash stud athlete with a strong jaw and a fat grin. And an everhard cock.

At sunset, as they turned off the Pacific Coast Highway and began the steep climb up Malibu Canyon Road, Mac soon saw Kyle's gray-blue fortress perched on top of the granite outcrop and said, "There it is."

"What?" Kevin asked.

"Kyle's place."

"That's a house?"

"Yeah, just a house," Mac chuckled. "But it's always reminded me of a UFO, in more ways that one."

"Some place."

"In a way, it's my house – " his voice drifted away. He was beginning to despise the fact that he was taking credit for everything Kyle had because he had discovered him. Now that Kyle had bought this house, he had become even more remote and loving him became even more difficult. But Kyle Cartwright was a habit Mac could not seem to break. He rested a warm hand on Kevin's knee. "You'll have an even bigger house one day, just keep on with your lessons."

Kevin put his hand on top of Mac's and squeezed. He liked Mac, the fact that Mac had patience with him when nobody, not his football coaches, his professors, his parents, or his numerous girlfriends, ever did. He was not a bright boy, he needed time to absorb things, but he was eager to learn and a hard worker.

Mac was happy Kevin had answered one of the bulletins he frequently fired off to colleges seeking students to continue their acting training in Los Angeles. It was a ploy that had worked well and brought Mac many a handsome young stud to interview. And Kevin's sexual ambiguity made him soar to the top of the list for "future development."

The chosen eventually ended up visiting Bird's Eye, the name Kyle gave to his house for its unobstructed one hundred-and-eighty-degree view of the mountains and the Pacific. Mac now regarded his ex-lover and greatest discovery as a mysterious instrument of passion used to seduce and enthrall young studs. Kyle was convinced that the studs who came to the beach completely understood their role and relished the attention and theatricality of it all. And tonight was more theatrical than most, because this was Kyle's last party before six weeks of sobriety. He had begun drinking earlier and the pills he was taking put him in a mood that Mac could only describe as "fey."

When Kyle took Kevin from the poolside pergola to "look at the view," Kevin was awed at how, at the edge, the cliff dropped away thousands of feet to the valley floor. "Behave or we'll throw you off," Kyle joked.

Kevin smiled. "I'll behave."

"Everyone does," Kyle said, linking his arm with Kevin's.

Mac, seated in one of the Douglas-fir-planked lounge chairs beside the pool, watched them as he listened to the Stylistics' singing "You Make Me Feel Brand New." Soon he was laughing and pouring himself another martini.

Kevin couldn't take it all in. The silver trays of canapes, the ever-fresh tulips of champagne, or the smoldering joints. He was accustomed to fraternity beer parties. His head was swivelling. "Was that - ?" he kept asking. He was aware of all he was missing in life - till now. Mac made him feel a part of it, and when Steve Sommers arrived, a roly-poly figure in a flowing silk caftan, Mac saw to it that Kevin was the first one Steve took to Kyle's bathroom to "entertain." Steve preferred Kyle's bathroom because it had mirrors on all sides and he could watch the young men's cocks sliding in and out of his mouth as he sat on the toilet and sucked them. In Kyle's bathroom, away from the main part of the house, he was also less likely to be disturbed.

When Steve was through blowing the new recruit, he joined Mac in a flute of bubbly and gave Kevin "two thumbs up."

"He tastes divine, Mac-y," the wealthy producer said, smacking his lips. "Good to the last drop."

"I know," Mac said, smiling; the boy was halfway home. All he needed now was to have sex with Kyle.

Even before the caterers had finished clearing up in the

kitchen, most of the guests had departed. Mac saw the last of them to their cars and by the time he returned to the house, Kyle had already taken Kevin into the music room where he had started a fire in the marble fireplace. Soon Kyle joined Kevin on the couch and began to caress and kiss him.

Mac came into the room quietly and sat near them, watching. He grew hard at the sight of Kyle indiscreetly forcing his tongue in and out of Kevin's mouth as his hands kneaded the youth's crotch.

Before long, Kevin's cock was revealed, an abundant sex, thick and long, and Kyle quickly went down on it. He would look up at Mac occasionally between sucks and it seemed as if his mentor was studying them, marking in his memory the image of their beautiful bodies made more so by the glow of the fire. Mac's disturbing presence lent a new eroticism to Kyle's pleasure. Indeed, when he was alone with someone else in the house, he would often imagine that Mac was there, watching, wanting to be humiliated in front of them.

But Mac was comparing the scene to others he had witnessed in the same room. Often he had left in a huff, and his young charges would remain in Malibu, sometimes for several days, before Kyle tired of them. Then Mac would drive back out to retrieve them. Often he found the young men bewildered, seeking answers to what they had done wrong when it appeared Kyle was having a wonderful time.

"He's easily bored," Mac would tell them. "I have to constantly send in reinforcements."

Finally, Kyle had sucked Kevin's cock to the point of suffocation and Kevin came, pouring cum down Kyle's willing throat. Once Kevin had finished, Kyle kept sucking and when it grew hard again, Kyle wanted Kevin to fuck him, to see once again Mac's raging anger as another man abused his asshole.

But tonight Mac wasn't going to play that game. He stood up and said, "Okay, that's enough. C'mon Kevin. Let's get the hell out of here." He had often in the past subjected himself to Kyle's unsuppressed moans filling the house and now he sought to wipe away the uneasy feelings that were going through him.

Kevin broke free from Kyle and stood before Mac. He took the older man's head in his hands and drew it to him, kissing

Mac violently as though he were fucking his mouth with his tongue. Kyle watched as Kevin's cock began throbbing eagerly, tempting Mac with its succulence.

Before long all three were on the couch, their bodies twitching with arousal under the luxurious caress of the leather beneath them. Mac pinched Kyle's nipples from behind as the young star put himself between the two other men. They were all on their knees, Kevin kneeling before Kyle's face, Mac kneeling behind him. Kevin's cock was so swollen it stood straight up, grazing his belly, and Kyle at first had difficulty getting it to straighten so he could get it in his mouth. "Let me warm it up again," Kyle said.

As he sucked Kevin's cock, Kyle's hips began moving in a slow, beautiful rhythm, rising and falling to meet the tempo of the music on the stereo. His moans were coming faster and louder and Mac could hear Kevin's own pleasure sounds mingling with Kyle's. Kevin bent over and rubbed Kyle's hips, which began to undulate under his caresses. Kyle was panting, stroking his own cock, as Mac began fucking him. Kevin's eyes were locked on Mac's cock as it slid in and out of Kyle. "I'm warming it up for you," Mac chuckled. Kevin beamed and they began kissing. Their lips locked together, they came almost simultaneously, thunderously.

Kyle let out a scream, his body racking with convulsions as Mac's heavy load shot into him and Kevin's eruption splashed in his face.

Mac pulled out and went to the bathroom, leaving Kevin and Kyle on the couch, wrapped in each other's arms.

"Well, did I behave?" Kevin asked.

"You did good." Kyle chuckled. "You'll hear that a lot in this town. Get used to it."

"Yeah, I could get used to this all right," he sighed, leaning back into Kyle's warm embrace.

When he returned, Mac said, "Okay, Kevin, c'mon, it's time to go."

"Kevin's going to stay," Kyle said. "Aren't you Kevin?"

Kevin blinked.

"I want to feel this big dick up my ass – Kyle said, lifting it from the boy's thigh and stroking it.

Mac tugged at Kevin's hand and said, "No, Kyle has to fly to

Texas Monday. He has to pack."

"I've got all day tomorrow to pack."

"With Kevin around, you'd never get any packing done."

"Oh yes," Kyle laughed, grabbing for Kevin's penis, "lots of packing."

Kevin smiled at Kyle, then at Mac.

Mac said, "Kevin, now."

Kevin shrugged and jerked himself away from Kyle.

"I'll see you when you get back," Kevin said. "Have fun in Texas."

"I will. The biggest cock in Hollywood is going with me."

"Who's that?" Kevin asked, searching for his briefs.

"Never mind." Mac chuckled. "Kyle could keep you here all night talking about all the big cocks of Hollywood."

Kevin looked at Kyle again, started to move back towards the couch, but Mac pushed him, urging him on before he had a chance to change his mind.

Before Mac left the music room, he bent over Kyle and kissed him on the forehead. "Be good."

"Don't worry. I'll be very good."

"I know."

Kyle lay on the sofa watching them disappear through the living room and out the front door. He hugged one of the leather pillows to his chest and closed his eyes. He was exhausted but not sleepy. He would have to go to his bathroom and find the sleeping pills. He was glad he had a pill for everything.

Well, he thought, almost everything.

FOUR

Kyle awakened early the next morning with a monumental headache, a milestone of a headache, and he made the long climb down the street to the Ocean. He needed to clear his head with a walk on the beach.

At about the same hour, Nico Mendoza was beginning his day as he always did when he was staying at his rented place in Malibu, with some exercise. As he jogged along the beach, his elbows held high, chest and stomach lurching forward, Nico saw Kyle walking serenely in the opposite direction. He was struck by the young man's beauty; indeed, he seemed even more handsome than he appeared on the screen. Before he left for his last business trip to Mexico, Nico had heard that Kyle had bought the Connelly place on the ridge for two million and was intrigued by the notion of having a young movie star as a neighbor. He had rented a small bungalow down the road for over a year and had only occasionally seen film stars in the shops, buying groceries and other necessities. They had not impressed him one way or another but this morning Kyle attracted him. Yet while the movie star appeared very real, to Nico his connection was a mythical one, understood in terms of inconceivable distances.

Kyle knew nothing about the Panamanian from Mexico who introduced himself as his neighbor but Nico knew much about Kyle. He had heard about the young man's notorious sex drive and his insatiable drug habits.

The instant of connection between the two men occurred when Kyle invited his new neighbor to see the improvements he had made since buying the Connelly place. Nico sensed that Kyle's vivaciousness was due to the drugs he was taking.

They went through the house very quickly and ended up by the pool. Nico, warm and perspiring, found the Jacuzzi Kyle had added to the area incredibly inviting. Unabashedly, Kyle stripped to the skin and jumped in. As Nico peeled away his sweatsuit Kyle thought the older man seemed attractively vigorous and had an exotic sexiness about him, with his deeply-set brown eyes, a brushy mustache, broad nose and a cleft chin. His build, Kyle thought, was that of an aging fighter, a stocky mixture of flab, hair and muscle and, most pleasing to Kyle, a huge uncut prick.

Relaxing in the swirling water, Nico talked about his recent trip to Mexico City, making vague illusions to the Mexican cops, the loud tourists, the drug smugglers. Kyle quickly grasped what Nico was telling him. Kyle disappeared for a few moments to take another hit of cocaine and fix them Bloody Marys.

"Yes, this is an amazing place," Nico said, leaning back after taking a long swallow of his drink. "It's like being in the tropics out here. Just like my little place in Acapulco."

Shadows of birds flying overhead glanced across the pool and Kyle picked up his sunglasses to look at them. "Yeah, it's great at sunset."

"I fear after you've lived here a while, you forget the sunsets and start watching TV."

"Or doing other things – " Kyle said. Lifting the sunglasses off his face, he decided there was a time for talk and a time for action, and he moved closer to Nico, so close that his guest suddenly grew uncomfortable, unsure what was expected of him in a situation with a celebrity. He had never been this close to a male movie star who was rumored to be gay. The thought of fucking him was inconceivable, yet the mere idea of it tantalized him. His cock grew hard and he made no attempt to conceal his excitement. Kyle stared at it. It was a nine-inch masterpiece of a cock with a fat brown bulb peeking out of a thick fold of foreskin.

Nico saw where Kyle's eyes were riveted and smiled. He picked up his glass. "To our friendship, may it mature and ripen," he toasted.

Kyle merely touched glasses with a half-swallowed "*Salud*." He was incredibly high, confused to the point of stupidity. He stroked Nico's cock. As he pushed back the heavy foreskin, he sighed, "Talk about ripe."

Nico, finishing his drink, resolved to end Kyle's confusion. "Pretty boy Kyle," he said, "my new friend, I am a man who likes to come right to the point."

"I can see that," Kyle chuckled, staring at the erection.

"I must confess I am charmed by you. I have seen your movies, heard you on the radio. And I must admit I have heard the stories about you – "

"The stories are just that, stories."

"Ha! We shall see. But if you don't mind my saying so, I am Senor Discretion himself."

"I'm glad to hear it."

Nico raised his empty glass, "To the two of us."

"To the two of us," Kyle mumbled, then finished his drink.

Their sex began in a quiet and controlled way. Nico was a methodical man. He could spend an afternoon having his cock sucked, or an entire morning fucking in every possible position. He stood up in the pool and straddled Kyle's chest.

"God what a cock!" Kyle exclaimed as Nico brought it to his lips. Nico held Kyle's head as he mouth-fucked him, gently at first and then a little deeper with each stroke.

Kyle's eyes popped wide open when Nico finally pulled his cock from his mouth and backed off, ready to begin the fuck.

"Oh, yeah," Kyle said, stroking it as he climbed out of the Jacuzzi. Kyle reclined on the chaise and undulated his hips in invitation.

Nico came over to Kyle with grim intent in his eyes. With fucking as well as sucking, Nico began gently, at first rubbing the rim of the head into the asscrack, teasing Kyle.

Finally, Kyle was moaning, begging for it, and Nico grabbed his hips and spread his ass, shoving it into the young man with one powerful thrust. Kyle cried out, "Oh, God!"

"¡Que' rico!" Nico laughed.

Slumping over, Kyle turned to watch over his shoulder as Nico pushed it all the way in, then pulled back and began rotating it in his rectum. Another deep thrust and he was on top of Kyle, his hairy chest rubbing on Kyle's gleaming, muscular back.

As Kyle clenched and unclenched his sphincter, Nico groaned and began fucking him so hard he fell flat to the chaise. While Nico huffed and puffed, swinging his hips from side to side, grinding into Kyle, he maneuvered himself with a sense of grandeur that inspired awe in Kyle. He even came grandly, small spasms leading to big ones, filling Kyle with copious sperm. Nico then rolled Kyle over onto his back and sunk his half-hard cock back into the burning ass and moved in and out gently while Kyle jacked himself off.

"I woke up with a helluva headache," Kyle said as Nico lifted himself up from the chaise. "All that's gone now. I feel wonderful."

"I am glad. Yes, I am always at your service," Nico said, shaking his spent cock.

Kyle, unwilling to give it up, stroked the cum-coated prick and drew it close to his mouth. As the cock began to harden again, Kyle sighed and closed his eyes. A warm glow came over him. "All this and Senor Discretion himself."

FIVE

Later that day, as the sun was setting, Carl Benson came to Bird's Eye. The songwriter said he was there to wish Kyle a safe journey, but Kyle knew it was a ploy to make his case again for Kyle to record a another album.

"...You owe Capitol that third album," Carl said after Kyle let him in the house and fixed him a drink. "And all you do is make movies."

"I make more money making movies," Kyle said, lying back down on his chaise by the pool. "I have to pay for this house, you know."

"But you're singing in this movie aren't you?"

"Yes. But it'll be a single. They're going to bring it out when the movie premieres."

"Who wrote the song?"

"Jimmy Webb."

"You know how to hurt a guy, don't you?" Carl was waving his cigarette, scattering the ashes toward Kyle, his hand trembling when he talked as if there were, just beneath the surface, all the right words, the Great Truths, straining to get out. He could write them down, put them to music, but he found it impossible to say them, especially to someone he adored as much as he adored Kyle. The words that did come were usually rushed, jammed together, and some people thought he stuttered, but it was his body jerking, forcing the words out. It was why, he said, he had to have people sing his songs, he could never get them right. Kyle, Carl Benson always said, got his songs right the first time, every time. And that wasn't all. When you went to bed with Kyle, he made you feel you could do no wrong. And he had not been to bed with Kyle for months.

"Is that what you came up here for, to whine?"

"Why do you hate me so?"

"I don't. I love you. But you're always whining. I get tired of it."

"I'm sorry. It just seems you've forgotten all your old friends, the people that helped you get all this."

Kyle got up to freshen his drink. "Didn't you make a ton of money? What more do you want?"

"You know what I want. The third album. Some of the scores for these stupid movies."

"See Mac," Kyle said, walking by Carl in the skimpy bright pink bikini that deftly outlined his crotch.

Carl sighed. Balding, with his delicate face and bicycle-tire of fat at the belt-line, he had always envied the star's lank, hard, tanned torso and he reached out to touch it. "That's the answer to everything. See Mac. I'm sick of seeing Mac. Mac can't give me this – " He stroked the soft bulge in the bikini.

Chuckling, Kyle pulled away and kept walking to the poolside bar. "Please, Carl, behave yourself. And I know that's what you really want. It's what you always want."

"What am I supposed to do, forget you?"

"It'd be better if you did."

"Better for you. Better for you if you never had to look at me again, never sing another one of my songs."

Kyle poured himself a tall vodka and tonic. "We're played out, Carl. And, as a songwriter, you're played out. Even you said you wrote better songs when you were miserable. Well, write some."

"I have. And I brought them. I'll leave them with you. Let me know."

"I'll take 'em to Texas with me, try 'em out on the crew."

"Say, what do you do all that time on location anyway?"

"Jerk off a lot," Kyle said, making himself comfortable again on the chaise. "You know I've gotta come at least twice a day."

"But if I know you, you won't just be jerking off alone. Vincent Lawrence is going with you."

"Mac tell you that?"

Carl nodded. "Mac tells me everything. We're both in the same boat."

Kyle ignored Carl and began stroking the bulge in his bikini.

"Yeah," he snickered as his cock swelled. "Old Faithful Vinnie'll provide a distraction."

"Distraction?" Carl sneered. "I was at a few of Steve's parties, remember. I know just how distracting Vinnie can be."

"That's right, you were. But you don't get into a party. That's why I didn't invite you last night."

"Was it fun?"

Kyle nodded. "Mac brought another of his discoveries."

"If you mean Kevin, I haven't met him yet."

"I doubt you will. He'll probably be replaced in a week. You know Mac." Kyle took a long swallow of his drink.

"No, I know you. That's the trouble." Carl finished his drink, set it on the table next to him. "Are you going to the apartment?"

"I have to. They're picking me up there in the morning."

Carl stared at the bulge in Kyle's bikini. "You're in no condition to drive. Let me take you."

"I knew you came up here for a reason."

Kyle kept the condominium apartment in Hollywood he bought when he moved out of Mac's house in the Hills. If he had a long day, he could stay there instead of driving all the way to Malibu. And he used it to entertain the men he ordered from the service. It was safer than bringing them to Malibu.

Kyle got his guitar, packed a few things in a bag and locked up the house. On the way into the city, Carl was quiet, letting Kyle talk. It seemed like old times to Carl, the two of them riding along with the top of Carl's black Mercedes open to the stars, Kyle's songs on the stereo.

Six years before, Mac had sent his young star to the composer and lyricist for voice training. Mac knew Carl was attracted to the same type of kid he was, but he knew the training Kyle would get was worth the risk. What Mac hadn't counted on was that Kyle would take delight doing some training of his own, teaching Carl to enjoy life.

Kyle and Carl made a strange couple when they went out together. In Kyle's favorite haunt in those days, the huge pastel-lit disco, Chances, he spun himself around, arms akimbo, heels kicking into others, pretending every song was James Brown.

Kyle thought it odd that a musician, someone as musical as

Carl, always danced the same movement, a neat triangle with his right foot – one, two, three, then a swing of the hip. Four, then back to triangle, his body, restrained and even, elbows tucked into his ribs, moving like a pendulum across the floor, tracing the same spots over and over.

Seen together, Kyle was everything Carl was not; his energy was boundless, Carl held it all in. Kyle would twirl about with sweat plying his long hair to his face, head bobbing in every direction, singing along to the music. He even danced in the calm between songs. To Carl, he often seemed somehow tragically lost, spinning star. He longed to help him, to save him.

Left to his own devices, Kyle realized early on that Carl would have been just as boring a fuck as he was a dancer. The youngster, then only seventeen, teased and taunted Carl as no boy ever had, and Carl was moved to fucking him with a ferocity that, when he recalled it later, shocked him and delighted him at the same time.

Tonight, while Carl smoked several cigarettes, Kyle smoked a joint and, the closer they got to town, the friendlier Kyle became. When they reached the condominium, Kyle had Carl's pants unzipped and was going down on him. Carl wouldn't let Kyle finish in the garage. He begged to go to the apartment: "Please, I want to fuck you. It's been so long."

It was a small apartment on the 20th floor, with a lovely view, on clear days, of the mountains to the east, but sparsely furnished. It was a place to rendezvous, not a place to impress.

Kyle disappeared into the bedroom with his Gibson guitar and his bag; Carl put on some music.

After a few moments, Kyle appeared holding a bottle of poppers and a fifth of brandy. After drinking some of the brandy, Kyle uncapped the bottle of poppers and held it under his nostrils.

Soon they were in bed and Carl was sliding several fingers in and out of Kyle's ass while Kyle sucked him to hardness. Then, on all fours, Kyle took an occasional hit off the poppers as Carl finally shoved his short, thick cock in him. Carl thought about the many orgies in the past and how when they were all having the kid he no longer seemed to be the celebrity Kyle Cartwright, but just another body, a beautiful body that was somehow being sacrificed. He preferred to have it this way, alone with Kyle, his music playing on the stereo, Kyle singing his songs.

"Please," Carl said after awhile, "get on your back. You know I like to look at your face when you're coming."

"Okay," Kyle said, wriggling around, keeping most of Carl's cock in him. He swept his leg over Carl's head and Carl settled in again. But now Kyle was feverish for it and Carl's thrusts were too gentle for him and he began lifting himself against Carl, hard and fast.

"God, it feels so damn good, Kyle. So damn good." Carl lifted Kyle up by the backs of his thighs as Kyle slammed his cock into his body. Carl smiled watching Kyle, amused at how much the young star enjoyed fucking his cock. It seemed like old times, and he cried like a baby when Kyle finally came, jacking himself off. Gasping, Kyle closed his eyes and stopped his thrusting, letting Carl gently fuck him again. He brought his hands around Carl's neck as Carl finally finished. "Oh, Kyle, I love you," Carl cried.

"Keep it in me," Kyle begged. "I want to go to sleep with you in me."

Carl was delighted to keep his cock inside Kyle as they clung to each other in the spartan bedroom. In a few minutes Carl was hard again and, as they lay on their sides, Carl gently fucked Kyle to orgasm again.

And tonight, Kyle fell fast asleep without taking a pill.

SIX

Carl and Kyle stood under the hot shower, soaping each other. Kyle knelt and began to take Carl's cock into his mouth, but Carl pulled him to his feet. "No, no. I'm raw from last night and you've got a plane to catch."
"But I need it. One for the road. One last time."
"It's always one last time. But there's always another time."
Kyle smiled. "Just you remember that."
"But I will kiss you goodbye."
Carl pressed his tongue into Kyle's mouth, demanding entry. Their cocks squeezed tightly together, Kyle moved his erection urgently against Carl's limp cock. Carl kept kissing Kyle, even as Kyle tried to pull away. Soon the soap had washed away and Carl finally released Kyle and turned off the shower. Kyle stood in the shower, massaging his cock and balls. Carl stepped out, grabbed a towel and, as he handed it to Kyle, Kyle shook his cock at him. "Will you at least make us breakfast?"
"Okay," Carl said, drying himself, "if you'll promise to sing my new songs to the crew."
"I promise," Kyle said, stepping from the shower and grabbing a towel. "Who knows, I might like 'em."
Carl served them scrambled eggs and toast on large white plates. It was all he could find in the refrigerator. They were eating when a buzz from the lobby interrupted them.
Vinnie was already in the white Mercedes limousine when it pulled up in front of Kyle's condominium at precisely noon. He waited for a few minutes and then, fearing Kyle was running late, told the driver he was going up and fetch him.
"I didn't know you two were back together," Vinnie said after

Kyle let him into the apartment.

"We aren't," Kyle said, rushing towards the bedroom. "I need to see you Vinnie, in here, please."

Kyle closed the door as soon as Vinnie was in the room. He swept Vinnie into his arms. "Why didn't you come to my party?"

"I had a date."

"More important than me?"

"I'm sorry."

As Vinnie pulled away, Kyle's hand dropped to his groin. "I've missed you. It's been two weeks."

"We'll be together for six weeks, Kyle."

Kyle dropped to his knees and began unzipping Vinnie's trousers.

"What the hell are you doing?"

"Just one for the road?"

"Look, the limo's out front, waiting. The plane's waiting at LAX."

"Let them wait. They aren't going anywhere without me. I'm the star, remember."

"In all my years, I've never met anybody who loved suckin' dick more than you."

Kyle now had Vinnie's limp dick in his hand. He looked up at Vinnie and smiled. "It's my favorite thing in the world. And *this*," he stroked the slowly hardening member, "this is the best there is, isn't it?"

Vinnie shook his head. He had been so long without sex and now the prospect lay ahead of having to refuse it at almost every turn. But this morning, Vinnie asked himself, what harm could it do? "Okay, but that's all you're getting until we get to Texas." Closing his eyes, he took Kyle's head in his hands. Wanting to get the show on the road, he would control the boy's sucking of him. As Kyle filled his mouth with the immense organ and began pumping his mouth back and forth on the shaft, Vinnie squirmed his hips, sending his prick deep down the young star's throat. Soon, with the hungry working of Kyle's tongue and lips on the huge cockhead, Vinnie's belly was rippling in spasm after spasm and he spent his load across Kyle's face, wetting his shirt and the carpet under them. Kyle hugged Vinnie to him, kissing the semi-flaccid cock.

A knock on the door interrupted their last moments of pleasure.

"Kyle," Carl said, "the driver's buzzing. What's going on?"

Kyle wiped his face with his hand. "I've gotta change my shirt. This one'll never do. I'll be out in a minute."

. . .

The studio had leased an L-1011 to fly the company to Texas. As it punched its way up through the haze and climbed out over the Pacific, Kyle looked out the window. As many times as he'd flown, he never got bored with the take-off. The air was slick and clear and, below them, the red of the mountains and the desert and the gray of the ocean looked clean, warm. Kyle was perfectly content. He patted Vinnie's knee.

"Thanks for coming along," he said.

"Well," Vinnie chuckled, "thanks for making me come."

Coffee and rolls were served. The young dark-haired flight attendant's smile was so wide he dimpled. Kyle asked where he was staying in San Antonio.

"The Hilton," came the reply.

"I bet you'll have fun there."

The attendant smiled. "Hope so."

Vinnie shook his head. "We're going to Brackettville."

Kyle shrugged.

The flight attendant looked at the obscene bulge in Kyle's jeans and smiled. Shaking his head, he said, "I don't know where that is, but I bet you'll have fun there."

"We'll try," Kyle chuckled, "but I'd rather be in San Antonio."

As the attendant bowed and began serving the rest of the party, Kyle turned to Vinnie. "We will have fun in Brackettville, won't we Vinnie?"

"If you call shooting a movie six days a week, twelve hours a day fun."

"At least we get Sundays off."

"Not me. I have a hunch I'm going to busy Sundays."

"But that won't be work."

"You call it what you want," Vinnie said, sliding a magazine out from the pocket in front of him.

They landed beneath a layer of overcast sky so thick and dark it looked like casket lining. A fleet of limousines, station wagons and trucks were waiting to take the company west to Brackettville. Kyle, hidden behind his Ray-Bans, waited at the baggage carousel while Vinnie went to the Avis counter where he picked up the keys to a red Mustang convertible. Kyle collected their luggage and waited while Vinnie brought the car around.

As they left the airport, Kyle took off his sunglasses and began fiddling with the radio, punching the buttons.

Finally, when Roberta Flack was singing, "Feel Like Makin' Love," Kyle was satisfied and stretched out in the bucket seat, his hand gently resting on Vinnie's groin.

Kyle was comfortable; the wide open spaces reminded him of home, of Hamilton, Montana, the isolated village of two thousand with one radio station, one four-way traffic light, and three-digit telephone numbers. Yes, he thought, he could stay in Brackettville for six weeks. Hell, he'd stayed in Hamilton for fourteen years. And in Hamilton he'd had Kale. In Brackettville, he'd have Vinnie. He chuckled to himself with the realization that, somehow, he'd always managed to have a big dick around when he needed one.

To Vinnie, after leaving San Antonio, it became a scorched, hardscrabble landscape that, much like show business, makes kin out of strangers and killers of friends.

SEVEN

The living quarters on location are assigned according to protocol and rank, like the quarters in a division headquarters town in France or Italy during World War II. Actress Catherine Campbell, hired to play Kyle's love interest, would arrive in two weeks and share a rented house with her make-up woman and stand-in. Kyle's co-star, Douglas Raymond, would have his own house, as would Grant King. The head cameraman, the assistant director, and less important supporting actors, the makeup men, the wardrobe mistress and the script girl, all stayed at hotels scattered around the area, including the Holiday Inn and the Motel 6 in Del Rio. Kyle, being the star, was given the nicest private house that could be rented, in this case the Sunset Ranch. He would live there with a maid and cook and drive seven miles north to the Alamo Movie Location every day in his rented convertible.

When they arrived at the ranch house, Vinnie left his bags in the Mustang.

"What's wrong?" Kyle asked.

"I'm not staying here. I'm staying in town at the Cattleman."

"What?"

"I think having me here every night would be a distraction. You'll need to concentrate on studying your lines for the next day, getting your rest."

"No. I want you here."

"I've made up my mind, Kyle. It'd be best if I stayed in town."

Kyle shrugged. "Not tonight. You can stay in town

tomorrow, but not tonight."

Reluctantly, Vinnie took his bags from the trunk of the Mustang. He was determined to win this point, but he could just as easily win it tomorrow as tonight. And besides, he was as horny for Kyle's ass as Kyle was for his cock.

The Sunset Ranch was comfortable and Kyle felt immediately at home there. After Consuela, the Mexican cook, made dinner, Kyle told her she could leave. He explained he would often be late arriving and she was to leave each night at six. "Just have dinner on the stove for me." He paused, looked at Vinnie. "For us."

After Consuela had left and they were eating barbecued skirt steak with brussels sprouts, Kyle brought up the living arrangements once again. This time Vinnie said, "You're insatiable, Kyle. If I'm around, you won't be able to concentrate on your performance."

"No. I'll be fine. Let me worry about my performance. You just worry about yours."

Vinnie stared at Kyle. "I'm here to work, too, you know, not just fuck you." He took a deep breath, then, slicing into his beef, he smiled and looked deeply into Kyle's eyes. "Say, this food is terrific. I tell you what, for both our sakes, I'll make a deal with you. I'll have dinner here three nights a week."

Kyle shook his head. "No. That won't work."

Vinnie stared at his food, a somber expression returning to his face. "Please, don't push me, Kyle."

Kyle looked up at the ceiling, then at Vinnie. He grinned. "And we'll spend Sunday together?"

Vinnie looked away. He wasn't smiling. "All day, if that's what it takes."

"If I only get it three nights a week, it'll take all Saturday night and all day Sunday."

"I guess I can, if that's what it takes. But I'm not a young man anymore, Kyle."

Kyle grinned. "But that's what I like about you. You've learned so much and you know just how to make it feel so *damn* good."

Vinnie chuckled. "At least I'm still good for something to somebody."

While Kyle cleared the table, Vinnie went into the bedroom and removed his clothes. If he was being treated like a stud bull, that's the way he'd act. He wasn't going to lift a finger around the place, just his cock.

He was lying on his back in the center of the bed, stroking his erection, when Kyle came into the bedroom and flung himself on the bed. Kyle groaned with happiness as he kissed the throbbing manmeat. His face flushed, he climbed over him and grasped the penis in his hand. "God, I love this."

Vinnie shook his head. "You love it too much, Kyle. Loving dick that much is going to get you into trouble."

"Some dick maybe, but not this one," Kyle said, touching the swollen ballsac, tracing the contours with his fingertips, then he began sucking in earnest. Soon the cock was hard enough to please him and he quickly stripped. He mounted the older man, straddling him with his knees. He squatted down, watching their reflection in the mirror across the room as he guided the prick between the cheeks of his ass. In moments, he was gasping with pleasure as the ring of his anus stretched to accommodate the excessive girth of it. Vinnie sighed as more and more of it slid into Kyle. Then it was finally completely inside of him, Kyle began jerking up and down on it and Vinnie reached out and ran his hands up and down the tanned limbs of the young star.

"You are a beauty, I've gotta admit that."

"Oh god, oh god, it's so fuckin' big - "

"I think you like fucking as much as you do sucking."

"Oh yes, yes I do," Kyle cried. "God, it feels so good. Biggest goddamn dick in the world and it feels so good."

Kyle's orgasm caught him by surprise. He was not even touching his cock. He began crying out, moving faster, like a wild man riding a stallion, the muscles of his anus contracting tightly around the cock. The increased friction caused Vinnie to begin his orgasm. Kyle's cock wobbled and spunk flew up and then splashed down on Vinnie's chest. As Kyle pressed his buttocks into Vinnie's stomach, the older man's sperm gushed into Kyle. Kyle continued milking the organ and it remained fairly erect. Finally, Vinnie withdrew the prick and stood up. Kyle remained on his knees and Vinnie pulled him over on the bed so that he could enter him again from where he stood. He enjoyed taking a man in the animal way. In this position, Kyle could still watch Vinnie in the mirror as he fucked him. Vinnie moved with his familiar rhythm, reaching down for a moment to open the young star a little wider. He pushed and filled him. Kyle grabbed his own cock and stroked it again to hardness.

"Oh god, oh god," Kyle kept groaning as Vinnie showed no mercy. The pleasure was intense and he almost wanted to move away from it but he could not. Instead he heaved his hips, jerking into him, and came. Again his cries drew Vinnie further and, arms around his torso, he held on, and was jerked and pulled towards his second orgasm as well.

Later, as Kyle rested his head against the older man's chest. he said, "I'll try to be good, honest I will."

"You've been good so far," Vinnie said, stroking Kyle's flaxen hair. "Very good. Now, kiss it goodnight."

Kyle laid across Vinnie and brought his lips to the cock, lying in repose against Vinnie's thigh. He kissed the head of it, then with his tongue lapped up the excess cum. Then, looking up at Vinnie, he slowly began working it into his mouth once again. Vinnie pulled it away and rolled over. "I said you could kiss it. That's all. Just kiss it. You have to learn to do exactly as I say."

Kyle kissed Vinnie's naked back, then leaned his head against his shoulder. "I will. I promise, I'll do exactly as you say."

"Then go to sleep now, Kyle."

"Yes, sir." Kyle rolled away from Vinnie and started to get up, to fetch a sleeping pill, but he slumped back down and fell soundly asleep, his hand clutching his penis, sticky with cum.

The next morning, Vinnie returned his bags to the trunk of the Mustang and Kyle didn't say a word. Kyle did not want to force Vinnie; he would let Vinnie come to him.

EIGHT

As almost all movies are, "El Dorado," was shot out of sequence. Grant King decided the most difficult scene, a burning hay wagon rolling down the street of the make-believe town and a stunt man, doubling for Kyle, jumping from it, would be gotten out of the way first.

Even though the stunt double did the hard work, Kyle still had to be on the set and had to roll around on the ground and come up swinging.

The shooting of this sequence took most of the first two days of the schedule and Kyle was exhausted each night. He made no entreaties to Vinnie to "come to supper."

Instead, he drew a hot bath for himself and sat in it studying the script for his upcoming scenes. The heat made his body swell with well-being. He remembered a Christmas Eve when he went out in the snow to chop down a tree and when he returned his mother snapped the icicles from his nose and ordered him to the bathtub. He giggled remembering Kale coming in and taking a pee and standing beside the tub while his little brother gave him head.

Kyle set the script on the floor and leaned back. He stroked his cock with a fierceness now, remembering Kale, the beauty of that cock, and his skin tingled as he came, jets of cum spewing out in the warm, sudsy water. Closing his eyes, he cursed his brother and wished that he were there, to see how right he was, how his cock had grown big like he said it would, and what a success he had made of his life.

But by Saturday night, Kyle was desperate. He and Vinnie barely got in the front door of the ranch house before Kyle's mouth closed on Vinnie's cock and he was working at it. As Vinnie looked down and watched the blond head bobbing before him, he realized again he was just a prop to Kyle's ardent action, having the last vestiges of honor sucked from him. He had allowed his penis to become the toy of a kid half his age. Still, he had to admit, Kyle was a pro. Vinnie stroked Kyle's hair. "I take it you've missed it?"

Kyle withdrew the erection and held it. "You wouldn't even come to my trailer – "

"We have to be discreet."

"Discreet shit, everybody knows."

Kyle's taut throat gulped and he took all of Vinnie in. As Vinnie came, he grew weak and he had to hold on to Kyle to keep from falling. He couldn't remember ever coming as hard or as fast in his life. He had missed it almost as much as Kyle had.

Hearing strange sounds outside the house, Vinnie tried to free himself but Kyle would not give up his soft toy.

"It's just the wind. Off the prairie. I've never heard winds like it. But I've gotten used to it. Like I've gotten used to this."

Kyle finally stopped sucking after Vinnie promised they would have a nice long fuck after supper. Kyle ate leisurely but Vinnie was ravenous after his stupendous orgasm. "*Tengo una hambre que parece dos,*" Vinnie said.

"I didn't know you knew Spanish."

"I don't, but I'm picking up some phrases at the hotel. Nice folks at the hotel. You should be staying there."

"No, you should be staying here."

Consuela had left what had become Kyle's favorite, albondigas de gallina. "Chicken balls," he laughed. He liked the sound of it as well as the taste.

"All of Consuela's food improves with cooking."

"It is good, I gotta admit."

"Consuela says, '*Barriga llena corazon contento.*'"

"You'll be gaining weight – "

"See, you should be staying here. No cooking like this in town."

"*Mas vale llegar a tiempo que ser invitado,*" Vinnie chuckled.

"Let's see, that's 'it's better to drop in at the right time than be invited?'"

"Right."

After finishing his favorite Consuela-prepared dessert, cocada, a coconut pudding, Kyle began clearing the table. Vinnie remained at the table, sipping his Coke. "It's at times like this I could use a brandy."

"Me too," Kyle said from the kitchen. "But I really feel better without it."

"You're still doing the other shit, though. I saw some of it in the bathroom."

Kyle didn't respond, he just kept rinsing the dishes. Vinnie got up and went into the kitchen. He stood behind Kyle and stroked his arms. "You should stop that, too, Kyle."

Kyle still did not respond.

Vinnie's hands moved to the asscheeks. He massaged them gently. "I may have to give this up if you don't."

"I have to give things up one at a time," Kyle said as Vinnie reached around his waist and undid his belt, then unzipped his pants. Kyle went on rinsing the dishes as his pants dropped to his ankles.

Vinnie's hands began kneading the now bare ass. As he hugged Kyle to his body, his erection rubbing into the asscrack, Kyle sighed. "I'll give the blow up if you'll move in here."

"Can't."

"Won't, you mean. You won't."

"No, I won't."

"Then I won't."

"What you *will* do is bend over – "

The fuck that started in the kitchen went to the living room, then the bedroom, and finally ended in the bathroom, where Vinnie had gone to shower after he had come. Kyle followed him and began sucking him as the water cascaded over his body. It was here, on his knees in the bathtub, that Kyle finally jerked himself to orgasm.

. . .

The exquisite face Kyle saw in the mirror the following morning drew him closer and he put down the cologne and leaned towards it. He dropped a little to the side and watched the reflection closely. He saw tears begin, the pouty lips turn to wistful smile. He was happy, sublimely happy now. He closed his eyes and folded his arms and began rocking, as if he was hearing a lullaby.

There were noises coming from the connecting bedroom. Vinnie was stirring. Last night, after their shower, he had gone to the second bedroom. He preferred sleeping alone.

After Kyle awoke, he lay in his bed imagining what it would be like to live here permanently, with Vinnie only a room away, that humongous cock, the cock that Kyle had adored before and loved even more now. The shape of it, the size of it, the smell of it, the taste of it. It was the most joked about cock in Hollywood but few really knew the truth about it, what it could do, who had enjoyed it. What Kyle knew provided fuel for his fantasies on the nights Vinnie wasn't at the ranch.

Yet, while Vinnie's reputation was well-deserved, he remained almost illusory, too much for Kyle to comprehend. Vinnie was not affectionate; he had never kissed Kyle and had touched him only fleetingly.

Suddenly, Vinnie appeared in the doorway of the bathroom. Kyle looked at his face, the splendidly tired, battered face with the laughing green eyes, that today had a placid look to match Kyle's own. Kyle smiled and his eyes fell, as they always did, to the cock. Even limp it was outrageous. His mouth watered for it once again.

Kyle fell to his knees before Vinnie. Saying nothing, Vinnie took Kyle's head in his hands and hugged it to his crotch. "Yeah, kiss it good morning, Kyle. Kiss it."

Kyle kissed the cock, prepared to take the head in his mouth.

"This'll have to do, Kyle. I want to go to town this afternoon. Everybody's meeting at the Cattleman."

"We'll see," Kyle teased, lifting the penis so he could slide some of the shaft in his mouth.

As Kyle gorged on the prick, Vinnie pushed, sending it deeper and Kyle gagged. For a long while, Kyle was all mouth, then his hands began to waver and clutch at Vinnie's skin. When he sensed Vinnie was close, Kyle grabbed his buttocks and Kyle looked up and saw Vinnie's head was tilted back and he began gasping. Kyle let go suddenly and the throbbing cock, released, spurted cum all over his face.

. . .

After lunch, Kyle agreed to go to the Cattleman Hotel. The crew was gathered on the veranda balcony, drinking and talking, and they watched Vinnie and Kyle as they drove up in the Mustang, mumbling things to each other they would never say out loud in front of Kyle.

While the others got drunk, Kyle and Vinnie sat near them drinking cola.

Late in the afternoon, Jim Donner checked into the hotel and joined the crew on the veranda. Kyle had expected him, but not for another week. Kyle knew that Donner, although calling himself a free-lance "photo journalist," was one of the most infamous of the paid informants for the *Hollywood Tattler*. He feared and resented the man but felt it best to tolerate him, even feed him occasional bits of gossip in return for silence. Kyle saw Donner as a man much like himself, a polymorphous man, for whom the world consisted of two kinds of people: those who could be used and those who could not, and they both made a systematic attempt to cultivate only the former. Donner had made several passes at Kyle in the past but, although Donner had a certain appeal – masculine, tall, slender, his hair gently graying at forty three, and with a certain animal grace about him – it was more interesting for Kyle to tease Donner than to give in to him.

Donner went about the hotel shaking hands with the crew and finally settled near Kyle and Vinnie.

"You're early," Kyle said, not smiling.

"I finished up early in Africa so I came here directly." He held Kyle steadily in his gaze. "I could hardly wait to get here."

"I can't imagine why," Kyle said, looking away, avoiding his stare.

"Oh, I love location shoots," he said. He went on to tell them when, twenty years before, fresh out of journalism school, he had joined a crew to film Ernest Hemingway on a hunting expedition. "I got along fine with old Hemingway," he said, "although he did strange things at times. Every morning, when he woke up, he would come out of his tent, carrying a bucket of soap and water. He would take off his pants and stand there, with everybody in the camp watching him, and proceed to wash his cock and balls with the soap and water."

"Don't give Vinnie ideas," one of the men laughed, overhearing the tale. "He'll be out in the hall every morning waving that thing."

"Hell, 'round here it pays to advertise," Vinnie joked.

Grinning, Kyle finished his bottle of Coke and looked about for the waiter to bring him another. The men had been served all afternoon by a boy named Bobby, the grandson of Colonel Patterson, the hotel's owner. Earlier, Bobby had told Kyle whenever he wasn't going to school or studying his lessons, he earned his allowance working at the hotel, doing errands for his mother, Kate Richards, who managed the hotel for her ailing, aged father.

It was obvious the boy was excited about having the crew staying there and he seemed to be in awe of Kyle. "I have all your records," he said.

"You mean, all of my two albums."

Bobby smiled. "Yeah, all of them."

Bobby was, like Kyle, slender and fine boned, but while Kyle was fair, Bobby was dark and had large glittering eyes, accentuated by thick expressive brows. And Bobby was so extraordinarily handsome that people would stare at him on the street. His features were, Kyle thought, perfect, as if carved, and he was so diminutive, he had a "please don't hurt me" quality that strangely excited Kyle.

"If he weren't so young, I'd have him in bed in no time," Kyle told Vinnie after the boy served them.

"Oh I don't know. I think he's old enough to know what he likes, and he's smitten with you. Everybody's aware of it."

Now when the boy entered the room, carrying drinks for two of the cameramen and Donner, Kyle fell strangely silent when Donner lifted his camera and snapped the boy's picture.

"You must pose for me, Bobby," Donner said, handing him a twenty dollar bill as a tip.

"Doing what?" Bobby asked mischievously.

"Anything you want," Donner laughed.

"Okay," the boy said, his hands on his hips. "Tell me when."

"Tomorrow?"

"I can't tomorrow. I'm going to be in the movie tomorrow. I got off from school to be one of the extras."

"Even better. I'll be there too and we can shoot you in your western get-up."

"Sounds like fun," Bobby said, rushing off.

Donner's eyes followed the boy in retreat, his splendid buttocks undulating in tight white bellbottoms. The journalist felt Kyle staring at him and turned around in his chair. "God, what a cutie. He's a natural, Kyle. You should get him a bigger part in the movie."

"I'll speak to Grant about it. I have to agree. I don't think I've ever seen a more beautiful child."

"*Child?* Hey, don't kid yourself," Donner said. "That kid knows what's happening. Besides, he's just a small person. Everybody can't be six foot tall, you know. How boring that would be."

"But to me he looks so innocent - "

"As innocent as you looked at about that age," Vinnie interjected. "And I remember quite well you knew what the fuck you were doing."

Kyle nodded and lifted his glass of Coke in salute. "Well, here's to knowing what the fuck you're doing."

Vinnie shook his head in exasperation. "May God help us."

As the afternoon wore on, the crew got drunker and Kyle grew more and more restless. He was anxious for Vinnie to drive him home. And fuck him again. But first they had to eat dinner at Snyder's restaurant. When Donner joined Kyle and Vinnie at their table, Kyle explained to Vinnie that Donner had been hired by Bergen and Mac to shot some publicity stills, mostly featuring him and Catherine Campbell. "It'll create a diversion," Mac said, "from all these rumors about your being gay."

Cutting his steak, Kyle eyed Donner suspiciously and asked, "Catherine doesn't get here until next week. What are you going to do in the meantime?"

"Take pictures of that little cutie."

"Leave him alone," Kyle said, surprising even himself with

his tone.

Donner snickered. "Hey, he's hardly your type, Kyle."

"I just meant, there are laws against that sort of thing."

"And when did breaking a law ever bother you?" Donner laughed.

Kyle shook his head and went about finishing his dinner as quickly as he could. While he and Vinnie ate, Donner talked about his profession. He told them how he preferred taking the pictures for a story to doing the writing. He relished the specifics of photography. In his spare time, he would spend hours composing still lifes before photographing them. He understood the difference between intention and effect in art, aware of the fact that no matter how hard something is willed into creation, the result is never exactly as planned, and he thrived on taking the spontaneous photograph that would eventually be heralded as an artistic masterpiece. He considered himself an artist, not simply a news photographer. "A photograph reflects a given moment in time, and yet the more specific it is, the more universal. You can understand that, Kyle. You're an artist. What you do in your acting is the same."

"Hell," Kyle chuckled, "I'm not an artist, I'm just a movie star."

. . .

After dinner, Vinnie drove Kyle to the ranch with the top down, Ringo Starr's "You're Sixteen" on the stereo. "This is getting to be my favorite song," Kyle joked.

"You're askin' for trouble, that's all I gotta say," Vinnie said, "goin' in for jailbait."

When they arrived, Vinnie stayed in the car.

"Aren't you coming in?" Kyle asked.

"I'm raw after last night, Kyle. I told you, three times a week. That's our deal."

"Hey, this is a new week."

Vinnie shook his head and turned off the ignition.

As Kyle lay on his stomach on the bed with Vinnie topping him, Kyle couldn't get Bobby out of his mind. He had always thought of himself exclusively as a bottom, but when he met Bobby, and saw everyone's reaction to the boy, especially Donner's, all he had been able to think about was what it would be like to make love to him, to kiss him, suck him, even fuck him. Finally, he gave himself up to the fantasy of what would have happened had they brought Bobby back with them.

He saw himself getting into position between Bobby's legs as Vinnie straddled the boy's head. The boy would lick Vinnie's balls, then push down on the topside of the mammoth organ so that it could slide into his mouth easily. Vinnie would lock his legs around the back of the boy's neck and push down. Being so little, Bobby would nearly choke on the cock.

Kyle would spend a few minutes on each of Bobby's splendid pectorals, grabbing them with both hands and forcing up so that they soon would resemble a woman's tits. He would suck the nipples violently.

Then Kyle would squeeze one cheek of Bobby's succulent ass with his hand as he got into position between his legs, holding himself up at an angle on his arms and not touching him. Slowly he would begin pushing his cock in so as not to hurt him. Then he would grab his legs, feeling them tremble as the cock slid in all the way. Kyle would feel the desperation when the boy clutched his ass, pushing, pushing, pushing.

When Vinnie finished, sending a stream of cum across the boy's face, Kyle would push Bobby onto his belly. The hole expanded now, Kyle would press, moving his hips slowly, carefully. He would hold himself steady and soon the cock would be halfway in. Bobby would moan and Kyle would stop moving momentarily, then begin again, slowly sliding in another inch. He would push in, draw out, slipping his hands around his ribs and twisting his nipples. He would begin moving faster, as the boy writhed, twisted, rotated his hips beneath him.

He would pump his all deeply into him, Bobby's taut muscles clutching him, and then he would collapse onto his back. Then Vinnie would lift Kyle from the boy and, stroking his renewed erection, he would mount the boy . . .

Just as he was imagining this scenario, Vinnie was close to orgasm and he spread his hands out flat on Kyle's ass, stretching the hole, opening it was wide as possible. Vinnie began breathing harder and, as he rammed his cock into Kyle's ass one last time that evening, Kyle came himself.

NINE

Kyle sauntered onto the set wearing faded jeans held up by a silver-buckled cowboy belt, scuffed cowboy boots, and a long-sleeved red cowboy shirt. He rocked back on his heels, cocked his head to one side and finally he grinned. His face lit up when he saw Bobby.

Kate Richards had brought Bobby to the location and she was as fascinated by the process of movie-making and as excited to be there as her son. The last major motion picture to be shot at the Alamo Movie Location was "Bandolero," in 1967, when Bobby was too young to appreciate it. That movie, starring James Stewart, Dean Martin and Racquel Welch, caused the most excitement in town since Stewart had been there seven years before to film "Two Ride Together."

As Kyle watched the boy being suited up for his scene, he thought: 'What a great sense of fun Bobby has.' He could not help but think of them in bed together, what fun they would have.

When Bobby was dressed, he and his mother joined Kyle in the canvas chairs off to the side.

"When will they start?" Bobby asked.

"When they're ready. Good and ready. I get paid for the waiting," Kyle joked, "the acting I do for free."

Kyle had learned to be patient, endure long hours of waiting for the shot, then do ten seconds of filming, then wait while the crew set up the next shot. He would usually strum his guitar and chat with the crew. Today, he entertained Bobby and his mother with some of the new songs Carl had given him and ended with a song that expressed the feelings he was having about Bobby at that moment better than he himself could articulate them: "Don't Let Me Be Lonely Tonight:

"Do me wrong, do me right
"Tell me lies but hold me tight
"Save your goodbyes for the morning light
"Don't let me be lonely tonight."

Later, Bobby told his mother he could listen to Kyle sing and talk all day, especially, he said, in a low voice, "Don't Let Me Be Lonely Tonight." The boy did not know Kyle's voice was a product of determination and hard work. Reverend Williams had another clergyman friend, Bill Ambler, who lived near Los Angeles, and when he was on a sabbatical in Washington state and heard Kyle sing, there was no question the man would take him back to the city and pursue a possible future for him in music. But Reverend Ambler was, Kyle found, in charge of a poor parish and had no real connections in Hollywood; if he hadn't left Ambler's parish that day and gone shoplifting in Beverly Hills, he never would have met Mac. Mac was the one who took Kyle to Carl. Kyle would sit for hours at Carl's Steinway trying to lower his voice. It was too high, hard, nervous. He had the straight-lipped, set mouth of a boy who had learned early to fight through things alone. Eventually, the voice dropped and developed the easy firmness and remarkable resonance that reminded many of the voice of Clark Gable. With that, his face muscles relaxed, his eyes opened wider, his forehead smoothed, and his now famous smile was born.

Grant King interrupted the little concert to talk to Kyle. He never gave instructions to an actor out loud. Instead, he would go over and put an arm around the actor and have him walk with him a few moments while he talked to him quietly. Kyle liked King's methods and he wanted to please him.

After giving his instructions to Kyle and the extras, Grant was ready, but there was still a great deal of fussing about setting up the stunt. There was a final check of camera angles, a sound check and a call to make sure the ambulance crew and doctor were standing close by.

"All right, everyone, let's have quiet please," the assistant director announced through his bullhorn.

"Everyone in their places?" Grant asked. "Then roll 'em."

"Slate it," the assistant said. There was a harsh clack of the slate and the slate man called out the scene and shot numbers.

"Speed," the sound man said.

"And...action."

The stuntman took a running start and launched himself through the upper half of a door. He crashed though on the side facing the camera, did a quick little roll when he hit the ground, then bounced up onto his feet.

The crowd broke into applause and cheers.

Now it was Kyle's turn to bounce up on his feet. He did it several ways, over a dozen takes, before King was finally satisfied.

Filthy now, dusting himself off, Kyle stepped over to where Bobby and his mother were sitting.

Spitting dirt, Kyle said, "Well, that's show biz."

Bobby said, "I love it."

As it did Kyle, show business exerted an irresistible attraction for Bobby. It also served as a protection; he felt safe committed to the childlike art of play acting. He could never understand why he felt so at ease in an imaginary role; it was as if all of the anxiety and terror he felt in real life melted away behind the footlights. He had no fear of performing in front of an audience. The technicalities of acting fascinated him. He listened to dialogue repeated over and over again. No effort seemed too great to achieve a heightened effect.

But, unlike Kyle, Bobby's acting talent ran in the family. Bobby's grandmother Maxine had moved from Brackettville in the fall of 1927, when she was sixteen. She went to Houston to take a steady job with the Gene Lewis Players, a stock company at the Palace Theater, at $75 a week and she soon became the company's leading lady and her pay was raised to $250 a week. It was there that she became involved with the son of a wealthy oilman, Clarence Bitting. She married and, although she retired from performing, her interest in the stage never left her. The couple tried unsuccessfully to have children and eventually, to keep herself occupied, she began an acting school.

In 1942, her husband joined the Army and fought in the War. Before he left, Maxine became pregnant. Their daughter, Katharine, was five when her father returned home a full colonel. The three visited Brackettville and decided to settle there to help run her parents' hotel.

Ten years later, on a visit to Houston to see her fraternal

grandparents, sixteen-year-old Kate met Robert Richards and fell in love. Her mother forbade her to marry and the rebellious girl became pregnant. She had the child, then returned to Brackettville when the relationship soured. No one in town knew she had never married Bobby's father.

Kate inherited her mother's love of the theater and they often travelled to Houston and San Antonio to see professional companies. After her mother died, Kate took a small studio in Del Rio and taught acting.

Now she considered Bobby her finest pupil. "He is the most poised thirteen-year-old actor we've ever witnessed," one reviewer remarked of one of the boy's early performances as the snottiest son in "Fly Away Home," a comedy by Dorothy Bennett and Irving White. "Nothing fazes him, simply charming," another said.

After shooting the day's scenes, Grant was charmed by Bobby as well. But that evening, viewing the dailies, Grant was stunned: The camera, he realized, loved Bobby Richards, loved him even more than it did Kyle Cartwright.

TEN

Kate Richards had a serene, easy way of talking. Her voice hummed behind every sentence and her words fell evenly into long, smooth phrases, as if she were reading them. Vinnie found himself listening to hear that hum, soft and comforting, rather like the background noise of air-conditioning. He would return from the location and sit with her on the veranda, talking late into the night.

Vinnie came to think of her as somehow distant, detached from the world, and he nourished that image, convinced her devotion to her father, her son and her work were only pieces of the facade she'd built, a cloister to retreat into. She had been more successful retreating from the world than he had and he admired her enormously, wanted to spend more time with her.

Near the end of the week, Kyle said, "You're not living up to your bargain." Vinnie had cancelled their rendezvous the night before.

"I'm sorry. I never should have made such a deal with you."

"Maybe you're sorry you even came to Texas."

"No, I'm very glad I did."

"Yeah, I've heard the guys talking. You're sniffing up to Bobby's mother."

"She was the Colonel's daughter before she was Bobby's mother. I prefer to think of her that way."

"I prefer not to think of her at all."

"I'm sorry."

"You should be. And tonight you can show me just how sorry you are."

"If you say so."

• • •

Vinnie had never dared go as far as he secretly wanted to with Kyle. After all, when he met Kyle, the boy was only 18 and he still regarded him as a youngster, even though he knew he probably had his share of sexual encounters. But tonight his impatience with Kyle's demands caused him to lash out in the only way he knew: with his enormous penis. If Kyle wanted sex, he'd give him sex. So much sex he wouldn't want it again any time soon.

Vinnie began as soon as they had finished supper. He let Kyle clear the table as usual. He went to the bedroom and prepared the love nest. He put Kyle's album on the stereo and dimmed the lights. He was lying in the middle of the bed, as usual, stroking his erection with the dildo Kyle had brought with him. Kyle had purchased the dildo just before he left at a shop in West Hollywood. He wanted one that was as long and fat as Vinnie's cock. Vinnie discovered the greased monster in a drawer in the bathroom when he was inspecting for cocaine. He left it sitting on the vanity for Kyle to find the next morning. Kyle never mentioned it.

Now Kyle smiled as he entered the bedroom and saw what Vinnie was doing. "The real and the faux, together for the first time," Kyle laughed.

"So this is what you do on my off-nights?"

"It's the best replica I could find."

"The head's not the same."

Kyle laid down on the bed between Vinnie's outstretched thighs and took the real penis in his hand. "No, and it doesn't taste the same either." He began licking the cock, nibbling on the head, and soon he had engulfed as much of it as he could take. "And it doesn't come. You like it when I come, don't you Kyle?'

Kyle nodded as he sucked.

"That's okay, but I want you on your back right where I am. You're going to suck it while I fuck you with this."

"All right!" Kyle shrieked, freeing the penis.

First Vinnie inserted the dildo only a couple of inches, then, straddling Kyle's chest, he began. Kyle went wild with the sensations. Vinnie emulated his own fucking, the short, quick jabs, then the long ones, then back to the short ones. Kyle just held his head still as Vinnie fucked his mouth while he fucked his ass with the dildo.

After a while, Vinnie removed his penis from Kyle's mouth and brought it to the anus, now well-lubricated and sore from the intense jabbing of the dildo. Vinnie showed no mercy with the entry. Kyle writhed in pain. Tears came to his eyes and he cried out.

But Vinnie did not fuck for long. He pulled almost all the way out and then, slowly, began inching the dildo into the ass alongside his prick. Kyle screamed but Vinnie would not stop. Inch after inch entered the flailing body of the young star. His fingers clutched his own ankles and he forced his legs as wide apart as he could get them. He thought he would black out from the pain. Vinnie began rocking, with about six inches of cock and dildo inside Kyle, and, to the accompaniment of the last song on the A side of Kyle's second album, "Come to Me," Vinnie did just that. He let go of the dildo and it slid out of the rectum as his cum spurted into Kyle.

"Oh god," Kyle said.

"Yeah, you like that. Oh, yeah, take it all, take it all, Kyle." He grabbed Kyle's legs and forced them back and then let go as he collapsed on top of the young man. His head was next to Kyle's, facing the wall. Kyle began licking his face, hugging him. Vinnie pulled up, withdrew his prick and stood next to the bed, wiping the blood off his cock with the sheet. Kyle slithered over to the edge of the bed and, his face in Vinnie's crotch, opened his mouth to receive it again. Vinnie dropped the sheet and began to slap Kyle across the face with the now flaccid cock.

"Not enough, was it?"

"No," Kyle said.

"No *what*?"

"No, *sir*."

"That's better. See, you're makin' it hard."

It was true, the cock was hardening again as Vinnie whipped Kyle's face with it. And it wasn't long before Vinnie permitted Kyle to suck it again. Kyle sat on the edge of the bed and jacked himself off while he sucked.

After Kyle had come, he continued to suck until Vinnie came

again, a small load but enough to satisfy Kyle. He yanked his cock from Kyle's mouth with a flourish, "That should keep you." Kyle swallowed the cum and laid back watching the older man go out of the room and heard the door to the other bedroom slam shut.

Kyle had a mother when he needed one; a brother when he needed one; a cock when he needed one. But having a lover was something that had eluded him. He had tried living with many men, even spent a few months with Mac but it never felt right. Now, here at the ranch, Vinnie felt right, that Kyle could live with him, could endure anything to please him, yet Vinnie did not love him. He was only serving him, doing nothing more, really, than the hustlers he paid in Hollywood. As he lay quietly in bed on the filthy sheets, his thoughts turned again to Bobby and the song, "Don't Let Me Be Lonesome Tonight."

ELEVEN

The following Saturday, Vinnie said he would be staying in town because he was taking Kate and Bobby to the Superbull, an annual bull riding event, early the next morning. He invited Kyle to join them but Kyle begged off. He had no desire to be part of the new "family." "I'm gettin' out of town," he said.

He left the set early on Saturday and, still dressed in his cowboy duds, drove to San Antonio.

He went to the Yellow Rose. The evening dragged. He spent most of it watching. One good prospect he talked with for several minutes had to get up early the next morning and, rising from the barstool, said: "Adios, as we Texans say. Happy hunting."

All of a sudden he felt lonesome. But soon there appeared someone new standing at the bar, ordering a drink. Immediately Kyle made up his mind. He could hardly wait for the tall, dark-skinned man with the soot-black hair and eyes like obsidian chips to notice him.

Frustrated, Kyle sent him a drink. With that, the man came over to him and introduced himself: "King."

"Prince," Kyle said with a wide grin.

King was amused: "I'm named after King Fisher, a legend in these parts. Who were you named after?"

"Prince, the singer, a legend in all parts."

"Fancy that," the stranger said without smiling. "Well, sir, since you're a stranger here I'll tell you about my namesake."

"I can hardly wait," Kyle said, staring at King's bulging crotch.

"Well, sir, King Fisher was killed in a bar right on this spot in 1884. And he didn't end any different from all the other wild guns before and after him. When the bullet with his name on it came along, he was there."

"Do you shoot?" Kyle asked, finally lifting his eyes from the bulge.

Now King chuckled. "Well, I've fired a few blanks but mostly I hit the target."

"What are we waiting for?"

"Damned if I know."

The cheap well vodka hit Kyle hard. He had been on the wagon too long. He found it difficult to walk; King put his arm around his waist and took him to his battered pickup truck.

"Did anybody ever tell you you look just like Kyle Cartwright?" King asked as he started the engine.

Kyle thought of what he always told Mac: "Yeah, nobody ever says to me, 'You're Kyle Cartwright,' they always say, 'Did anybody ever tell you you look just like Kyle Cartwright.'" Now he chuckled. "Ha! I sure get that a lot."

"Yeah, when I walked in and saw you at the bar I said, 'Hey, I'm gonna meet him. And then I'm gonna go to bed with Kyle Cartwright.'" He stroked Kyle's left thigh.

Kyle brought his hand over King's and squeezed it. "I'm sorry I'm not Kyle Cartwright."

King smiled. "So am I."

King's cock was exactly as Kyle had imagined it would be: long, dark and uncut. King didn't get a chance to undress. Kyle was on his knees as soon as they entered the trailer King owned in a park near the edge of town. It was a filthy place, but Kyle thought it fitting for the fucking he got there was even more brutal than the one Vinnie had inflicted upon him two nights before. It seemed as if King simply could not stop. Long, long into the night the screwing continued. Kyle came and then came again. King didn't. He just kept on. Kyle would stop him momentarily, to change position; the relentless King never went soft. Kyle thought he was insatiable, but in King he had met his match. He thought once again about the indispensability of these men who fucked him. He had enjoyed Vinnie's fucking but this big Texan was incredible. The ravaging of his ass brought a chill to his stomach, it was a horror that was purely sensual, and he felt equal to it: he could take all this man had to give. The edge, the exclusiveness of his feelings for Vinnie had now been blunted by this tower of masculinity, this tall, rough stud who could not stop fucking him.

Finally, just before dawn, King began a furious ramming, bursting fully into the ass, up to the very base of the penis. King's orgasm started somewhere in his bowels, growing in size and strength with every thrust.

"Ooooooh," Kyle cried out. He was now lying flat, exhausted, on his stomach.

Sweat gathering on his brow, King's lips parted and he panted, writhing his hips, lost in convulsions as he hurtled his body hard against Kyle, grasping the sweaty sides of his waist and pulling the young man back onto his crotch. The splendid orgasm spread through his body, blanking his mind. Kyle had never felt anything like it; King seemed as if he was having an epileptic fit, his cum lost in a flood deep in Kyle's rectum. King slowly came out of Kyle moments later and fell onto his back, fully, finally drained. He rolled over and took Kyle in his arms and kissed his shoulder blade. And then they both fell happily asleep.

    Around noon, King awoke to Kyle's caressing of his chest.

"How do you feel?" King asked.

"Fine. I feel fine," Kyle answered, tracing the lines of muscle. He brushed back his hair and kissed King long and hard; then his hand moved down his body until it rested heavily, warmly on the thick, limp penis. The cock stirred immediately and King returned the kiss with passion. Kyle's fingers twined gently around the flabby hunk of flesh, tickling, caressing, pinching. Soon it had been rekindled into the complete and massive rigidity that had thrilled him the night before. His fingers left it, coursing softly, gently down and over the flopping balls, brushing them, exploring.

King wriggled and his thighs tensed. He pushed his hips up and Kyle's warm, demanding lips found their place on his cock.

"You don't mind bein' hurt, do you?"

"No. Not if you mean when you're fucking me. I love being filled completely like that. Having someone really enjoy me. And for so long."

"Not many here can take it."

Kyle rolled over on his stomach. King brushed his hand

down the smooth, tanned back, his eyes feasting on plump, perfectly formed buttocks. His hand felt them, cupped them so that he could spit between them.

"Are all the asses this nice up in Seattle?" With strangers, Kyle always reverted to being a straying choir boy from Washington state.

"No, not anymore than all the cocks in Texas are as big as yours."

"How many Texas cocks you had?"

"Yours is the first."

King chuckled. "Well, then, think what fun you'll have finding out."

"I only want one, this one," Kyle said, reaching behind him, grasping the penis.

King rolled against him and slithered into him. Kyle's squirming, his tightening and relaxing, made the entry easy. King spread the young star's thighs wide. Kyle wriggled a bit, adjusting to the thickness of it as it slid into him. King pressed his hips down and Kyle opened his thighs even wider so that they stretched out on either side of King. Kyle cried out. King felt a sudden, sharp containment of the unusually thick base of the cock. His cock had been thrust to its limits. It needed to be contained its whole length and King needed to curb his sadistic desire to leave it there. He pulled back a bit, then pushed back in, then out, in a gentle rhythm, his teeth clenched, eyes closed in ecstasy. He felt he was demolishing the insides of this beautiful young man, the passage so tight and giving at the same time. Kyle's fingers dug into the mattress, his buttocks stopped writhing and relaxed to become a flattened cushion for King. In a few minutes, Kyle pushed himself up onto his knees and King knelt between the stretched thighs. He was only halfway in when he came. It was not as strong an orgasm as the night before but it thrilled Kyle nonetheless.

While Kyle showered and shaved, King made breakfast. As Kyle entered the tiny kitchen with a towel draped around his waist, King, nude, pointed to the plateful of food.

"Steak 'n' eggs," King said. "A real Texas breakfast."

"Looks delicious."

King looked up from the buttering of the toast and took all of his guest in. He grinned. "You're the one that looks delicious. I've ain't seen a boy prettier than you, I swear it, 'cept maybe Kyle Cartwright. Damned if you aren't a dead ringer for him."

Kyle picked up the plate and carried it to the table by the window. "Maybe I should go to Hollywood. I could double in his movies. But I can't sing."

King, carrying the plate of toast to the table, laughed. "Shit, neither can he, least not the kinda songs I like. Did you ever see that John Wayne picture he was in? Dumbest piece of shit I ever saw. Cowboys my ass."

"No," Kyle said, smiling and reaching for the bottle of catsup. "I never go to the movies."

"What *do* you do anyway?" King asked, returning to the counter to get his food.

"I'm in college, working on my masters' degree."

"In what?"

"Fucking."

King, laughing, sat down. "Well, I swear you graduated last night, kid. Now eat up."

"Yes, sir."

They ate their breakfast in silence. When Kyle was finished he pushed his plate away and rested his elbows on the table, with his head in his hands, watching King cut his last bite of steak.

"I've got a plane to catch, but - " he brought his hand to King's knee, then caressed his thigh. "Can I kiss it goodbye?"

"Damned if you aren't the horniest critter I ever met - "

As Kyle pushed himself back from the table and fell to his knees, King parted his thighs. Kyle reached out and drew the cock up, still wet with grease and cum. He took a deep breath and opened his mouth. King pushed up with his hips and the cock was once again invading Kyle's mouth.

King had known few boys who were as proficient in arousing him to such maddening sensations. He was only too willing to let Kyle do whatever pleased him, and he sunk back into his chair and watched as Kyle buried his head between his legs, trying with lips and tongue and finger to bring him off once again. As if he had a fever, Kyle's fingers ran continuously over the older man's body, eager to know every inch of him.

Suddenly King's whole frame was shaking, as if he was being

possessed against his will. He put his legs around Kyle's head and hugged him to his crotch. Kyle pulled back just as the cum shot from the cockhead so that he could thoroughly enjoy the show. It was not a heavy load but the convulsions of King's body made it thrilling for Kyle. Then, pulling the skin tight against the shaft, he licked the penis clean.

As King stood at the door of the trailer preparing to take Kyle back to the bar to get his car he asked, "What'd you say your name was?"

"Prince. The Prince and his King, don't you remember?"

"Sheee-t, I'll never forget," King said, taking Kyle roughly in his arms and kissing him with great passion. It was a kiss Kyle would never forget: A Texas-size kiss from a man with a Texas-size dick.

With the top down and the collar of his jacket turned up, Kyle began following the sun homeward.

About thirty miles from San Antonio, he came to Hondo. He remembered the town from the previous day because of its name: one of his favorite movies starring his former co-star John Wayne was "Hondo," and today it amused him that it was also Spanish for "deep." He felt he had been probed to his deepest, what with Vinnie's fuck and then King's. The pain remained with him, caused him not to want to sit for long periods, and he looked for a place where he might stretch his legs. Passing through town and continuing west, he began seeing the signs offering wildlife photo tours at the Exotic Game Ranch and the dinosaur track exhibit in Hondo Creek. He laughed out loud; the resourcefulness of Americans to create tourist attractions never failed to amuse him. Finally he pulled in at the Whitetail Lodge to get gas and walk a bit.

He noticed the restaurant there was offering "BUNUELOS: Light-as-a-Feather Mexican Pancakes." Kyle could never resist pancakes.

From his seat at the counter, he could see the boyish dishwasher glancing his way. There was a glint of recognition in his eye, almost as if he knew who Kyle was.

After finishing his pancakes, which were served the Mexican way, broken in a soup bowl, smothered in brown sugar syrup with cinnamon, he praised the cook and asked her to write down the recipe for Consuela.

He was ordering a large cup of coffee to go when the dishwasher came through the door and picked up a bucket of dirty dishes. As he turned to carry them to the back, he gave Kyle the same look, the look of recognition, perhaps even of desire.

Kyle smiled, gave a little nod.

The boy hesitated a moment, took a deep breath, then went into the kitchen.

Kyle asked the waitress to put a little more coffee in the styrofoam cup he was taking with him, hoping the boy would come back through the door. Then he checked the arithmetic of his bill twice, then a third time. The waitress was growing impatient. Finally, he paid the bill. Just then, the dishwasher was back, getting more dishes. He walked all the way down to the end of the counter, near the door. As he passed the boy, Kyle asked the way to the men's room, even though he already knew.

"In there," the boy said, nodding towards the door to the left of the entrance. As he bent down to pick up what he come for, he was grinning.

Kyle set his steaming cup of coffee on the porcelain urinal and his piss flowed effortlessly. He was finishing when the dishwasher opened the door part way, feigned embarrassment, started to leave. Their eyes met. Kyle smiled, "Come in."

Grinning, the boy locked the door behind him.

As Kyle turned from the urinal, his cock was already erect. Swiftly the boy dropped to his knees before him. As he sucked, the kid reminded Kyle of the endless wells he had passed on the highway, pumping continuously, expertly sucking the oil from the earth, and Kyle's orgasm was a gusher. He tried to draw the boy off his cock but he would not let up, he was intent on not missing a drop. Kyle stifled his moans as the dishwasher kept going at it.

"Hey, that's great but they'll be wondering what happened to you," Kyle said, breathing heavily, playing with the boy's hair.

He looked up into Kyle's eyes, still stroking the sopping wet cock. "I know. You just passin' through?"

"Yes."

"Are you spending the night?"

"I hadn't planned on it."
"I get off at seven."
Kyle nodded.
"Why don't you get a lodge here and I'll see you later."
"It'll be the little red Mustang convertible parked in front."
The boy stood and Kyle made a move for his hard-on.
"I'll be missed," the boy said.
Kyle hugged and kissed him.
The boy was startled and he beamed. "See you at seven."
It was a good hour and a half drive back to the Sunset Ranch but Kyle figured if he left by ten that night he'd have no problem.
The lodge was very comfortable and he took a long soak in the tub. He was turned on by the slender youth who was such a good cocksucker. How lonely it must be, he thought, to be living in Hondo, Texas, and be gay.

"...You look so familiar," the boy said, setting down the can of soda pop he had brought with him.
"A lot of people say that. I guess look like a lot of people." Kyle was perfectly relaxed, lying on the bed, a towel wrapped around his middle.
The boy lowered himself to the bed. "Kyle Cartwright is who you look like, except he has longer hair."
"Yeah. Some people say I could be his brother."
"He's a sexy guy. I saw him in a movie with John Wayne - "
"'Silver City'?"
"Yeah, that was the one. He's so cool. Do you think he's gay?"
"Shit, in Hollywood, you never know."
The boy's thick, black eyebrows shot up to the dark sweep of his hair. "I heard Montgomery Clift is gay. Do you think so?"
"Like I said, in Hollywood, you never know."
The boy began toying with the towel that surrounded Kyle, finally loosening it and slowly dragging it back until Kyle's limp cock was exposed. "I know one thing, they'd love your cock in Hollywood." He fell towards Kyle, his head coming to rest on Kyle's thigh.
As the dishwasher began sucking, Kyle grinned and stroked the boy's long black hair. "Yeah, they just might," he chuckled.

Kyle quickly became hard and the boy continued sucking, now even more excited by Kyle than he had been earlier in the men's room.

It was the first time in many weeks that Kyle was playing the passive role in oral sex. He watched intently as his cock glided lusciously in and out of the boy's mouth. After awhile, the boy rose up and began kissing Kyle's flat stomach, his pectorals, and nursing on the nipples. Kyle drew the boy to him and felt his hot breath on his face, the soft lips that quivered and then the tongue that filled his mouth as he brought the cock to his asshole. Slowly, the boy sat on it, then began thrusting up and down with rapid strokes, jacking himself off in the process.

Every part of Kyle seemed to explode as he felt the heated rush of his orgasm. He opened his eyes and for an instant thought he saw Bobby instead of the dishwasher, sighing as his ass opened and closed in spasms to take all of Kyle's heavy load.

TWELVE

Kyle could not let the dishwasher go. They fucked well into the night and Kyle left Hondo early in the morning, going to the location directly and arriving a little after nine. When he pulled up in front of his trailer, Vinnie was waiting.

"Well, you look as if you'd been ridden hard and put away wet."

"Thank you," Kyle said slamming the door of the car.

"Have fun?" Vinnie smirked.

"Yeah, how 'bout you?" Kyle asked, unlocking the door of the trailer and swinging it open.

"I think I'm in love."

"Oh? I think I am too." Kyle said, following the older man into the trailer.

"Then we're even."

"Not quite," Kyle said, bolting the door. "You still have to live up to your bargain."

"You want it now, here?" Vinnie asked, groping himself playfully.

"Don't be silly. But tonight, come tonight for dinner."

"No," Vinnie said, fluffing Kyle's hair. "I'm coming *after* dinner. I just know I'm gonna to be *very* hungry."

Kyle let Vinnie out of the trailer and closed the door. Why the sudden change? Kyle asked himself. Vinnie said he was in love, in love with Kate, surely. But why the sudden interest in what Kyle was up to? Vinnie's ambivalence had thrown him off balance again. What was Vinnie up to? Perhaps the man liked nothing more than to play with other people's minds. Or perhaps it was: if you can't fuck the one you love, fuck the one you're near. But what Vinnie didn't know was that Kyle had just had some of the best sex in recent memory and being fucked by Vinnie was the furthest thing from his mind...and now Bobby was knocking on the door of the trailer.

"Can I come in?" Bobby asked.

In Hollywood, between takes, the doors of the sound stages are opened and cast and crew spill out onto the streets of the lot. If an actor disappears with someone in his trailer, people are bound to notice and comment about it. It was no different on location and Kyle had no intention of giving the gossips any more to chew on than they had already.

"No, just stay there. I'm coming out."

When Kyle opened the door, Bobby had stepped away and was rocking back and forth on his heels. He was already dressed for the crowd scene. Kyle knew Grant had called in the scriptwriter Bart Leahy and had him look at the dailies featuring Bobby. They agreed to give a couple of lines to the boy and invented a piece of business in which the youngster would sneak into the saloon to look at the singer, played by Catherine Campbell, who had finally arrived at Brackettville with her entourage.

"How's my little cowboy?" Kyle asked.

"Ready."

Kyle chuckled, remembering how many times he had thought of Bobby while the dishwasher was working his magic over him. But Bobby looked even more delicious today than he had in his fantasies. "You have to meet your leading lady," Kyle said, leading Bobby towards the set.

Catherine was waiting for the wardrobe mistress, sitting in her canvas chair, trim in a white shirt, blue jeans, tightly curled blonde hair, without makeup. She took a Kool from the pack and lit it with a cheap lighter.

Kyle was startled. He had always pictured her at his side at Chasen's, extracting a Dunhill Blue from its box and lighting it with a gold lighter from Tiffany's given to her by one of her many admirers. Kyle had only met her twice, once at a Golden Globes award ceremony and then at a premiere. He liked her; she understood without him telling her that he was a homosexual but she was still terribly attracted to him.

Kyle introduced Bobby and, after the boy had gone, Catherine exhaled and asked Kyle, "How are you?"

"How do I look?"

She was amused by him. "You always want to know that and I don't know why. You always look wonderful."

"So do you."

She did look marvelous today, Kyle thought. Real. Not dressed for a premiere or a party. It was as if she was just anybody. Or perhaps nobody. Maybe she wasn't anybody at all, like the critics said, that she was a void. A dumb blonde.

"I talked to Donner," she said. "We're doing our 'thing' at the ranch tomorrow."

"And Donner's gonna take pictures of us doing it? Do we have to?" he chuckled.

"For the sake of our careers," she said. She was four years older than Kyle and all the columnists said they made a wonderful couple, a sentiment that was hardly lost on Mac. He had gotten Catherine's agent to agree that the two stars would pose for Donner and conduct a joint interview to promote the film. Donner had already peddled the story to *Ladies Home Journal*. Catherine and Kyle would also be on the cover.

"For the sake of my reputation, you mean."

"Whatever you say. You know I never believe anything until I can see for myself."

"You're something, you know that?" He squeezed her hand.

She smiled. "So are you."

. . .

That night, Vinnie drove the Mustang back to the ranch with Kyle stretched out beside him. They drove in silence, listening to the music on the radio.

Consuela had dinner waiting on the stove. While Kyle fixed their plates, Vinnie took a shower. He came into the dining room with only a towel draped off one shoulder. Kyle was seated at the head of the table, eating.

"Am I losing my touch?" Vinnie asked, lowering himself into his place at the table.

"Why?"

"You let me get in the front door tonight. In fact, you even let me shower alone."

"I told you, I'm in love."

"Oh?"

"Let's face it, you're only a cock. A big, wonderful cock, but only a cock. Sometimes, a guy needs more."

Vinnie grinned. "You mean you've found it?"

"Let's put it this way, I'm beginning to think it's possible."

Vinnie changed the subject, talking about the filming while they finished their dinner.

As usual, Kyle cleared the table while Vinnie went to the bedroom. The older man was lying on the bed nude, playing with his erection, when Kyle entered.

Kyle stood over the bed, his hands on his hips. "I've changed my mind. I just don't want to get fucked tonight. I've been fucked too much lately."

"Okay."

Kyle took a deep breath, threw up his arms. "In fact, this was a mistake tonight. It's too soon. Why don't you come tomorrow night?"

"You're not going to let this go to waste, Kyle," he said, waving it at him.

"Yes I am. It's time I did," Kyle said, turning on his heels and swiftly leaving the room.

Vinnie found him in the living room, sitting on the couch watching television. He stood before him, stroking his erection. "You suck me off tonight or you're never going to get it again."

"Why are you acting like this? I told you, this was a mistake tonight." Kyle tried to ignore him by watching the movie on TV, but Vinnie moved in front of the set, blocking his view.

"Come on, you little shit, get on your knees and get over here."

"No."

"Kyle, I'm warning you - " Vinnie said, swinging his cock back and forth like a pendulum.

"No," Kyle pouted, now enjoying the game.

"Kyle - " Vinnie said, slowly moving towards him.

"No." Kyle put his hands over his face and held back his laughter.

Vinnie whipped him with his prick, first one side of the head, then the other, back and forth. The flogging continued let me shower alone."

"I told you, I'm in love."

"Oh?"

"Let's face it, you're only a cock. A big, wonderful cock, but only a cock. Sometimes, a guy needs more."

Vinnie grinned. "You mean you've found it?"

"Let's put it this way, I'm beginning to think it's possible."

Vinnie changed the subject, talking about the filming while they finished their dinner.

As usual, Kyle cleared the table while Vinnie went to the bedroom. The older man was lying on the bed nude, playing with his erection, when Kyle entered.

Kyle stood over the bed, his hands on his hips. "I've changed my mind. I just don't want to get fucked tonight. I've been fucked too much lately."

"Okay."

Kyle took a deep breath, threw up his arms. "In fact, this was a mistake tonight. It's too soon. Why don't you come tomorrow night?"

"You're not going to let this go to waste, Kyle," he said, waving it at him.

"Yes I am. It's time I did," Kyle said, turning on his heels and swiftly leaving the room.

Vinnie found him in the living room, sitting on the couch watching television. He stood before him, stroking his erection. "You suck me off tonight or you're never going to get it again."

"Why are you acting like this? I told you, this was a mistake tonight." Kyle tried to ignore him by watching the movie on TV, but Vinnie moved in front of the set, blocking his view.

"Come on, you little shit, get on your knees and get over here."

"No."

"Kyle, I'm warning you - " Vinnie said, swinging his cock back and forth like a pendulum.

"No," Kyle pouted, now enjoying the game.

"Kyle - " Vinnie said, slowly moving towards him.

"No." Kyle put his hands over his face and held back his laughter.

Vinnie whipped him with his prick, first one side of the head, then the other, back and forth. The flogging continued for several minutes. Precum dripped from the inflamed cock and covered Kyle's fingers. Vinnie grabbed Kyle's wrists and pulled his hands away from his face. "Open your goddamn mouth."

"No." Kyle said, pursing his lips.

"You know you want it."

"No. No more."

Vinnie took Kyle's head in his hands, brought it close to his cock.

"Beg for it, you piece of shit!"

"No," Kyle said, trying to pull back.

"Beg!"

Kyle shook his head resignedly, licked the cum-slick head of it. "All right." He cleared his throat. "Please – "

"Please *what*?"

"Please, *sir*."

"That's better. Open."

Holding Kyle by the ears, Vinnie began. First the head, then two or three inches of the shaft. He dragged Kyle's head back and forth, fucking his mouth with the throbbing cock.

Kyle unbuttoned his jeans, pulled out his own cock and began masturbating.

Vinnie was charging into Kyle's mouth with such ferocity that Kyle was afraid the older man would come and he pulled back, let the cock vibrate in front of him.

"Please, don't come," Kyle begged.

"You'll get it when I'm ready."

"No, please don't come now."

"I will if I want." Vinnie slapped him hard across the face with it, saliva flying off of it.

"No."

"No, *what*?"

"No, *sir*."

"That's better." Vinnie stop stroking his penis but it was no use: the cum flew from it, splattering Kyle's face, rolling down his chin, dripping onto his own cock.

But Vinnie was not through. He held Kyle's head and rammed the cock back into his mouth again. Kyle sucked on it as he jacked off but even after he came he did not want to give it up. Vinnie started chuckling sardonically. "If all those teenage girls could see you now, cum all over your face, sucking that big dick like there was no tomorrow – "

"They'd love it as much as I do."

"But would they still love you?"

Kyle ignored his tormentor and took the cock back into his mouth again.

But Vinnie was finished. "No more," he said, pulling away from Kyle and going to the bathroom. When he came out, toweling his cock, Kyle was lying on the bed, his ass in the air, a smile on his face. Vinnie smiled back, a smile without warmth and affection, and he said, "I told you, no more."

Kyle brought his hands to the cheeks of his ass and spread them. "It's all ready for you. I like it best after you've come."

"Oh, shit," Vinnie said, climbing on the bed. "I wish I didn't like fuckin' you so much."

When Vinnie was fully in him, Kyle could not remember the cock being as huge and hard as it felt tonight. He gasped in pain and each gasp seemed to excite Vinnie more and more, until finally Kyle let out a scream, muffled into the pillowcase, and Vinnie came again. He collapsed against Kyle and they were silent, his weight crushing him. Kyle hugged a pillow to his chest and curled around it. He stuffed a corner of the pillow slip into his mouth. He'd be damned if he'd let Vinnie hear him cry.

THIRTEEN

"You look wonderful together," Donner kept saying all through the photio session. He was obviously infatuated with Kyle, flattering him with the best positions, angles, lighting. He had once written, "Even in clothes he's naked. It's the open look, athletic repose and parted lips. He's got animal magnetism down to a science."

Now, watching Kyle comb his hair to get ready for the next set-up, Donner thought of something more he would add for the new story: "Just by practicing sullen looks as he combs his hair in the mirror, he has perfected the art of saying everything by saying nothing at all." He was moved to mutter under his breath, "I love you, you bastard."

Kyle turned. "What?"

"I said, don't do anything more. You look perfect."

"As a cowboy, he is perfect," Donner wrote another time. "He has a loose cowboy's gait, lean body, piercing blue eyes, shaggy blond hair, an aura of mystery and insufferable arrogance."

"Are you getting everything you need?"

"Except the shot I really want."

If there existed a picture of Kyle Cartwright nude, Donner couldn't find it, and he'd spent a couple of years trying. He had a file on every actor and his collection held many surprises. But the one he wanted most eluded him.

"Not for all the money in the world," Kyle said.

. . .

Kyle invited Donner and Catherine and her make-up girl to join him for dinner. Consuela stayed to serve them and made it a festive occasion by serving Mexican wine.

Kyle placed his hand over the glass when she came around to his place. "I'm on the wagon till this damn thing is over, maybe forever."

"Oh, go on. A little wine can't hurt," Donner said.

"My trouble is, I never want just a little of anything."

"So I've heard," Catherine said.

"You don't know the half of it - " Donner said.

"Let's change the subject," Kyle interrupted.

"Just when it was getting interesting," Catherine said.

"The trouble with Donner is, nothing's off the record," Kyle said.

"That's not so. I have lots of secrets I keep and you of all people should know that."

"And you never could take a joke."

"Why don't you two kiss and make up?" Catherine chuckled.

"It's more fun fighting with him," Kyle said.

Donner turned to Catherine. "I wish he *would* fight me. That might be fun."

"I live in Hollywood," Catherine smiled. "I know what you mean. All the best looking men are gay or already married."

"That never stopped you," Kyle chuckled.

"No," Catherine winked. "Never stopped me from dreaming."

After the women had left, Donner stood at the door, reluctant to go. "Did you mean that?" he asked.

"Mean what?"

"That it was more fun to fight me?"

"Yes. Just think what would happen if I stopped fighting."

"I've dreamed about it."

Kyle smiled and gently pushed him out the door. "Sweet dreams, Jim."

Consuela had left what remained of the wine on the counter. Kyle took it with him to the bathroom. He was still hurting and he took a long soak in the tub, sipping the wine. He thought about Catherine, how lovely she was, how much he had enjoyed their love scene that morning, how much he had enjoyed posing with her. She was not like Kale's whores. She was lovely. He closed his eyes and began stroking himself. But he could not let go of the vision of his brother atop the whore, or the whore straddling his brother's chest, jumping up and down on his big cock.

Kyle finished the bottle of wine and went back to the kitchen. He found another bottle under the sink and proceeded to finish it as well.

FOURTEEN

"You're late!" Vinnie screamed at Kyle. "And look at you. You look like shit."
"I feel like shit."
"Grant's pissed. I'm pissed. You're going to get us both fired."
"They can't fire me, the damn picture's almost finished."
"You're finished if you don't pull yourself together. You're back on the bottle again. I can tell."
"That's right, you're an expert. And there's nothing worse than a reformed drunk."

When Kyle arrived on the set, Grant took him aside and told him he had talked with Bergen. There was to be no more tardiness. Kyle promised to behave. Kyle's scene with Douglas Raymond had been re-scheduled until after lunch. Raymond had cut Kyle down several times with his sharp tongue. For one scene, Kyle wasn't getting into the anger Grant was calling for and Raymond spoke to Kyle alone: "I've been meaning to talk to you."
"Oh?"
"They say you give damn good head."
Kyle's face flushed but he held back his temper.
"They say that's one way to get ahead."
Kyle drew a deep breath. "Then why don't you try it?" he sputtered and stalked off the set.
Grant was fast behind him. "Now you've got it. Get back there and let's do it again."
Douglas Raymond was fifty-eight and had appeared in over forty films in the U.S. and England, along the way serving and

being wounded in World War II and being decorated as something of a war hero. He had no use for the young singer he was hired to appear with and called him "the sissy." Aloof, dignified and educated at Oxford, Raymond was of the old school who believed actors should learn their lines and follow the script. Lately he had been appearing with many of the so-called "Method" actors and had no stomach for them and feared Kyle, with little training in acting, would be even worse. But, after a few days of shooting, Raymond conceded perhaps Kyle wasn't so bad after all. "At least," he said, "the boy follows the script, such as it is."

The script, as concocted by at least three different writers, involved a Federal agent who was on his way north with gold the Mexicans paid for armaments. He stops overnight in El Dorado, where a drifter tries to rob him. Both men are killed in a brutal struggle. As the town's sheriff, Raymond must guard the gold until Federal agents arrive to confiscate it. The sheriff receives word that an outlaw gang has learned of the gold's existence and is on their way to El Dorado. In the tradition of "High Noon," the sheriff attempts his hire deputies to help him but no one will sign on. Later, the sheriff enters the saloon just as a gunfight ensues between a young drifter and a ranch hand. The drifter shoots but does not kill the ranch hand. Seeing how good the young man is with a gun, the sheriff asks him to help defend the gold and the town. The drifter refuses but later he saves the sheriff's life. After a romantic interlude with the saloon's singer, who also appeals to him to help her friend the lawman, he finally agrees to help.

Raymond had most of the scenes in the film and wanted to get what he termed the "dreary" location shooting over with as quickly as possible. He was furious with Kyle for delaying the picture.

"Cocksucking little turd!" Raymond mumbled when he saw Kyle.

Kyle ignored him. He too wanted to get this dreariness over with as soon as possible and get back to Hollywood, the only place in the world he really felt safe.

FIFTEEN

On Saturday Bobby arrived early to do his scene with Catherine. When it was over, Kyle praised the boy and before he left with Kate, Kyle asked asked Bobby to walk with him back to his trailer. "Do you know something fun that we could do tomorrow?" Kyle asked.

Bobby stopped. Kyle stopped. Bobby looked up, into Kyle's eyes. "You want to do something with me?"

Kyle blushed, looked away, continued walking. "Yeah, you know like the Superbull or something."

Bobby grinned, his pace quickened. He was almost skipping. "I think so."

"Like what?"

"Shopping. I love to go shopping. We could go to Eagle Pass. All the neat stores are in Eagle Pass."

Kyle shook his head. "I can't just go *shopping*, Bobby."

Bobby smiled. "Why not?"

"I'll be recognized."

"No, you'll be with me. You'll be safe."

Kyle started giggling and Bobby giggled too and they giggled all the way to the trailer. Kyle stifled the impulse to invite Bobby in. "Well, see you tomorrow."

"Will you bring your guitar?"

"Of course."

Kyle arrived early, before noon, and Bobby suggested they first go to the park.

"The park?" Kyle asked incredulously.

"It's nice. They got lots of old Texas stuff there. And a place where you can play your guitar."

"Hey, I'm not doing a concert, you know – "

"I know. Just for me. They have a spot where we'll be alone. You'll see. "

It was chilly and Kyle was glad he'd worn a sweater under his buckskin jacket and Bobby pulled the hood up on his jacket. Kyle had Bobby buy a bag of M&M's at the grocery store and they shared them as they toured the ten restored buildings of the fort that housed 10,000 troops during the Villa revolution in Mexico and World War I.

When they finished the tour, it had warmed up and was sunny. They found a grassy slope away from the crowd, and Kyle strummed his guitar and sang some of the new songs Carl had given him. But these were not the songs Bobby wanted to hear.

"You've got the records – " Kyle protested.

"Records are nice but this is better."

Kyle resigned himself to the fact that he wasn't going to be able to refuse Bobby anything and he also realized Bobby somehow intuitively knew that. But when Bobby asked to hear another chorus of "Don't Let Me Lonesome Tonight," which he said he couldn't get on the albums and which had fast become his new favorite, Kyle simply set his guitar down and put his arm loosely around Bobby's shoulder. Bobby snuggled closer to Kyle; he had never felt so content. He kept asking Kyle questions and Kyle answered them as best he could. But every time Kyle would ask Bobby a question, Bobby would quickly ask him another; he was eager to know all about the many aspects of movie-making, recording, Hollywood, and Kyle's life in general that Kyle finally relaxed and allowed himself to be "interviewed."

They spent the rest of the day in Eagle Pass, going from store to store at Mall de Las Aguilas. Bobby wouldn't let Kyle buy him anything. "I don't need anything, I just like to look, see what's new." Kyle simply shrugged. With his dark glasses and his blond hair stuffed under his Stetson, and acting like a silly kid with Bobby, Kyle passed unnoticed. Then they decided to go into Mexico. In Piedras Negras, at the drug store on Hidalgo Street, Kyle insisted on buying Bobby every magazine that had his picture in it. When Kyle took his glasses off to pay the bill, the young Mexican salesgirl said, "You're Kyle Cartwright. I thought it was you. Doing a movie over at the Alamo, aren't you?"

"Yup," Kyle said with a smile.

"We read about it in the paper." The salesgirl had Kyle autograph a copy of 16 that had a spread on "A Day at the Beach with Kyle Cartwright." Bobby said he already had that issue and it was his favorite.

"My biggest fan," Kyle said, smiling at the boy.

"I can see that," the girl said, looking at Bobby, then Kyle, then back again.

As they left the drug store, Kyle asked Bobby what he'd like for dinner.

"The Mexican place on Morelos is good," Bobby said.

"No. I get Mexican every night."

"Okay, there's a Burger King in Eagle Pass."

"I think we can do a bit better than that. I noticed the La Quinta has a restaurant. It might be nice."

"The Colonial. Yeah, I know it. But it's expensive. Mom took me there for my birthday."

"Good. Then let's celebrate it a second time."

"Okay," Bobby beamed.

Over rare steaks, fries and Cokes, while Bobby was chewing, Kyle began asking questions.

". . .I'll bet you have lots of girlfriends – "

"Yeah, all my friends are girls."

"That's not what I meant."

"But it's true. It's always been like that. They like me and I like them."

"But you do have buddies – boy pals, don't you?"

"Only Butch."

"*Butch?*" Kyle nearly choked on his dinner roll.

"Yeah, he's about six feet tall and two hundred pounds." Kyle nodded. "Butch."

"When you're as little as I am, you gotta have a buddy like Butch around."

"And what do you do in exchange for this, ah – protection?"

"I help him out when he needs it."

Kyle smiled. Bobby smiled. Then they started giggling again and just then the waitress bought them refills on their Cokes.

After she left, Bobby asked, "I bet you have lots of girlfriends, like the ones in the pictures with you, like at the beach and the premieres and stuff – "

Kyle chuckled. "Yeah, I have to fight 'em off." Kyle explained what he meant by telling Bobby about the only time he was really terrified in his life. He had signed to do five appearances on behalf of the release of the second album and opening night on the tour was at Public Hall in Cleveland, Ohio. There were thousands of screaming, hand-clapping, foot-stomping, singing, dancing fans, and for the first time Kyle came face-to-face with his stardom. The crowds were receptive to his music and his performance that night was over the top; he even tossed his sweat-drenched shirt into the audience to have it caught by a young girl who, Kyle joked, probably wore it to bed that night and masturbated to his image.

When the concert was over, he did not go to his dressing room. Instead, he was escorted away by a large team of thick-necked secuirty guards, who formed a flying V in front of him and streamrolled over everyone who attempted to get in their way. But once outside the hall, the screaming fans broke through and the young star was mauled, losing handfuls of hair and his jacket. Finally the guards were able to stuff him into a waiting van and off he went to the airport and on to Philadelphia. "That's why a day like this is so special," Kyle told Bobby.

Suddenly the waitresses were gathering around the table as a busboy brought in two huge pieces of birthday cake, one with a lighted candle. Bobby started giggling again and Kyle joined the chorus of the birthday song. After Bobby blew out the candle and the waitressses had left, Kyle asked, "So what did you wish for?"

"That Kyle Cartwright would sing me 'Happy Birthday' again some time. This has been the happiest birthday of my life."

Kyle smiled. "Sure, Bobby. That's an easy one. Any year. You just name it."

When they returned to the Cattleman, Bobby invited Kyle to come in.

"No," Kyle said, gunning the engine. "I got an early call tomorrow. The movies don't wait, you know, just the actors do."

"Please? I want to show you something."

Kyle looked into Bobby's suddenly sad eyes as the boy stood beside the car clutching the magazines to his chest and, shrugging, he turned off the ignition. "Oh, okay. What the hell, it's your birthday."

They entered the hotel and Kyle followed Bobby up the main stairs. "Where are we going?" he asked.

"To my room."

"Well – "

Bobby turned, smiled at Kyle, who, standing down two steps, was now the same the same height as the boy. "I want to show you something in my room."

Kyle smiled and shrugged once more.

Bobby went to the far end of the hallway and opened a door that led to the family living area. Once the grand suite in the hotel's better days, Kate had fashioned it into a homey parlor and three bedrooms. Bobby had the smallest bedroom, utterly tiny it seemed to Kyle when he entered it; there was barely enough room to squeeze past the twin bed that was shoved against a wall and covered with a brightly colored Indian quilt.

Bobby dropped the magazines on the bed and flung open the door to his closet. "See," he said, beaming. A poster of Kyle covered the back of the closet door.

Kyle chuckled and shook his head. "You mean they sell those in Texas?"

"They sell them everywhere. I saw them this afternoon. I read in a movie magazine that it is the biggest selling poster in the whole world."

"All I know is I'm tired of looking at it."

"I'll never be tired of looking at it."

Kyle shook his head. "C'mon, close the door."

"And I have the poster alive right here in my bedroom. Crazy, eh?"

Kyle put his hand on the knob of the door. "Crazy." He was fighting his every impulse to close the door, lock it and take Bobby in his arms and kiss him. "Okay, I've seen it – "

"And here," Bobby said, going over to the maple chest of drawers. A record player was on top and records stacked neatly behind it. He picked up two albums and flashed them at Kyle.

"See, I have them. Will you autograph them for me?"

Kyle shook his head again. He could refuse Bobby nothing. "Sure." He left the door partly open and came towards Bobby, who thrust out the albums. Kyle stood awkwardly next to the bed, then lowered himself on to it. Perched on the edge, he took the pen Bobby proffered and, with a flourish, signed the album jackets. "There, 'To my buddy Bobby, All the best, Kyle Cartwright.' Okay?"

Bobby held up the first album. "Gosh, wait'll I show Marianne."

"Marianne?"

"Yeah. She's as big a fan of yours as I am."

"Well, I doubt that but tell her to come by next Sunday and I'll sign her albums too."

"Okay." Bobby set the first album down on the bed and picked up the magazines. "And these?" Kyle shook his head again but signed each magazine. Bobby opened a drawer and pulled out a battered copy of *16*; he flipped it open to the spread of Kyle at the beach. "And here, right on this part."

Chuckling, Kyle signed the full page color photograph of him leaning against a pier, his crotch splendidly bunched in white swim trunks. He had to admit it was the best picture of himself that had ever been taken, except perhaps the poster. Mac liked it so much he got the original print and had it framed and hung in his office in Hollywood alongside the poster.

Bobby opened the closet door again. "And sign my poster too, okay?"

"Hey, I got to get goin' Bobby," Kyle said, standing up, leaving the magazine lying open on the bed.

"I know, I know. It'll only take a second."

They stood tightly together before the opened closet as Kyle signed the poster of himself bare-chested, in tight jeans, turning away, so that his ass was prominently displayed.

"Oh, there you are," Kate said, suddenly appearing at the threshold, pushing the door all the way open.

Bobby turned and smiled at his mother. "Kyle's signing *everything*."

"Did you have a nice day?"

"Great!" Bobby said, all enthusiasm, walking over to his mother. "You can come in my room, Mom, it's okay."

"No. It's off limits, remember?"

Kyle turned and smiled at Kate. "Kid needs some privacy, right?"

"Yes, Mr. Cartwright. One of Bobby's jobs around here is to keep this room in order."

Kyle looked about and nodded. "He does a good job."

Kate ran her hand through Bobby's hair. "Yes, he's a good boy."

Kyle smiled and, looking down into Bobby's anxious eyes, he said, "He certainly is."

Kate walked Kyle to the front door of the hotel, thanking him for spending the day with her son.

"It was my pleasure, Kate. He's a great kid."

"Thank you. I've tried, I really have."

Bobby stood at the window and watched Kyle get in the Mustang and drive off into the night. He was stroking himself through the fabric of his jeans as he went to the bed. He stripped and laid down next to the magazine. The image of Kyle sitting on the edge of his bed, signing his picture came back to him in a rush and he impulsively kissed the photo. He spread the magazine out again and took his erection in his hand and began, once again, to masturbate to the photo, now made even more desirable than it had ever been.

When Kyle returned to the ranch, he could not sleep. Visions of Bobby filled his mind. Tossing off the sheet, he stroked his cock as he remembered a time so long ago . . .

. . . He had lived at the parish house for three months when The Reverend said he had to go to his cabin to get it ready for a retreat he was having for married couples in a couple of weeks. "I sure could use some help," he said to Kyle. The Reverend had not made a move towards Kyle in all that time and Kyle thought it might have been the presence of the housekeeper that caused The Reverend to ignore him. Kyle had tried to arrange it so they would be alone together on several occasions but nothing happened. Now, The Reverend himself was making the move. Kyle was thrilled at the prospect of a couple of days alone with The Reverend.

The clergyman drove his old Cadillac very fast on the rain soaked country road. They passed the country club, then a little grocery store and finally Kyle could see the river. Water oaks and willows bent down to the water. In a few minutes, they arrived at what The Reverend called "the camp."

The rain cascaded over them as they hurried to the cabin. Once inside, The Reverend said, "You better get out of those wet things."

Kyle nodded and went to the lavatory off the kitchen. The Reverend went to the bathroom off the bedroom. Kyle changed into the pair of shorts he knew showed him off and a T-shirt he had outgrown two years before. He wanted The Reverend to like what he saw, to want what he saw, right from the start.

When Kyle came out of the bathroom, The Reverend was fixing sandwiches. He looked over his shoulder, taking Kyle in. "That's better, eh?"

"Yeah," Kyle said, putting his hands behind him and slipping them into the back pockets of his shorts, pulling the fabric even tighter at the crotch. The Reverend looked down at the bulge and swallowed hard, then returned to making the sandwiches.

They sat at the kitchen table eating and The Reverend had a couple of beers while Kyle finished a bottle of Mountain Dew.

When the sun broke through, The Reverend decided they should go for a ride in the boat. As they walked out onto the dock, their weight and the current made the water-rotted slats creak under them.

As they pulled out, Kyle looked back at the cabin. A tree at the end of the porch had hidden a huge wisteria wine, heavy with bloom. The vine crawled along the roof and was slowly taking the porch down. Kyle thought it was the loveliest place he'd ever seen. He wanted to stay there forever, with a man as kind as The Reverend.

Kyle sat huddled in the bow, and the current took them in a long line across and down the river. It began clouding up again and Kyle began to shiver.

"Come back here with me," The Reverend said. "You'll catch your death. This weather is crazy."

He joined him in the stern, their thighs pressing tightly together. The Reverend draped his arm over Kyle's shoulder and they continued to drift down the river. The Reverend talked about how his father used to bring him up here and they would go fishing together and how sorry he was he'd never married and had children. "But I've had many of God's children up here over the years and we always had a good time."

Kyle slipped his arm around his heavy waist and clung to him.

When it began drizzling again, The Reverend started the outboard and they raced back to the cabin. Kyle went to the bathroom again to get out of his wet clothes. He wrapped himself in one of the big towels and came back into the kitchen. The Reverend was sitting at the table drinking whiskey. Kyle had another Mountain Dew.

The Reverend told Kyle the history of the camp, how his father had bought it many years before and he and his buddies came there every weekend.

While he fixed pork and beans, The Reverend told Kyle some of his father's favorite old fish stories. The Reverend drank while Kyle ate the supper he had fixed.

Later, they sat on the screened porch by the river and listened to the rain fall on the water. Before long, it seemed The Reverend passed through drunkenness to the dream of clarity on the other side that drinkers seek and seldom find, the place of peace where everything is possible. He began talking about the boys he had brought to the camp, how much fun they had together, how he missed them. Finally, he went over to sit next to Kyle. The Reverend said the green wicker chairs and settees were old when they were brought out to the fishing camp and after years of neglect they had become sprung and flattened so that when he sat down on the settee next to Kyle, they fell easily together. Kyle let his head fall to the Reverend's chest. The Reverend sighed and began caressing Kyle's shiny blond hair. Soon he drew him tight against his body.

"It's so peaceful here," Kyle said. He was exhilarated by a sense of being in a deserted world. It was as if they were lost creatures, having only each other. They sat there, hugging, for several minutes until The Reverend decided to get the beds ready.

To Kyle, the bedroom of the place seemed somehow haunted, haunted with the smell of old fishermen. The tin roof had leaked and left the bare mattress streaked and he saw, or hoped he saw, that it had been stained with the semen of boys The Reverend had brought there when it was dark and fucked them as the rain came down. The Reverend covered the bed with a sheet and took blankets from a chest. Fluffing a pillow after he put a case on it, he said, "I'll make this up for you and I'll sleep on the couch in the living room."

"Bed's big enough for both of us," Kyle said, hopefully, now helping make the bed up.

"Kyle, we need to talk. Sit down."

Kyle lowered himself to the mattress and The Reverend put his arm on his shoulder.

"There's such a thing as being too eager, Kyle. I've known almost from the first day you came to live at the parish what the story is. I guess the liquor's loosened my tongue so I could tell you this. It's for your own good that you not show your eagerness so much."

"I'm sorry." Kyle looked away, tears began to roll down his cheeks. "I can't help it. It's the way I was brought up, to go after what I want."

"It's good, but temperance in all things. Be patient and all will come to you."

Kyle hugged The Reverend about the waist, his crotch in his face. He rubbed his head into The Reverend, who pushed Kyle back and said, "Enough now. Get into bed."

"Please, I don't want to sleep in here alone."

The Reverend smiled. "I understand. I'll sleep here with you, if that's what you want."

Kyle slipped the towel away and slid under the covers.

While The Reverend took off his shirt and escaped from his pants, Kyle closed his eyes and started playing with himself.

Lying a few inches from each other, they listened to the rain on the roof.

"I'm sorry it's raining," The Reverend said.

"It's kind of nice," Kyle said, rolling over and looking at him. The Reverend had the sheet pulled up only to his navel and his chest was hairy and strong. Tentatively, Kyle ran his fingers across it. The Reverend rolled towards him, facing him, and Kyle left his hand on his chest. The Reverend took Kyle's fingers in his own and brought them to his lips, kissing them one by one. Soon he was sucking them. "You're a good boy," he whispered.

Since it was not just his fingers Kyle wanted sucked, he took the Reverend's hand and brought it to his crotch. "I can be very good."

"I'm sure," The Reverend chuckled, his fingers gently stroking Kyle's erection. "My, you're a big boy. I bet the girls love this."

"I don't know. Haven't been with a girl yet. What about guys? Do you think they'd like it?"

"Guys who know what's good for 'em will. The others, who cares?"

The Reverend flung the covers back and leaned over Kyle's trembling body. Taking the head of it in his mouth, he began licking, nibbling.

"Taste good?" Kyle asked.

"Hmmmm," he answered, filling his mouth with it. He got on his knees and bent over Kyle. His mouth and hand working deliberately, in a practiced way, he brought the horny teenager off in moments. It was the most intense orgasm Kyle could remember since he had been with Kale. The Reverend left it in his mouth even after Kyle had come. Kissing it, licking it, making a fuss over it.

Kyle ran his hands up the Reverend's thighs and he begged to suck him.

"Very well," The Reverend said, lifting himself over Kyle, his crotch in his face. He propped the pillow behind Kyle's head and, his hands planted on the wall behind him, he brought his cock to Kyle's lips. In the dim light, Kyle closely examined the balls, the cock, the pubic hairs. It was not as big as Kale's, but he thought it was a fine cock. It was not fully hard but when it slipped between Kyle's lips, it began to stiffen. The Reverend began slowly, working it in and out. Kyle rested his hands on the fleshy cheeks of his butt. Before long, Kyle just held his mouth open while his mouth was being fucked. The Reverend tried, but he couldn't come. "It's the booze," he said. "And all the excitement." He slipped under the covers again, holding Kyle tightly in his arms.

"Can I try it again tomorrow?" Kyle asked.

"Sure, first thing."

But first things first, Kyle found out the following morning, when he awoke with The Reverend between his thighs, running his fingers up and down, then lifting his erection to his mouth.

"What we do here at the cabin will be our little secret," The Reverend said. "I know you can keep a secret."

Kyle sighed and nodded.

"Good. I'll let you do me in a minute. I want to see you come again. Seeing you come again will make me hard."

And so Kyle came for The Reverend.

Later that day, after all the chores were finished, Kyle took a shower and when he had finished, he went to the bedroom and lay face down on the bed. He called out to The Reverend.

Kyle's excitement had never been so keen. The Reverend had his hand on his sex, his fingers rubbing his cock as he moved his cock up and down the asscrack.

The pleasure for The Reverend had never been this acute. He had never been with anyone so sensual. He could feel Kyle's rectum gripping the cock, the heat of their connection washing over him. His face was bright red. Kyle pushed back forcefully, and The Reverend entered him all the way. He looked in the mirror to see the holy man's eyes fixed on the round buttocks, the stretched mouth of his anus. He gripped the cock even more tightly, squeezing the penis as hard as he could. He felt the crisis was near and his ass muscles constricted without his willing it, milking the cock.

"Oh God help me!" The Reverend cried. It was a phrase The Reverend would use many, many times after that.

Now, re-living his days with The Reverend, Kyle came and he was finally able to fall into a half slumber, but the nagging doubts about Bobby and his overwhelming attraction to him returned and eventually he took a sleeping pill.

SIXTEEN

Later in the week, when Kyle hurt his leg during an especially arduous scene, Bobby was there to massage it for him.

"You're so good at this. Is this what you do for Butch?" Kyle asked.

"Sometimes. Butch plays football and gets hurt a lot."

"So he needs a lot of massages?"

"Sometimes too many. It interferes with helping my mother at the hotel and with her drama classes."

"You're a busy boy. Now you're even in the movies."

"In the movies with Kyle Cartwright."

"You *are* in that one scene when I'm walking down the street."

"I am?"

"Unless they cut it out."

"Don't cut it out. Hold still." Donner happened to be hanging around the set and snapped a picture of Bobby applying his nimble fingers to Kyle's leg and up onto his thigh.

"Yeah, no pictures on the set without permission," Kyle grunted.

"Okay, okay. I'm on my way out anyhow. See you in Hollywood, Kyle."

"Yeah, see ya."

But Kyle began to worry that Donner would use the picture against him and, after finishing dinner and a bottle of wine, he drove into town to confront the photographer. He found him at Bloom's Bar on Main Street.

"I thought you were leaving," Kyle said, sliding onto a stool next to Donner.

"I was. But I sensed there could be another story here, a story so different from the one I am writing that I decided to hang around a bit longer."

"I don't think that's a very good idea."

"So what's the problem?" Donner said, ordering another bourbon that Kyle paid for.

"Today you took a photograph that might give people the wrong idea."

"Yeah, people do have lurid imaginations."

Kyle finished a vodka neat and ordered another. "I'd like to buy the film from you. In fact, I'll buy you a plane ticket out of here."

"You have nothing to fear from me, Kyle, except for the fact that I'm as nuts about the kid as you are. So if you don't want him, how 'bout giving me a second chance."

"A second chance?"

"I thought you knew."

"No, I don't know. What am I supposed to know?"

"You and the kid are together so much, I thought - "

"What did you think?"

"Well, that he does for you what he did for me."

"What the - " Kyle's face flushed. He clenched his fists. "No, maybe I don't want to know."

"Well, you don't stay at the hotel. I guess you wouldn't know about it, unless he told you, or someone else did."

Kyle drank the vodka in one gulp. "What is it that everyone knows that I don't?"

"That the kid sucks a mean dick."

Kyle stared at the man with stupefaction. He thought he might explode with rage. "You're a fuckin' liar."

"Hardly. It's like one of the cameramen said, 'That kid's mouth ain't a pussy but, what the hell, it takes the edge off.'"

Trembling, Kyle stood up. "Okay, you've said enough. I've gotta go." He tossed a twenty on the bar and staggered out of the bar. He stood unsteadily on the sidewalk and looked across the street at the hotel. There were lights on in several of the rooms. He rushed into the lobby and up the stairs. He pounded on the door to Vinnie's room.

"Yes?" Vinnie called out.

Kyle could hear the sounds from the television. "It's me. I've gotta see you."

The older man unlocked the door and opened it a crack. "What's wrong?"

"I've gotta see you." One of his eyebrows rose sharply.

"Not here, Kyle. We agreed. Not here."

Kyle plowed his fingers through his hair and blew out a gust of air. "No, it's about Bobby."

Now Vinnie opened the door all the way. After Kyle was inside, he closed the door behind him.

Kyle stood in front of Vinnie's bed, looking down at the floor. "I just heard he sucks a mean dick."

"Oh?" Vinnie said, his hands on his hips.

Kyle turned, glanced down at the absurdly long cock hanging enticingly before him. Kyle closed his eyes, not wanting to imagine Bobby sucking it. "Oh?" Kyle exploded. "Is that all you can say? *Oh?*"

"What's so difficult to understand?" Vinnie asked, walking over to the television, turning it off. "A lot of men stay here off and on. The kid says he's been doing it for a long time and he likes it. But I put a stop to it the night he came to this room."

Kyle opened his mouth to make a sharp retort, but suddenly realized he didn't have one. He closed his mouth quickly and looked away. Tears began to roll down his cheeks. The vodka was beginning to have its full effect. He was lightheaded. He thought he might faint. He gripped the edge of the nearest chair in an effort to remain standing.

Vinnie moved slowly toward him, advancing on Kyle until he could smell the liquor on the young star's breath, "You're drunk and acting like a jealous lover. What the hell did you do with him when you took him to the park?"

"Shut up! You're disgusting."

"Disgusting huh?" He laughed, repeating the word several times as though he found it more amusing each time he said it. He wrenched Kyle away from the chair and tried to take him into his arms. Shaking his head defiantly, Kyle struggled to be released but Vinnie was more powerful and he pushed Kyle onto the bed. Kyle tried to stand up but Vinnie shoved him back down. "Leave the boys alone, Kyle. You've got the men to take care of." He took a clump of Kyle's hair in his hand and yanked his head back. Kyle's jaw opened.

"You're the one's that disgusting."

"No," Kyle cried as Vinnie brought Kyle's mouth and the head of his cock together.

"Yes! C'mon, show me just how disgusting you can be."

The harder Kyle fought to free himself, the more Vinnie twisted his body, forcing his cock into his mouth, down his throat. Kyle's first notion was to bite Vinnie but when he was shoved onto his back with the monstrous thing moving in and out of his mouth he found himself grabbing Vinnie's ass, anxious for it, as if to do it would somehow eradicate the lies the men were telling about Bobby.

Vinnie's orgasm was fast in coming and Kyle took every drop.

When he came back into the bedroom after washing himself, Vinnie said, "Kyle, take my advice: he's a cute kid but give yourself a break, don't get involved,"

Kyle glanced at Vinnie, his skepticism plain.

Vinnie gave a noncommittal shrug.

Kyle glowered at him with exasperation. "I've gotta go."

"You're not driving anywhere in your condition. You're going to have to spend the night here with me whether I like it or not."

"Won't I be in the way, I mean, isn't Kate due any second to get her fuck, or is it Bobby's turn tonight?"

Vinnie reached for the lamp on the nightstand and switched it off. "Like I said, you're the one that's disgusting. Grow up, Kyle."

Kyle lay still on the bed gazing at the ceiling. Then he began rubbing his hand back and forth across his abdomen.

Vinnie got into bed and propped himself up on his elbow and looked down at Kyle. "I had heard you never knew when the kid was going to come knocking on your door asking if you wanted a massage and I was told if you didn't want him you just don't answer and he goes away."

"On to the next door?"

"I dunno. I suppose."

"Like a maid that puts a chocolate on your pillow?"

Vinnie shook his head. "You're disgusting. But when it happened to me, I let him in and had a good talk with him.

He's a sweet kid and I think I'm in love with his mother, so I felt I had a duty – "

"You – in love?"

"Yeah, 'bout time, don't ya think? And she's a mighty pretty woman, that Kate. Anyhow, I told Bobby if I ever heard that he did it again, I'd give him a whipping he'd never forget." Vinnie ruffed Kyle's hair. "Get some sleep. We have any early call tomorrow."

Kyle lay quietly in the darkness listening. Soon Vinnie, lying flat on his back, his head propped up on two pillows, was snoring lightly beside him.

Kyle could not close his eyes. He heard footsteps. He began trembling. Someone passed by the door. Then he thought he heard a knock but it was only a faint one. A door opened and closed down the hall. He lifted himself up, thought about going to the door, even into the hall to investigate, but he slumped back down, as if from a felling blow.

The next day, Kyle and Vinnie left the hotel before anyone else was awake.

SEVENTEEN

Kyle spent a troubled Saturday night. He drank too much Mexican wine and passed out in the bathtub. The next afternoon, nursing a hangover, he came to town, going directly to the Cattleman to confront Bobby. But the boy was nowhere in sight; he had errands to run for his mother Rufe, the hotel's black porter, told Kyle.

Kyle joined the others at Snyder's restaurant, taking his usual place next to Vinnie, but he barely spoke through dinner. Donner, he was told, had left town. "Thank God," he muttered.

Kyle left the table before dessert was served. Slowly he walked back to the Cattleman, lost in thought, but his pace quickened when he saw Bobby was waiting for him on the veranda.

When their eyes connected for a moment, Kyle looked at the boy uneasily, then cast his eyes downward.

"Rufe said you were looking for me," Bobby said, smiling. Marianne left her albums for you to sign – "

"Yeah, I was lookin' for you but it's late." Kyle shrugged laconically, glanced at his wristwatch. "I have to get back to the ranch. Early call tomorrow."

"All right," Bobby faltered, turned away.

Kyle shook his head resignedly. "Bobby – "

The boy turned and faced him again. "Yeah?"

"Let's go for a ride."

Once in the Mustang, heading to the ranch, Kyle began shaking his head with misgiving. "What will your mother say if you've left with me without telling her?"

"She saw us leave. She trusts you. She thinks you're the greatest. Just like I do."

"Damn!" Kyle's temper snapped. "I can't believe what I heard about you."

Instantly suspicious, Bobby asked, "What did you hear?"

"That you're not as innocent as you appear."

Bobby laughed nervously. "I appear innocent?"

"To me."

"I'm not." His voice was soft, the words spoken like a warning. "But what did you hear?"

Kyle winced. His eyes cut to the boy's sharply.

"I was afraid of this. It happens all the time," Bobby said, on the verge of tears.

"What happens?"

"They find out and then they don't like me any more."

"And just what do they find out, Bobby?"

"That I like boys."

"But you said you liked girls."

"As friends. I usually don't have sex with girls. Just boys."

"Well, it may come as a shock but I like boys instead of girls too. For sex."

"I was hoping that. With all my heart, I was hoping that."

Tears now welled in Kyle's eyes. He slid his arm around Bobby and drew him close. Steering the car with one hand, he ran his fingers through Bobby's hair. "But is it true, what I heard? I need to know."

"Is what true?"

"That you go to men's rooms at night, to give them massages and – ?"

"Not any more. Vinnie told me that if I kept doing it he would tell you – "

"Well, if it makes any difference, he didn't tell me."

"I'm glad. I like Vinnie."

Kyle gripped the wheel tightly. "Did you and Vinnie - ?"

"No. I was going to but Vinnie had heard what was going on and when I went to his room that's when he warned me. I stopped after that."

"How long have you been doing that, going to guy's rooms?"

"For a long time. It started with Mr. Austin, the salesmen for the supply company. He loved getting one of my massages. After they changed his route, he'd still come to Brackettville just to stay at the hotel. He was very nice. He bought me all kinds of neat presents – "

"Stop! No, I guess I don't want to know."

"Okay."

"Look, what's done is done. Now we have to think of what we're going to do now."

"What *are* we going to do?" Bobby asked, his hand dropping to Kyle's groin.

Kyle shook his head. "I don't know."

Bobby's lips twitched with the effort of suppressing a smile.

Again, Kyle gripped the steering wheel tightly with one hand and guided Bobby's hand with the other. "Just how old are you, my beautiful little Bobby?"

Smiling broadly now as he caressed the bulge in Kyle's jeans, Bobby replied, "Old enough."

Kyle's nearness in the quiet, still house overwhelmed Bobby. Because Kyle was holding him so close, looking down at him so intently with his laser beam blue eyes, Bobby was a little afraid of him. He swallowed with difficulty, wanting to move away, but unable to, wanting to look away but incapable of it. For Bobby, it was a fantasy come true. Kyle was even handsomer than he was on the screen, in the magazines or in the poster or on album covers. To Bobby, Kyle was the most beautiful man in the world.

For Kyle, it had been inevitable. Sooner or later. He had longed for this moment as one longs for something one's reality simply cannot bear. Yet there was something horribly wrong in that longing, that desire. He argued against himself. The arguments trailed him, chased him, unresolved.

But now that Kyle had the boy alone, at the ranch, he could not imagine he could do anything to him that had not been done already, yet he was still hesitant. Bobby removed his last shred of doubt by telling him that he saw how troubled he was, how exhausted, and he wanted to give him a massage.

In the bedroom, as his clothes came off, Kyle caught the boy watching him closely, examining his body, smiling.

Kyle chuckled and snapped the elastic of his white briefs. "I'm ready."

"So am I," Bobby said, smacking his lips. Once Kyle was lying face down on the bed, he realized Bobby's full mastery was startling, too marvelous to stop. It would have been like cutting the hands of a gifted magician. Kyle could no longer resist. The boy was spinning his own kind of spell. Kyle's stomach fluttered weightlessly, yet his limbs felt heavy. His skin tingled as Bobby ran his hands up and down the smooth skin of his back. His bones seemed to have liquified as Bobby applied pressure to his aching joints.

Unable to take much more, Kyle rolled over.

Brazenly, the boy's lips grazed his belly, dug into his navel.

"Damn, Bobby," Kyle muttered as he gazed down at him.

Slowly Bobby made his way up Kyle's body, kissing, licking, sucking. Finally Bobby placed his lips on Kyle's, lightly at first, then harder. The boy even knew how to kiss, Kyle thought. Kyle felt the kiss straight through his body to his toes.

Bobby cupped Kyle's head between his hands and titled it back like he meant business. Kyle felt he could handle this, after all, it was only a kid. But Bobby was an astonishingly practiced lover: Before Kyle realized quite how Bobby had accomplished it, his lips had been seduced to part and he was receiving his tongue. Receiving was the proper word. Bobby hadn't forced his way inside Kyle's mouth. He didn't make hit or miss stabs at the seam of his lips, he just entered, non-aggressively, and explored his mouth leisurely, tasted thoroughly, stroked lazily. Kyle's cock responded, throbbing as it lay snug in his briefs.

As Bobby strung a necklace of kisses across Kyle's throat, he wanted to tell him how many times he had dreamed of doing this, but soon he was sticking his tongue so deeply into Kyle's mouth again he couldn't speak.

Kyle luxuriated in the rhythm of the youth's hands as he lightened the pressure and tapped up and down his upper body, pressing and squeezing each area before removing his touch entirely.

"Lay still for a minute. I'm going to take a quick shower and then come back for this..." His hands stroked the outline of the obscene bulge in the briefs. More than anything he wanted to suck the cock at that very moment but he had worked all day at the hotel and run errands; he felt dirty and he wanted to be clean for Kyle Cartwright.

Kyle heard the shower running, bathroom sounds, the light

click off and the door open.

Bobby entered the bedroom naked. Kyle sighed as he watched the boy approach the bed. He was filled with a mixture of disbelief, fear and longing. Bobby, he thought, was more adorable than he had ever imagined a kid could be. His little body was as perfectly formed as his face. His cock was small but entirely in proportion with the rest of him.

As the boy approached the bed, he reeked of Kyle's favorite Grey Flannel cologne. Kyle smiled.

Bobby gently caressed Kyle's stomach, then climbed between Kyle's thighs. Slowly he began lowering the briefs. As Kyle's erection was revealed, Bobby kissed it, first the head, then all the way down the shaft to the pubic hairs. He climbed away for a moment to remove the briefs entirely, then made himself comfortable again between Kyle's thighs. He seized the erect penis with his fingers and licked it.

"Hmmmm, yes," Kyle moaned. "Oh yes."

Bobby's fingers weren't massaging to loosen muscle now. With his mouth, he applied just the right amount of pressure and a delightful degree of suction. Kyle could scarcely believe it: Little Bobby was even better at cocksucking than he was, he had to admit, simply because Kyle was so unprepared for it. He began feeling a feverish ache in his loins. He was close to coming. But Bobby wouldn't let him. Not quite yet. Bobby went at the ballsac with great abandon, licking, sucking, kissing.

Finally, Kyle could take no more and it was the most intense orgasm he could remember. Bobby had reduced him to gurgling infancy. Kyle nursed on Bobby's gentle touch, suckled after his attention like a child unwilling to have his mother far from his sight.

Bobby lay atop Kyle and their mouths came together, their lips rested together. They were now glued together.

"Did you enjoy it?" Bobby asked finally, caressing Kyle's cheek.

"Oh yes."

"I'm glad because I wanted to please you most of all."

"You have pleased me, more than I can ever say," Kyle said, giving him a peck on the cheek.

"I love you."

"Don't talk like that."

"It's the truth."

"Then I love you, too. And I was pleased most of all." Their kiss was long and, in his happiness, Bobby started to cry. He did not sob, tears just ran down his cheeks. Kyle wiped them away and kissed his freckled nose. He reached between their bodies and took Bobby's erection in his hand.

"You want me?" Bobby asked, his eyes wide.

"Yes."

"No one's ever wanted me before."

"Shit − ?'

Bobby shook his head.

Kyle beamed. "But I do."

Kyle squirmed down to put Bobby's crotch in his face. He kissed Bobby's erection and took it in his hand. It was a lovely penis, he thought. Not long, not thick, but perfect. It was cleanly cut and the balls were lightly furred. Kyle sucked on the balls first, then the cock. He was prepared to suck it for hours but Bobby came instantly. Kyle swallowed all of the sperm that just seemed to keep on coming.

Fully satisfied that he had taken it all, Kyle drew himself up next to Bobby and the boy looped his arms around his neck. Bobby was ecstatic beyond all comprehension. Kyle Cartwright had sucked him to orgasm. Kyle had triumphed: he made the boy come, the boy who said he loved him, really loved him. They kissed with great passion and adoration.

"Really, no one's ever wanted you before?" Kyle asked after several moments.

"Maybe they did, but I never wanted them to touch me, I guess. I just wanted to do it, to watch them as I made them happy."

Kyle was not going to pursue it, but still he had to know. "Have you ever had anyone," he hesitated, "Well − " Kyle slid a finger down into Bobby's asscrack.

Bobby closed his eyes, shook his head. "Oh, no."

"Thank god." Kyle breathed deeply.

Kyle sat up and ran his hands over Bobby's body, still not quite believing there could be such a perfect little form.

Bobby reached up and laid his hand against Kyle's cheek. At the touch of the boy's hand, Kyle groaned with pleasure. He took each finger and kissed them, sucked them. His eyes misted at the thoughts he was having. No one had ever blown Bobby's cock, no one had ever fucked him, he had never fucked anyone. There was so much they could share that he was overwhelmed with tenderness. He couldn't help himself: "Yes, I adore you, Bobby," he said, smiling. "I do."

"I'm glad. I can't really believe it yet, but I'm glad."

Showering together, they soaped each other and as the suds were rinsing off their bodies, they held each other and kissed passionately. As their cocks became erect again, Kyle knelt and took Bobby again. After Bobby had come, he insisted on making Kyle come again as well.

When they were dressed and leaving the ranch, Kyle's hands came up and framed Bobby's face. His thumbs took turns sweeping across his lips. Then his mouth settled on his. It was warm, undemanding, fluid. He slipped his arms around his waist and drew him up against him as he angled his head to one side and deepened the kiss. A tide of heat reverberated through their bodies, pooling between their thighs, in their groins. They were hard again. Kyle tasted Bobby again and again, then pulled away and worked his way into his ear. Bobby felt the warm, damp stroke of his tongue and gave a soft cry. He stumbled backward. No one had ever made love to him before. And this wasn't just anybody, this was Kyle Cartwright - singer, movie star, the man in the poster that hung on the back of his closet door. Every girl's dreamboat.

Kyle pulled him down, covering his body with his own, plowing his fingers through the boy's hair. He kissed him as though he was starving for love. Kyle was astonished that this felt so right, so good. His erection was firm against Bobby's own.

And there, on the carpet runner in front of the door, Kyle drew Bobby's penis again from his pants and sucked it to orgasm. He could not let the boy go. He wanted to suck him all night long but he could not.

"Patience," Kyle muttered, wiping the excess cum from his lips. "We'll have to be patient. There's only two more weeks to this misery, then you're coming to Hollywood with me."

"What?" Bobby said, zipping up.

"I said, you're going back to Hollywood with me."

"But how?"

"I'll figure a way," Kyle said, hugging him. "Leave it all to me."

"Oh Kyle," Bobby sighed, his eyes worshipful, hopeful.

Tears in his eyes, Bobby's cum still on his lips, Kyle kissed him madly and Bobby's passion matched his own.

EIGHTEEN

Kyle was late. He had taken Bobby back to the hotel, gone in to sign Marianne's albums, and couldn't leave without closing the bedroom door and kissing Bobby goodnight. He returned after midnight and kept recounting the events of the day until he came again. Still he could not sleep and had to take a pill.

Now Grant would be angry with him, report him to Bergen. He could be placed on suspension. He bolted out the door and clambered down the steps to the car. He jammed the key into the ignition, shoved the transmission into gear, and floored the accelerator. The rear wheels skidded on the gravel.

Arriving on the set, he apologized profusely and Grant laughed. "We don't need you till after lunch, Kyle. Don't you remember?"

"Oh God, now I do." Kyle shook his head and walked slowly to his trailer.

But he couldn't stand being in trailer alone. He smoked a joint and then came back out and had lunch with the crew.

Back on the set, as he watched Raymond finishing his scene, his mind wandered. He wondered where Bobby was, what he was doing, and if he felt as lonely as he did at that very moment. Suddenly he looked up and there was Bobby with the group, suiting up, getting ready for the next scene, a crowd scene.

As Kyle started to walk over to the boy, he made eye contact but it didn't last as long as a blink before he looked away. Seeing the boy with the others, with his mother, Kyle was embarrassed now about what had happened, what he had said. Behind Kyle's imperious expression, Bobby detected nervousness, near desperation.

Kyle had on his cowboy hat and now he pulled it low on his

brows. Meeting Bobby's eyes again, he touched the brim with the tips of his two fingers before stepping away to take his place on the set.

After Kyle finished his scene, he went directly to his trailer. He was through for the day. Soon, Bobby was knocking on the door. Kyle opened it and when Bobby swung his worshipful gaze up to his it had such impact, Kyle had difficulty recovering his breath. "Come in," he finally managed.

Once inside, Bobby did not merely kiss him, he made love to his mouth. When Bobby kissed him, he could tell instinctively that the power of his passion was unknown to him. Once Bobby made up his mind to kiss, he poured his all into it. Kyle's mouth became the soft core of his world. Kyle took Bobby's firm buns in his hands and squeezed them. If that were true of a kiss then what more could he expect - ?

He snapped his wandering thoughts away from treacherous territory. The strength of Bobby's sensuality had probably scared off a lot of men because it posed a threat none of them could afford, Kyle most of all.

Kyle pulled away, out of Bobby's arms. He shot him a withering glance over his shoulder. Cursing under his breath, he removed his Stetson and placed it on the couch. He took a deep breath and looked into Bobby's eyes. "I take full responsibility for starting something I shouldn't have. I apologize."

"I don't understand," Bobby said, starting to tremble.

"I've had a chance to think - "

Bobby turned away, reached for the door knob.

Kyle rushed over to him. "Don't leave. I want to talk to you about this - "

Bobby was crying. Kyle took him in his arms. He smiled. "Oh, shit, I don't care what happens. God help me but I adore you, Bobby. I must have you with me."

Their kiss was the longest and most passionate yet, their hands roaming over each other's bodies with a fiery intensity. Their groins rubbing together, Kyle thought he would come in his pants; Bobby did, and when he pulled away, he pointed to the wet mess. "How am I gonna leave now?"

"I guess you're not," Kyle said, unzipping his pants.

Bobby dropped to his knees before Kyle and eagerly opened

his mouth. As Kyle watched, Bobby performed his magic. He was incredible, Kyle thought, so young, yet so experienced. He closed his eyes and was close to coming when they were intrrupted by a knock on the door, Vinnie shouting Kyle's name.

Kyle stood against the door shoving his cock back into his trousers. Bobby stood up and wiped his lips with the back of his hand.

"Yeah?"

"Is Bobby in there with you?"

Now Kyle opened the door slowly. "Yeah."

"We're goin' back to town now. Will you bring him in later?"

"I guess I could."

"You are having him for dinner tonight, aren't you?" Vinnie said with a grin.

"Oh, yeah, of course. Consuela made something special just for him," he lied.

Kyle opened the door a little wider. Kate was standing next to Vinnie, smiling.

"That's so nice of you, Mr. Cartwright."

"No trouble at all," Kyle said.

Bobby came up next to Kyle. "I'll be back early."

"You have school tomorrow," his mother said. "You've missed enough already."

"I know."

Kate nodded and, taking Vinnie's hand, they turned and walked away.

Kyle eased the door shut and leaned against it, catching his breath. "I don't believe it."

Bobby started giggling. "That's so nice of you, Mr. Cartwright," he said, mimicking his mother.

They left the trailer hurriedly and roared off in the Mustang. But Kyle did not want to go to the ranch while Consuela was still there so he stopped in a secluded area where he could watch the house from a distance.

After Kyle had turned off the ignition, Bobby groped Kyle and asked, "Can I finish now?"

Kyle put his arm around Bobby and chuckled, "Something tells me we've only just begun."

NINETEEN

Over the next few days, Kyle felt the pressure build inside him, the raw hungry desire that defied his control, that defied every rational thought, every warning made by others. Occasionally, the pressure made his breathing difficult and he had to work for every swallow of air. He had lusted before but had never had this seemingly uncontrollable craving, this obsession to possess another human being. It was not just to experience erotic pleasure but to satisfy a more powerful, inexplicable need.

But how to accomplish it? That is what nagged at Kyle. Then, less than a week before the location shooting was to wrap, he got a message from Jay Julian's secretary. The producer was coming to Texas to see Kyle.

It was at a party in Beverly Hills in 1969 that Kyle first met Jay. The older man's face was pleasant, almost handsome. Kyle watched as the intense man who wore Italian silk suits and could say yes to a movie and yes to an actor ease his way around the room, smiling graciously, saying little, nodding. Jay's hand was everywhere, Kyle saw, but he never left a fingerprint. When his hand touched Kyle's, Kyle trembled.

Jay looked at the ice cubes in Kyle's now empty glass. "You must be drinking what I'm drinking."

"Mineral water?"

"The only thing I'm allowed these days."

"Me too."

"You because of your young age, me because of my old age. We have much in common."

Jay signaled a waiter. "Two Perriers."

The waiter nodded, smiled at Kyle, and left them alone

again.
"Macaulay has told me much about you, about this new record you have coming out."
"I had fun making it."
"Then it must be good. I've learned that if it's fun, it's good."
"I think it is."
"You're a sweet kid. We must get together."
Kyle smiled.
"My wife is going to Paris to do some shopping soon. I'll call you."
Kyle, still smiling, nodded.

Jay Julian lived in a Cotswold manor house, set on an acre of land in Beverly Hills, surrounded by iron railings, painted white. Kyle honked his horn. A buzzer went off and the gate opened. He went up the flagstone steps. Jay opened the door himself, gesturing for Kyle to enter the high, beamed hall filled with sunlight. Jay's large hand was outstretched. "Great to see ya again. Great to see ya."
"Thank you."
"My wife's gone to Paris. I gave the servants the day off so we could be alone together. Come, let's go to my study."
Jay sat in a wing-backed Queen Anne chair. "Make yourself comfortable, there, on the couch. Let me have a long look at you."
Kyle looked about, at the Picassos, the family photographs.
Jay took a long cigar from the table next to him, offering it to Kyle.
"No, thank you. I don't smoke."
"Good for you," he said, lighting his cigar. "It's a gruesome habit. Gruesome."
Staring at Kyle, Jay took a few puffs. Finally he said, "You're here because I've got this John Wayne picture, based on a novel nobody ever heard of but we have a good paperback deal. It's gonna be big, but I want to make it bigger."
Kyle leaned forward, knowing full well that Jay would quickly make it clear the price he must pay. "That's what I understand."
"Yeah, but you in the picture, it's good. Teenage singer. It's irresistible, bring John Wayne up-to-date, ya know?"

"Yeah."

"Yes. You have to get into pictures. We're picture people, Kyle. Always been in pictures. The best people are in pictures. None of this television shit. That's for amateurs."

"Yes, I know."

He set down his cigar, got up and went to a vast partners desk with a scarlet leather top and a phone with a bank of six buttons and picked up a script. "Here, I want you to read this."

Kyle stood up, approached the desk.

"You'd play the kid, Chance. Not a big part, but enough. Yes, you study it, and go see our casting director in a coupla days. Read for him, pose for the camera. No big deal."

Kyle took the script.

"I can see you are very beautiful. In a way, you resemble me when I was your age. Jews in Warsaw in those days were supposed to be little, dark. But not me. No, I was blond, large for my age." He sighed. "I know what it means to be different."

Kyle looked down at Jay. Kyle found his large, soft cow-eyes somehow hurt and fighting tears, yet his strange, animalistic mouth was strong.

Jay's eyes flashed wildly as he looked up at Kyle. "And I hear you're not only different from all the others, you're very good."

Kyle nodded, glanced back down at the script. "It depends."

"Yes, very good indeed."

As Kyle looked down at him Jay wanted to find if those pink lips on that pouty mouth of Kyle Cartwright's were as warm and alive as they looked. He said, "My father used to say, 'Jay, you're too easy with people. You'll never be a trader.' But I fooled him. I found out what people wanted. I know what you want. Do you know what I want?"

Kyle smiled.

"I want to kiss you. Right now." He stood up and took the back of Kyle's head in his hand and drew him across the desk. They kissed for a long moment, then Jay let go, stepped back. "You taste wonderful. I bet you taste wonderful all over."

Jay held the door open for Kyle. "This is the guest bedroom. We can be comfortable here."

Kyle stood still, just inside the door. Jay locked the door and slowly moved across the room. He sat on the edge of the bed.

"Come, let me have another look at you."

His hands slipped gently down Kyle's body, caressing every inch until they finally settled on the crotch. He kneaded the swelling bulge, lowered the zipper.

It was strange to Kyle, having a man do this. This rarely happened. Most of the time, the men just wanted to be serviced, to be blown. Quick, easy. This had swiftly become something more. He stood watching Jay in silence, his heart thudding in his throat. He dared not speak.

Slowly, Kyle's semi-hard penis was revealed. Jay held it, stroked it, admired it for several moments. "Yes, you are very beautiful..." he pulled up Kyle's shirt, ran his hand over the ribbed abdomen, "...all over."

Kyle drew a deep breath. "Thank you."

Kyle's cock swelled to its full length as Jay stroked it. With his other hand, Jay unzipped his own trousers and withdrew his prick.

"It would be a sweet gesture if you'd see what you could do with this. I haven't been able to do anything with it for years." Jay let go of Kyle's cock and leaned back on the bed, propped up by his elbows.

Kyle squatted, then fell to his knees between Jay's outstretched thighs. He finished undoing Jay's pants and pulled them off his body.

"I have overstayed my welcome on God's earth," Jay said as Kyle settled back down on the floor before him. "It saddens me. It is disgusting, but you are making such a fine gesture..."

Jay's cock was fairly large, with heavy balls, and, even though it never got fully hard, it did respond to Kyle's machinations. Jay began to pant and give eager cries as he neared orgasm. Kyle moved his mouth on it anxiously, wanting to please. Jay was delighted with Kyle's rhythmic throb of acceptance, the deep, prolonged sucking, and he thrust his penis down into Kyle's throat and groaned.

When Jay came, it was without sperm, but it was an orgasm that made his entire body shudder. He was pleased. "Oh, that was wonderful. You are very talented." He hugged Kyle to him. "It is at times like this that I know it is good being a Jew in this town, making good pictures. The goyim, they drift through life, everything comes easy. For us, life is sharpened. When life is hard, the roses are redder, the smell sweeter, the boys more talented."

Kyle stood up and Jay put his arms around his waist. Kyle's cock had gone limp during the long blowjob. Jay took it in his hand again and stroked it. "And the cocks more beautiful." His head was down, the cock pressed against his lips. "Yah, yah, we have time, plenty of time."

Jay's tongue folded, unfolded, folded again, sucking at the tender young cock and Kyle came vigorously. Jay held the last gulp of sperm in his mouth a moment and let it trickle down his throat in a warm, satisfying stream.

Two days later, Kyle received a call from Jay. "I want you to come to New York," he said, "meet some people."

"Okay."

"Good. I'm going tonight. I'll see you on Saturday. Call my secretary, Mrs. Travis, tomorrow. She'll arrange it. I always stay at the Plaza."

"It'll be fun."

"Then it'll be good."

And it was good. Two days later, Kyle was making his first trip to New York City. A limousine was waiting for him at La Guardia to take him to Jay's suite at the Plaza.

"Sex, money and power, that's the Holy Trinity," Jay told Kyle at dinner. "It's always been. And those who understand that fare better in life. I can help you, smooth the path for you."

Studio executives, Mac had told Kyle, fall into two categories: those who once considered a life in art and those who used to be agents. Julian considered himself an artist first, a businessman second. But it was he who decided what scripts to buy, whom to hire, the decisions that count. He made the big money, the profits and the half-million dollar fee upfront.

Jay was used to having the best of everything and, like many rich men, under the impression that his comforts, even his pleasures were necessary to his business. A man who thought in billions could hardly be expected to worry about the details. The cut flowers, the private jet, the limousines, were deductible expenses. He could buy anything but there was nothing he needed to buy.

After drinks, Jay told Kyle, "We'll start with some caviar. It's the only food I know that's like sex. No matter how much I eat, I always want more."

"Do you come to New York a lot?"

"Very rarely. Only when I must."

A platoon of waiters was taking care of them.

"Why do they fuss over us so much," Kyle asked, "If you don't come here very often?"

"Because I am rich. And I'm loyal. I mention this place to everyone I know. And, because I always bring beautiful people with me. Nothing a restaurant hates more than ugly people. I have dined here with some of the most beautiful women in the world. And now I am here with you."

They watched the waiter slice the coulibiac, then Jay tasted it. "Excellent," he said, beaming at the maitre d'. The maitre d' and the waiters nodded.

"A restaurant is the only place where people are happy because you're happy," he said, thoroughly chewing his tiny portion of salmon.

Kyle took a huge mouthful.

Jay chuckled. "Do not bite off more than you can chew," he told Kyle. "Only amateurs do that."

Later, Jay turned his attention to the platter of cheeses the waiter brought to the table. Under the table, he took Kyle's hand and squeezed it gently, describing the various cheeses, approving his selection of a goat cheese.

After Jay signed the check and tipped everyone a twenty on their way out, Kyle, astonished, asked, "Are you always kind to strangers?"

"It's one of the few pleasures of being rich. Organized charities bore me. I prefer sudden gestures."

Kyle provided a sudden gesture of his own when they returned to the suite: feeling high on the wine and the gentle benevolence of his host, as soon as they returned to the hotel, he took Jay in his arms and kissed him full on the mouth. Kyle groped the crotch, then dropped to his knees.

As Kyle lowered the zipper of Jay's trousers, Jay took the youth's head in his hands. "It is I who should be on his knees, dear child. Get up." But Kyle would not stop. He hauled out the smooth cock, about five inches soft, with a mushroom head.

"Lick it," Jay begged. "Please, get it hard."

Kyle licked the head and laved the entire cock with his spit. He stroked it and it grew another four inches.

"Oh, yeah. Suck my nuts."

Kyle pulled the trousers apart and brought his mouth to the balls, the size of jumbo eggs. As he sucked both of them into his mouth, he continued stroking the pulsing erection. Precum formed on the head as Kyle worked the balls over. When he pulled away and returned to the cock, he slid it halfway into his mouth, then all the way down his throat. Jay pulled at Kyle's hair as the suck continued, moaning all through it, "Oh yeah, god. Oh yeah."

Kyle teased the underside of the cock and added pressure on the cockhead, then backed off until he had just the head of it in his mouth. He wrapped the fingers of one hand around the base while the other hand went to work on Jay's balls. He moved his hands and lips simultaneously until the older man could take no more and insisted they go to the bed.

The suck continued but Kyle wanted to ride the cock. He got naked and greased himself, then returned to the bed. Jay had gone limp but Kyle brought it back to near hardness quickly and then climbed over Jay. Jay groaned as he watched his cock disappear into Kyle. He stroked Kyle's erection as the youth crouched over him. Thrust after thrust, Jay's cock was plunged into the boy, and with each deep penetration, Jay was writhing and moaning wildly, Kyle bucking with ecstasy.

When Kyle was close, Jay begged him to let him take it in his mouth, so Kyle moved up, letting the prick slip from his asshole, and Kyle face-fucked the moaning, gasping man. That was all it took. Kyle's back arched, his cock swelled and he cried out, his sounds intense as his body thundered with the orgasm, the orgasm the Jay was taking into his mouth and down his throat. Jay pushed hard on the firm buttocks, determined to keep the boy at that plateau of incredible joy as long as possible.

Panting, Kyle lay next to Jay for several minutes, a soft sheen of sweat coating his bronzed young body, playing with the glistening cock that had just pleasured him so much. Jay's trembling limbs alerted him that the man was enjoying himself, although the orgasm was a dry one.

After Kyle washed, he joined Jay in bed but he found it

difficult to sleep. Jay's wife was used to her husband's fits of insomnia, his restlessness, and teeth-grinding. Jay suggested Kyle sleep in the second bedroom of the suite.

When Kyle woke in the morning, Jay was already dressed, sitting in the living room with a cup of coffee in one hand and the *New York Times* in the other. He was reading intently and only acknowledged Kyle with a nod.

Kyle poured himself a cup of coffee and sat beside Jay. "What's wrong?"

"The world. The whole world's gone mad. Sharon Tate's been murdered."

"Who?" Kyle asked.

"Sharon, Roman Polanski's wife. He's in Europe. I'm having Mrs. Travis find him for me. I want to help if I can."

"Murdered?"

"A bunch of them, in a rented house. Awful thing." Jay handed Kyle the newspaper.

"Murdered," Kyle muttered, staring at the headlines.

"Hard to believe something like that happening in Hollywood. You know, in Hollywood everything is so insular, comfortable. It shields you from reality. There's no feeling among a lot of those people as to how the world really works. Everything's there for them. That's why I have to come here every once in a while, to remind me. Most people in Hollywood never want to come to New York, they hate it here, but I have to come here. And that's why I wanted to bring you here, so you could see how it really is for people."

New York City to Kyle meant exploration and adventure. He was young and fearless and had three days to discover what Jay called "reality." He found it in the gay bars, in the baths, on the street. He would return to the hotel exhausted but with still enough youthful vigor to please Jay.

The reality of it was, Jay enjoyed watching more than anything, and that night they went to a party where a man would be putting on "quite a show," Jay said with a wink.

Jay took Kyle to a pied-a-terre on Park Avenue owned by a diamond merchant from Brussels, David Friedman, whom Jay had known for twenty years. Kyle was ushered into what his host called a "formal" apartment, full of antique mirrors, empire-style furniture, and Oriental rugs. "It's a city residence, after all. My place in Cannes is much sparer and more open. It looks out to the ocean, with no carpets and lighter colors."

After pouring the visitors drinks, David led them into what he called his "back room," a long, narrow bedroom that had been converted into a playroom, with settees and huge overstuffed ottomans covered in richly patterned fabrics. Music was blaring from speakers hidden in the walls, which were covered on each side by mirrored glass.

Kyle nodded politely; he could not hear any of the other men's names as he was being introduced and, besides, his attention was focused on the black man dancing to the tune of Little Eva doing "The Locomotion" at the far end of the dimly lit room. Carrying their drinks, Kyle and Jay sat on the ottoman closest to the dancer. One of the men passed a joint to Kyle and he inhaled it gratefully as the black swirled around him, dressed only in white briefs. Jay called the man Joseph and told Kyle he was making a name for himself in porn films being filmed in New York. Joseph reminded Kyle of a long, lean, sleek panther, racing through the city in other people's fantasies, and he thought how hard such a life must be.

After Kyle finished the joint and his drink, Joseph motioned for him to join him. No sooner had Kyle begun to dance than Joseph's hands were up under Kyle's T-shirt, his fingertips toying with the boy's nipples, making them stiff. Kyle looked into the man's dark eyes, which seemed to him to be lumps of coal ignited by fire, and he cringed.

Joseph sensed the boy's nervousness. As Lesley Gore began singing "It's My Party," Joseph said, "It's gonna be fine, young fella," undoing the buttons of Kyle's jeans, shoving them down his thighs. Kyle reached for the elastic band of Joseph's briefs but the black grabbed his wrist and held it. "Wait," he commanded.

David moved forward and reclined next to Jay on the ottoman nearest to the two young men so that he could have a choice view. The other four men seated behind them were now stroking their pricks.

"He wants it, Joseph," Jay said, loud enough for the man to hear.

"And he's gonna get it," the black man hollered so that all could hear. "But he's gotta wait. No sense rushin' it."

"Aren't you being paid by the hour?" Kyle asked, feeling playful now.

"By the job. And you're a job, believe me. Any white boy's a job to me." He danced around him, slapped his ass." You gotta take so much time breakin' 'em in."

"Oh, he's plenty broken in," Jay chuckled.

"Not for this he ain't," Joseph said, tantalizing Kyle by patting the huge bulge in his Jockeys. He put his hand on top of Kyle's head and pushed down. Kyle dropped to his knees. Joseph pushed Kyle's head into his crotch, burying his nose deep into the musk-smelling bulge in the damp cotton. Kyle began tracing with his tongue the curves of the big balls and the lengthening, thickening column of the prick and soon the heavy round knob of the enormous cock slid from the fabric. The black began gyrating to the music again, this time to The Chiffons doing "He's So Fine," tormenting Kyle, moving away from him.

Kyle pulled his T-shirt up and off, then sat on the floor to remove his jeans and tennis shoes entirely. Joseph moved in, straddling Kyle, snapping the elastic waistband of his briefs and lowering them a bit. Kyle reached for it, Joseph jumped back. The men laughed. Joseph turned so his back was to Kyle and lowered the briefs all the way and stepped from them. He danced about for a few moments, his hand stroking his cock, until finally he was before Kyle again and he released the mammoth organ. Kyle's eyes bulged. He had never seen anything so monstrous. His mouth flapped open. He could hear Jay chuckling and the other men began cheering, urging him to touch it, suck it, do something with it.

But it was Joseph who called the plays: he put a hand on Kyle's head and drew Kyle's mouth and his erection together. "Do me, baby, do me!" As it began sliding into Kyle's mouth, the men cheered again and a couple of them clapped.

"My god," Jay screamed, "he's gonna take it all."

But Joseph wouldn't let him - not just yet. He backed away and began slapping Kyle's face with it. "Smack! Whack!..." the men yelled as each side of Kyle's face took a beating of the most delicious kind.

Kyle closed his eyes and grabbed for Joseph's thighs. He was successful in encircling the man, drawing him to him, and the cock was pinned against his cheek and the hairy, sweaty thigh of the black. Eagerly Kyle kissed, nibbled and licked the erection until he managed to get the head of it back in his mouth and begin sucking again.

The men in the back moved closer, hovering right behind where Jay and David remained reclining, with their cocks also out, stroking them wildly.

Kyle's suck-show lasted several minutes until Joseph withdrew and started to dance again, this time to The Ad Libs' "The Boy from New York City," eventually coming round behind Kyle. He put one foot on Kyle's neck, forcing him down, lifting his ass into the air. He spit into the crack and rammed two fingers in, to his knuckles, and soon he was driving in a third finger. Kyle cried out. Joseph withdrew the fingers and swatted his ass.

"Fuck him!" someone cried.

Joseph nodded, changing from cat to human and back again, returning to the reality of it only when Jay and the others would groan. He parted the asscheeks and slammed into Kyle with the huge pole, sinking it into Kyle until his balls slammed with a thud against the asscheeks. Kyle howled and dug at the carpet. The other men cheered, moved even closer. Jay stood and joined them as they gathered round the two performers, stroking, squealing, moaning, carrying on all over each other. As Joseph pounded in again and again, Kyle opened his eyes to see the feet and legs of the men surrounding them. He grabbed the torso of one of the men and rose up to take his dick into his mouth and begin sucking. The man came instantly, then another moved into position, Joseph all the while keeping an astonishing rhythm.

As the fourth man finished outside of Kyle's mouth, Kyle, tongue curved, lapped up the milkiness running down the man's leg. When finally the fifth man was before him, Kyle knew it was Jay and he just held him fast as Joseph was finishing. At this point, though traumatized by the incredible pain in his anus, he was still turned on and, jacking himself off, he craned his neck so that he could see the spectacle as the cock was slid from his asshole in the midst of the orgasm. Cum flew onto his backside and ran down onto the carpet. Jay sighed, "What a fine gesture," and lifted Kyle up and kissed him full on the mouth as the Paris Sisters were breaking into

"Will You Love Me Tomorrow?"

Kyle had quickly discovered that sex was not as important as it was made out to be in Hollywood. Once he had blown someone and they discovered his ability, he was talked about, brought in to meet others. Rarely did he have sex with the same man twice. There were exceptions, of course, and Jay Julian was one.

Now Jay was an independent producer, making the films he wanted to make, and he was flying into San Antonio in his Gulfstream jet on his way back from New York. He called Kyle and told him he was scouting locations for his next film, although he had already decided on Santa Fe; he didn't want Kyle to know he had had lunch with Bergen and now was worried about Kyle's behavior on the set.

"You look good." Jay's hand covered Kyle's and he squeezed it gently as they rode in from the airport in the Mustang.

"I should. I'm in love."

"What?"

"Yes. But he's only a kid!"

"You're not in love," Jay chuckled, "you've lost your mind."

"Maybe. But I'm so glad you came here because you can fix it."

"I'm no psychiatrist."

"No. I don't need a psychiatrist. I need you. Put him in this new picture with me. Make it possible for him to come to Hollywood."

Jay patted the back of Kyle's hand. "Only if I meet him first."

Consuela stayed on to serve dinner to Kyle and his guest. Kyle told her to spare no expense: she made pigeon with rice, Spanish style, with shrimp, clams and crabmeat, and Jay was delighted. She served Perrier water and Mexican kisses for dessert.

After the cook left, Jay sat quietly on the porch, smoking his cigar as the sun was setting. Kyle lighted a joint.

"You're never completely sober any more, are you?" Jay asked him.

"Not if I can help it."

"Is your life so bad?"

"No, it's good. It really is, this just makes it even better. It relaxes me."

"I've never asked you, when did it start, the drink? You were drinking Perrier the day I met you."

"On the road, for the first record, the first album. It was unbelievable, those guys in the band, the other guys that were along. It was a party, for two months, it was a party."

Jay frowned. "And you haven't been sober since."

Kyle chuckled. "Not if I can help it."

"Well, I was glad to see you've stopped drinking for the picture. That's something."

"Bergen insisted on it."

"As do I. But a little in moderation is all right."

Kyle shook his head. "I can't seem to do anything in moderation."

"You're young. All young people want everything all at once. I did, and I wore myself out. It wasn't until six years ago that I was able to – " He hesitated, took a few puffs of his cigar.

"I was there, remember?" Kyle said, grinning mischievously.

"You've been there ever since, and that's why I'm here now," Jay said, resting his hand on Kyle's knee and squeezing it. "Kyle, I'll never forget your fine gestures. And you are such a beautiful boy."

Kyle made Jay comfortable in the room Vinnie had used, then took a shower. As he stood under the spray, he thought of other showers of recent memory, of Bobby, how they stood here soaping each other, sucking each other, kissing, and he became erect. Jay appeared in the doorway, his robe wrapped tightly about him. Kyle knew the routine; he had left the light on, the door open, his album on the stereo. Jay, he knew, preferred the first album to the second and "A Lot of Lovin'" most of all of his songs. Kyle had given him an autographed copies of the first pressing of the album which Jay gave to his granddaughters.

The master bath at the ranch was almost as heavily mirrored as his own bathroom in Malibu, so Jay could easily watch as Kyle stroked himself to hardness. Kyle thought about Bobby all through it, how delighted Jay would be to watch the two of them making love. Ever the resourceful actor, Kyle made a little show for Jay, pretending Bobby was there, using his hands the way Bobby used his, pinching, squeezing, stroking.

Jay moved closer to get a better view. He undid his robe and let it fall open. He stroked his cock as he watched Kyle perform.

Kyle bent over to adjust the temperature of the water and his gasp was soft as he felt a single digit gently enter his moist ass. Jay's finger withdrew all the way, then plunged in again. Kyle remained bent and Jay stripped off his robe, got into the tub behind Kyle. The warm water slicked over them as Jay soaped his hand and explored the smooth terrain of Kyle's perfect form, finding every crevice and massaging it. Kyle turned and faced Jay as the older man soaped and plucked at Kyle's hard nipples. His hands quickly dropped to the cock and he soaped the erection. Then, falling to his knees, slid the erection into his mouth. He slid a finger into the puckered asshole as he sucked, quickly provoking a climax.

As the cum began splattering from the cockhead, Kyle again slammed it into Jay's mouth and, taking the older man's head in his hands, fucked his face with it.

Kyle left Jay alone in the bathroom. He got on the bed and lay face down, his ass high in the air. He heard the lights click off and the sound of footfalls. Before long he felt the tongue, the wet, coarse tongue that by now was so familiar. The soft hands spread his asscheeks and the tongue invaded him, niping, licking, sucking. The lips went to the buttocks, down his flanks, back to the anus. The mouth adored the young flesh and left it sopping. The half-hard cock slid up and down in the moist crevice and finally the head of it was inserted. Kyle groaned but said nothing. An inch or two entered, the fuck was attempted, stopped, then attempted again. The mouth returned to the anus and now the cheeks were pressed tightly together and the fucking continued with the tongue. In a few moments, short gasps were heard and then silence. Jay lifted himself off the bed. Kyle lay still. Jay started to walk away but returned to the bed, bent over and kissed the asscheeks goodnight. Finally he went to the other bedroom and gently closed the door behind him.

The next day, Kyle took Jay to the set where they watched the dailies of "El Dorado," then Kyle invited Grant and Jay back to the ranch where Consuela had lunch waiting.

Seeing Jay on the set, talking with Grant, Kyle felt he was not seeing the same person who had eaten his ass the night before. There was no physical change, nothing in his face to suggest a new happiness or unhappiness. Whatever occurred was like a change in the lighting, like seeing a room in the dim light and then seeing it on a sunny day. Jay was one of the most powerful men in Hollywood, one of the richest men in America, and he commanded attention and respect wherever he went simply because of that, but today it was more, Kyle saw, much more. Jay was serenely happy; he had just been with his "boy." Kyle saw too that Jay knew exactly what to say and when to say it, how to press and how to hold back. He remembered what Grant had said about Catherine, "You never got close to her." That was the way he felt about Jay in the beginning. No matter where he stood, it seemed he was somehow out of reach. Untouchable. Yet, the night before, they shared an intimacy few men know. And today Jay would glance at Kyle and smile, then go on talking with the others, and Kyle understood just how much he meant to Jay.

Jay had noticed a change in Kyle as well, that Kyle had crossed a line, stepping over into the same kind of atmosphere that enveloped him. So young, Kyle had always felt rather than reflected, had acted rather than waited. Now there seemed to be a new confidence about him, a sweetness that Jay had never seen before. "You're acting like a man in love now," he said while Grant was in the bathroom.

"Oh?"

"Yes. You used to be like a bomb with the fuse ready to blow. If things didn't go your way, you caused a problem. But today on the set you were in charge, caring about everything about the picture. It's good. You know, there's a thing inside us, it says, I may want to love someone, to reach out and touch someone, but I can't. I have to go my own way. But now you stopped going your own way. You've reached out. It's wonderful to see. I can hardly wait to meet Bobby. He must be some kid."

"He is. But I'll let you see for yourself."

After they ate, Jay napped while Kyle took Grant back to the location and went on to Brackettville get Bobby.

Bobby was thrilled to see Kyle, who got him excused early from his classes to meet Jay Julian.

On the way to the ranch, Kyle told Bobby who the producer was and how important the man was to him.

"Why do you want me to meet him?" Bobby asked, resting his head on Kyle's shoulder.

"I think the two most important people in my life right now should meet each other, don't you?"

"Do you love him?"

"In a way. Not the way I do you, more like a father, you know."

"Yeah," Bobby said, "I know."

When they arrived at the ranch, Bobby came into the living room smiling, holding Kyle's hand.

Jay beamed appreciatively. "Young love," he muttered.

The two youths sat on the couch across from Jay.

Seeing Bobby in person, Jay was impressed: "Grant showed me the dailies. Yes, you are extraordinary. But it takes more than looks, more than talent. What you need to know is that you got to give to get. You may say, fine, but what if I don't want to give, what if the price is too high? Then we go on to the next one, the one who's just getting off the bus."

"He won't have to take the bus." Kyle said flatly.

"He's a lucky kid."

"He knows that."

"I hope so."

Bobby looked at the man carefully. He didn't want to insult him but if he'd ask him to give him a blowjob right there and then, he wouldn't have known what to say. Jay overwhelmed Bobby; he had never seen anyone puffing such a big cigar, so totally sure of himself. He was quiet for fear of making an untoward remark. This man was important to Kyle and Bobby was eager to make a good impression.

Kyle looked at his watch apprehensively. "Jay's plane is waiting."

"Yes," Jay said, rising from his chair. "I only came down here to check on my boy here and I find out he's in more trouble than I thought." He chuckled as he ran his hand across Bobby's smooth, pink cheek and he winked. "Oh, but such beautiful trouble."

On the way to the airport, Jay turned to look at Bobby sitting in the back seat. "Yes, you are a sweetheart," he said. Then he turned to Kyle. "I don't know if I'm the best person in the world to give advice, Kyle, god knows most people think I've made a terrible mess outta my life, two divorces, two daughters who don't speak to me, a wife who spends all my money but won't sleep with me, but when I look at Bobby, I think if that's what you two want to do, you should do it. You should fight for each other.

"You know, all we have is this moment. You have to fight for what you want. We Jews always fight. Nothing is ever right for us. Jews were stoned three thousands of years ago and will be stoned thousands of years from now. It's the same for gay people. The gays and the Jews, we will always have to fight."

On the way back to Brackettville, Bobby rested his head on Kyle's shoulder and massaged his groin. "I like Mr. Julian," Bobby said. "I'd like to see him again."

"You will. Didn't you hear him say he'd see you in Hollywood?"

"He – you – *really* want me to go out there?"

"Yes. More than you can ever imagine."

"But how?"

"Leave it to me. I'll make your mom an offer she can't refuse."

TWENTY

"You're not serious?" Vinnie asked as he and Kyle got out of the Mustang in front of the hotel. A storm had come up and the crew was let go early. Kyle told Vinnie he was taking him back to the hotel. Once in the car, he told Vinnie his plan to ask Kate if the boy could come to Hollywood and stay with him at least for the duration of the shooting of Jay Julian's new film.

"Yes. Yes I am serious."

"This is crazy, Kyle. You're acting like a big baby."

"Babies don't get horny."

"God, you're asking for it."

"I'm tired of all this. I don't want to waste any more time. Get out of my way. I'm going to see Kate."

"I've told her, you know. I had to."

"What did you tell her?"

"That you like men, not women. But that we all are supposed to protect your image."

Kyle bounded up the steps and rushed across the veranda to the front door. He turned and glowered at Vinnie. "Thanks. I don't need any more of your help."

Shaking his head disgustedly, Vinnie said, "Kid, you're gonna need all the help you can get."

. . .

"I've been around the theater most of my life, Mr. Cartwright," Kate said, stacking some papers on her desk in her office.

"Call me Kyle."

She nodded. "Okay, Kyle. We people in the theater aren't like other people. We have a better understanding of things. Have greater imaginations. Bobby has a gift, Mr. Cartwright. A real gift. And he's told me what you want to do. At first, I wasn't sure. I thought he was kidding. And then he came back from San Antonio saying that Jay Julian had given him a tour of his jet. That Jay Julian wants him to be in his next movie. Now I now I know you are serious."

"We are, but –"

"And Vinnie has told me about you."

Kyle looked away. It always comes down to that, his gayness, he thought, grinding the heel of one of his boots into the floor.

"And I know Bobby, better than he thinks I do. He needs to get out of this place if he's going to do anything with his talent. You could take him out of here."

"I could, yes," Kyle said, his eyes back on Kate, blinking wildly. "But at what cost?"

"What cost?"

"You say you know your son. I wonder if you know as much as you think. That you know what he's *really* about."

She nodded. "Oh, yes, I know. And I know he's got a wonderful imagination. He got that from me, Mr. Cartwright. And I know what he's capable of. He can make up the wildest stories. But, yes, I know the truth about him, if that's what you mean." Although not a beautiful woman, Kate had a serenity about her that Kyle envied. She reminded him of his own mother, the mother he sometimes wished, fleetingly, he had never left in Montana. It made him wonder what had become of her.

"It doesn't bother you what he does, I mean – ?"

"It bothers his grandfather that he's gay, if that's what you mean. A lot. But it doesn't bother me. I just want him to be happy, to succeed in life."

Kyle cleared his thought with a sense of finality. "So you'll let him come to California?"

She nodded, then smiled. "For a little while, to see if he really likes it. A day at a time. Vinnie doesn't agree with me but Bobby's all excited about it and I think it would be a wonderful chance for him."

"It would be, but Vinnie – "

"Don't worry, I'll handle Vinnie."

"Well," Kyle said, moving to the edge of his chair, "I promise you I'll take care of Bobby as if he was my own brother."

"He adoress you, Mr. Cartwright. He told me so. And now I can see you care about him."

Kyle stiffened. "I'll see to it no harm comes to him."

"Just keep caring about him, Mr. Cartwright. Just keep caring."

Kate wanted a life for Bobby that she felt had been denied her, a life befitting someone of good breeding and disposition, the life of a "thoroughbred." Now that her son might be going to Hollywood, to be in the movies, Jay Julian's movies, she was thrilled.

Kyle was ecstatic. In Hollywood, the greatest aphrodisiac is the ability to put someone on camera.

As Kyle left the hotel, he saw Vinnie waiting by the Mustang. It had stopped raining, the sky parted and the sun was setting brilliantly in the west. Kyle grinned.

"Yeah," Vinnie said, "I know what she told you. And here I was looking forward to being a father. Now you've stolen the kid from me."

Kyle chuckled, "Look at it this way, you've gained a son-in-law."

. . .

Sitting in his wheelchair, the Colonel had carried on about General Pershing for an hour. Back at the hotel earlier than usual, the members of the crew felt trapped. They had had enough. They began talking about going across the border and having some fun.

"I'd love to go," the Colonel joined in. "But can't you see I'm old now? I'm old. I'm not like I was. When I was young I had a way with the women. Walkin' down the streets of Bar-le-Duc as if I owned 'em. Not a mama's boy like Bobby. Stinkin' little mama's boy! Gutless little sonofabitch." The old man grabbed Bobby as he came in the front door carrying his school books and passed him. He had waited to come home until the thundershowers had stopped. The Colonel began shaking him.

"Maybe I can shake some sense into you!"

"He's got me," Bobby yelled, dropping his books. "Crazy old man's got me! Help!"

"Why can't you leave the boy alone?" Kate said, sweeping into the lobby and separating them.

"Here, Colonel," one of the crew members said, "have a drink."

"Thanks," the Colonel said, taking a deep swallow of bourbon.

After grabbing up his books, Bobby ran up the stairs to the safety of his own room.

Suddenly, the Colonel began trashing about violently, spitting the booze all over his shirt.

"What's wrong with the Colonel?" one of the crew asked.

Rufe went to him. "Oh, mah God! Colonel Patterson, you okay?"

"Is he dead?"

"Help me, God in heaven, help me," the Colonel cried.

Kate felt the old man's pulse. "No, his heart's still beating but he looks terrible. Rufe, better get him up to his room and wait with him until the doctor can get here."

Rufe shook his head. Sometimes he thought his "boss lady" was as crazy as her father. No doctor could help the old man any more. "Runs in de familee," he'd tell his wife. "She gits up in the mornin' mad at the rooster an' goes to bed at night cussin' the owl."

Rufe wheeled the old man to the stairs and carried him up from there.

"It won't be long now," Kate said to no one in particular as she went back to the front desk.

"Crazy old fool," one of the crew muttered.

"For God's sake, take a look around you," another said. "Whattaya see? Domino players, stumble bums, mama's boys, pimply-faced kids, and crazy old men. What a place!"

"But Kyle likes those mama's boys."

"Yeah, virgin territory! He's used up all the virgins in Hollywood!"

They all laughed.

"Just where the hell do we fit in?"

"We? We don't fit in here."

"Then, let's go over to Mexico and get laid. I bet we fit in there just fine!"

"I'm with you!"

The crew passed Vinnie on the way out. He declined their invitation to spend the night in Mexico and entered the lobby. He went over to Kate, who was now in tears. "What's wrong?"

"The Colonel. I've had to call the doctor again."

"Everything will be fine. You'll see."

"I'm not so sure. I told Kyle Bobby could go to California."

"You know what I think."

"Do you mind so terribly?" She patted his cheek.

"I do, but if that's what you want, well, you're his mother. But you won't recognize the kid in a year, mark my words. He won't be the same."

"That's what I'm counting on. If he stays here, he'll just be another sissy. Out there, with Kyle, he just might be somebody."

Vinnie chuckled. "He'll be somebody alright. Kyle Cartwright's little – "

Kate brought a finger to Vinnie's lips, then took him in her arms and embraced him. "Don't say it. Don't say anything more. Bobby's so excited about this, if I don't let him go I'll live to regret it."

Their kiss was long, interrupted by Rufe, humming "Red River Valley," coming down the stairs and shuffling back into the lobby. He began picking up. "Ah'll jest straighten thangs up and lock de back door."

"You just do that little old thing, Rufe," Kate chuckled, leaving Vinnie's arms. "And I'll get something started for dinner while we're waiting for the doctor."

"You're a good woman, Kate," Vinnie shrugged as he followed her to the kitchen. "Crazy, but what the hell, ain't we all, one way or another?"

TWENTY-ONE

Grant brought "El Dorado" in on time and under budget. Bergen sent a check to throw a proper wrap party. Grant asked Kate to put on the biggest party Brackettville had ever seen. She ordered a tent and had Snyder's put on a Texas-style spread behind the hotel. Vinnie volunteered to serve as bartender: "You need somebody who won't drink up all your liquor."

"You're a dear," she beamed. Vinnie had told her he was staying on in Brackettville; the movie location could use a cinematographer part-time and she could use his help at the hotel, "Now that you're losing a son." He was bitter about Bobby's being with Kyle but he agreed not to argue about it further. Kate had become enraptured with Vinnie. Finally, a week ago, he had slept with her and she found him a maker of love beyond all her wildest dreams. And the penis, well, it just went on forever, she told a girlfriend.

"I guess Kyle Cartwright's coming to Brackettville was the best thing that ever could have happened," the girlfriend said.

"Yes, it's amazing how things work out," Kate agreed.

Kyle arrived at the party late. He patiently signed some autographs for the townsfolk who were all invited to the party and celebrated with a vodka and tonic. Bobby was helping with the ice and every time he passed Kyle, he'd flash him a wicked little smile and smack his lips. Kyle would smile back and shake his head.

As Vinnie was pouring Kyle another drink, he broke the news to Kyle that he wouldn't be returning with the crew to Hollywood.

"You're sure?" Kyle said.

He nodded. "You don't need me anymore, you'll have Bobby to look after you."

Kyle chuckled. "But who'll look after Bobby?"

Vinnie looked across the room to see Bobby joking with one of the crew members Vinnie was sure the boy had serviced in the night early on. "Oh, I'm sure he'll find somebody."

Around eight, Kyle went to the Mustang and drove down Main Street, past the laundromat, and turned into the parking lot where Bobby said he would meet him. Kyle waited only five minutes before Bobby was opening the door and getting into the car. He had barely slammed the door shut before Kyle was all over him, hugging him, kissing him violently. Bobby pulled back. "Hey, we gotta get outta here."

"You're right. No sense taking any chances now."

As they speeded to the ranch, Bobby sighed. "You really have to go tomorrow?"

"Everybody's gotta be on that plane. I wish you could go, but it's better this way."

Bobby unzipped Kyle's trousers and drew the cock from the fabric. As he lowered his head over it, Kyle held his head with one hand and steered the car with the other. By the time they reached the ranch, he had come but Bobby would not stop sucking.

"Hey, you'll wear it out."

"That's what I'm hoping. So you'll save it all till I get there."

Kyle took him in his arms and held him tightly. "I will." Then, as if he was singing, he added, "I'll be savin' all my love for you."

When they arrived at the ranch, they went straight to bed. In their favorite 69 position, as usual, Bobby came first and, after sucking Kyle until he came, the boy lay back and fell asleep. Kyle went to the bathroom and when he returned to the bedroom, he was about to wake Bobby when he became overwhelmed. It was a feeling he had never known before. The euphoria of the weekend, of wrapping the picture, the party, the kindness of Kate and the other townsfolk – and at last being able to drink freely – had exhilarated him. His heated, passionate sex with Bobby had now mellowed him and he was at peace. It was an absolute peace. He could not imagine a boy as beautiful as Bobby, let alone such a person loving him, trusting him so completely.

Bobby was sleeping curled around a king size pillow. Kyle sat cross-legged on the bed and watched the boy sleep. He had not realized how hungry he had been for this until at last he had it. He hadn't known what he was looking for until he found it.

Kyle's waiting was over: Bobby Richards was coming to Hollywood, to Bird's Eye, to his bed.

TWENTY-TWO

"Hear my voice/Where you are," Kyle sang into the phone. "Take a train/Steal a car/Hop a freight/Grab a star/Come back to me - "

"What is that song?"

"Yes. It's new. Alan Jay Lerner. I think I'll put it on my next album. Do you like it?"

"I'm not sure. Sing some more."

"Catch a plane/Catch a breeze," Kyle went on. "On your hands/On your knees - "

Bobby laughed. "On my knees all right!"

"Swim or fly/Only please/Come back to me. Have you gone to the moon?/Or a corner saloon/Or to rack and to ruin?"

"No!" Bobby shouted into the phone.

"I don't care/This is where you should be/From the hills/From the shore/Ride the wind/To my door/Turn the highway to dust/Break the law if you must/Only please just/Come back to me."

"Okay."

Bobby looked forward to Kyle's nightly call. Kyle said he was singing him to sleep. "But I can never sleep after your call. You know what I have to do."

"Just be careful, don't wear it out."

"Don't *you* wear it out."

". . .A visit is just a visit," Kyle teased Bobby over the phone the night before the boy's plane was to leave for Los Angeles.

"Okay. How long a visit?"

"Could be a day, a week. Maybe two."
"But I have to know how to pack."
"Well," Kyle chuckled, "why don't you just bring everything."
"My bike too?"
Kyle chuckled. "No, I'll buy you a bike here."
". . .I love you," Bobby said before hanging up.
"I know," Kyle said. "Damned if I don't know that. And I adore you." Kyle could not bring himself to tell him how much he really cared about him. Not yet. He had to have Bobby in his arms in order to tell him how much he missed him, how much he really adored him, how much it would mean to him to have him there, in the house, in his bed. And he had kept his promise. As hard as it was for him, he had, except for a visit from Nico, who had brought some coke to Bird's Eye and stayed for a short fuck, saved all his love for Bobby.

The next evening, shortly after midnight, Bobby's plane landed at LAX and Kyle met him at the gate. They hugged; it was warm, like father and son.

Once in the Corvette with the top down, Bobby's bags piled high behind them, secured with straps on the luggage rack, they inched along in traffic on the freeway. Kyle steered the car with one hand so he could hold the boy's hand with the other. He was a little drunk, he knew, and excited with the prospect of holding Bobby in his arms once again. He took a few deep breaths and tried to clear his head. Driving carefully and not too fast, Kyle headed toward the freeway that would take them to Malibu.

As traffic cleared, Bobby snaked an arm around Kyle's neck and his hand, as it always did when they were together, went to Kyle's crotch and he began massaging. He unzipped Kyle's trousers and pulled his cock free. His head went down into his lap and his lips closed over it.. After a few minutes of Bobby's sucking, Kyle pulled off the highway in a secluded spot. He leaned back against the headrest and ran his fingers through Bobby's hair. The boy concentrated on his work, moving his head up and down, making little noises.

Kyle was again astonished how much the boy knew about pleasing a man, how much he could do with lips and tongue. He came violently, but Bobby held onto him, sucking, kissing, stroking, until the spasms stopped. Reluctantly, he tucked his penis back into his trousers and zipped him up.

Kyle continued on to the beach, humming along with the song on the stereo, his own song, "A Lotta Lovin'." It was difficult to imagine how things could be any better.

. . .

At last alone in Kyle's bedroom at Bird's Eye, Kyle's right hand tightened on Bobby's as his left reached down and caught the youth's chin between his fingers, gently lifting it up. A shudder ran through Bobby's body when Kyle's flesh pressed against his. Bobby reached down and felt Kyle's erection throbbing again, ready for action. They gazed into each other's eyes, saying nothing. Bobby's cheeks flushed red as he stood on his tiptoes, his head barely coming to Kyle's chin. Their lips met and they both knew this time they couldn't stop.

Bobby lay on his back, his knees up and legs spread. With one hand, Kyle fondled Bobby while the index finger of the other hand played at the opening. Even the gentle probing of one finger caused Bobby to cry out. He applied more grease. He twisted it in about an inch. Bobby's sphincter squeezed the finger and his legs trembled. Kyle could tell Bobby was in anguish. Kyle could not bear to see him cry. He withdrew his finger. "We'll try again tomorrow."

He swept him up in his arms and held him. Felt his heart pounding.

"It's just that somebody tried it once, a kid, not much older than me, and, well, it hurt and I'm scared."

"I understand." They kissed, passionately. Kyle had never kissed anyone as heatedly as he did Bobby. At last, he thought, for the first time in his life, he had to admit it: he was in love.

. . .

The next day, Kyle ached all over.

"Tell me where you feel it and we can work it out," Bobby said, thrilled to be spending his first day at Bird's Eye. First they took a swim in the pool and then Bobby fixed breakfast while Kyle sat in the Jacuzzi. Kyle had gone back to working out every day after he had returned from Brackettville and, with the strain of finishing the movie and Bobby's impending arrival, he was full of tension. The Jacuzzi helped, but not enough.

    Now Bobby was finding the knots that suddenly felt like scars to Kyle; he pressed his fingers into places so sore that Kyle bit the insides of his cheeks to keep from screaming. He was good, as good as Kyle had remembered. Kyle rolled over onto his back and Bobby's palms traveled up the inside of Kyle's thighs. As he slid his tongue over his chest, Kyle sighed. Bobby worked the muscles in his neck and shoulders, all the way down his arms, and bit his nipples. He rubbed his cock against Kyle's, teasing. They both had erections again. It seemed to Kyle Bobby always had an erection. Bobby's mouth went to Kyle's cock and stayed there for almost an hour. Kyle would come, but Bobby would not give him up. The phone rang three times. The first caller, Mac, left a message. The second caller, someone at the studio, left a message. The third caller, the catering company, said they would be "coming at four."

    Listening to the messages while Bobby sucked him, Kyle laughed at the last one. "I'll probably be coming then too."

    "Catering?" Bobby asked, taking a breather.

    "Your welcoming committee will be here at seven."

    He licked Kyle's cock. "Cool. But this is all the welcoming committee I need."

    In the splendor of the bedroom at Bird's Eye, every sound was magnified, bigger than life. They kissed and sucked and made love for three hours. Their senses were stirred, every movement was important and intense. They dallied and caressed, their beautiful young bodies fitting together so perfectly, so gracefully, it seemed they had been made for each other. Their lovemaking was so passionate and they clung together so tightly, a ray of sunlight could not have come betwen them. At last relaxing against the big pilows covered with immaculate white-starched covers, Kyle stared solemnly at the ceiling. An impish smile was on Bobby's face as he suddenly got up and walked into the bathroom. Kyle turned and saw the boy standing at the toilet, the doorway outlining his tiny yet perfect body. As he lay there silently watching his beloved taking a piss, his stomach growled; he realized they had had nothing to eat since breakfast. A gust of wind rattled the windowpanes fiercely as Kyle leapt from the bed and went into the bathroom to stand behind Bobby.

"How's a pizza sound?"

"A pizza?"

"There's a place in the village that delivers," he said, clutching Bobby's shoulders and kissing the top of his head.

"Okay."

"How do you like it?"

"With extra cheese."

"You got it," Kyle said, starting to leave.

Bobby grabbed his arm and smiled. "I do, don't I?"

"What?"

"Got it, got it all."

Kyle took him in his arms and hugged him tightly. "You sure do." And as they kissed, Bobby's cock became hard again and Kyle lowered himself to the floor and took it in his hand. "Does this thing ever go soft?"

"Not when I'm with you."

A little after seven, Bobby left the bedroom and found Bird's Eye beautiful with people. He didn't know who they were but they were as colorful as the royal flush his Grandpa always was hoping for. Kyle had had the caterers decorate the house as if it was Christmas. "Christmas in July," he said when he made the invitations over the phone.

There were so many smiling faces, so much chatter, that Bobby was momentarily lost in it, floating through the room with Kyle's hand at his elbow.

The caterers had hired two musclebound waiters for the occasion and they wore sequined bikinis and black bow ties as they carried silver trays of steaming hors d'oeuvres. Bobby was afraid of the waiters. Not only were they spectacular physical specimens, they were offering him food he couldn't identify. Kyle stopped one of the waiters and made Bobby sample each item on the tray: A block of artichoke heart with crab and hollandaise sauce. An oyster. Smoked salmon. He named the various cheeses and made Bobby sample the smelliest one. At last he laughed and said, "A snail!" as he held it up for Bobby.

Bobby had to close his eyes for that one.
Kyle left Bobby at the pool to get another drink. Bobby was quickly worn down by the gaiety around the pool and he wandered to avoid attention to himself. He examined the flowers and grew dizzy with the startling scents. At the very edge of the property, peering over, he discovered the part of the house that was supported by steel struts. As he looked further down, he felt a hand graze his buttocks. He started and turned to see Kyle, holding a vodka on-the-rocks and beaming.
"Don't jump, please don't jump," Kyle laughed. He put his arm around the boy's waist. "Sometimes I wish I were a stunt man so I could dive off, time and time again. But movie stars only get to do it once."
"It would be a terrible way to go, wouldn't it?"
Kyle nodded. "Me, I want to go out sucking. That's the only way. I want it on my tombstone like that, 'He died with a cock in his mouth.'" His hand squeezed the boy's ass gently and he left it there. "Or maybe, 'With his cock up Bobby's ass?'"
"I want to - " Bobby hugged him. "So much I want it - "
"I know. I want it too. And we will."
"Promise?"
"I promise." They kissed passionately. "We gotta get back to our guests. Come, I have to introduce you to Mac."

As Kyle and Bobby approached Mac, hand-in-hand, Kyle said, "Where's Kevin Casey, or whatever his name is?"
"Why, isn't one enough for you?" Mac said, shaking his head.
"When it's Bobby, one's plenty. I was only thinking of you."
"That'll be the day."
Mac's eyes were riveted on Bobby's face.
Kyle turned to Bobby. "Careful, he's in one of his moods."
Kyle left Bobby in Mac's care and went off to take another snort of coke.
"You smell wonderful," Mac told Bobby.
Bobby blushed. "Kyle's Grey Flannel."
"It smells differently on you - better somehow."
Bobby turned away, looked for Kyle.
"I've been watching you since I got here," Mac went on, "and I've been stalking you for ten minutes." He pointed to the mistletoe. "Kiss me."

Bobby shrugged and gave Mac a gentle peck on the lips.

"Hey," Mac chuckled, "I saw the way you were kissing Kyle. You can do a little better than that for your agent."

Bobby shrugged again and let Mac kiss him for several moments.

"You smell wonderful and you taste wonderful," Mac sighed when they finally separated.

Bobby smiled.

Just then, Steve Sommers, in a tropical print caftan, swept up. "I'm in love already," he said, shoving an oyster into his mouth as his eyes raked Bobby's body. Bobby was wearing the best clothes he owned: black dress slacks and a white boys' Polo shirt Kyle had bought him. Kyle bought a dozen of them, one in every color they had, and left them stacked in the bedroom for Bobby. "They were on sale," he told the boy. Still, Bobby was self-concious, wanting to fit in but knowing he couldn't, not yet, perhaps ever.

"Everybody's talking about Bobby," Mac said.

Steve put his arm around the boy. "And I'm the only one who wants to talk *with* him. Come - "

A few minutes later, as the shade of evening wiped the pool, Kyle came up to Mac. He had a frown on his face.

"Feeling bad?" Mac wrinkled his forehead, sipped his drink.

"Hell no. I have so many drugs zipping through my veins I couldn't feel bad if I wanted to."

"You should be feeling wonderful," Mac said. "Without question the cutest boy in the world is in love with you."

"He's sure getting all the attention, isn't he? Say, where is he?"

Mac tilted his head toward the pool house. "Steve took him over there."

Kyle, flushed with anger, cried, "You let him?"

"I have no say."

Kyle began to shake. "I told you this one was different. He doesn't need Steve Sommers."

"Everyone in this town needs Steve Sommers, Kyle. If anybody should know that, you should."

"Shut the fuck up!" Kyle screamed, smashing his glass to the ground and rushing into the house.

...Steve closed the door and bolted it. Bobby stood in the amber light that streamed in from the west through the windows. It honeyed his skin and Steve thought how ridiculous it was that this boy should be so beautiful. He was unspeakably lovely. He stepped up to him and groped his crotch. Bobby hung his head. Steve brought his hand to Bobby's chin and titled his head back. He looked down at the boy's fresh, shiny face and smiled. "You're afraid of monsters, aren't you?"

Bobby nodded.

"Everybody at this party is a monster and they all want you, you know that?"

Bobby nodded again. Tears were coming. He began to tremble.

"Don't be nervous." Steve smiled and ran his hands up Bobby's arms. "And don't be afraid of the monsters or they'll eat you alive." Steve began unzipping Bobby's trousers. Bobby brought his hand to Steve's to stop him. At first, Steve stared at him incredulously, then he smiled. "I won't do this now if you don't want me to. I can wait. I am *very* patient."

A tear flowed down Bobby's cheek. "I'm sorry. I've only been here a day."

"I know." His pudgy fingers slid between the teeth of the zipper. He knelt down and pressed his face to the front of Bobby's underwear, licking through the heavy cotton. Slowly his hand moved into the briefs, to stroke the soft skin of the penis. He placed his other hand on Bobby's ass and hugged the boy close to him. "I just suck. That's all I do. I want to make love to your cock. I know it's a beautiful cock."

Kyle had gone over the guest list with Bobby. Mac, the agent. Assorted actors, mostly unemployed, writers, directors, hangers-on. And Steve Sommers. He told Bobby that Steve was one of the wealthiest people in Hollywood, having produced one of the longest-running musicals in Broadway history, which he subsequently made into a movie which became one of the biggest boxoffice successes ever. Since then, Steve didn't have to work but he invested in projects that interested him. If Steve was involved in the project, it got made. If Steve liked you, you got calls from casting directors, auditions, often the part. "He'll try to seduce you," Kyle said. Then he hesitated as B o b b y looked at him questioningly. "But you don't need him."

Now Bobby was pulling away from Steve. "Maybe later. After I figure all this out."

Chuckling, Steve stood up. "When you figure it all out, let me know. I haven't been able to and I've been here longer than you've been alive."

As Bobby zipped up his pants, he smiled. "I really like you."

Steve smiled. "You're the first kid that's ever said that to me." He draped his arm around Bobby's shoulder. "I think we're going to get along just fine, Bobby."

As they left the pool house, arm-in-arm, Mac greeted them. Steve said to Mac, "Most kids this boy's age are so boring. They're like commercials and I've been waiting for the movie. I tell you, Mac, I think this little kid's the movie."

Bobby looked about and asked, "Where's Kyle?"

Mac tilted his head toward the house. "I feel like a goddam traffic cop."

Bobby went into the house. Kyle wasn't in the living room or the kitchen. He went to music room. In the corner, in the dark, two men were fucking. They were both dark-haired. Bobby closed the door and went on to Kyle's bedroom. Opening the door shyly, he looked beyond the bed to the bathroom. Kyle was there, leaning against the wall, head tilted up, eyes closed. Bobby went to him. The toilet was full of vomit. His shirt was in bad condition.

"Kyle?"

"Go away, Bobby. I want to be sick by myself."

"Please, what's wrong?"

"Go back to our guests. *Your* guests. This is *your* party. Your coming out party. And how you've come out! Christ!"

Kyle fell silent. He stared with deep concentration. He was in a place he occupied alone. But Bobby would not be ignored. He tugged at Kyle and finally Kyle stood, pale and long, against the wall. His clothes hung loosely on his body. For the first time Bobby thought Kyle looked sick and old, so very old for 24. Bobby had no trouble imagining he knew Kyle well. But now he wasn't sure. He turned the water on in the bathtub, and undid the buttons on Kyle's shirt and pulled it off of him. Kyle knelt against the side of the tub, his face beneath the facet spray. Bobby leaned over him and soaped his shoulders, neck and chest. Kyle swallowed water from the faucet and spit. He dunked his head deeper, wetting his hair. He took the soap and scrubbed his face. As he leaned away from the tub and ran a hand through his wet hair, Bobby handed him a towel. Drying himself, Kyle stood, unsteadily, and took Bobby in his arms.

"How was Steve?"

"I did just like you said. He said we were going to get along fine."

Kyle shook his head. "God, I love you," he said.

"I love you," Bobby said, hugging him, lowering his head to Kyle's smooth, naked chest. He wanted to prove himself worthy. He wanted to study, to become what Kyle wanted him to be, whatever that was.

Music was playing throughout the house. Frankie Valli: "My Eyes Adored You." They went into the bedroom and began to dance a slow dance, tightly against each other, Bobby holding Kyle up. Hugging, kissing, rubbing. As they danced, Bobby finished undressing Kyle and they went to the bed. "But our guests," Kyle protested.

"You should lie down. Rest."

Kyle told Bobby to tell Mac he was sick and to get everyone out of the house. "I'm afraid I spoiled your party," Kyle said.

"I think my party's just beginning," Bobby said, kissing Kyle's cock before he left the room.

When he returned to the bedroom, Bobby bent down and kissed his lover, shoving his tongue between his lips as hard as he could. He began to kiss Kyle's body all over, finally working his way again to the penis. He took it in his mouth but it would not harden. "Just let me suck you off," Kyle said after a few moments.

Bobby quickly mounted Kyle's head. "Yeah," Kyle said. "Damn thing's always hard."

Bobby did all the work for him, furiously face-fucking him, and, soon, Bobby was drenching Kyle's face with cum. Kyle hugged the boy's crotch to his face and licked it clean, then passed out.

. . .

Bobby opened his eyes and listened hard. There were noises,

sounds he was not accustomed to. The room was dark and he wasn't sure where he was; then he recognized the sound. He sprang out of bed and swept open the drapes. He blinked in the intense light of the morning. Birds were perched on a limb of a Cypress tree that spanned the entire length of the picture window. The birds were singing. He could almost hear the Ocean. Little Bobby Richards was in California. In Malibu, at Bird's Eye. In Kyle Cartwight's bedroom. He went to the phone and punched in the numbers.

It was nearly noon in Brackettville.

"How are things?" Kate asked.

"Great. Birds are singing outside my window. And where I don't have windows, there are mirrors."

"And how's Kyle?"

"He's gone to the studio. He says he's doing what's called 'post-synchronization.'"

"You're there alone?"

"Yeah. No big deal." He went on to tell his mother about his plane trip and the party the night before, the people he met. After a few minutes, Kate said, "Be careful, Bobby. I love you."

Bobby held the phone in his hand for a moment, as if to keep his mother close to him for a while longer. He hated to admit it, he missed her already. And even Grandpa. But he held back his tears. He was in paradise, with the man he loved. Everything would be fine.

He dropped the receiver back into its cradle and reached into the drawer next to the bed. He withdrew the dildo Kyle kept there. It was about eight inches long and flesh-colored. He greased himself and then slowly began to play with the dildo probing his asshole while he jacked off. Slowly he inserted the latex monster an inch, then two. He came. He closed his eyes. He would practice with the dildo until he could take all of it and then he would be ready for all Kyle had to give him.

Coming had made him hungry. As he slipped on a pair of shorts, his stomach was growling. But he decided to go to the kitchen the long way, by way of the pool, taking the late morning air deeply into his lungs. Without the crowd of people, without Kyle, the place was just a house, a big, beautiful place to be sure, but just a place. And, he remembered, this was still only a visit.

TWENTY-THREE

Kyle hummed in tune with the stereo as he approached the city limits. Barry White was singing "Can't Get Enough." It was how Kyle felt at that moment, and how he wanted to go on feeling for as long as he could. It was a cold evening, a raw north wind was blowing but the skies were clear. He was in a sunny mood. He was in love. He came bouncing into Bird's Eye, smiling and rosy-cheeked.

Bobby was not in the music room, not by the pool. He called out to him. He heard a faint sob, coming from his bedroom.

Bobby was lying on the bed, naked, clutching a pillow. His eyes were red from crying.

"What the hell - "

"Look at me." He rolled over and raised and lowered the pillow in rapid succession.

Kyle stared incredulously at the scratches, the bruises, splotches of dried blood.

"Now I'm just a piece of shit," Bobby sobbed.

As Kyle came near the bed, Bobby lunged for him. They fought, Kyle hitting Bobby with blows that had no power, trying to subdue him. The breath whooshed from his body when Kyle grabbed one of his arms and yanked him down onto the bed. Bobby grabbed the pillow. Kyle wrestled the pillow away from him and tossed it aside.

"What the hell's the matter with you? What's happened? Tell me."

Bobby again began to buck and kick and flail his arms. Kyle anchored his legs to the bed by throwing one of his arms across his thighs. Bobby tried to knee him in the groin. He managed

to elude him, but barely.

Astonished, he gazed down at the beautiful youth on the bed. "Behave now."

He bound his wrists together with a sheet and pulled them over his head, stapling them to the mattress with his own hard fingers.

Little Bobby squirmed beneath him, trying to get away. His eyes narrowed with loathing, he glared up at Kyle, whose face was bent low over his.

"Why did you let it happen?" Bobby cried.

"What the fuck are you talking about? I didn't let anything happen."

His denial only made Bobby more furious. He renewed his efforts to get away. "You've made a fool of me. I hate you."

One of Kyle's hands still had his wrists pinned to the mattress. The fingers of the other sank into his hair and settled against his scalp.

"I love you. God help me, I love you. Now tell me what's happened."

"Your friend Nico came with a present for you. I let him in."

"Oh shit."

"I fought him but he was so strong." Bobby broke down, sobbing hysterically.

Kyle let him loose, but Bobby needed to be held and reached out for Kyle. Their embrace lasted for several minutes, both overwhelmed by the sadness that it would never quite be the same with them again.

Even though Bobby told Nico that Kyle was at the studio and he didn't know how long he would be, the dealer insisted on waiting. He asked for a glass of wine. He knew where the bar was. Bobby went back to the pool. When the boy finished swimming his laps, Nico was waiting on the chaise. He was naked, stroking his cock. Bobby started to run to the bedroom. Nico chased him. The more Bobby resisted, the more determined Nico became. He took a blow to the stomach without even tensing. Bobby grabbed for a wine glass and it smacked on the floor, shattering it into hundreds of daggers of glass.

Nico managed to wrestle Bobby back to the chaise and held

him, rocking back and forth. He raced his hands over Bobby's back as if he were looking for something. He held Bobby down with an arm across his chest, pinning him to the cushion, and he tore the bikini from the boy's body. He laughed when he saw Bobby's erection. He rolled him over and, his hand planted in the middle of Bobby's back, probed the anus with his finger. He found it prepared and he began to chuckle again.

"You were waiting for me, eh?"

"No," Bobby screamed. "No."

"Oh, yeah, Kyle. You were ready for Kyle. Well, this'll get you good 'n' ready."

He mounted Bobby and guided the huge, uncut erection into the crack, roughly entering him.

Bobby cried out and his fingers clutched the cushion. He tried to crawl up the cushion but Nico held him down.

"No! Be still...Ah, there...Oh, yes..." Nico sighed as each inch of flesh was introduced into Bobby's tight hole. When Nico had stuffed all of it into the boy, he placed his hands on top of Bobby's and lay across his back.

The thrusting was heated for several minutes and Nico kissed the back of Bobby's head all through it. Bobby closed his eyes and tried to hold back the tears.

When Nico was close, he pulled Bobby up so that he was on his knees and the boy cried out again, tried to pull away. Nico held him fast, his nails digging into Bobby's tender flesh, madly kissing his bare shoulders.

As he started his orgasm, Nico began a litany of groaned expletives in Spanish, clutching Bobby tightly to him. Bobby's entire body reverberated as he felt the enormous jolts from Nico's cock and the warmth spreading through him. Held so tightly that he could scarcely breathe, with Nico squeezing his tensed nipples, Bobby felt sensations that were so foreign to him, so exciting. He was overcome by it and looked down to see his own cock spurting cum without his even touching it.

Nico lowered Bobby back down to the cushion and removed his cock. Left empty, Bobby began sobbing. He realized he wanted Nico to stay in him, to start again. He had enjoyed it after all and he suddenly felt ashamed. His eyes followed Nico as the older man hurriedly went to the pool house. A few moments later, he came back to where Bobby was lying on the chaise, his eyes tightly closed. Quietly, Nico pulled on his clothes and left the house. Bobby lay still for several more minutes, re-living each moment of the attack. Finally, he rolled over and took his erect cock in his hand and proceeded to come again.

Bobby would tell Kyle very little about the attack, but he would re-live the moments with Nico over and over in his mind and every time the doorbell would ring, Bobby secretly wondered if it was him.

Epilogue

A dozen red roses arrived at the house every day for a week after the attack. But there was no card.

Kyle had gone to Nico's house but no one answered the door. The place appeared to have been abandoned in haste, junk mail still in the box. He called Nico but the machine picked up. He left a message: "Call me." He tried the beeper but there was no call back until about a week later. Nico reached Kyle at the studio and they agreed to meet for a drink at five.

". . .I like to come right to the point," Nico said after they had been served.

"I remember."

"It was some bad shit, that blow," Nico told Kyle.

"You're telling me. It made me sick at my own party."

"I was sick in the head. I was crazy for a week. That little hustler staying with you – "

"He's not a hustler – " Kyle snapped.

"Yes, I see that now, I thought that after I had done it, but you understand, he is such, how do you say, a cock tease – "

"What?"

"Yes, anybody looking like that...I never dreamed he was a virgin."

Kyle took a sip of his vodka, felt the tingle as it rushed down his throat. He shook his head. "I don't think we should see each other for a while."

Nico nodded. "I understand. I go back to Acapulco, then to Panama. I have some things to attend to. But when I return I will make it right."

Kyle took a long swallow of vodka, then set the glass on the

table. He took a deep breath and smiled. "I think you ought to make it right right now."
"Oh?"
"At my apartment."
"Your apartment?"
"A few blocks from here. It's my fun house."
Nico nodded. " You can trust me to make it right."
"I know, Senor Discretion himself."

Once Kyle had overcome his jealous rage at the thought of Nico taking liberties with Bobby, he began to imagine the scene that afternoon. Having had Nico himself twice before, he knew how good the stud could be. And today Nico did not disappoint him.

They went about it in utter silence. Primed by the coke Nico always carried with him ("Only the best for my Kyle," he said, pouring it on the table), they went at it furiously, carelessly. For those few moments, they existed only for each other. Kyle threw himself into it with considerable abandon, stunning himself with how much he had needed it.

Nico charged into him, seemingly inexhaustible, until Kyle had come, and then, pushing Kyle flat onto the mattress, the stud proceeded to do push-ups over his body, with just one to three inches of the rigid tool in Kyle at a time, until he was close, then he lowered himself over Kyle completely, driving all of it into him, and Kyle moaned in uncontrollable ecstasy as the cum filled him.

Later, climbing into his car, Nico promised, "I will see you when I return."

"I hope so," Kyle sighed as he stood in the parking garage and watched as Nico's rented Cadillac disappeared into the heavy traffic. Kyle muttered to himself. "God, I love that big dick." But Kyle was not to see Nico again. Rumor had it that he had stayed in Panama to work directly for Noriega, negotiating deals with the Cartel. Kyle went back to using his former dealer, Frank, a skinny, ugly young man who worked as a grip at the studio but made his real money trafficking in drugs. He too had a big dick and Kyle would usually give him a blowjob in exchange for better quality drugs, a lower price, or both.

Kyle and Bobby started work on Jay's new film, "Gun Shy," going to Santa Fe to shoot the exteriors. To avoid the crew, they stayed in a guest house far from the location but that only fueled rumors. Kyle didn't care, he was with Bobby, and this was their honeymoon.

Kyle saw to it that Bobby was in a couple of extra scenes and was given supporting player billing. "If Gregory Peck could give Audrey Hepburn star billing, I ought to be able to get Bobby in below the title," he told Jay when he came to visit them on location.

Jay laughed. "In fact, Bobby looks a lot like Hepburn did in that picture. Remember when Peck is waking her up that morning?"

"Yes," Kyle smiled, "he is even lovely in the morning. You like him, don't you, Jay?"

"Everybody likes him. You may be in trouble."

Kyle nodded enthusiastically. "Some trouble to be in ain't it?"

Jay smiled. "Tell me, is he still a virgin?"

"As far as I know," Kyle, said, looking away. Kyle thought of Nico, of how that side of him, the side that needed to be fucked by as big a man as possible, could not be monogamous. As much as he adored Bobby and as much as Bobby thrilled him in a way he had never known, it was not enough. But he was confident he could deal with his sexual needs in his own private way, not letting it interfere with his relationship with Bobby. After the attack, Kyle did not broach the subject of anal sex to Bobby; he decided when Bobby was ready, they would do it. Meanwhile, he contented himself with Bobby's incredibly luxuriant massages and masterful blowjobs. And sometimes, as Bobby's eager mouth closed over his penis, Kyle wondered just how long he would be able to keep the secret, astonishing as it seemed, that Bobby was even better at giving head than he was.

When they returned to Hollywood, Kyle had Mac call Leonard Pierson at *Teenybopper* magazine, who agreed to meet Bobby and consider him for a cover story.

"He's even more photogenic than Kyle," Mac raved.

"Hmmmm. That's just we need," Len said, smacking his lips, "some fresh meat."

"Time –
He's waiting in the wings
He speaks of senseless things
His trick is you and me, boy."

- David Bowie, 1973

TEEN IDOL

*"Hollywood swallows its children.
It bears them, suckles them and suddenly
leaps upon them from the rear and gulps them down."*

— *Writer Budd Schulberg*

Note

"Memories," somebody once told me, are "pretty picture postcards in your mind." Some of these "postcards" might not be "pretty" to some people but they are to me and are all part of my quest to grasp the significance of where I have been, to get a better handle on where I'm going. That has meant telling my side of the story – and do it before somebody else beats me to it.

Although I'm telling my story as it happened, I'm also telling it in anecdotes as I remember them, compressing time and relocating some events. And I've changed everyone's name. You'll see why.

- *Bobby Richards*

Preface

I wasn't prepared for how quickly it all happened. One day I was in Texas, riding my bike to school. The next day I was riding a horse, playing a bit part in a movie, "El Dorado," a western starring my idol, Kyle Cartwright. And it seemed as if the very next day I was here in Hollywood, driving my red Porsche.

Kyle thought I had "potential" and he brought me here. It was just for a visit, to see how it went, and it went pretty well. I was in Kyle's next movie, "Gun Shy," filmed in Santa Fe. He made some room for me at Bird's Eye, his place in the mountains overlooking the beach at Malibu. He had the pool house, a glorified room for people to change in, made over for me. And I didn't have to go to school any more, my tutor came to me. But I did have to leave Bird's Eye for acting lessons, dancing lessons, singing lessons, even fencing lessons. Kyle wanted me to be prepared. I was going to be a star, he said, and he'd like nothing more than to have *two* stars in the family. That's what he said – in the beginning.

ONE

Sunday, June 20, 1976
    I wake up slowly, very slowly, sliding my feet to the coldest part of the sheets. I get up and open the curtains, get back in bed, and look out. I love the view, the Pacific Ocean shimmering in the sun. Bird's Eye. What a place.
    I'm horny. I want to come, to come *now*. It'll take the edge off till Kyle comes home. When I jackoff, I start by rewinding my mind to the last scene: Last night, in Kyle's bedroom.

    ...It started as it usually does, with an argument over drugs. He has given in, letting me share a joint with him, but sometimes he has used everything up – or I have, when he's not here – and we have to go out and find some more. The dealer, Frank, works at the studio and lives in the part of town near where the Vietnamese immigrants have settled. So we have to drive into town and make a buy. I go with Kyle now. I didn't used to and then he wouldn't come home for hours.
    I like to be as close to him as I can, as often as I can. From the first time we made love that night back in Texas, it seems as if we've been living inside each other's skin. Even before I had pieced together the sad history of Kyle's life, I felt I'd known him forever. He was, after all, my idol, the man whose poster I had hanging on the back of my closet door in my bedroom. We became lovers but it's more than that, it's as if we're one person, joined, and nothing can ever separate us.
    On our way to get the drugs, I blew his cock while we drove. I love Kyle's cock. It's not that it's big, it's just that it's perfect. A perfect sucking cock. A nice head and a shaft that gets bigger as it goes down to the base. Kyle kept his foot hard on the gas

pedal as I did him the way he likes it, with lots of licking and nibbling, and after he came I just held him in my mouth, waiting until he was ready to start again. I could feel us turning off the freeway and Kyle said we were almost there.

I zipped him up and waited for him when he went in and saw Frank. He would usually stay fifteen or twenty minutes. I never knew why and didn't ask. I supposed he gave Frank a blowjob, although he said Frank was skinny and ugly, he had a big dick and Kyle likes big dicks. Anyhow, it lowers the price of the drugs.

Kyle was high when he came back out to the car. He and Frank had shared a joint...and whatever. Now it was my turn to drive, Kyle's turn to suck. He enjoys it more when he's stoned, takes his time, makes love to my cock. I had come twice by the time we were back at Bird's Eye.

While I lit up, Kyle took a shower. When he came out of the bathroom, I was ready for him. He likes it when I lie flat on the bed and pretend I'm asleep, as if he's surprising me when he mounts me and starts working over my ass. What was surprising on this night was how much he enjoyed eating my ass. He stayed at it for several minutes before he stuck his cock in me. I'd come twice so I was in no hurry, I didn't even jack-off while he was doing it. I just watched him in the mirror, getting off on the pleasure he gets fucking me. I'm the only one he fucks. He does everything with everybody else, I know, but that. That's something that's ours and ours alone. And at some point, when he's close, he likes to roll me over. I always lie back with my eyes closed, loving every minute because Kyle knows all sorts of good angles, his hands never fumbling, going over my whole body, and when he comes I part my eyes just slightly because it is too much to look at him, he is so handsome, even with his mouth loose and pink and parted, his eyes closed, letting it all out, giving it all to me. And last night, I came again while he was coming. His cock soft but still in me, he leaned over and lapped up my cum. He says he loves the taste of my cum. I tell him I love the taste of his too but most of the time it's buried deep in my ass.

And I come again, now, just remembering it, and I'm ready to go out and jump in the pool. I'll do some laps, then go to the kitchen. Kyle gets a special coffee from France and it's always there waiting for me. He got up hours ago and went off to the recording studio. He's working on a new album. Thank God.

I have a different coffee cup every day, depending on how I feel. My favorite cup has a picture of Kyle painted on it and his autograph. I love that cup. I love Kyle. Kyle: movie star, recording star, star of my life. They say that, in California, the sun shines to light up the stars. And Kyle's the brightest star in the world, if you ask me.

The movies made in Hollywood kept alive all these myths about the West: golden opportunities, free individuals, free sex in the sunshine, and happy endings. For me, they were just that, myths, until Kyle brought me here. Now I know they aren't myths, but to have it all, you've got to bend a bit. Sometimes, more than a bit.

I finish my coffee and go back to my room. Today I decide to go shopping. In California, poverty is a sin; success is wealth. They say that in Northern California, people hide their wealth behind tall hedges; in Southern California, it's all displayed. The size of one's front lawn shows the owner's control over enough youth, water and wealth to keep the grass green. Here in Malibu, your wealth is displayed by the number of feet of beach you own. But we don't own any; we live above them all, in the hills, so we can peer down on them as the waves wash their houses into the sea. And I've learned that a lot of those nice houses are changing hands. The Asians who once worked the land in California are now buying it and the Mexicans who owned it originally are now trimming the bushes. The rest of us make movies or television shows or record new albums. Or go shopping, which is what I like to do the most, other than have sex.

After we got back to Hollywood from shooting "Gun Shy," I made a few commercials and went for some casting calls, but, basically, I haven't worked in six months. I thought not working every day would bother me but it hasn't yet; there's been so much to do, so much to see. But I do love to act. It seems since I don't have to worry about where my next meal is coming from, I've learned to relax. Kyle's managers invested his money well. He says he doesn't really ever have to work again but he wants to. He's worried about the poor box office showing of his last two movies. That's why he's started a third album. He's a better singer than an actor anyway, so I'm happy he's doing it. He said, "Okay, I'll do it if it makes you happy." He'll do *anything* to make me happy. That's why he bought me a Porsche. It makes me happy driving my Porsche when I go shopping.

In California, there is so much light, everything is lost in the brightness. That's why we all wear dark glasses. I slip mine on and back out of the garage, then hit the button to lower the door. Through the gate, down the steep climb to the Pacific Coast Highway, and I'm on my way.

The best sights in California are the ones that disappear: the towers of mirrored glass reflecting sun; the gold of the sun as it vanishes; instant buildings that are put up only to be torn down, or to fall down in the next earthquake.

I can hardly wait to get downtown. I speed up, pass everybody. If you drive fast enough the view is a blur, but if you go faster the landscape stands still and you just float through it. We had a friend of Kyle's from New York, an artist named John Dugan, visiting for a few days. He drives even faster than I do. And he is always making these big pronouncements about Los Angeles. He said, "Like any brilliant art, the results are better if you go fast, if the images aren't finished." I wrote that down. I try to write everything people say that sounds important down in my notebooks. It helps me to remember it and I may use it later.

Today I'm going to Melrose, to shop for more clothes I don't need, and have some lunch. Then maybe I'll spot a boy on the street and have some fun. Like this afternoon I see there's a hot number just a bit taller than me in very tight white shorts just walking along. I make a little show of trying to park and then go on, turn around, drive by again, and wave.

"Cocksucker!" he hollers after me.

"Got that right," I say, but only to myself. I wish I could stop, pick him up, suck his dick, but Kyle says it's too dangerous. First, because of the car, second, because of who I am, whoever that is, and if I'm going to get anywhere in this town, I must be discreet which means that we only deal with people who have everything to lose by not cooperating.

And later this afternoon, someone very cooperative is waiting at the apartment. Kyle's apartment is leased by the company so that if anybody inquires at the front desk they're told that there's no Kyle Cartwright as a tenant. It's convenient when you want to meet someone and not have to take them all the way out to Malibu. And Kyle insists on security. He was in shock after Sal Mineo was murdered in the carport of his building in West Hollywood last February. "He was just in the wrong place at the wrong time," Kyle said. I asked him if he'd been to bed with Mineo and he said, "No, not that I wouldn't have liked to, but he told me that it was too difficult to keep it a secret. But then, as if to prove his word, I heard he was seeing Rock Hudson and Peter Lawford. I figured, those guys were his type, so what would he want with me? Then I heard he had a crush on Michael York, so I guess I just wasn't in the right place at the right time with him."

But there were many who were in the right place at the right time, although he wouldn't talk about it. Our first night at the apartment, Kyle put out a new toothbrush for me, still in its cellophane wrapper. I was pleased until I opened the medicine cabinet and found a half dozen more wrapped toothbrushes, in different colors.

I asked him how many guys he'd brought there. He shrugged. "If I told you ten you wouldn't believe me. If I told you a thousand you wouldn't believe me. But those guys didn't mean a thing. It was just sex. Not like what we have."

Kyle says if some of those guys ever got to Malibu they might never want to leave. *Those guys*, I've found out, are mostly young "actors" looking for work; but most of the acting they've done is in New York, making porn films. All of the films Kyle has shown me at Bird's Eye are terrible, blurry things, and little acting is done in them. Now most of these guys are in Hollywood dancing at the gay theater on Sunset and going to parties, trying to get into movies - any kind of movies.

The kid this afternoon is called Jed. Kyle saw him last week. He liked him because he has a huge dick. Kyle's obsessed with big dicks. I can take them or leave them. To be fucked by a big dick hurts me terribly because I'm so little. I am only five feet four in my stocking feet, and everything is in proportion.

Now Jed, who sort of resembles Mickey Rooney in the "Andy

Hardy" movies only tall, is looking at me in that strange way these guys have, wondering what in the world I'm doing here. I don't shave yet so I appear to be maybe fourteen years old tops. If any of them asked me right out why I was there I wouldn't know what to say except that Kyle wants it this way. I do whatever Kyle says.

"...Yeah, suck that big dick," Kyle groans, holding it up for me.

I approach it tentatively. It's uncut and I don't know yet whether I like them this way or not. This one is nice because when it's erect and you pull the foreskin back you'd never know it was there. The head is quite large and tastes pretty good. Kyle got it all worked up and now Jed's working on Kyle's cock. Jed's lying between us and Kyle and I are taking turns sucking the big one. I pray Kyle won't ask me to take it up my ass. I'd rather watch him try to take it, but I'm afraid he already took it, last week, and now it's my turn.

"Wouldn't you like this up there?" Kyle says as he waves it at me, drooling saliva on the kid's hairy thigh.

I sigh. "I suppose I could try."

"Good boy."

Jed gets into position. If I have to take this thing I want to see it so I'm lying on my back. Kyle spreads my legs apart and Jed lines it up. Kyle finger-fucked me with the grease so I'm good and ready, but mentally I'm not. Kyle's been wanting this more and more and so I've been enjoying it less and less.

For about six months it was wonderful. There wasn't anybody else. Except for the time Kyle's dealer, Nico, came to the house. I'd only been there a short time and Kyle was at the studio doing post-synchronization on "El Dorado." Nico wanted to wait. I saw no harm in that. Besides, he was good-looking and had come with a package for Kyle. I went back to my swimming and he made himself a drink. He knew where the bar was.

When I got out of the pool, he was sitting on a chaise naked. Talk about big uncut dicks! My eyes bulged. I couldn't take my eyes off it. I sat down on another chaise and started a conversation, but he didn't want that. He wanted me. Any other time it would have been exciting but right then, with me just there a short time and being so wild about Kyle, I wanted to avoid this guy. I fought him and got pretty beaten up because he was high on bad coke and there was no reasoning with him. When he had torn off my bikini and felt my ass he thought I was ready for something, but what I had been doing was practicing, trying to take Kyle's dildo, the thick eight-incher. When Nico first started sliding it in, I thought I was going to pass out or get sick. I cried. I remember grabbing onto the chaise as he entered me fully. By then, he wasn't trying to be rough, it was just the size of it. In fact, once he got into it, it became less painful and I even got an erection. I came while he was doing it, without even touching my cock.

When I got up after he'd gone, I was all wet and sticky, bruised and bloody. I just went to bed and cried. Kyle was very nice about it, cleaning me up, kissing me, telling me everything would be all right. But I felt as if I had lost something that afternoon.

Kyle said that once Nico knew I was his lover, not a prostitute he felt guilty about raping me. He sent a dozen red roses every day for a week afterward, but we never saw him again. Kyle said he went back to Panama to work for Noreiga.

And then Dugan arrived. In his mid-30's and attractive in an intellectual, artistic sort of way, he and Kyle had a thing for about a week in New York a year before and it was Dugan's second trip to California. He hated the place and only came out to see Kyle and go with him to orgies. When Dugan discovered I was there, he was disappointed because Kyle didn't seem to have any interest in going to orgies. "Bobby and I have our own orgy," Kyle told him.

The first two days of Dugan's visit went without incident. I let him use my bedroom and I slept with Kyle. And then they started doing coke. Kyle won't let me do any so all I could do was smoke a joint, which made me horny. When they were really high, Kyle's suggestion that we all go swimming soon became something else. And for the first time Kyle had to actually watch me get fucked by another guy. As long as I was sucking him while Dugan was fucking me, it was okay, but after he'd come, he disappeared into his own bedroom and left Dugan and me in my bedroom. It was the first time I'd been alone with someone other than Kyle at Bird's Eye and that night I stayed with Dugan. It was the wrong thing to do but it was nice for a change. Dugan was dark, just a bit taller than me, hairy and chunky, the opposite of Kyle, and I was surprised how easily we cuddled together, his thick cock up my ass.

The next day, Kyle was in a terrible mood and took Dugan to the airport. While he was gone, I sat in my room surrounded by things that had become a part of me. There was really a large part of me there, but right then I felt that I should just go back to Texas and finish high school. But when Kyle came back and I was packing, he told me I couldn't go, that we would work things out, that maybe we needed to have other guys involved with us. He said he would take care of it. What that meant was, we would be meeting guys for sex, but only at the apartment, in a situation that Kyle could control. I agreed. After all, after Kyle, Nico and Dugan, fucking was getting to feel pretty good.

Now big ol' farmboy Jed's feeling pretty good right from the start. He's a real pro at this. Kyle is a good fuck but this guy, well, he's got a style all his own: slow, deliberate, easy. And this big dick...

God, I'm coming already. Kyle's taking my cum. God, I can't stop coming!

Kyle laps it up off my chest, my cock.

"Shit, look at that," Jed says as it just keeps coming. Kyle can't take it all, there's so much. And I just came this morning.

"...You were a good boy," Kyle says on our way home. He left his Corvette at the apartment; I have to go to a meeting tomorrow so I'll drive him into town. I love dropping him off at the recording studio. The last time I went there I met David Cassidy, got his autograph. Kyle knows lots of neat guys.

The Next Day

"Television. You've gotta get on television, kid," Leonard Pierson's telling me. He is meeting me for lunch at the Brown Derby.

"We've had this conversation before," I say.

Macaulay Kinton, Kyle's manager and now mine too, set it up months ago that I would meet Len, the publisher of *Teenybopper* magazine. "The first meeting's always very public,"

Mac said. "He'll take you to lunch, get familiar. If he likes you, he may invite you to come back to his apartment."

Len did invite me back but I didn't go. When you're Kyle Cartwright's lover, everything takes on a different perspective, at least it did at the time. Like when I first met Steve Sommers, the rich producer who wears caftans everywhere and looks like he's visiting from Saudi Arabia. He said he only wanted to give me a blowjob, but I played it like Kyle said to, politely refusing. "Keep him coming back," Kyle said. And it worked. We didn't see him for weeks and then, at a party, I found him, holed up in the bathroom, snorting and sucking everybody who came in. Again I refused. Being just one of a passing parade of pricks didn't turn me on, so there was nothing for me to do but leave.

Now I'm telling Len about all the people I'd seen and I still don't have steady work.

"This is a high-stakes business," he says. "Confrontation, that's all it is. The truth is it's your job to swallow what gets dished out. If you're going to take it personally, you're not tough enough to make it."

"I can be tough. It may not look like it, but I can."

"Okay," he smiles. "But it's TV now. It's all TV. I can't do anything until you get a series."

"Jay Julian says TV is for amateurs."

"Jay Julian's worth a hundred million. He can say anything he likes. You, you gotta get on TV. Then we'll start the ball rolling."

"Kyle gets thousands of fan letters a week and he's not on TV."

"Kyle's on the radio. He's got hit records. He's been in movies with John Wayne. That poster of him as sold a half a million."

"He's very sexy in that poster."

"You could be too. Your face is extraordinary, you just need the right clothes, the right look."

It was at that point that I realized I hadn't considered my "look." Other than a few things Kyle had bought me, I was still dressing like a little cowpoke from Texas. It was then that I went shopping – and I've been shopping ever since.

TWO

Later That Day
"Television," I say.
"I suppose," Kyle says. "Mac's always wanted you to do it but Jay says you should wait, take parts in movies. What do you want to do?"
"Television."
Kyle said Sam Pappas was looking for a new kid to help the ratings on an old TV series, "Home Life." Pappas was head of production for CineWorld, the first studio to go into TV in the fifties. Now they were part of a conglomerate, into trucking, steel, rental car companies. And they still have more shows on the networks than anyone else.
But they kept the studio running because "Mr. Pappas" ("Call me 'Sam,' kid.") was there and he represented a big block of stock. Besides, he told me, the tax setup made it necessary for them to expand every year, with new shows, new properties. If they didn't, they'd have to pay it all to the government. I made a note of it in my notebook.

Two Weeks Later
"How'd it go?" Kyle asks as I return from Sam Pappas' house. Kyle is sunning himself by the pool, reading *Variety*.
"Okay. I got the part." I go over to the poolside bar and drop some ice in a glass, then pour myself a Coke.
"I knew you would."
"I had the part before I went there, didn't I?"
"No. It all depended - " He folds the paper over and drops it on the ground.
"Depended on whether I cooperated?" I turn and face him.
"That's the name of the game, remember?"

"How could I forget?" I turn around, my back to him. I can't let him see my tears.

"Hey, what's the matter?"

I sip my Coke. "He says he wants to see me again."

"Oh?"

I look over my shoulder. "But what if I don't want to see him again?"

He shrugs. "You must have been very good to him."

I stare into my glass of Coke. "It doesn't matter to you, does it?"

"What?"

"What they do to me?" I try to hold back my tears.

"Of course it does. But, look, I've been there. I know it doesn't mean anything. It's just doing them a favor, for a favor in return. I've done some things I'd rather not have done, gone places I'd rather not have gone, just to be cooperative. If word gets out you're uncooperative, you might as well forget it."

He senses my frustration and is soon standing behind me, massaging my neck. "Now it's my turn," he says, digging into the skin. He turns me around, takes me into his arms and kisses me.

"Yeah," he says, wiping away my tears, "it bothers me. I wouldn't be human if it didn't, but I've got to be grown up about it. You're what they want. And as long as you're enjoying it, it's okay."

"As long as I'm enjoying it?"

"Right. The minute you stop enjoying it, stop doing it."

"Wouldn't that be 'being uncooperative?'"

He kisses my forehead. "No, that'd be keepin' your sanity."

Always after I have been out being "cooperative," I want him more intensely than ever. My feelings for him haven't changed. In fact, they have deepened. I truly love this guy. With every fiber of my being, I want only him. Yet I know that's impossible, given the circumstances, the way he has lived, the way he continues to live, whether I am here or not.

Sam Pappas first saw me at his office, told me he'd think about using me on one of his series. Then he called Mac and wanted me to drive down to his place in Laguna Beach. He said he wanted me to visit him there, that he liked having meetings there, it was more "casual." And besides, I knew, his wife was at his house in Beverly Hills.

Sam was wearing his usual poker face but his eyes were reading me; inside my head, I thought.

"I hear you're no talker," he said, pouring himself a tall Scotch. I had a Coke. "No loose mouth to blab things around. I hear you cooperate."

"Yeah," I sighed, settling back into a big armchair. "I always cooperate."

"That's m'boy! You'll go far in this business, kid." He sank down on the arm of the chair and patted my knee. "Any friend of Kyle's ends up bein' a friend of mine."

I waited for him to go on but he didn't. He just looked at me, with all the shades pulled down in his eyes. His face was saying absolutely nothing. He was waiting for me.

I looked past him, out the window, toward the sea. The view was spectacular. It should have been. I had read that the place set him back two million. Still, it wasn't the view I had from Bird's Eye. And Pappas wasn't Kyle. But you can't have everything.

"Great view," I finally mumbled.

And soon his hand left my knee and was caressing my cheek, fluffing my hair. "Nothing compared to the view I have."

"...The face," he said later as he held my head with his long, bony fingers. "You've got the face."

"Glad you like it."

"*Like it?* I love it! Just kissin' it makes me come!"

"So I've noticed."

He'd come twice. Once just moving across me, between my thighs, and again inside my ass. I hadn't come yet. I didn't want to come yet. I wanted him to have a good time. He kissed me on the mouth again and I could feel his big cock harden against my belly. I wrapped my legs around him and he squirmed into position. His cock slid in easily. Our lips parted and he said, "You love to get fucked."

"Oh, yes, oh, yes," I moaned, bringing my arms around his neck. I tightened the muscles of my ass as he pumped his flesh back into me.

"Kyle fucking you good?"

I pulled him close to me and whispered in his ear, "I'm no talker, remember?"

He nodded. "I hope to hell he is. You're good." Then he held my chin to look at me one last time. "'Faces,' that's what Gloria Swanson said, and they did have faces back then, in the old days. Lotsa class. You got class, kid, to go with that face. Walk down any street in any city any time of day. How many faces do you see? Real faces, I mean, the kind that light up the screen? I hate to put you in TV because we can't give you the close-ups you deserve. But your time will come."

Pappas was right: Now I love to get fucked. I like the older guys better than those porn actors Kyle hires. The older guys seem to enjoy it more and that makes me enjoy it more.

But nothing compares to the first time. I could write a lot about the first fuck with Kyle but it would never be the same as the thought of it. The very thought of it turns me on even now. Perhaps it always will. I had always wanted to do it but I thought it would come on gradually, with someone trying to do it for months and finally they did.

But my first *real* fuck was the sudden, impulsive, slambang thing with the huge Panamanian. Although technically it was the first one, I would rather not count it as the first. I like to think Nico just opened the path for Kyle.

It was about two months after Nico that Kyle introduced me to poppers: "This is what you need. I'm sorry I didn't think of this before. I gave up using them because they give me a headache, but they might be fine for you."

I took my place on the bed, lying on my stomach, clutching a pillow. Kyle prepared me with Vaseline and then, resting with his hard cock poised at the entrance, he leaned forward and placed the bottle of poppers under one nostril and blocked up the other. He inhaled deeply, then he did the other nostril. Then he handed me the bottle. I pressed the poppers to my own nose, took two hits, then quickly screwed the cap back on and set the bottle on the nightstand. I looked into the mirror to see Kyle over me, spreading me apart as his cock began filling my ass. The euphoric effect of the poppers surged through me and there was little pain.

Kyle groaned and slowly worked his cock deeper into my

butthole. "Oh, god," he cried when it is all the way in.
I hugged the pillow to my chest and moaned.

As the popper high passed, he really settled into it and it was as if I had discovered a different kind of appetite, a kind of hunger for his cock up my ass. I loved watching him fuck me from behind, loved helping him have his orgasm, loved it when he pulled me up as he was coming. All of it made my desire for him become more intense than ever. There was nothing I wouldn't do for him.

Now Kyle's holding my head in his hands and is kissing me, the way he always does, with great passion, as if the cameras are rolling. We are in another scene. I think, to Kyle, life has become a movie.

THREE

Sunday, July 25, 1976

Lately, Sundays have been the saddest days of the week for me. It's because of Kyle. Starting work on the third album may have been good for him but it's been bad for me. For us. Now he goes away for days. And he never calls. I'm going out of my mind. Trouble is, I'm lonely. Kids my own age have always bored me. I didn't belong. The trouble is, I don't know where to turn. The trouble is with me.

When Kyle does come back he says he's been with the guys who play in the group that backs up his singing. He says they know he's gay but they're comfortable with it. He says he doesn't have sex with any of them but I know Kyle.

If I don't start the series soon I don't what I'll do. I can't go back to Texas, that would be admitting defeat – maybe I'll just go crazy.

The Next Day

I look at Kyle with his musician friends, showing off, but then of course, why shouldn't he: he's twenty five, handsome, and has sun-bleached blond hair. Well-muscled, soft smooth skin on his stomach, his back, inside the curves of his long arms. His body hair is of a perfect length, perfectly placed. His hair is longer now, but not too long, and he resembles a young lion. And he is a star. Records. He had a number-one single, an album, a second album, a sell-out tour. Four movies. To me, he's the blondest, brightest star in the world.

He gently, absent-mindedly teases his crotch in that funny way of his, like I've seen Negro men do, making sure it's all still there. Mac says Kyle's "like a walking copulation" and it's true.

To watch him gives me the same kind of pleasure as when he's fucking me. It is an absolute perfection, like none I have ever experienced.

Now he bends his upper body and his muscles bulge under his skin. The muscles I have so often massaged. He straightens up and points at me, sitting over here, pretending I'm reading. He's talking about me. I can tell when he's talking about me because he gets this funny look on his face as if he's telling a dirty joke. He lifts his glass of vodka, it's tumblers full now, up, as if he's offering it to me. But he knows I hate liquor. Hate it all the more because he likes it so much.

Then his lips turn cruel, as he tells these guys about me. I try to read the lips, the lips that have travelled the extent of my body, that know every inch of me. I drop my hand to my crotch, to hide my erection. God, he does have a talent for making love. Everyone who's been blown by him or fucked him knows it. He has patience. Infinite patience. He will go at it until they come. He has more patience than I, to be able to do everything he does with people for whom he feels no attraction. But then *he* is the attraction, the *main* attraction.

Kyle showed up, finally, his pals in tow. They were going swimming, he announced, passing me without even a kiss. But first they needed drinks. He served them, then came back to the kitchen. I was fixing dinner.

He announced the album was finished! But there was one more song to sing and he invited me to come along. It'll be the first time I've been in the studio in months. He wants me to see him sing what he calls, our song: "Come Back to Me." He sang it to me every night when we were first separated, waiting for me to finish school. I guess it will always sum up our relationship, either he's singing it or I am.

He told me to fix dinner for everybody, then we'd go to the recording studio. Then he started to leave the kitchen, still without even touching me. It was if I was his servant.

"Kyle – " I reached out to him, touched his arm.

"Hey, the guys might see – "

"I thought you said they knew – "

"They do know, but not about us. Not that I like – " He looked away, took a deep breath, then went on, "*little boys.*"

"Well, then, who am supposed to be exactly?"
"My roommate. " He shrugged. "You know, my *roommate*."
"And they're supposed to believe that?"
I pressed into him, so badly wanting a kiss. He looked down into my eyes, kissed me lightly on the lips. "Okay, now be a good boy and get dinner together. Everybody's hungry."

Now that they have eaten, I'm sitting here watching him make jokes, probably about me. I wonder what the guys think. I don't care really but just seeing them makes me imagine they know more than Kyle gives them credit for. They are a strange group: the drummer, an Italian kid named Tony, skinny, in need of a shave; Jake, keyboard, the hunkiest of the lot. And Jeff, the quiet one. Except when he's playing his guitar. When they're on stage, it's the dueling guitars. I wonder if, in the dressing room, it isn't the dueling dicks.

People say they're themselves no matter who they're with but I know now that's bullshit. Kyle has taught me it pays to be a lot of different things to different people.

. . .

"...Ride the rail
Come by mail,
C.O.D.
Leave a sign on your door,
Out to lunch
Evermore.
In a Rolls or a van,
Wrapped in mink
Or Saran,
Any way that you can,
Come back to me."

He's singing the song directly to me. Now he doesn't seem to care if the guys notice or not. He gets very romantic when he sings it and tonight is no exception. Kyle once told me he doesn't like to spend a lot of time analyzing what he does or how. "It's natural," he said. "It's either there or it isn't. There's no way to learn. It's as natural as breathin'. I know a lot of people struggle, study and are coached. I can't relate to that. I worked with a couple of people when I first came here, but basically I just get up and sing. I've been doing this since I was in the church choir and I don't worry about how I'm going to do it. I just do it." And he *is* doing it tonight. I know the musicians don't care who he is singing to as long as he does it.

"The best yet," Jake tells him.

"I told you I was savin' the best for last."

He's ignoring me again but I don't care. Not now. Not after that. If I ever doubted he loved me . . .

"Where are we going?" I ask as we get into the Corvette in the parking lot.

"Jake's place. To celebrate."

"Oh, no."

"Oh, c'mon. You'll love Jake's old lady."

And I do. Right off. There is something appealingly trashy about Jake's "old lady." She has dyed hair, auburn, and a thin-lipped mouth, painted shocking pink. I can see the line of the elastic of her panties through her tight white slacks. At the door I shake her soft hand. Millie. She winks at me, leads me into the kitchen, where I fix a Coke. Kyle goes with the guys into the living room.

"Kyle's really beautiful when he's happy, isn't he?" she says.

"Yeah," I say, sipping my Coke. Someone has to stay sober.

"Now I know why he's happy – "

"Oh?"

"Meeting you, I can see. You're what he needs."

"I don't know what he needs. He doesn't know what he needs."

"Yes he does, and he found it. Just don't strangle him. When you're married to a musician like I am, that's the first thing you learn."

She caresses my cheek. "You're even cuter than he is, though. That could be a problem, but remember, he'll always come back to you. You know that, he'll always do that."

"I hope so." I think I'll start a page in my notebook: "Lessons in Lovin' from A Musician's Wife."

"Come on, into my bedroom – " She says, taking my hand.

"What?"

"Oh, don't worry," she says, patting my hand gently, "I just think you'll appreciate my collection."

Her collection leaves me speechless is what it does. White plaster penises. A whole wall of them.

"Well, what do you think of this one?" she asks, lifting one off the shelf.

I take it in my hand. "It's nice."

She laughs. "You don't recognize your own lover's dick?"

"Well, I thought it looked familiar but – " I turn it over a Kyle's signature is there all right, in purple ink.

"Some aren't signed, but Kyle's a sweetheart. It was tough though, having him keep it hard long enough for the plaster to set. It was a challenge, but then – " She blushes, giggles a little.

"Then what?" I am stroking the plaster cast.

"Well, we had a guy visiting here when this was done, oh, a couple of years ago at least now, and Kyle had the hots for him and, well, Kyle stayed hard all the while he blew the guy."

"There's only one thing he likes better than giving head – "

"I wouldn't know about that, but the guys tell stories and I've heard some. But he's slowed down now. He's got you. A boy like you could be a full time job all by himself."

I chuckle. "No, it's *Kyle* that's a full time job, when he's there." I put Kyle's cast down and pick up the biggest one on the shelf. "Who is *this*?"

"Jimi Hendrix. He was a lot of fun."

"I'll bet. I've never been with one, a Negro, I mean. Closest I ever got was Rufe, the guy that worked at our hotel. I would've done him in a minute, but he was straight."

"Hey. nobody's straight, honey, especially out here."

"This is *quite* a collection. You should start a museum with this."

"Down on Melrose. It'd be a real tourist attraction now wouldn't it? But they're all my own, you know, I'd rather not share them with anyone."

She takes my hand and leads me back down the hallway, past the pictures of Jake on stage during one of Kyle's concerts and other gigs. In the living room, the men are smoking and listening to a track from the new album.

"This one'll go to number one," Jake says, shaking his head with the beat, tapping his fingers on the table in front of him. He is sexy in his own way. I wish now I would have asked to see *his* plaster cast. I sit down and begin to wonder how he feels having to look at all those other guy's dicks in his bedroom when he smiles at me and says, "You're gonna be a star, kid. Cutest little thing I've ever seen. 'Cept for Millie, and she's a girl."

"All girl," Kyle chirps.

Millie slides down on the arm of the chair I'm sitting in and strokes my hair. "He is adorable isn't he?"

Kyle finishes the joint he's been sucking on and jumps up. "We've gotta run."

"Party's just startin'," Jake says.

"Yeah, I know. But I gotta get the kid home. It's past his bedtime."

On our way back to Bird's Eye, Kyle has dropped his head on my shoulder. "They both wanted to fuck you, you know that, don't you?"

"No."

"Sure you did. You love it. You love it that everyone wants to fuck you. Nico, Dugan, all those big dicks at the apartment. Everybody. But nobody *really* fucks you but me. Right?"

He kisses my chin, works his tongue into my ear. I grip the wheel. I want to stop, make love, but I don't.

"Sure, Kyle. Nobody *really* does it right except you. If you're around, that is. Where do you go, what do you do?" I ask.

"When?"

"With those guys."

"We just hang out, ball some chicks."

"You did?"

"Yeah! Like I told you, I've been blown by a chick before. And maybe lie on the bed while they move up and down over me, somethin' like that. Anyhow, the other night I fucked my first chick. Kid you not! I *really* fucked her. Fucked the livin' *shit* out of her!"

"No!" I act surprised but at this point nothing surprises me any more.

"Honest! 'Course, Jake had been in her first and he wanted

me to have some, and, well, I wanted to show 'em that I could do it. You know, on the tour I'd leave them, it was easy, 'cause I had my own suite. But here, when they invite me along, shit, I don't have anywhere else to go – "

"No, I guess you don't. Nowhere to go."

"Hey, it wasn't so bad, that cunt. She loved it. I tell you, she loved it." All the while he's telling me this, he's massaging my groin.

"I believe it." Of course she loved it. It was Kyle Cartwright fucking her. Who wouldn't enjoy it?

"And then I stuck it to this other one that was given Jerry a blowjob." Now he's squeezing my erection.

"Oh, no!"

"Yeah, I took her from behind. She loved it too."

"I'll bet." Now I push him away. "I bet Millie loved suckin' it too."

He leans over again, drops his hand back in my crotch. "Quite a collection isn't it? She'll want to do yours one day – when you grow up."

I push him away again.

"Hey, you aren't jealous of some smelly old pussies, are you?"

"Hardly."

"Good boy." He strokes my erection. "God, you are a *good* boy. I need to be reminded every once in awhile don't I?"

"I guess."

He runs his hand through my hair. "God, I love you." He finally pulls open my pants. "And this! God, I love this dick!"

"Imagine how you'll love it when I grow up."

"I hope you never grow up. This is just perfect. Craziest thing I ever saw. It never goes soft." He lowers his mouth over it.

I put my hand on his head and shove.

. . .

I kiss him more than I should now, just to remind him. Lately, he does need a lot of reminding. And when he pushes me away, telling me he's too tired now, I embrace him, and in moments we are wrapped around each other and moving together toward the moment when the final pleasure comes, when he comes inside my ass.

The image of him fucking a woman hangs on. It had been our thing, that he never fucked anybody but me. But now –

Oh, well, I think, it was just a pussy. Just some stupid cunt whores that the guys had picked up to fuck. Still –

Now, as he's fucking me, I think he's the better for it; he's charging into me like he's really missed it.

And he's not too stoned to come. I stroke myself, I need to come again. It's a competition now to see who can come first. He knows I'll always win but he keeps trying. I can't help it. I'm just a horny teenager, after all.

FOUR

Monday, August 9, 1976

"You got it, Bobby," Mac says to me in his office. "You're now on 'Home Life.'"

Mac stalled, lied, said I was busy, out of town. He waited until their final, panicked hour before agreeing to deliver the answer to their prayers: Me.

Mac told me there was nothing worse than being seen in the middle of a cattle call: "By the time you get on, the producers are courteous and good-humored but they have heard the shit a thousand times and they're numb, gaga, but not desperate enough to really pay attention. The only hope is to go on last. That's where the agent comes in."

"And Mr. Pappas?" I said.

"Seeing Pappas gets you in the door, but once you're in, you've gotta deliver."

"Oh, I'll deliver."

I am so excited I find myself driving north toward Trancas, way beyond Malibu, before I collect myself enough to decide to go home. I turn the Porsche and head back to Bird's Eye, pressing the pedal to the floor.

I start fantasizing about what kind of sex Kyle and I will have once I get home, to celebrate the series, but the sound of a siren and the sight of flashing lights in my rearview mirror brings me back to reality. I brake instantly but one glance at the speedometer tells me I'm in trouble. I am only doing fifty but several moments have passed. I pull over to the curb, roll down the window and take a deep breath.

"In a hurry?" the cop asks. He's ugly with a beer belly coming on rapidly, not my idea of the kind of officer of the law I want giving me tickets.

"Yes, kind of."

"See your license, please?" he says in a friendly way.

I hand it over. He disappears, goes back to his car and uses the radio. Then he sits in his car for what seems like forever before gets out and shoves the ticket in my face. "You live around here. You should know this is a residential area. Speed limit here is twenty-five, not *seventy*-five."

"Nobody does twenty-five here."

"That's no excuse for breaking the law yourself. You've gotten two of these since you've been in California. But you go to traffic school and we can get this one taken off your record. You know, four of these and we take away your license. And you wouldn't want that, would you?"

"No, sir."

What I *would* want is to be caught by one of those cops I see on TV, and have him take me to his own traffic school – in the back seat of his squad car.

The cop follows me all the way to Bird's Eye. I have a hunch he is checking whether I even have permission to drive this car. The addresses on the registration and my license match but cops are always suspicious. After I put my card in the box at the gate and it opens, I hit the accelerator, laying skid marks on the pavement. But he doesn't follow me any further, just sits in his car watching the gates close behind me.

The Corvette isn't in the garage. There is no note. I will have to celebrate all by myself. I'll start with a joint. Then have some dinner and then – where is that cop when I really need him?

FIVE

Monday, August 30, 1976

I love clothes. I've been on "Home Life" a couple of weeks and just got a paycheck. I'm trying to figure out what to buy. All my clothes are lined up, on the right hangers, color coordinated. My shirts go from white to pale blue to beige to brown to yellow to red to black. Someone designed most of my clothes. I'm so little that they have to be tailored. They're art. They shouldn't be abused. It would be a crime to toss them on the floor. My shoes go gradually according to how I wear them: beach shoes, sports shoes, the evening ones.

Kyle's messy. Sometimes, I'll go to his closet and straighten it up, totally do it over. It drives him nuts. But I know what I'm doing. He has the greatest Armani jackets. He's learned a lot about clothes since he's been in show business, but it took awhile because he's not one you can tell a lot to. He has to find out on his own.

Tonight I'm dressing for dinner. I'm wearing my own new Armani jacket. Jay likes it and tells me so. He's come for dinner. It's his first time at Bird's Eye in weeks; he came to celebrate my being on the series.

"Television!" Jay says over and over, but without malice because he's happy for me now. He says: "So I called Sam from Vegas. I said, 'You're not takin' this kid away from me,' and he said, 'I already have.' I laughed and he said, 'I'm saving the close-ups for you, Jay.' Close-ups? The *close-ups?*"

"The face. The kid's got the face," Kyle says.

Jay and Kyle always do this when I'm around, talk about me as if I wasn't even there, or just a vase or picture on the wall or something.

Jay looks at me now. "The face that'll pretty soon be on the cover of every teen magazine in the country." He smiles at me. "Yes, such a face."

Kyle nods. "And he's such a *good* little boy."

After dinner, Kyle and I prepare to make love in the music room on the couch. Jay sits in a chair across the room nursing a brandy and puffing on his cigar. We put classical music on the stereo just for him. Schubert.

Kyle dims the lights and then slowly undresses me. He treats me as if I was a little doll, dressing me, undressing me.

The first time Jay visited it was warm enough to swim in the pool and we did a nude ballet for him. He left before we started fucking. Now it appears he intends to stay through all of it. Kyle told me not to be nervous. "Jay just likes to watch," he said.

"So do I," I said, thinking of the number of times I lay quietly on the bed while some porn actor fucked Kyle. At first, Kyle would never let me touch the guy or let the guy touch me. But gradually he drew me in, made me a part of the action. The first time another guy fucked me with Kyle there he was lying across me so that his dick was in my mouth and he could watch the porn actor's big cock going in and out. It was after that he had mirrors installed over the beds at Bird's Eye and the apartment. Kyle and I have mirrors all over the place. We like to catch glimpses all the time, just to be sure.

Now it's as if we're fucking before a mirror, our images reflected in Jay's gleaming eyes. He's put out his cigar and finished his brandy. He unzips his pants and takes his cock out. Even soft, it's big. I figured it would have to be. Everything about Jay Julian is big. Big body, big expense account, big heart. Now it's a big semi-hard-on that's preceding him as he slowly makes his way across the room. It finds a home in Kyle's ass. A familiar home I presume, although I've never asked. After the first jolt, Jay settles into Kyle's rhythm and it feels like I'm getting fucked by both of them at once. I'm lying on my stomach on the huge leather couch and all their weight is on top of me, pushing me into the cushions. I close my eyes and let my limbs go limp. I came when Kyle entered me but I'm still hard. Kyle finishes first but just relaxes on top of me, letting Jay have his fun. No one has said a word. Finally, Jay makes some little gasps and then pulls out of Kyle. After he zips up, he quietly leaves the room.

"Did he come?" I ask.

"As much as he ever does. He loves it though. Will you let him do you sometime?"

"Do I have a choice?"

"Of course you do. You wanted every one of those dicks at the apartment, I know you did. I saw how much you enjoyed it."

"Only because you were there, watching it."

"Well, with these other guys, well, it's the same, only if you want to. Whether I'm there or not."

He rolls me over and we embrace. I say, "Only if you want me to. It's not up to me."

"Yes it is. I've been trying to tell you that from the beginning. It's all up to you."

I let him believe it, if that's what he wants to do. I just kiss him. We're still kissing when Jay enters the room again. This time he's naked, stroking himself. Kyle lifts himself off of me and smiles at Jay. I roll over and get on my knees, my ass high in the air. If I have to take Jay, it'll have to be this way. Kyle gets on his knees in front of me and I take his cock in my mouth. I begin sucking as Jay gets behind me, rubs my ass gently and brings his mouth to the crack. His tongue enters. He's licking Kyle's cum out of my ass! Nobody's ever eaten my ass out like this! Meanwhile, he's playing with my balls, then my cock, reaching under me, massaging. I can't help myself: I come all over his hand.

"Don't tell me the kid came again," Kyle says, lifting his dick from my mouth.

"You did say he was a good little boy," Jay says, and then he goes back to licking my ass and Kyle shoves his dick back into my mouth.

The Next Day

"What's wrong?" Kyle asks me.

"Nothing," I say, looking up from my book. I'm studying Shakespeare. Kyle says he likes it when I study literature. He's never read any of it and doesn't intend to, but he likes me to tell him about it. He even likes me to read to him. And I like it when he sings to me, or even just hums. We're a perfect pair.

"You're so quiet," he says. "You're like a mouse. Always watching me, never saying anything."

"I don't know what to say."

"We live here together. You're my boy. I want vibes. I want somebody to talk to me. All day you've been in here, reading."

"I'm sorry." He's acting crazy again. High again. I wish he'd leave the coke alone but he won't.

"You're on coke."

"Everyone's on coke. It raises your level."

"It's all going wrong. Stop, please."

"It's been going wrong for a long time. You just didn't notice."

He stands still, silhouetted against the late afternoon light.

A man can't pretend sex but now he says that's what he's been doing, pretending. "But I'm sick of pretending with you. You know what I want. I want you to give it to me. You!"

He lifts me up out of my chair. My book drops to the floor. He starts shaking me. "Fight me, Bobby. Fight me, then fuck me. Fuck the livin' shit out of me."

I fight all right – to get away from him. He holds me tight. I fight some more. I grab at his arms, dig in with my nails. He is grinning. It is an evil grin. I don't like it when he smiles like this. I can't look at him. I keep struggling to get out of his grasp but he has his arms wrapped around me and is pushing all of the wind out of me. I start to cry. He can't stand it when I cry. He lets go of me and I fall to the floor before him, sobbing.

He gets down on his knees and takes me in his arms. He has a splendid erection now and I stroke it.

"God, I want fun. I need to have some fun. Fuck me, Bobby."

I wondered how long it would take before he got around to this. I feel so inferior. I know he likes a big dick. He likes a powerful fuck. I've seen him getting fucked. He goes crazy when somebody's letting him have it. But I don't feel that way about it. I take my time. I make love to him, the way he made love to me that first night he fucked me, really fucked me. I will never forget that night as long as I live. After so many aborted attempts, I finally was able to let him shove it in all the way. It didn't last long, but when he came, I came too and we held each other and cried and then we did it with me on my back and we both came again. I never loved him more than I did on that night.

Now I'm in him fully. His height is in his legs so when we lie here, wrapped in each other's arms, my cock moving in and out of his asshole, we can kiss easily and I keep on kissing him, his lips, his face, his ears, his shoulders. All through it I just keep kissing him. When I start to come, he tightens the grip his legs have on me and I keep my cock in him. I have an advantage: I can keep it hard and come again quicker than he can now. I keep this up for a couple of hours until he's so raw he can't take it anymore. And he says he needs another hit.

I ask if I can have a hit. No, I'm too little. "I'm big enough to fuck you," I say.

He ignores me, goes on snorting. Is there any end to it?

Back in bed, he lies on his stomach, tells me to fuck him from behind. I give him a massage instead. This drives him wild, begging for a fuck and not getting it.

"But I just fucked you for two hours. Can't we give it a rest?"

"You're just mad about Jay. I told you you didn't have to do it."

"I'm not mad about it."

"You are. You didn't enjoy it."

"I did. It could have been worse. He's very gentle."

"He loved it. He told me so on the way out to his car. He's going to give you a part in his next picture. Hell, there isn't even a part for *me* in his next picture but there's a part for you."

I stop massaging his neck. "Oh, what's it about?"

"A science fiction thing about a kid who is kidnapped by aliens. He thinks you'd be perfect."

I roll him over and kiss him. "I would be perfect. That sounds like the story of my life, only Kyle Cartwright kidnapped me."

He spreads his legs. "It shoulda been the aliens."

I hold him by the ankles and, as my hard-on invades his ass again, I smile: "I know."

SIX

Tuesday, September 7, 1976

I had a scare the other day. I was driving home after filming and a squad car followed me out of Hollywood and for a few miles on the freeway. I had been speeding but they didn't stop me. Relieved, I made up my mind: I would do what I had to do, go to that most dreaded thing in California, Traffic School. I had to move fast; I only had a few days before my grace period would be up. But if I was going to do it, I would make it fun. Little did I know how much fun it would be.

The yellow pages was filled with ads for Traffic Schools, something for everybody: kids, singles, old people. But none bold enough to advertise that it was for homosexuals. One school advertised it was run by comedians for comedians. At least they wouldn't put me to sleep, I decided. I called and said I was a comic actor, was working on a TV series. That qualified me. As it turned out, anything would have qualified me. All they wanted was my money.

All I wanted was to get it over with. I told Kyle I was going shopping. I arrived at the old building on Pico and climbed the stairs to the room where class was held. When I opened the door, the instructor, a policeman, or somebody dressed as a policeman, said, "You're two seconds late. Another second and you'd have to take another class."

"Sorry," I said, slouching and taking the only available seat, upfront but off to one side.

The instructor was a policeman all right, but he was also a comedian, of sorts. And I couldn't imagine anything worse than being locked in a stuffy room with a bunch of strangers, the high and low of society, and a cop trying to be funny. But then the instructor made me feel even worse when he said, "Don't even *attempt* to cheat me out of a *single* minute of your four hundred and eighty minutes in class."

I never thought the first break would come. When it did, the girls all left first and then a few of the guys. I closed my eyes, thinking maybe I could nap, when there was a tap on my shoulder. "Excuse me," a voice said.

I turned around. A gray-haired, distinguished-looking man in a beautifully tailored dark blue suit and wearing some great cologne I couldn't identify was grinning at me.

"How's Kyle?"

"Who?" I was dumbfounded.

"Kyle. I saw you with him at Steve Sommers' party. You two didn't stay very long."

"I'm sorry. I don't remember."

"You wouldn't have. You had stars in your eyes. You were so much in love. You hardly left his side."

"I still am."

He hadn't stopped grinning. "I thought I knew Kyle. He was the last person I would ever think would fall in love. "

Just then the others returned and the man moved back to his chair.

The lunch break finally arrived and the man met me at door.

"I didn't get your name," I said, extending my hand.

"Martin. Martin Dyer."

The name meant absolutely nothing to me. I'm afraid that was obvious.

"I'm in promotion," he said, straightening his silk tie. "I put tours together. I did Kyle's first tour."

I imagined that he had probably taken quite a tour of Kyle as well and I smiled. "Small world."

"It is isn't it? Say, let's have lunch."

"Okay. I'm starved."

He lead me out across the street and to a waiting limousine, a white stretch Cadillac with darkly tinted windows. I shook my head. "They take your license away?"

"No, but they're threatening. But I have plenty of time."

"Not me. I've only got a week to go. I waited till the last minute."

"You kids always do," he said, opening the door wide for me. "Come, have some lunch."

Lunch, I found, was in the car. It was a spread fit for someone who promoted tours. Big star tours. But the tour he was promoting today was of my body: His hand dropped casually on my knee as he handed me the salt for the chicken; the endless refills of my wine glass, despite my protests that I don't drink; the reference to Kyle enjoying the view from his terrace overlooking the Pacific.

He was full of talk about Kyle's tour and the one he had just completed for Led Zeppelin.

"I'm not into rock 'n' roll," I said. "I'm into Kyle's music."

"Yes, of course you are. And Kyle's was a great tour. Those little girls bought everything we had."

"Like what?"

"T-shirts mostly and programs, buttons. We call it merchandising. That's where the money is. That's why I bought the factory."

"I have the poster. I didn't know there was a T-shirt or any of that other stuff."

"You wouldn't, unless you went to a concert. They're all true souvenirs."

"I've never been to a concert. Any concert, much less Kyle's."

"He'll do another one, if he ever makes another album."

"He is. He just finished the last track."

"Well, that is good news. I'll have to call him."

"Oh, we'd better get back," I said, checking my watch. I was flustered. The thought of this man calling Kyle and telling him about seeing me here shocked my wine-soaked brain back to reality.

"Oh, why?" he asked. "We're having such a good time."

"No. I've got to complete this thing."

"There's always next Saturday. You said you had a week." He put his hand on my knee and left it there.

"But – "

"I know. Let's go to the warehouse and I'll give you whatever I have left of Kyle's stuff. I can't think of anybody who deserves it more." He patted my knee.

"Well, maybe – "

"Joe," he said, lowering the partition between the front seat and the back, "let's go to the warehouse, the one downtown."

"How many are there?" I asked.

"What?"

"Warehouses?"

"I have so many I forget where they all are. But Joe remembers. He remembers everything."

As the chauffeur turned and smiled at me, I really noticed him for the first time. He had the regulation black cap and white shirt and black tie but he really looked as if he should have been wearing a football uniform. He had the mean, square-jawed, steely-eyed look of a linebacker. And he could probably put me in one of his pant legs and have room to spare. I decided there was no sense arguing; I would go to the warehouse.

As Joe eased the car into traffic, Martin said, "Joe doubles as one of my security people when we're doing a tour."

"I'd be secure with him around."

"He's also good with the leg work. He 'walks' the route from where the limo lets our stars at the door through the back lobbies and service elevators to the hall where they're to appear. Mob scenes can be rough."

"Kyle told me about one time in Cleveland – "

"It was Joe that saved him that day. Grabbed him by the hair and got him into the van. If he hadn't there might still be parts of your boyfriend in Ohio."

Everybody, it seemed, had had their hands on Kyle one time or another.

We arrived at the Dyer warehouse, or rather the Wonderland Productions warehouse. "Joe and I aren't here every day but we're always here to help get the football to the end zone from the two-yard line," he said.

As we climbed out of the limo, his hand was zeroing in on *my* end-zone. I had a feeling I might be getting more than a T-shirt in the warehouse. Joe got out of the car and came around to unlock one of the large glass doors at the entrance to the building. It was then that I saw what a towering hulk he really was. There was so much muscle that he really should have had his shirts custom made, but then I decided he liked the idea that everything bulged the way it did because, as he held the door open for me, his hand drifted down to his crotch and he made a little show of adjusting his equipment.

"Jockstrap too tight?" I asked playfully.

"Yeah, they can't seem to make 'em big enough."

"They don't make 'em small enough for me," I said.

Martin turned and, grinning, said, "I knew you boys would hit it off."

"I bet Joe hits it off with everybody."

"I get my share," Joe said, opening another door.

Martin led me down a corridor to a big store room with stacks and stacks of T-shirts and boxes and boxes of other things Martin called "merchandising."

"I've got Kyle's stuff in this file cabinet," Martin said, pulling out a drawer. "There's not much left but you're welcome to it."

"You're also welcome to finish the wine," Joe said, miraculously re-appearing with the lunch basket and wine bottles.

"Oh, no, I've had too much already."

But he had already poured some for me and another glass for Martin, who told him to finish the rest himself. Joe took the bottle, raised it and swallowed what remained in one long gulp.

I looked at the T-shirts for Led Zeppelin, Eric Clapton, even one for Jimi Hendrix. This got my attention. "You did a tour for Hendrix?"

"No, we just handled the merchandising. Those Negro acts are trouble. I have another company that handles them. Why, you a fan?"

"Sort of. I saw one of his souvenirs the other day."

He wasn't paying any attention to me, which was just as well because I wasn't about to tell him about Millie's collection; he probably would have gone over there and signed her on.

"Here we go," Martin said, pulling from the drawer a large envelope. "All yours."

I opened it: Two T-shirts, a big button, and a program with lots of pictures I had never seen before. Kyle didn't even have this stuff at the house. "Thanks. This is neat."

"What's neat is *you*. Kyle's a lucky guy."

Martin came up behind me as I was looking at my new treasures and put his hands on my arms in a gentle, undemanding way. I knew what he wanted. What he wanted from the beginning. I just kept looking at the pictures in the program, seeing how far he would go. His hands dropped to my waist, then went back up my torso, coming to rest under my arms. He began rubbing his crotch into my ass. "Yeah," he sighed, "Kyle's a lucky guy."

"Yeah," I said. "But he doesn't show it a lot of the time."

"I'll bet you need someone to show you a *lot* of appreciation."

"Well, I'm just a teenager. I have this constant need – "

"I wouldn't want it any other way."

Constant need or not, I pulled away from him. He didn't cling to me; he let me pick up the souvenirs and, as I turned to face him, said, "You haven't finished your wine."

"Oh, I've had enough. I don't drink much."

"Here," Joe said, "have the rest." He stepped over to me and handed me the glass.

I put my package down and took the wine. "Maybe just a little."

Joe stood still, his hands falling again to his crotch.

I looked down and smiled. "You really shouldn't get a hard-on when you're wearing a jockstrap."

"Yeah, it hurts like hell."

"Why don't you fix it?"

"I thought you'd do it for me." With that, he began unbuckling his belt. Then his zipper came down and he stood there waiting for me.

I finished what remained of the wine and set the glass on the table. So, I thought, this is the guy that saved Kyle in Cleveland. I began to imagine the scenes they must have had together and how crazy this was; here I was four years later, with what remained of the tour in a folder behind me, about to go down on Kyle's savior. I had to at least look at what was hurting him.

I stepped over to him and squeezed the hardness I found bunched in the jockstrap.

"It's beginning to feel better already," Joe said as I ran my fingers across it.

At this point, Martin, who had been off to the side watching us, came up behind me. He didn't touch me until I had bent over to reveal Joe's erection. As it came flopping out from the pouch, Martin began squeezing my buns. Joe's cock wasn't particularly long but it was very thick, heavily-veined and cleanly cut. I remained bent at the waist and began fellating him while Martin undid my pants and slipped them down my hips. His mouth went to my ass and he began tonguing me while I worked Joe's cock over as well as I could in that position. Martin ate out my ass with even more enthusiastically than Jay had. These guys are incredible with this, I thought. I practically came when he started playing with me and he sensed this. He said, "Hey, Joe I think the kid's ready."

"Okay," Joe said, pulling his cock out of my mouth and barking, "Hang on to the counter there, boy."

I did as I was told, with Martin taking off his jacket and dropping down on his butt on the floor, his legs stretched out between my legs, my crotch in his face. Joe stood over us and held me by the shoulders. He just let his dick find its way to the target. He didn't ease it in, he just barrelled ahead and I groaned, wishing I had some poppers but thankful I'd had the wine. When it was all the way in, Martin put his hands on Joe's buttocks and they began a rhythm that had me coming in moments.

I cried out and Joe said, "Get ready Marty."

Martin swallowed all my cum and kept my dick in his mouth while Joe continued. I looked over my shoulder to see him put his hands on my asscheeks and lean back, enjoying the sight of his dick going in and out. I imagined Kyle in the same position as me, going crazy as he was being fucked with the thick prick, and that got me hard again. Martin would not let go of my cock until I had come a second time, just before Joe finished inside of me.

After we washed up, they invited me back to Martin's place in Beverly Hills but I told them I had to get back to Bird's Eye. I confessed that Kyle thought I was shopping, not going to Traffic School.

"Well, you *were* shopping," Martin said, handing me the package of Kyle's souvenirs.

"Yeah," I said, rubbing my battered, cum-filled ass, "collecting all kinds of souvenirs."

As Joe pulled up next to my Porsche in the parking lot at Traffic School, Martin said, "You shouldn't drive that car if you want to avoid tickets. They'll pull you over just on general principle. Even standing still you look like you're breaking the speed limit."

"But I love my car."

He chuckled. "That's what makes you so damn cute. You love *everything*."

Martin was right, I *do* love everything, at least everything that's happened to me so far. Except coming home to an empty house. Kyle was gone again, but at least this time he left a note: "Out with Jake for some pussy. Don't wait up."

. . .

"It's tough on the street, eh?" I ask as I shove the key the girl has handed me into the lock and we enter the dark, dank motel room. She knew just where to go. "I get a special rate," she said.

"I can handle it," I say.

Her name is Racquel, "Like in Welch."

"Okay," I say. If that's what she wants

... I saw her walking along on Santa Monica. I knew what she was selling. Suddenly, I got the urge to buy some. After finding Kyle's note, I hide my souvenirs, took a shower, ate some dinner, and off I went. There were a couple of boys hanging out on the corners but I had been with guys all afternoon. What I wanted was to at last have some pussy. If Kyle can handle a pussy, I ought to be able to. I liked Racquel's looks: almost as short as me, with big boobs, making her appear as if she was about to topple over. She brought my hand inside her blouse to feel her tits as I drove here to the motel.

From the bathroom comes the rushing sound of an open faucet. The room feels like a closet. Mirrors, though, are everywhere. On the double bed the sheets are clean but well-worn. The light is dim, bleak. I think of all the people that must have fucked with that dim light on, the orgies the mirrors must have witnessed, the bouncing the bed has taken.

Now she comes out of the bathroom, dressed only in black lace panties. She approaches me as I lie still on the bed, my head propped up by pillows.

She bites me briefly, licks me, bends me, makes me submit totally to her will. I have the urge to bring my lips to the painted lips of the mouth now screaming obscenities, the tongue and teeth chafing my nipples, turning my skin into a flaming hell. Her hands crawl over my skin and slowly I open my thighs to her. She laps at my cock, then my ass. The way she is tonguing me reminds of Kyle. The images blur in my mind; I cry out, "Fuck me!"

"Oh, baby wants to get fucked? I thought so when I first saw ya."

I open my eyes. She is staring at me, a grin beginning.
"Oh, baby, do I have a surprise for you."

I look down, between my outstretched thighs. There, in her hand, pulled from the panties is a dark, uncut cock of a very respectable length and thickness.

"Jesus!" I shout.

"I had Jesus last night, honey. Tonight I got you."

He enters me swiftly, as if he thinks I might try to stop him. The idea of it so stuns me that I lose my erection, but soon get it again as he holds my feet with his hands, pulls my legs apart, and plows into me, the tits flapping up and down, whack, whack. I can't help it, I start giggling. I haven't giggled in so long; I am really getting into it. He must think I'm crazy. I must be crazy. My amusement makes him lean forward, for a better angle, to fuck me harder.

I close my eyes and want to keep thinking about Kyle or Joe but each jolt of his cock brings me back to life.

My legs intertwined around him, his hands roaming my back his he rocks me back and forth, his long polished nails scraping me, trying to leave their mark, the marks of the man (or whatever) who did this to me. His violent mauling of me, coupled with the fucking I had earlier from Joe, makes my eyes cloud over with pain and his hands grasp my hips to thrust himself deep inside of me one last time.

An incredible whore, he grips my erection and jacks me off, holding his orgasm until he knows I'm coming. As the rush roars through my body, I decide he really is great, except for the tits and the wig.

"Oh, my, oh my," he says, seeing the globs of cum spurting

from me. "You *were* horny."

"I'm like this all the time. I'm just a teenager, you know."

. . . I lie on the bed and watch him dress.

"Hey little teenager, you okay?"

I nod, close my eyes, open them. Try to smile. I have a thousand questions but don't have the heart to ask.

"Say, honey, I gotta get goin'," he says, looking into the mirror, checking the crotch.

"Okay." I lift myself from the bed and pull some loose twenty dollar bills from the back pocket of my jeans.

"Thanks," he says. "See ya around."

And he is gone. I stand there in my filthiness, my heart pounding, surprised now at the sudden emptiness.

The Next Afternoon

There is no hiding the marks. Kyle doesn't ask any questions. And neither do I. I guess we are both afraid of the answers. There is no one to blame.

Now while I am preparing to fuck him he says there are bigger dicks, but nobody can do it longer than I can. "It's always hard," he says as he guides it in, "I don't know why but it's always hard."

I feel like telling him he'd be hard too if he'd stay off the coke and forget all the stupid pussy, but I just take all my anger at him out on his ass. He seems to like it.

SEVEN

Tuesday, September 28, 1976

I'm creating a new character on an old sitcom, twenty-two episodes guaranteed. The show's frail plots are kept alive entirely by sex jokes which never fail to make me laugh. They say we're the raciest show on television. Some stations in the Bible Belt are threatening to ban the show. And now it is threatening to get even racier because there has been another new character introduced on "Home Life:" my girlfriend. Pamela Brown has been hired for six episodes with an option so they must be planning on my getting her pregnant or something.

Pamela is a combination of every one of the girls I knew really well back in Texas. The day I met her, for rehearsal, she was wearing a wrinkled man's blue oxford cloth shirt, baggy corduroy jeans, a single long reddish brown braid down her back and no makeup. My first reaction was: tomboy. I liked her immediately. Which was good, because we were supposed to be crazy about each other, panting all over each other. By the thirteenth take, I could feel an erection stirring. But I was thinking of Kyle with her, fucking her.

Yesterday the errand boy delivered the gifts for the cast sent in by fans from all over the world. I couldn't believe most of it was for me. I had stuffed animals, candy, cookies, a recorded message on an audio cassette ("Hi, Bobby, this is Joyce from Newark."), and a T-shirt, two sizes too big, with "Christ Is The Answer!" painted on it. I was the only one who kept his treasures from the fans; the rest of the cast gave everything away to the Mexican clean-up crew.

Today I am supposed to be "on hold," in other words, not in any scenes but available. Kyle hasn't been home for days and I fall into a deep funk and smoke a joint. A big joint. I am out of it when the phone rings. The studio has re-arranged things and they want me in to do my big scene with Pamela that will end the episode. If I show up stoned, I fear, it could end my career.

Still, I am feeling very high, almost invincible. I can do it, probably be better than ever. Even show them how it's done. Show Pamela how it's done.

I jump in my Porsche and take off. It is not rush hour so the traffic is manageable. Still, I am not so stoned I don't know I have to obey the speed limit, whatever it is. But the pot has its effect on me because it seems the trip takes forever. When I finally get to the studio, I keep making suggestions until the director tells me, not very politely, to shut the fuck up. We go on with the scene as it is written, but Pamela gets a lot of laughs out of it.

When we are finished and walking off the set, she asks,, "How did you like it?"

"What?"

"Kissing a girl."

"I've kissed a lot of girls before."

"So have I. You and I were made for each other."

She has heard the rumors about me, that I am Kyle's lover and I have other friends in "high places," but mostly she is interested in having me come to dinner.

"But why?"

"I want you to meet *my* lover."

Pamela is playing a teenager but, like me, she has always looked young for her age. She is really 24, and her lover, Frankie, is 30. Frankie is slender, pleasant-looking with big horn-rimmed glasses. She is from New York and Pamela says she acts like all New Yorkers: alert, intelligent, fearless. When I tell them I know a New Yorker, the famous artist John Dugan, they don't seem to be impressed. They probably don't know anything about art. By the looks of their place, it's doubtful they know a Monet from a Manet. I do, because I read a book about it. Dugan sent me a bunch of art books. I laughed about it –

Nico sent flowers and Dugan sent books. What is it with these guys? What is it with *me*?

The girls live in a little house in the Hollywood Hills with a retaining wall for a backyard. They installed a Jacuzzi and they invite me to join them for a soak after dinner. But we never make it to the Jacuzzi. They never even serve dessert, but they probably think of me as the dessert. Things start with a sudden exchange of glances, grins, nods and off to the bedroom we go, with their clothes dropping as they lead me along.

They begin with gentle, innocent kisses, then, after they pull the house painter's pants I wore on the set down past my butt, they cover me everywhere with more little, ladylike kisses. I feel so safe, with just the hint of their tongues, just for a moment, here and there, on my neck, across my chest, on my shoulders. And then they start kissing each other. I have never seen two women make love before. They are very busy with each other, licking and slurping away merrily while I get naked. Soon they are nearly naked themselves, their slips just loose confusions of nylon around their waists.

They fall to their bed and take me with them. Between them, it's as if I was melting, becoming warm and shapeless as they twist me to suit their desires, a quivering thing in their arms, my cock surprisingly hard, eager. Both of them press close against me, squirming and wriggling. There's a lot of kissing and holding and caressing. Then they start talking again while playing with my cock. Pamela bubbles with delight at seeing me naked. She kisses my cock and says she likes it and wants to feel it inside her; she is so happy with it that she promptly backs down on it. Frankie goes right on kissing her as she bounces up and down on me. Then they switch and Frankie does some bouncing. At least I don't have to look at their tits slapping up and down.

After a while, Pamela gets on all fours and has me enter her from behind. After I bang away for a few minutes, Pamela is groaning and moaning and I think she's ready to have Frankie get fucked but Frankie's very happy just having Pamela eat her out. I want to come, try to come, but for the first time in my life, it just isn't working. I am growing bored and restless. I decide to fake an orgasm and get the hell out of here. On the way home, I decide, as far as I am concerned, Kyle deserves all the pussy he gets.

Back at Bird's Eye, I find Anna May has left me another note. No note from Kyle, but a note from the maid. It's been my day for women. Anna May comes in and tidies up, makes everything right. I used to go to the beach, wearing my "Jaws" T-shirt, when she was in the house. It takes her all day. Now that I'm working I'm gone before she gets here, return after she's left. She leaves me little notes all the time. She misses me, I miss her. I always enjoyed our little talks.

Now I'll call her up to talk. I call my mother every week but I can't *talk* to her; I can only, now, *lie* to her. I hate lying but I don't want her to know how bad I feel about Kyle's disappearances. So I talk to Anna May, who is like Confucius, dropping these sayings on me which make me think. I don't need any fortune cookies, I have Anna May.

Her name really isn't Anna May, Kyle just nicknamed her that because she looks like Anna May Wong. And, being Japanese, she's little like me so we understand each other. I can meet her at eye-level.

She taught me how to do stir-fry, which is Kyle's favorite now. I cook some Mexican dishes too but not often any more. Mostly I just do fish or steak. And, lately, mostly for myself.

I love to do the shopping for the groceries, of course, because I get to go to the neat market we have here. It's a fun place because you never know who you are going meet. George C. Scott, Charles Bronson and his wife Jill Ireland, who's really nice, and Larry Hagman and his wife Mai, who is also very nice, all shop at the store. I get along with the ladies, of course, and the men simply nod because they don't know me but think they should. The thing is, nobody acts as if anybody is anybody, we're just shopping. The clerks, however, are another thing, especially when it comes to me. There is one special one, a hunky blond surfer-type whose name is Freddy, who always wants to help me, taking my bags to the car. This is nice because I get to look at him walking ahead of me. His ass is as nice as Kyle's and I fantasize about fucking him. Incredible as it may seem, I think I'm becoming versatile.

Anna May says in her note that Mac's accountant, Kyle's accountant, *my* accountant, Ned Schuyler, didn't send her check on time. Maybe Ned's getting forgetful. I think it's time I pay him a visit. I like to know who I'm dealing with.

The Next Afternoon
I decide to stop at Mac's house first, because it's on the way to the address I have for Ned. While both Mac and Ned have made millions for their stars and for themselves, they both keep low profiles. Mac lives simply. It's a nice house on a tree-lined street and it's kept very neat by Kevin Casey, Mac's young live-in lover. He does a few TV commercials, appears in print ads, but mostly just takes care of Mac. When I first met Kevin at one of Kyle's parties, I liked him immediately. He reminded me of every star football player in school, especially Butch, who was my all-time favorite protector. When you're little like I am, you have to have a *protector*. After I met Kevin, Kyle made the remark that the kid loved to get blown. From that I took it that Kyle had done the deed. That got me going. If Kyle could do it, I could. And I wondered if Kevin would really like it as much as Butch used to like it. That was the price of Butch's protection, and I never minded paying the bill.

Kevin is mowing the lawn! I can't believe it! They could easily afford a Japanese gardener, but Kevin says it's good exercise. Obviously, by the well-muscled look of him in just his little baby blue nylon shorts. He also says he's almost finished and asks me to go in and fix us both something to drink.

At least he didn't ask me to help him mow. The house is, as usual, spotless and it's almost a crime to spill a drop of the Coke that I pour into two glasses over ice.

I carry the drinks out into the walled garden with its narrow, twenty-foot long black slate pool and Jacuzzi. Mac calls it a "lap pool." They don't have any backyard, just ivy, lemon and cypress trees in containers. I am sitting under the canopy that opens out from the house to shade the seating area when Kevin comes rushing in, all sweaty and grinning mischievously. He says he's surprised to see me and chugs down his Coke in a couple gulps as I explain I'm on my way to see the accountant.

"Ned doesn't like to be surprised. You'd better call him from here."

"I'll risk it. It's more fun when you're not expecting things."

"Like now. I sure never expected to see you here without

your husband."

"I just thought it was about time we got to know each other. After all, we're like one big happy family."

"If you say so. But I've just got to jump in the pool."

"Go ahead. I might join you."

He jumps in wearing his nylon shorts but before long he's taken them off and tossed them onto the deck in front of me.

"Your turn," he says.

I decide the accountant will keep, Kevin won't.

...Our bodies are shiny with sweat; we are laughing, gasping, dizzy with the craziness of it. Two young guys without their older lovers, taking turns sucking each other. At first Kevin fucked me but, after about five minutes, he got on his back on the couch and wanted me to fuck him. Now I'm close and Kevin knows it. He joins my rhythm and whispers little encouraging things into my ear as I let loose with my most gigantic come in weeks. It has been building up since I couldn't get off on pussy.

I roll off of him and, chuckling to myself, lie on the carpet in a stupor for I don't know how long while sounds of ecstasy come from the couch above me. Kevin's jacking off without me! Somewhere I find the strength to get back up on the couch, just in time to take his load into my mouth.

"Wow," he says, "we have to do this again."

"Yeah, but not today," I say, kissing his big cock one last time. "Remember, I've got to see the accountant."

. . .

"Who?" asks the voice on the intercom. Ned lives in a big apartment building and conducts his business out of his home. He has an office, Mac says, but rarely goes there. He hates to drive and, if you hate to drive, you're dead in L.A.

"Bobby Richards," I say.

The only response is a loud buzz at the door. I go in and take the elevator to the 20th floor. It's an older building but it has a nice layout. Nothing pretentious. Nice prints on the walls.

The man who opens the door and lets me in doesn't look like what I think an accountant should look like. I thought all accountants wore dark blue suits and pin-striped ties. Ned greets me in his gym shorts. He's been working on the treadmill, he says, good for his heart. It's obviously good for *something*, I think, admiring the physique by God. He looks like Kevin might look in ten years if he really worked hard at it. No, this is no accountant, this is my new personal trainer. Kyle said I could have a personal trainer when I got old enough. Every movie star has a personal trainer; this is the guy I want, once I get into the movies.

"What seems to be the problem?" he asks, wiping the sweat off his massive chest. I feel like telling him, Wait, I'll lick it off.

"Anna May. You know, Miss Wong at the house? She didn't get her check."

"You drove all the way here to tell me that?"

"I was in the neighborhood."

He's grinning at me. I grin back. "Anyhow, I think I should meet the man who handles all my money."

"I see. *All* your money," he says sarcastically, as if I don't have any. I'm not in Kyle's league, but I'm not doing too badly.

He offers me something to drink. I follow him into the kitchen. He serves us grapefruit juice.

"I'm sorry about Anna," he says, chugging it down. "It's important to keep her happy. She's trustworthy. You know, in Hollywood, everybody has a friend who knows a person who works for Someone, so it's essential we keep her happy. I'll check on it."

"Thanks."

He finishes his juice and walks back into the living room. I follow.

"I've been preoccupied lately," he says. "Moving investments around. The way Kyle's been spending it, we may all be out of job very soon."

"Oh?"

He smiles. "Well, don't you worry your pretty little head about it. It's my problem. I'm just getting tired of it, that's all." He's leading me to the door. I really have no desire to leave now. I stop in the middle of the living room. He stops, turns, looks at me quizzically.

"Kyle would have to have an accountant that looks like you do," I say.

"Yes, and he would have to have taken a lover that looks like you do." He looks me up and down. "I warned Mac about this in the beginning, but I must admit I'm pretty impressed. I saw your pictures but you're even cuter in person."

I wanted this mutual admiration thing to start getting out of hand but what he was saying about the money interested me. First things first. "I thought Kyle had good investments."

"He does, but he can't live off the income. He keeps going into the principal. It's enough to drive me crazy, but it's his money. I really have no control over it. But I do all I can."

"I'm the one who doesn't have any control – " I step over to him, reach out, run my finger across the bulge in his shorts.

"I knew there must have been a reason he brought you back here all the way from Texas – "

"This is the reason Kyle brought me back here," I say, massaging Ned's thighs. I am lying between them, his cock straight up, bobbing close to my mouth, begging to be sucked. I try to imagine the number of times Kyle's sucked this cock. How can I do better than that? I decide to tease him, to just ignore the cock as I kiss, fondle and suck the balls, massage his thighs, and kiss every inch of his tanned skin all the way up to the navel, pressing the cock against my body, making him gasp.

"This can't be happening," he says as I start sucking it. "I could never get anywhere with Kyle, and I wanted to in the beginning, believe me I did, in the worst way. God he was beautiful. But now, I've got his little cutie sucking my cock. No, this just can't be happening."

It is happening, all right, but I suddenly realize I may be making a huge mistake. But Kyle told me to do this only it if I'd enjoy it and I am enjoying this. A lot. This dick is so suckable. Big head, thick shaft. About seven inches of beautiful, cut dick. Kyle doesn't know what he missed with this one. I want it up my ass but after an hour with Kevin, I think I'll give Ned a reason to invite me back. I just take his load in my mouth and make my exit. Ned promises me Anna May will get her check on time from now on.

EIGHT

Tuesday, November 30, 1976

Jay said my part in "Space Travellers" would be filmed during what we thought would be the hiatus for "Home Life," but then word came that the show had been cancelled after all. I was numb. I somehow felt responsible for singlehandedly ending the series. Kyle tried to make me feel better by telling me we were going to Las Vegas with Jay in his Gulfstream jet but it didn't help.

It wasn't until we were in Jay's big suite at the Hilton that I began to cheer up. It's hard to stay sad around Jay. No expense was spared to make my first weekend in the gambling capitol a big success. They say money can't buy happiness but I'm not so sure. One thing for sure, Jay knows how to spread it around.

At dinner, Jay said, "I want Bobby to come to New York," he said, "meet some people."

Kyle snickered. "Seems I've heard that one before."

"You liked it, he'll like it." Jay took a long sip of white wine. He drank rarely, but at dinner he liked a little wine. Kyle was already four glasses ahead of him and had ordered another bottle.

"Sex, money and power, that's the Holy Trinity," Jay told me when the steaks are served. "It's always been. And those who understand that fare better in life. You need to meet more people, Bobby. Good people, who can help you."

Kyle snickered again. "Jay, you must use these lines on every boy you meet."

"Only special ones. In fact, this is only the second time."

"I can't believe that," Kyle said, shaking his head.

"Believe what you like. You were the first, Bobby is the

second. You two together, it is good."

After dinner we strolled through the arcade and went into a jewelry shop. Jay wanted to buy me something, a gold neck chain to match the one he bought Kyle. The salesgirl, an older woman with bangs, asked Kyle, "Say, aren't you some singer or other?"

"*Some* singer," Jay laughed.

"Or other," Kyle sniffed.

Another salesgirl looked at me strangely, as if she was saying, "He's so short; he didn't look that short on television," but didn't say anything, just smiled as Jay gave her his American Express card.

Later, we were at the Desert Inn, which Jay called the "DI," at our table in the Crystal Room, when a big guy dressed in a lime green polyester suit comes up and hollers, "Kyle Cartwright!"

"Yeah?" Kyle said, feeling no pain at that point in the evening.

"Can I have your autograph? It's for the wife, back there." He turned and waved towards the back of the huge room. "She's too embarrassed to ask you herself."

"Sure," Kyle said, taking the book and pen.

"My wife loves you. I even like you too. Sometimes."

"Thank you," Kyle said. "Your wife's name?"

"Bobbie."

"Oh," Kyle snickered winking at me.

As Kyle scrawled out his autograph, the guy looked down at me. "Are you a singer too?"

"He's the kid on 'Home Life,' Bobby Richards," Jay said.

"Never watch television," the man said, totally unimpressed.

Jay went on: "He's also going to star in my next picture, 'Space Travellers.'"

The man shrugged. "Never go to the movies anymore."

Kyle laughed. "But they do listen to the radio," he said to Jay.

"No, records," the man said. "My wife listens to your records all the time. Drives me crazy."

"Good," Kyle said, handing the man the autograph book.

After we finished laughing, Kyle said, "If it weren't for people like that, I'd be pumping gas in Montana." We all laughed again and Jay filled my glass with champagne. "We are celebrating, you know," he said. "Next time we're here, he'll know who you are, believe me."

We were in Las Vegas to see Sammy Davis Jr.'s show. Jay wanted to talk to him about a film he had in the works and Kyle was anxious to see the singer in person. We all enjoyed the show, especially his "Mr. Bojangles" number, which Jay said was always the showstopper. "But the best night of all," Jay recalled, his eyes flashing, "was when Sinatra was at Caesar's Palace and Sammy walked on stage during 'The Lady Is a Tramp.' It brought the house down. I'll never forget it."

Later we went to Sammy's suite and he greeted us warmly. I liked Sammy (*Mr. Davis* to me, of course, until he told me otherwise, which he did right away) – I could look him straight in the eye. He was one of the few people I'd met in show business who was the same height I am.

Davis had just finished filming "Gone With the West," a western with James Caan and Aldo Ray and told Jay he was happy he didn't want him for another western. "But you look so good on a horse," Kyle joked.

"No," Sammy said, "*you're* the one who looks good on a horse. Duke taught you. *Sinatra* taught me."

But Sinatra taught Sammy very well, Kyle said when he and I went out onto the balcony to let Jay and Sammy talk. He said that Frank knew all the tricks of the trade. The best camera angles, how to catch the light, frame a shot, all the stuff Kyle had learned from John Wayne, and he taught me. But, most of all, Frank taught Sammy how to ride a horse. It's different than if you were just riding out on the range. You have to sit high and straight on the saddle, and tighten up on the stirrups so you don't bounce up and down, and try to hold the saddle horn, especially if you are riding away from the camera. "But getting on and off a horse is more important than anything else," Kyle said. "Some people never learn." Wayne told him that when George Stevens wanted that great leap off the horse in "Shane," Palance could never get it right so they ended up having him leap off the horse and ran the film backward.

"And I can say that Kyle Cartwright taught me, handed down from John Wayne."

"If Duke only knew – ," Jay chuckled as he joined us on the

balcony. "Sammy's tired. We'd better go."

"Will he do your picture?" Kyle asked.

"Sure. Sammy will do *anybody's* picture who has the money to pay him. He's been in more stinkers than anybody I can think of."

Jay counted off the "stinkers" while we were riding down in the elevator. "Here's maybe the best stage personality there is and he's trapped in these stupid movies."

"You don't get a 'Porgy and Bess' every day, Jay," Kyle said.

"And I don't get Kyle and Bobby together every night, either," Jay said, taking our hands in his. "It is good."

Back at the Hilton, I was thinking about Sammy and asked Kyle, "Is it true about Negroes, you know, that they have such big dicks?"

Jay laughed. "Kyle should know. He had one in New York that I'll never forget."

Kyle was still feeling pretty good and in the living room of the suite he put on some music and entertained us with the entire scene as he remembered it. He and Jay had been to a party and the Negro was the entertainment – or rather, Kyle and the Negro. At least re-living it got Kyle turned on and I suppose I was a poor substitute for the Negro as I slammed my cock into him while Jay sucked on his cock until he came, but Kyle never complained. I didn't come inside of Kyle; I let Jay take my cum too. After all, he'd been kind enough to take me to Las Vegas on his private jet, introduce me to Sammy Davis, Jr. and buy me a gold neck chain.

NINE

Tuesday, December 21, 1976
"Kyle'll be fine," Jay says. He's come to Bird's Eye for dinner. Just the two of us. Kyle's gone again. He didn't say where he was going.

But I'm worried. Kyle has signed to do a tour to promote the album. It'll take him to London, Paris, Bangkok, Manila, and Tokyo. The second album sold more overseas than in the U.S. They're calling it the "Feel the Wave" tour, after a line from the song, "Come Back to Me." They didn't want to call it the "Come Back" tour. "I've never been away," Kyle said, even though he hadn't made a movie in nearly two years and hadn't recorded an album in over three years.

I was worried too when Kyle said Martin Dyer was coming to Bird's Eye to talk about the tour. But it went very well. Martin acted as if he'd never laid eyes on me before. I politely left them alone in the music room and went out to the driveway to see if Martin had driven his own car.

Joe was sitting behind the wheel of the limousine, reading a paperback novel. He had the lamp on, his door open, his leg dangling out. "Why don't you come in?" I asked.

"Martin likes me to wait while he's talking business. If he needs me, he knows where to find me."

"Will you be going on Kyle's tour?"

"That's up to Kyle. He usually likes somebody new. He was through with me after about the second night."

I dropped down onto the edge of the door frame, next to his leg, and ran my hand along his thigh. "That's hard to believe."

"You're a horny little bastard."

"When there's something around to be horny about."
"Does Kyle know where you are?"
"Why don't we go for a drive?"
"No. Martin might need me."
"Okay." I groped him. "Why don't you turn that light out?"
In the darkness, his cock glistened with my saliva after I sucked him to full hardness. "Anybody coming?" I asked.
"Yeah, me. Why don't you finish it?"
That was all I needed. Intoxicated by the musky smell of his crotch, the thickness of his prick, the thrill of blowing somebody right in the driveway with Kyle inside the house, I took him deep and played with his balls, went back and forth on the thick prick, forcing it out of him. He came with such ferociousness I couldn't take it all and the cum dribbled out of my mouth and dropped onto his pants. Keeping the load of cum in my mouth, I stood up and ran back into the house. In the privacy of my bedroom, I spit his cum out on my own cock and jerked off remembering each and every inch of Joe's fat prick. What fun Kyle would be having, I thought, with Joe along to "protect" him.

"Yeah, Kyle'll be fine," Jay now keeps saying as he sucks me off. It's his dessert. I didn't have time to make any.
I believe everything Jay says. He has an instinct for knowing what properties to buy. He'd had a few disasters, like the western Kyle and I were in together, but mostly he has hits. The money keeps rolling in and he keeps spreading it around. He began going to New York so often that he bought an apartment on Park Avenue. The trip he promised me never happened because I had to start the movie right away.
"It was the TV," Jay admitted. "I showed 'em the TV stuff and they liked it. They want you to read for them." I read, then went back and read again. They seemed to like me.
Now, after I come, I let him start on my ass. He says he can't decide which part of me tastes better. I come again before he's through.

The Next Day
Kyle is back. He starts decorating for Christmas. Just having him here is present enough, I say, but, no, we have to go

shopping. He never goes shopping with me, so it is a treat. We go to Giorgio Armani's, slipping in the back door and going to the private rooms. Nothing is too good for me. The clerks, men and women, are all smiles. They love us. Kyle has the bills sent to Ned. Doesn't matter. I'll take most of it back as soon as he's gone on the tour.

Before he met me, Kyle said that every year he got the holiday blues. The year before we met, he said, he was so blue he called it his "Black Christmas." He really thought he might kill himself. "The good die young," he said. But the first year we were together he was full of giddiness: we spent thousands decorating. And on presents for me.

Now, this Christmas, it's me feeling homesick. For Texas, the Cattleman. Home, Jay once told me, is where you go when you've run out of places, but then find you can't go there again. Jay said to just click my heels together three times and say: there's no place like it. But I told him I was happy in Oz. He laughed. I think he has begun to think of himself as the Wizard.

At Christmas at the Cattleman, I'd roam through the silent, empty rooms and spy on an occasional guest. School was out so I'd help Mom vacuum or make the sagging, U-shaped beds. It was always a mystery to most folks how my grandpa, the Colonel, managed to keep the place in business all these years, since his paying guests seemed to be so few and far between. Before Brackettville became a movie location, the only people who ever stayed in the dark, closet-sized rooms were occasional salesmen on their way through who are just too tired to drive any more, or a truck driver who'd just gotten lost. When my mother took over, she made the rooms homier and put a TV in every one of them and business picked up. And when I began visiting the rooms of the traveling salesmen and truck drivers to give them massages, we started to get a lot of repeat business.

I still think about Mom and Texas every day. From Bird's Eye I can see the Pacific Coast Highway and I think I can take it any time I want, even today if I wanted to. I could do just like my father did, pack a bag and disappear in a cloud of dust. Only I'd be driving my Porsche.

But Mom understands why I can't leave. She knows how

much I love it here. "You act because that is the thing that makes you happy," she said. "It isn't a choice. You need to do it. But do it well. I always say, 'If you bake bread, make beautiful bread.'" I asked her to send one of her fresh-baked loaves of my favorite raisin-nut bread to me for Christmas.

She's thrilled about my being on television. "You know," she said the other day (it was about the hundredth time I'd heard it, but I listened anyway), "I can't remember how many years of stock I did, and auditioning and looking. It was just when off-Broadway was coming up. I would work anywhere, anywhere at all, because that's what I needed to do. And that can take the place of almost anything else in your life. It took me years before I began, because it seemed the whole period was stretching and wanting to stretch but I never really thought I was doing it because of this or that. Anywhere it was, I was acting, sometimes terribly, but I was acting. We were the original Method people. We were boring to be around because we never stopped going to class. God forbid we would ever have to go out and look for a job. We had found out what we wanted to do! We just talked it to death." I chuckled to myself. She was *still* talking it to death! Someday, she says, as soon as the Colonel, who, it seems, has always been sick, trapped in a wheelchair and the orneriest bastard in Texas, dies, she'll come to visit me – us. I told her I'd take her shopping on Rodeo Drive.

TEN

Tuesday, February 8, 1977

Three weeks ago, Kyle went to New York with Martin and Joe to start the tour, leaving me to make it through "Space Travellers" alone.

Well, not entirely alone. I will have the help of Harper "Bud" Logan, the picture's director. "He's the best," Jay said. "He'll work wonders with you." Little did I know what wonders Bud would work with me.

When I first met him, Bud reminded me of Gary Cooper, with his long, chiseled face, strong jaw, cool gray eyes, and the thick shock of light-brown hair that falls straight across his high forehead. He even wears cowboy clothes: faded blue jeans over freshly polished black boots, a plaid flannel shirt, and a tan suede jacket. He has a permanent tan from swimming in his pool at his house in Beverly Hills that he shares with his wife and two daughters.

At six-foot-three, he towers over me and I feel safe, protected in his enormous shadow. Of course, I lusted for him immediately. I longed to see if his cock was in proportion with the rest of him the way mine is. His huge hands would always linger on my shoulder as he gave me direction and his smile told me I was doing well. "Be cool," he'd say. "Take your time." I could imagine him saying that to me while he was fucking me. It got so that I would fantasize about Bud instead of Kyle when I put the dildo to my ass at night before I went to bed.

He took me to dinner one night early in the schedule and told me: "Your character is in almost every scene. We need someone who can convey the emotional subtext of what's going on and not be intimidated by the hardware. When you read for me, it was simple: you were *it*. But when someone reads for you that early, you don't believe it. So I tried loads and loads of boys, but we came right back to you."

And coming back to me is what he kept doing, all through it. If I hadn't been told he was happily married, I'd have thought he was coming *on* to me.

Then the third week of the shoot Bud asked me to come with him to the place where all the animation had been done, off the studio grounds in downtown Los Angeles. He felt it would be good for me to see how it all came together. Bud was on the leading edge of computerization in film and had experimented with it when he was going to UCLA Film School, where he also taught when he wasn't making a picture. I had never met anyone as intelligent and so absorbed with their work. I wanted to please him in any way I could. "These people can do some marvelous things. They do tree bark, grass blowing and water rippling. But they have only begun with computer-generated humans. They tell me hair is *very* hard."

He was always dropping these lines, as if they were cues for me. Was I supposed to respond with a wisecrack just as full of innuendo? I didn't; I just smiled.

We went to Compumagic in Bud's black 1950 Barchetta convertible, a classic that he said he would never part with. "I could buy three new Jags for what I've paid to keep this going, but I love it."

He said the name meant "the little boat" in Italian; to me, it was more like a gigantic cock on wheels. I couldn't resist it. He laughed, "That reminds me. I know all about you but you really don't know anything about me."

"You mean about your big cock?"

He laughed again. "Who told you?"

"It's hard to hide it with the jeans you wear."

"Thank god I'm a happily married man, Bobby, or I'd let you find out."

"Thank god I'm happily married, too, or I'd try."

"Well, where's Kyle today?"

"I guess in Bangkok. I – " I hesitated. I didn't want to betray just how much I was hurting at that point. I heard from Kyle every couple of days but now, nothing. But I was not about to try to find him.

"Those tours must be crazy," Bud said. "I wouldn't do that no matter what they paid me, but Kyle's young, he can handle it."

Bud wasn't old in years, barely forty, but he was *very* old in the way he regarded himself. He was settled in his home life, settled at the top of his profession, had loads of money. And I was so young, so unsettled, just getting started, with no money to speak of. He was big, I was little. It was a perfect match. Opposites attract.

It began like so many other times: with a good massage.

Bud had hurt his back at the studio but insisted on keeping our dinner date with Jay. He had trouble getting in and out of the low-slung sports car. I recommend a Bobby special and he just laughed. But I was so horny for him I wouldn't let up. Jay helped immensely, suggesting to Bud that if he ever had a Bobby special, he'd never settle for anything less. With all the cocktails and wine, Bud was feeling pretty good when the valet brought the car to the entrance. He didn't get a chance to protest when I told Jay I'd find my own way home. I was in the car in a flash.

"Tell me where it hurts and I can work it out," I said. I dug deep into him, drawing the tension out, as if his muscles were towels and I was wringing them out, one by one. But the muscle I most wanted to wring out was hidden under his body. I had him roll over and as my palms travelled up the insides of his thighs, he met them and guided them to his cock. It was every bit as big as I had hoped it would be, and a perfect thickness. I teased it, played with it, and finally took it into my mouth. He held my head as I sucked it, going wild with it, almost as if he'd never had a blowjob before. I wanted to suck on it all night but what I really wanted to do was get fucked by him. He was ready. My massage, and my blowjob, had their desired effect. He was so excited he was ready to burst with it. I thought it would be easier for him if I just sat on his dick from behind as he lay on the bed after his massage, his hard-on wobbling, eager. In his position, his cock felt thicker than any I'd ever had, even thicker than Joe's. I took it slow, easy, inch by inch, until he was completely in me and then I let him watch it going in and out. Finally he couldn't stand it anymore; he had to have me in his arms, driving it into me.

At first, he was a very considerate lover, asking me all through it if he was hurting me. He was, terribly, but I didn't tell him for fear he'd stop and I wanted to feel him coming inside of me. He tried to be gentle. He treated me as if I was a doll. His little fuck doll.

Now Bud's turned into a madman; we barely get into the apartment before he's all over me. The directions on the set are mild compared to the direction he gives me here at the apartment. But something's happening with him tonight. Something strange. Tonight *he* wants to get fucked.

...A mixture of shit and lube drips from his asshole onto my thigh. He's on his knees, his face smashed into the pillow. His wrists lie still in the small of his back, bound by the leather restraints he bought earlier in the week. If this helps him do it, okay. He said it was all about control, and their resistance to control. "You control me, Bobby," he said. "I'll try to keep you under control," I said.

Now I'm pumping Kyle's dildo into Bud's tight ass and jacking him off at the same time, deep into the rhythm of fucking. When he's finally coming, I ease the dildo out of his ass and snap the hook off the restraints. He drops to the mattress exhausted but I am not done with him. I lie on top of him and grind myself against him, working my cock into his swollen asshole. I grab his hair and pull hard, just to see his mouth fall open. I rock back and forth on my knees, rubbing the tip of my cock up and down his asscrack.

"Fuck me," he begs.

I shove it all the way in with one easy jolt. He gets a grip on my thighs and pushes my cock deeper into his ass. He whimpers. I grab his hair and jerk him, rolling him over. He makes a loud noise and I dive at him, slamming my cock into him to the hilt. His tongue slides up and down my neck and chin as I fuck him. He laps up my sweat, brings his hands to my ass, pushing me deeper. We kiss, our tongues flicking in and out, darting around. As I come, he clings to me, not wanting me to, to hold on, keep on, but it is no use. As I finish, I take his head in my hands and press it into mine, and I shower him with little kisses, sliding my tongue over his lips, his nose, his cheeks, back and forth in the slick, hairy darkness that is his chest.

Finally I am able to pull away from him and, smiling, I look at him. He is smiling too, even though tears are rolling down his cheeks. "God, I love you, Bobby," he says. "I *really* love you."

I run my fingers through his hair. "I know. It's scary, isn't it?"

. . .

Scary too was Roman Polanski's arrest for rape. Jay was sick. He called me up, just to talk about it: "He was photographing this girl, this 13-year-old, for *Vogue* and she does this to him. It's as if you turned Kyle in."

He went on to tell me how the director was considered kinky even as a teenager. "I remember him telling me that he was seventeen when he had his first fuck. He took this 14-year-old girl to her mother's bedroom and he suggested they do it on the floor. 'I scored a point,' he told me, 'she thought it was kinky. But the reason I didn't want to do it in the bed is because her mother died there a few days before.' He's got a great sense of humor. He'll be fine. I remember one time he told me, 'At some point, I picked up a very bad reputation.'"

It was after that phone call that I began to really worry about *my* reputation. Bud was also worried, fearing I might turn *him* in. We talked about it and we didn't see each other again – for two nights.

ELEVEN

Monday, April 4, 1977
　My part on "Space Travellers," of being superimposed over all that animation, wrapped early and Jay called me from New York to thank me. "It was all Bud," I told him.
　"Bud tells me he loves you so much he wants to leave his wife for you."
　"He does?"
　"He was joking of course."
　"Yeah, of course."
　"But I think it's time you get out of there, come to New York, meet some people"
　"I'd like that. At least I could see Kyle." My lover had come off the tour, declared it a success and was staying in Manhattan "for just a few days."
　"I don't see much of him when I'm here," Jay said. "He's always out. You come here, maybe he'll be in."

　I was on a flight two days later, dreading it, yet excited about it. Kyle had called once or twice in the past week, asking how things were going, how was the house. Finally he got around to asking about Bud Logan. "Hollywood's really small town, Bobby. I ran into Linda Reynolds at Studio 54 the other night and she told me how things were on that cozy little set of yours."
　"Oh?"
　"In case you don't know, Linda works for the same company Logan does and they share the same crew. The crew talks, you

know."

I didn't think it needed to be explained. Kyle does his thing, I should be able to do mine. But somehow this affair has spun out of control. It's become something more scary than I could ever have imagined. Bud keeps playing Mary MacGregor's "Torn Between Two Lovers." I'm sick of hearing it.

A week before the filming was over, Bud brought dinner to the apartment and, after fucking, we ate. He told me he had thought about leaving his wife, that she was becoming impossible. "Wives know these things. I've told her I've been busy with the picture but she knows it's not the same when we're in bed together."

I blinked. It was the first time I had even considered he was still fucking his wife. When did he do it? When he went home after doing it to me was he doing it to her? Did she smell me all over him as he climbed into bed?

"I've had little flings before, with starlets, but nothing has ever been like this – " He smiled and caressed my cheek. He had a way of saying things very quietly and seriously, hardly moving his lips at all, making me stop to really listen to what he was saying. He rarely smiled or paid compliments so you knew when he did, he meant it.

"I'm glad."

"But because it's so different. You're right, it's scary. I think I've always wondered what it would like, I just had to find the right person to do it with."

"Well, now that you've done it – " I had read all about romances between actors and actresses, actresses and their directors, and so on while a movie is being made. But now I was involved with a director and the movie was almost over. I wanted it to go on, but yet I didn't.

He took me in his arms. "I want to keep on seeing you, Bobby. I really do. But what can we do, we're both married?"

"Yeah," I said, looking away. I tried not to think of Kyle while I was with Bud but it was impossible.

"By the way, where is Kyle?"

"He's was on tour. Now he's back in New York."

He nodded and looked away, mumbling, "You love him, I know."

"Yes. But it's different with him. He was the first man I ever really loved. I loved him even before I met him. I had his poster on the back of my door in my bedroom. I used to listen to his records all the time. Then he came to Brackettville – "

"Please," Bud said. He didn't want to hear any more about Kyle. He pulled away from me and slid out of the bed. He stood still, breathing deeply. "I don't want this to end but it has to, you know that." He said nothing more, just went to the bathroom. When he came out, he began dressing and I lay there watching him. He looked so sad I began to cry, not sobbing, just tears running down my cheeks.

When he was dressed, he lowered himself to the bed and swept me up into his arms again. "Don't do this," he said. "Don't make it worse than it is. Who knows, maybe tomorrow everything will be different. I'd still like to see you – if you'll let me."

I nodded and laid my head on his chest. Hugging him to me, I said, "You better go now. Your wife will be wondering what's happened to you."

. . .

In New York, at the apartment on Park Avenue, I felt like I was going to be put on trial for my affair with Bud. But Jay made light of it, saying it was good for the picture, and went out for an appointment, leaving Kyle and me alone. My suitcases were still in the vestibule but I was in bed, going down on Kyle before he could even get his shoes off. I decided it was the only way, to be so desperate for him that he would realize there was nothing – or no one – that could come between us, least of all a married man.

"God, you really did miss me," he said, running his fingers through my hair as I sucked him to hardness.

Yes, I had missed him, but I said nothing as I undressed him. How much I missed him stunned me. Who is the real me? I am asking that more and more. Kyle reduces me to speechlessness. I am putty in his hands. Or I am desperate for him, pawing him, clawing at him, can't get my fill.

He fell back on the enormous pillows, enjoying his blowjob. My fingers travelled over his skin as they always had, caressing, digging in, finally scratching as he came in my mouth.

He pulled me up and I lay across his stomach, the cum dripping from my lips as I kissed him. He rolled me over and got between my thighs. He began his own worshipping of my cock and balls. His technique was different than mine: slower, more deliberate, and it always ended up with his tongue in my ass, getting it ready for the assault of his prick.

By the time he was hard again and entering me, I was so close to coming I couldn't stop myself, I just let it go. My cock bobbed around wildly as he began thrusting his penis into me, and the cum flew everywhere. When he was all the way in, he took me in his arms and held me, kissed me, first on the forehead, then the nose and finally the lips. Since we both had come, the fuck lasted a long time that afternoon. I was tired from my flight but it didn't matter, we both wanted it to last as long as possible. Finally I could hear him yell and feel his cock shivering inside me. As he flooded me with his jism, I pressed my butt tight against him, keeping his cock in me, and I came, again without even touching my dick.

. . .

Jay, of course, has the master bedroom, a magnificent place that reflects his wife's taste, as does the entire apartment, even though they had a famous decorator do it. Kyle and I are together in the room Kyle likes best at the apartment. It is really the library, wood-panelled and with soft lighting. It has a sofa that becomes a bed but when Kyle is here it is never put back, it is always open, ready for action. And we gave it a workout. It was raining all the time and Kyle stayed at the apartment for two days; we spent most of it in bed.

In the late afternoon of the second day, the fire in my ass that had been building with every hour was forcing me to an incredible orgasm when suddenly Kyle pulled off of me. Jay had come into the room, rapping first, then entering. Kyle's cock slid away so that only the head of it was left in me. He looked at Jay, who was going to his desk. Jay used the room as an office so he would have to come in and out but we didn't mind. Mostly, we knew, it was only a pretext, to watch us. Jay sat at his desk and started going through the drawers, ignoring us. The shades were drawn and he didn't turn on a light; I doubted he could see what he was looking for even if he found it. I raised my face and kissed Kyle's lips and just then his cock flew into me again, the weight of him crashing against me and he kept pressing in and in, impaling me. Kyle came, stretching the ring of my asshole with his cock, and I screamed out with the pain, having had him so many times in so few hours.

Before long, I was on my stomach with my legs spread wide apart and Jay was lapping at my sore asshole, his spit cool, soothing. As he moved up the length of the cleft of my ass, Kyle climbed onto the bed and I raised my head slightly so that his cock was poised at my lips. Slowly he slid it carefully into my mouth, stopping when three inches of it was in me. I enjoyed the sweet taste of it, covered with his cum, and I sucked it for a long time while Jay busied himself at my ass. Finally, Jay was ready and my ass twitched as he sank it into me, his balls slamming with a thud against my asscheeks. I kept sucking Kyle as Jay did push-ups over my body, sweat dripping from his forehead onto my naked back. Kyle held my head in his hands, trying to match Jay's rhythm. My arms encircled Kyle and I hugged him to me as Jay continued. The pain brought tears to my eyes but I kept sucking on Kyle, who kept murmuring, "My boy, my little boy," all through it.

. . .

After two days together, Kyle said he had to leave the apartment. He had an appointment to see a producer about replacing an actor in a musical play Off-Broadway, "Joseph and the Amazing Technicolor Dreamcoat." I was excited for him and helped him get dressed in his best Armani. He hadn't snorted anything and had drunk very little. He looked wonderful and I told him so.

"That's what your lovin' does for me," he said.

I decided to go shopping. I discovered Manhattan was a fantastic place to go shopping. I could shop for hours and never buy anything and I went up one side of Fifth Avenue and down the other.

When I returned to the apartment, no one was there. Jay eventually came in and we waited around for Kyle before going to dinner. I was very anxious and Jay had me drink a brandy. That night, alone in the library, I cried myself to sleep.

The next day, I was straightening up the room and when I put a pair of Kyle's pants on a hangar, a business card fell out. I was amused by the wording: "Max. Massage by the Magic Fingers." I called the number, made an appointment. I realized I hadn't had a massage since Mr. Austin, a salesman for the supply company, stayed at the hotel and taught me everything I know about pleasing a man. I thought a massage just might get my mind off my absent lover.

Max's "office" was in the Village, at the end of a long basement hallway. I was late and a towering, muscular man of perhaps fifty, bald with white pants and a white tank top stood waiting for me with his arms crossed. His hands were meaty, his brow damp and his accent Eastern European. He had me undress and lie on his table in the sterile, dimly lit room. Classical music was playing on the stereo. He said he worked without oils. At first he made chopping blows to my chest, then started squeezing and pulling my body parts, altering his chops and squeezes and strokes according to what he felt. Tension left me momentarily as he went about his business. Suddenly I heard him open a jar and then I felt his finger, coated with oil, gently taunting my asshole.

I moaned.

"Hurt?"

"No."

"Do you want a *complete* massage?"

"Yes."

"It will be fifty dollars extra."

"That's fine."

His hands squeezed my asscheeks. They burned and quivered, still hurting from the fuckings Kyle had been giving me.

One fat finger began burrowing up my asshole. Another fat finger rubbed the cleft. He tickled the rim of my rectum. His finger dilated the pucker of my ass. Finally, his finger twirled maddeningly. I arched and pushed back on it. My hole spread wider and two, then three fingers went in. He twisted and bent his digits deep inside me. I thought I was going to shit. He was massaging my insides as no one ever had. But it was only a prelude to the big event. His fingers left my ass and he stepped in front of me. Slowly he unzipped his pants and let them fall. A fist-fat, uncut cock was rising out a dark, lush bush, the meaty nozzle of foreskin gradually disappearing as it grew harder. Soon his cock was even with the table. Huge hairy balls hung below the prick and I played with them while my mouth went to the swollen, bulbous-headed penis. I flicked my tongue around it, teasing the hole. Then he pushed it forward, sending it deep into my waiting mouth. After a few thrusts, he swung one arm back and one of his fat fingers found my asshole again. My nose buried in his sweaty hair, I was mouthing the root of his cock. It seemed he had a dozen hands; they were everywhere. As I sucked, he finger-fucked me and, when I started to came, my ass muscle clamped down tight on the finger.

"No," he said, nostrils flaring, "not yet." He withdrew the finger and, my jaws aching, I let go of the prick.

He took off his pants and climbed onto the table. Slowly at first, he pushed all the way in, then pulled back. There was pain for a few seconds but once he got a rhythm going I was able to relax again. My gasps as he fucked me were nothing compared to the cries he let out when he finally started heaving and came. "God, oh, God." After taking several deep breaths he stopped fucking and pulled out. My asshole ached with the sudden vacancy. Standing next to the table, he rolled me over and held my cock with those fat fingers, massaging, pulling, making me come. He licked the shaft, welcoming my cum. He mouthed my thrashing balls, popping each in and out of his mouth, covering them with spit. Exhausted, I lay on the table for a few moments. I heard bathroom noises and then he was back, massaging my stomach. "That was the first side. Now we do this side." By the time he was done, my cock was erect again, bobbing and jerking like a child begging for attention.

"Do you want relief again?"

"Yes."

"There'll be no extra charge. It isn't often I get teenage dick here. And such a pretty one at that." His mouth clamped down on my penis and wouldn't let it go. He began a flicking, darting, teasing action across the crown much like what I was accustomed to receiving from Kyle. Then he bathed my nutsack again. He twisted my nipples as he worked over my cock until I came a second time.

At the door, as I handed him two fifties, he told me the next time the massage would be on the house. I promised I'd be back.

Kyle still had not returned to the apartment. Jay told me not to worry, that Kyle did that all the time when he was there. "But not when *I'm* here. Why does he do this to me?"

Jay shrugged his shoulders. "He's just a boy. You are both boys. Beautiful boys playing with each other."

Then Jay told me the studio had called and I was wanted for some post-synchronization on "Space Travellers." He said he would take me back on his jet. He said, "I have to get back for the Academy Awards."

"When are they?"

"The 28th. And we're having a party for Stallone and all the 'Rocky' people. The picture is going to win, I just know it."

People in Hollywood called him a genius so often that after a while he began believing it. He told me that he found he had a power over others that big money brings and came to feel that most people were weak and needed to be controlled. They had to be controlled, otherwise they would be lost. These people, he realized, were drawn to a person like him and he took advantage of every opportunity. That, he said, was the secret, to be ready to take advantage of the opportunities. Then he smiled and said, "Oh, I haven't done too badly but, I'll be honest with you: If I had a choice, I'd come back very good-looking, with a great body and really stupid. Then the world is your oyster."

When I returned to Bird's Eye, the message light was winking on the answering machine. Kyle had called. "I miss you," he said. I called him back right away. He had signed to do the show. He would start rehearsals in a week. He had a minimum engagement of six months. He didn't say where he had been or what he had done. I didn't mention Max and his magic fingers.

"How's Bud?" he asked.

"It's over. I told you that."
"But now you're back there – "
"This will only take a week or so, then I'll come back."
"No, I'll be too busy. I'll be in rehearsal."
"No, I'll come back."

. . .

I've now been here two days and have attended one rehearsal. Kyle is a bundle of nerves. It's his first musical play, a far cry from his concert gigs and filming a picture. But it is Tim Rice and Andrew Lloyd Webber at their best, a nice little show. What started out as a fifteen minute school production is very impressive with Kyle being nearly naked most of the time. He says he's awful. I think he's magnificent.

But not in bed. The night I arrived he wanted only to be fucked. He could get it up but couldn't keep it up. After I came, he went to sleep. The next night he said he wanted to take me to a party. I'm too young to get into the bars so this would have to do. "There's always a party on Saturday night at David Friedman's."

Kyle said it was at the diamond merchant's apartment that he danced with the Negro. "Will he be there tonight?" I asked, my eyes wide.

"You never know with David. He takes what he can get."

That, I found, was true. David, a portly man in his 50's with an obvious toupee and even more obvious wealth, judging by the art hanging on the walls and all the antiques, greeted us and led us to the front bedroom, where we could change and "get comfy," which meant wearing a towel. This was a new innovation, Kyle said, making the men feel "more comfortable," but I was growing more uncomfortable with each passing moment. Kyle led me to what David had called "the back room," a long, narrow, dimly lit room with little couches and ottomans. The loud disco music made it impossible for me to make out anyone's name but Kyle seemed to know everyone and they were delighted to find he had brought someone new with him. This made me more antsy than ever. Big joints were passed around and Kyle and I made ourselves as comfortable as possible on one of the settees. Suddenly David turned on a spotlight at the end of the room. The entertainment, I supposed, was about to begin.

"Don't Knock My Love" by Diana Ross and Marvin Gaye began and Kyle went to get us drinks. I wanted a Coke. When he came back, he handed me the soda pop and then stood behind me, massaging my neck and shoulders. I felt like telling him Max did it better but when he whispered into my ear, "That feels good doesn't it?" I nodded. I gulped my drink, my eyes fixed on the muscular, dark-haired go-go boy who seemed to materialize out of nowhere. He was dressed in Levis and a tank-top but they quickly were removed. His body was great and he seemed excited about dancing before an appreciative audience of balding men with eyeglasses. The men howled, almost in unison, when he pulled his cock out of the only thing he was still wearing, a filthy jockstrap. Keeping the strap on, but with his cock dangling out of one side, he passed among the men, letting them touch him, feel him, kiss him, until he ended up in front of us. Up close, I could see what he had was dark, heavily-veined, about seven inches of semi-hardness. I would have sucked it if he had offered to me but, instead, he took my hand and pulled me up. I reached out for Kyle but he waved my hand away. "Get it on," he yelled. My towel fell from my body as this six-foot stud dragged me into the spotlight.

"Get Down Tonight" by K. C. and the Sunshine Band proved the perfect accompaniment to what came next – me. I couldn't help it. My cock was erect by the time the stud started dancing with me and he just dropped down and took me. I think he was as stunned by my immediate gratification as I was, because he held on to my buns and dragged me down with him, keeping me in his mouth all the way and continuing to suck while I collapsed on the floor. "Shake Your Booty" was next and that's what the go-go boy did, prancing around above me, his lovely cock wiggling and waggling above me.

Suddenly, Kyle was there, dancing right along with him, his erection tenting out of his towel at a rakish angle. The stud pulled Kyle's towel away completely and dropped to his knees again, taking all of Kyle in one mouthful. The men were all cheering as I gripped Kyle's legs and brought myself next to the stud and we shared the cock. I was so happy to see it so hard, so ready. I wanted him to fuck me but the go-go boy was way ahead of me, leaping up, turning around, spreading it. From my vantage point, I was able to guide it in, although it obviously didn't need any help from me. Kyle stood still, letting the go-go boy fuck himself with it, while I played with Kyle's balls with one hand and the dancer's cock and balls with the other. The men were all gathered around by this time, towels off, and jerking along with us. One of the men knelt down in front of the dancer and took the cock I was playing with into his mouth. A man started to play with Kyle's asshole and another knelt down and began to lick it and tongue it. With this, Kyle came, pulling out of the dancer and letting his sperm fly across the kid's back. I wrapped my arms around his legs and hugged him. He reached down and pulled me up, kissed me full on the mouth and then, without saying a word, led me out of the room. I turned around to see the men had completely surrounded the dancer.

Back at the apartment, Kyle said he was pleased I had gone along with him and behaved exactly as he wanted me to. "You were a good boy," he said, unbuckling my pants. "Now fuck the shit out of me."

I go shopping during the day. New York has quickly become, for me, the shopping capitol of the universe. Jay had said no place pulls out the stops quite like New York and I am finding that true. From Bloomingdale's to Macy's to Christopher Street, I make every stop. One day, on Christopher, just after noon, I was cruised by fifteen guys in a single block. I didn't stop. I was on my way to feel Max's magic fingers. True to his word, the second time was on the house. But the surprise was gone. I decided that, even though I was invited back as often as I liked – for free – I needed to be surprised.

There have been no surprises on Park Avenue either. Kyle didn't show up for two days, and when he did he was whipped. He'd stopped off after rehearsal and had a few at a bar he knew. He passed out in the bedroom and I packed my bags.

Now it's morning and I manage to wake him up enough to tell him I have to go back to Hollywood for a photo shoot for *Teenybopper* magazine to promote "Space Travellers." They are rushing the film into release on the July 4th weekend to take advantage of summer vacations. It was either that or delay it to Christmas and fierce competition.

I tell Kyle he'll be fine; he is so good in the show but he can't see it. There is no reasoning with him.

TWELVE

Two Weeks Later
When Kyle came home unexpectedly, Bud Logan was in the swimming pool. Nude. I was cooking dinner in the kitchen. Kyle never said a word, he just went to his bedroom and slammed the door. Bud, who has been working night and day trying to meet the deadline for the release of "Space Travellers," had come here for a break – a fuck, some dinner, then maybe another fuck. It was after the first fuck that he jumped in the pool and I went to tend to dinner. With Kyle's arrival, Bud left in a hurry. That night I slept alone, dreaming about the second fuck Bud and I would have had. It was my turn to be top. That's the way it's gotten to be, first him, then me, but sometimes I'm just too exhausted from taking it to give it, so a rest – or some food – between fucks really helps. Bud's decided he doesn't really need a wife, he gets everything from me. I tell him we *both* need her. He understands.

"I thought it was over," Kyle said the next morning when he came out to get his coffee.

"It is. Now it is. He was just here saying goodbye."

"Then let's celebrate," Kyle said. He said he had a week's layoff from the show before he actually took over the lead. He wanted to just be with me.

Almost caught in the act with Bud, I didn't feel like celebrating but he decided we needed to get away, to take a vacation, all the way to Santa Barbara.

We took the Porsche. I was bearing down a steep mountain curve. A granite wall suddenly appeared on my right. A precipitous drop yawned at me from the left. I shifted into fifth, accelerated and thrilled to the thrust as we hit the curve at ninety.

Kyle screamed, "Christ!"

White-knuckled, I clenched the steering wheel. Blood throbbed in my skull. We were having our first big argument. I wanted to fuck whomever I wanted. He could. I should.

"Are you crazy? Slow down," Kyle said.

"Yes. I guess I am crazy. But I want to know."

"Want to know what for chrissakes?"

"Why is it all right for you to fuck anybody you please but it's not all right for me?"

"I don't want to discuss it now."

"But *I* want to."

"Okay. But slow down."

I slowed down. To seventy.

"Okay."

"It's just that you're so public about it...fucking your fucking director for chrissakes. A fucking married man. Even I've never done that! And he's the biggest fucking director in the fucking business right now! How much more fucking public can you get?"

I tried to remain calm. "We didn't do it in public."

"You might as well have. Everyone in town knows about it. How do you think that makes me feel?"

"I'm sorry. I didn't think you had any feelings left for me that could be hurt. You watched guys fuck me, you sent me to be fucked by old men – "

"I'm sorry. I didn't know I was hurting you. You acted as if you were enjoying it. Every *fucking* minute of it."

"I didn't say that. I did enjoy it, but it seemed as if you just gave me up to them."

He shook his head violently. "No, no! Look, I found you, I brought you here. You're mine. I'll never, ever give you up."

Santa Barbara's Spring Arts Festival was going on and we ate chili and went on the carnival rides. It was the nicest day we had had together in a long time. That night, in our room at the Biltmore, with his cock finally up my ass, he told me he felt closer to me than ever before. I told him I did, too. He said it was as if we had created a whole new image of ourselves as lovers, that we had survived a difficult period and we were somehow stronger for it. I agreed to give up Bud; but I lied. It is a terrible thing to lie but at that moment I thought it was best. I knew I couldn't stop seeing Bud. I didn't want to stop seeing Bud. I couldn't explain why to myself, let alone to Kyle.

Kyle said it didn't bother him to watch me get fucked by somebody else, in fact it turned him on, but to hear that I was two-timing him while he was three thousand miles away was more than he wanted to deal with. I apologized. I told him the thing with Bud had just gotten out of hand.

He said while he had been fucked, and fucked often, while he was away, he never fucked anybody, that was, as always, saved just for me. I knew that much was true. He had never enjoyed fucking someone until I came along and once he started, he couldn't stop. It was the same thing again in Santa Barbara. After two days of fucking, my ass burned but I didn't complain.

When we returned to Bird's Eye he told me the truth: He had been fired from the musical. He had arrived drunk once too often. The story was in the trades the next day and he disappeared for two days. When he did show up, he insisted that we go to the apartment downtown. It is our first time there in months. He had ordered a stud from the service and wanted me to meet him. His name was Paul and I let him in the apartment. Kyle was sitting in a chair and called him over. The stud rubbed his chinos against Kyle's face, teasing him. Kyle unzipped his pants and pressed his face into the front of his underwear. When Kyle began licking him through the heavy cotton, I went into the bathroom to get ready. When I came out, nude, my asshole greased, my poppers in my hand, Paul's hard-on was thumping against his sweaty Jockeys, tantalizing me. When I dropped down on the bed, the kid mounted me and shoved the musky pouch in my face. I licked the contours of the huge prick and nibbled at the bulge. I wanted it in me. Slowly I pulled the cotton away and it throbbed before me. It was at least eight inches of nicely trimmed meat.

"Suck it," Kyle ordered. He was now nude and he squatted on the bed watching as I strained to take it all. The straining continued when, after Kyle and I sucked Paul for a while, I got on my knees and Paul began fucking me. When he started, it didn't hurt except right at first; the poppers helped and I'm getting used to the huge ones now, after Bud. It was a long, slow fuck and I really enjoyed it, especially with Kyle there, shoving his cock in my mouth, coming when Paul did. It was the first time he had come since we'd been in Santa Barbara.

Now the kid's gone and we're on our way back to Bird's Eye. "All I really need is one really good movie and I'll never have to work again," Kyle says now but I don't think he means it.

Jay sends over scripts but it's no use. Kyle won't even read through them. I read them, though, and tell him what I think.

He finds something wrong with every one of them. There was a role in one picture that would have been perfect for him but they gave it to William Katt. Jay told him there were already too many blond boys around right now. He had better stick to recording.

"Yeah," he says to me, "now you're the movie star in the family." Jay had brought the trailer for "Space Travellers" to the house and showed it to us. He kept playing it over and over until Kyle got up and went to his room. "He'd better get used to it. We've got a blockbuster here. We've already signed Bud to do the sequel."

"The sequel?"

"Of course, you're already signed. It was in your contract, don't you remember?"

"No, I don't keep track of things like contracts and stuff."

"You'd better," Jay said. "You're going to be big business, Bobby. Big."

THIRTEEN

Friday, May 6, 1977

Yesterday started out as a rotten day for fucking – for doing anything at all. It was cold and rainy in New York. I was staying at the Plaza; Jay's wife was using the apartment. And alone in the Big City, I was bored out of my mind. I was tired of waiting for yet another interview, yet another photo session to be over. But acting is the art of waiting, Jay told me. "You're always waiting," he said. "Waiting to pick up a cue, for the crew to set up a shot, for the right role." What I was waiting for was to return to Bird's Eye. To Kyle. But all my interviews were done. The last thing that remained was to be photographed by Charles Adams for the layout that would appear in *Interview*, timed to hit the newsstands as "Space Travellers" opened nationally over the Fourth of July weekend. Bud had finished the picture and the preview audiences love it, he says. All I've been able to do is talk to him on the phone, he's been so busy. He's still working on it, he said, cutting, cutting, cutting. "Just don't cut me out!" I hollered. He laughed like hell. "You're the whole picture, you little shit." Bud's so damn nice.

I pinched the fire from the end of the joint. Then, as usual, I chewed the roach and swallowed it. It was all I would allow myself before the photo shoot. Not that I needed a high for this performance. I looked in the mirror. I was adorable, I had to admit it. That's what the girls at my wardrobe fitting were all saying. "He's just so cute!" "He's even cuter in person than on TV."

The doorman called me a cab, then moved aside after I tipped him. The driver, with curly brown hair under his hat and a big belly, kept watching me in the rearview mirror.

"Hey," the driver said after a few moments, "ain't you that kid on 'Home Life?'"

"I *used* to be that kid. They cancelled the show, you know. One season with me and it was their last. Yeah, I killed that show."

He laughed heartily. "Hey, you were great! My daughter, she's got your picture on her door. On the fuckin' door! Bigger than life!" He shook his head. "Imagine, little Bobby Richards in my cab! She'll just die!" When we arrived at the photographers' studio on West 57th Street, I stuck a twenty out to him. "No, no. Ride's on me if you'll give me your autograph for my little daughter."

"On what?"

"Here - on this receipt." He held the pad out to me with the stub of a pencil. "Here, right here."

"What's her name?"

"Belinda. To Belinda from Bobby! She'll fuckin' die!"

"Sure," I said. I signed it: "Love To Belinda - Bobby Richards."

Looking in the mirror as the make-up woman was doing her thing, I saw the photographer's assistant, Ben, staring at me. I stared back. At that moment, I knew we were destined to fuck. And I thought it was a going to be lousy day.

While Ben was reloading for Adams, I let my arms fall to my sides and submitted to the hair people and the makeup people, and then I drifted around the stage, glancing back over my shoulder at Ben. No one was saying very much. The clicking of the shutter and the whirring of the speed loader were punctuated now and then by the unwrapping of a fresh roll of film, which sent narcotic little puffs of photographic chemicals wafting into the air. I was on a high.

Adams, a tall, good-looking man with wavy gray hair, consulted with the hair people and the makeup people and with the stylist, twisting his wedding ring while he listened, and ticking off instructions for them on his stout fingers. Having completed his rounds, he said to me, "Chemistry on a shoot is very important. When the chemistry isn't right, the shoot just comes off stiff. Just glossy. No sentiment. That's the difference between good and bad fashion photography –

sentiment."

"I feel we have good chemistry here," I said, looking directly at Ben.

Adams smiled. "Good. How about some with your shirt off?"

Ben nodded.

"Okay," I said.

I posed and posed and then they had to change the backdrop. I put on a shirt and came over and sat at the food table. I eagerly took the cigarette that the makeup person, who had plum-colored hair, had lit for me. If I couldn't have a joint, I'd have the next best thing. In a few moments, Ben came over and told us they were ready again.

My shirt came off quickly and, in a final flash, I turned and dropped my pants. Adams clicked away. He said it would make a great poster.

I saw Ben in the background, staring. I knew then that he knew it too – we would be fucking before the day was over.

The photography session lasted until nearly ten.

"Party?" Ben asked me as I was preparing to leave.

Without a moment's hesitancy I found myself saying, "Why not?"

. . .

Passing the time, still standing with Ben by the bar, finishing a Coke, I looked over the crowd. There were about fifty people there in the loft, a huge place, painted all white. Occasionally the door would open and someone would drift in or out. I suppose I looked as if I would rather be almost anywhere else in the world, especially when Ben got into deep conversation with a tall, blond woman. But then her friend came up and they put their arms around each other, making no secret of their attraction for each other. I relaxed and moved away, found a place to sit down. Ben shared a joke with the lovebirds, his eyes searching the room until he found me. He went on looking at me for a few moments from across the room, then when I smiled at him, he grinned.

He was easily the handsomest man in the room, I thought, and his movements resembled those of a graceful cat. The manner in which he used his hands, his impetuous eyes, his perfect body, he was an imposing hunk, more the type to be before the camera than behind it. He looked away, glanced curiously about the room, then began walking toward me. When he reached me he stood there, looking down at me. I hate having people look down at me. There are few people I don't have to bend backward to look at even when I'm standing up, so I sat quietly, looking straight ahead, trying mightily to ignore the big bulge at his crotch.

He slid down next to me on the couch, a fresh glass of wine in his hand, a Coke for me. "Having fun?" he asked, taking a sip of the wine.

"Yeah."

"You'd have more fun if I let everybody know who you are."

"These people don't watch TV," I said, sipping my Coke.

"No, but all I gotta do is say, here's the kid on TV and then the buzz'd start. I've done it before. You know that singer, the kid with Legion?" He tugged his chin. "Frank his name is. Yeah, Frank. Like in hot dog." He winked. "Nice kid, too. We did this big layout for *Rolling Stone.* Boy, get him to a party and he becomes the party."

I looked away. "I'm sure. But I'm afraid I'm not much of a party person."

"Just like your character in that show, what was the name of it?"

"I've been trying to block it out."

He took a small sip from his glass.

"But hey, you were so cute, running around in nothing but your Jockey shorts."

"Not on that show – "

"Then it was swimming trunks."

"Once. Say, you really did watch it –

"And now you're going to be a movie star. How does it feel?"

"I don't know. I don't know how a star's supposed to feel."

"Great. You're supposed to feel great! Cute kid like you."

"If you only knew – "

He winked. "I know more'n you think."

Just then, someone he knew called him over to the pool table. Right when it was getting interesting. For the next half hour it was almost quiet. Even the balls on the pool table didn't seem to click as loudly. It was good being there, with Ben. I hardly noticed the time go by. Watching him shoot a game of pool with another guy was the perfect antidote for thinking about how lonely I was, what the future might hold. He won handily. He got another drink, then slid down next to me again. Closer than ever. I didn't budge. "You were saying you knew something about me, more than I thought you did."

"Forget it," he said.

"No. I won't. What've you heard?"

"Nothing." He looked away, waved at somebody. "I haven't heard anything. It's just a feeling I get."

I sat upright and stared down at him. "I guess I'm not such a good actor after all."

"There's a saying, it takes one to know one."

I sighed. It was a deep sigh, one of recognition, of relief. "I'm glad it does."

"You're glad? I'm fuckin' ecstatic!" He took my hand in his and held it. "You are one cute little boy."

He handed me a joint. It seemed like sharing a joint with him was a kind of final hope that if I could get him stoned enough, that we could get stoned together, that maybe he would overcome his fear and just ask me if I wanted to fuck. Finally, I said, "Are you as good at shooting your load as you are shooting pool and shooting pictures?"

He grinned. "Better."

. . .

It took me a long moment to realize the phone was ringing. Ben reached for it but it wasn't where it was supposed to be. "Happens all the time. Stuff keeps moving around," he muttered.

Rubbing my eyes, I asked myself 'What was wrong with this hotel? I left strict orders never to call me before noon.' Then I realized I wasn't at my hotel. I was in Ben's bedroom. I sat up, took a deep breath, and watched Ben finally find the phone and answer it. He stood over the bed, his meaty cock semi-flaccid.

"'Hlo..." he said. I reached over and stroked his long, thick prick.

A pause.

"Yeah, you woke me. What time is it anyway?"

I glanced at the clock on the nightstand. It was eleven.

Twenty-four hours had passed. Yesterday had been, all things considered, a wonderful day, especially for fucking. When his cock was finally revealed, I thought of Kyle, wishing he could see this amazing young man, this stud with the biggest cock I have ever seen. Ben is even bigger than Bud! My God!

After kissing me passionately with his full lips, Ben slowly began to unbutton my shirt, his puzzling, maddening smile never seeming to leave his face. It was as if he was in awe of me, while it was I who was in awe of him, my hands having found the incredibly solid evidence of his passion within the folds of his trousers in the cab on the way to his apartment.

But Kyle's image was fleeting as I made myself comfortable, my mouth over his cock. My tongue flicked over the huge head and then I took three inches or so of it into my mouth. I was jerking my own cock and soon an orgasm was filling every nerve of my body. He pushed down hard on my head, making me taste his precum. Then he rolled me over and hung my legs over his massive shoulders.

"Damn, you're cute," he said, lining his cock up. "I've been wanting to do this ever since you dropped your pants at the studio."

The pleasurable sensation of having him slowly insert the cock into my ass made it impossible for me to respond with anything intelligible. On a high, I was compliant, opening up to him, wanting him in every way. He put his lips to my mouth and kissed me. He took my lower lip between his teeth and bit until he drew blood as he pressed himself all the way into me.

"Do it," I finally managed to groan. "Fuck me!" I gave in to his blinding sensuality. He moved magically over me and I lifted my body to meet the sensations every thrust brought. I let my head fall back and he sucked on my throat as he continued to furiously attack my ass. His strong hands held my hips and forced them in circles that moved on the axis of the huge prick. When he came, a shiver of recognition, of memory, ran through my body. He came as Kyle did in the beginning, pulling out, setting the cock free, the cum flying in all directions, then inserting it again while it still retained some of its hardness, then continuing, building to a second climax.

Now, in the light of late morning, Ben stands before me,

finishing his conversation on the phone.

I continue to play with his cock. It rises to meet my every stroke. As it reaches its full hardness and I become filled with ecstasy as I suck it, I somehow have the feeling I am going to miss my plane back to Los Angeles.

As Ben begins running his free hand through my hair, I know, somehow, it is going to be another wonderful day for fucking. And before it's over, Ben will have to agree to come out for the premiere of "Space Travellers." And wait'll Kyle gets a load of this cock. My God!

FOURTEEN

Sunday, July 3, 1977
    Kyle got a load of Ben's cock all right. A couple of loads, at least. And now everything has changed. Yet it's the same. I'm alone again at Bird's Eye.
    Fearing another incident such as the one with Dugan, I told Kyle ahead of time exactly why Ben was coming here and staying at Bird's Eye: So that he could enjoy Ben's cock as I had.
    "That big eh?"
    I nodded. He smiled. "Well, if you say so."
    Ben had called to ask if I meant it, he should come to Hollywood for the premiere? I said I really meant it and I was sending him the ticket. "But what about Kyle?"
    "Kyle's fine." But I lied. Kyle was far from fine. He was disappearing again for days. Having Ben with us would either make things worse or better, I wasn't sure which but I had to chance it. Ben was too good to let go. I told him I would tell Kyle that he was coming out to shoot the premiere for *Interview*. "Well, maybe I could. I'll bring it up to Adams. He'd never do that but there's no reason I couldn't."
    At first Kyle eyed Ben suspiciously but then a curious thing happened: they somehow clicked. It wasn't anything either of them consciously did, it just came upon them. I was fixing dinner and they were sitting beside the pool sharing a joint. After a beastly hot day, the air had cooled and they got to talking about New York, people they knew, the bars, Studio 54, and the subject eventually got around to fucking. Kyle said he thought he knew all the best tops in New York.
    "Well, you missed one," I said, coming out from the kitchen.
    "Yeah, Bobby says I missed 'The Biggest Thrill in New York.' That true?" Kyle asked.

Ben just shrugged.

Kyle got up from where he was sitting and dropped down in front of Ben. "Well, there's only one way to find out."

I stood behind Ben, massaging his shoulders, as Kyle slowly unbuckled Ben's trousers and unzipped them. Ben brought his hands up to my arms and gripped me tightly. I stopped what I was doing to stare at Kyle as he revealed the cock. His gasp was audible. Seeing it again, all pink and shining with the pulse of desire, I was eager to suck it myself, but I let Kyle lead the way. He caressed Ben, pulled on the cock gently, teasing, running his hands over the length of him, playing at the tip. As it rose to full hardness, he deep-throated it a couple of times before looking up at me. Seeing the eagerness in my eyes, he motioned for me to join him.

It was even bigger and more delicious than I had remembered. As Kyle's mouth went to the balls, I was able to take it deep down my throat without gagging. Kyle and I kissed each other, then the cock, then Ben.

When we got to Kyle's bedroom, Kyle wanted it so badly, I let him go first. I lay next to them on the bed, watching Kyle, on his back, his legs spread wide, having a wonderful time. Then he wanted to fuck me while Ben was fucking him. Ben got up and Kyle rolled over, swiftly entering me. Ben returned to Kyle's asshole with a thunderous jolt and it seemed as if I was being fucked by both of them at once.

My eyes met Kyle's: wild, fiery. Then my eyes met Ben's: calm, intense, watching. I could have taken his cock all night but Kyle stopped after awhile and told me he wanted me on my knees. In this position, I jacked myself off. Feeling me coming sent Kyle over the edge. After he came, I stayed on my knees and Ben entered me. The control, the dexterity, and forcefulness which Ben had displayed in our past encounter was again amazing. Every part of his body was entirely subdued and regulated. He was every inch the determined stud. I met thrust with thrust as powerfully as I could until we both cried out at almost the same moment. But Kyle wasn't through. He took Ben's cock from my ass and sucked it back to full hardness again. Then, Ben lying on his back, Kyle had me squat on the prick and after it was in, Kyle brought his cock to the heart of the action, teasing me at the opening. He worked the head of it in, it plopped out, he worked in again, a little bit at a time, and, little by little, the shaft until he thrust it hard into me, entering fully alongside Ben's cock. I let out a soft moan of pleasure. Kyle moved inside me, our bodies snug together. As the fucking continued, I cried out, surprised at the intensity of our sex, the feelings of my body. We moved as one, breathing as if we were athletes in a race, supremely excited, mouths finding mouths, until we all came again.

The night left me sore and bruised. The two of them had threatened to split me open. Finally, I left them together and went to my own room. I woke early and jumped in the pool.

Then, slowly, I made my way to Kyle's bedroom. Now, instead of Dugan in my room, it was my guest who ended up in the master bedroom. I stood at the door, not wanting to disturb them, listening to hear if they were awake. I heard nothing so I went to fix breakfast. An hour later, I went back again. Now I heard bathroom sounds.

I knocked and opened the door. Kyle was still in bed, asleep. The door to the bathroom was open and I could see Ben was in the shower. I quietly walked across the room, went into the bathroom and closed the door. I stood there, watching Ben through the steamy glass, rinsing himself. When he was finished and opened the door, I tossed him a towel. He grinned sheepishly and immediately started drying his cock and balls.

"First things first?" I asked, approaching him.

"Just getting it ready for you."

"It doesn't look like it needs any help – "

As I slid it into my mouth, Ben said, "God, you two guys are incredible. I've never seen any two people so hungry for dick."

I slid it out and smiled. "When it's this dick, who wouldn't be hungry all the time?"

. . .

Jay had a limo come out and pick us up. Catherine Campbell, who had starred with Kyle in "El Dorado," was his date for the evening and brought her make-up girl along, who was delighted with Ben. Pamela was happy to be my "date" and when she got into the car, Kyle opened the champagne and they all drank to my becoming a movie star. All I wanted to do was get it over with. After smoking all day and getting fucked repeatedly by Ben and Kyle, I was exhausted.

But Ben was having fun. "I feel free here. I don't really feel as free in New York. Out here, you don't need to worry about what color is in this year."

"Green," Kyle said, "the color that's always in out here. The color of money."

At the theater, the music came up, then the titles. My name, huge, on the screen. Kyle squeezed my hand. Pamela, sitting on the other side me, did too.

"A tale of alien abduction."

I didn't think I would enjoy the movie, seeing it all the way through, but I did. I kept thinking of how much trouble every effect was, how I had to do things without any props because the props were all put in later. It got to the point that I felt I was appearing in a cartoon. Still, the audience liked it and Jay seemed pleased, gliding about the theater smiling, thanking everyone for coming.

It was an unbearably warm, muggy evening. The room at the Beverly Hilton was crowded with people, making it even more uncomfortable.

They were all enjoying themselves in their own way and Pamela and I sat at a special table with Bud and Jay, who had brought a couple of starlets along as their dates. If I weren't feeling so sick, I'd have found it all very funny. I was anxious when Bud walked in, fearful of Kyle's reaction, but he was too preoccupied with Ben to even look our way. I nodded from time to time in their direction while my attention had to be given to Bud, who was in a dark mood, with Kyle in the room. It was the first time Bud had actually seen him, other than rushing through the house the day he was swimming in the pool. And now with Kyle just across a crowded room with Ben at his side, Bud wanted to know, "What's going on?" I smiled. "Just a friend." As the waiters plied him with more wine, he became ever moodier and he said all he wanted to do was leave.

The wine continued to flow into my glass as well and I became first giddy and then dizzy.

As the heat grew more intense, the candles leaped before me and I was dimly conscious of Bud mumbling something in my ear. I loosened my collar but there was no coolness, just moist, hot air hit my skin. I felt even more dizzy and felt myself gradually slipping away. Bud took me by the arm and, after making my apologies to everybody at our table and getting Jay to agree to see all the girls home, he led me out into the main room and then to the parking garage through the back entrance, saying there were photographers in front of the place, watching the limos.

He sat me down on the ground while the valet got his car and we sped away into the hot night.

The next morning I awoke with my first real hangover. Every time I blinked my head ached. Every inch of me was in pain. And to make matters worse, I was not at Bird's Eye. Bud had stopped at the first motel he came to. I staggered to my feet and fell back down, then tried again. I could hear the shower, Bud was awake. I went into the bathroom and splashed cold water on my face. He pushed the shower curtain back and said, "Well, still alive I see."

"Oh, shit," I moaned, and went back to bed. The next thing I remember, Bud was massaging my back, then my arms, my legs and ending up at my ass. Sex was the last thing on my mind but when he started sucking on me, shoving his tongue deeply into my ass, I got an erection. My head was pounding but what he was doing was so pleasurable I just let him continue. It had been weeks since we had been together, yet it seemed as if we had never parted. My limbs seemed to melt away entirely under the pressure of his fingers.

He moved rhythmically in time with my own motions and I tightened and lifted my ass when I felt a quickening of his thrusting, the signal of his coming. I reached back with my fingers to grasp it, to keep the big one in me as long as possible. I rose finding myself dizzy in another way, hungry for food, and we went to a nearby restaurant where I made short work of steak and eggs, juice, two sticky buns, and coffee.

Going back out into the sultry air, dressed in only the pants of the tuxedo and the white ruffled shirt, I thought I was going to get sick again, but I revived when I was safely back in the cool motel room. I dropped onto the bed and Bud joined me, holding me, kissing me, until I fell asleep.

Later, rather than drive me all the way out to Malibu, Bud called the limo service. I told him not to check out of the motel because I might have to come back there after Kyle had thrown me out of the house for being abducted, not by aliens, but by the world's greatest director. Bud laughed. "I may be thrown out too, remember. I also promised not to see you any more."

When I arrived at Bird's Eye, Ben and Kyle were in the pool, swimming and horsing around. They were both nude. Ben saw me first. "Hey, look who's here!"

"What the hell happened to you? I've been worried sick," Kyle said, lifting himself out of the pool. He had an erection.

"It looks like it."

He took me in his arms. "Oh, baby, you don't look too good."

"I don't feel too good."

"Come into the pool. It'll do you good."

What really did me good was smoking a joint and then getting fucked by the both of them. We did it right out on the terrace. Kyle was first, then Ben. Then Ben fucking Kyle, Kyle fucking me. Then me fucking Kyle while Ben was fucking me. It was electric. We finished in Kyle's bed and I feel asleep.

When I awoke it was after midnight and there was no one in the house. The Corvette was gone. In my own room, I went back to sleep. They were big boys, they could take care of themselves.

"I have to get back," Ben said the next morning, joining me in my room for coffee. "I'm helping Adams with a show of his work. One of your pictures is in it. One of the ones he did for the *Interview* layout that they didn't publish."

"My ass shot?" I asked.

He nodded. "But don't worry; he's a great photographer and it's laid back. I want to be as good as he is one day."

He looked straight and clearly into my eyes. "I asked him once what he tried to do with his work."

"And?"

"Well, he said he tried to photograph the space between who someone is and who they think they are."

"Did he do that with my ass?"

He laughed. "Yes."

"And who do I think I am, I wonder?"

"Well, now you're Bobby Richards the movie star. Have you seen the reviews?"

I suddenly realized I hadn't read the newspapers or watched television since the premiere. Jay had a stack of newspapers delivered and Ben had opened them all to the coverage on the opening of "Space Travellers." My picture was in every newspaper, along with one or two of the aliens. There were also some pictures of the crowds; the movie had opened big in New York and Los Angeles with lines stretching around the block.

The reviews were equally incredible. I was hardly the star of the movie, the special effects were, but every notice was a decent one. My favorite was the *Times*' critic, saying my role was "disarmingly played."

I was thrilled. I leapt into Ben's arms and he began kissing me, deeply, with great passion.

"Where did you go last night?" I said, finally settling into his arms.

"A couple of clubs. But Kyle can't handle all that shit," Ben said. "In New York, you can just get a cab and go home, but here, well, it's scary. You have to drive everywhere and he almost killed us. I ended up driving."

"I know. I worry about him, but what can I do?"

Ben shrugged. "He'll work himself out of it. I think he was a bit shaken up when he saw you on the big screen. I was too. You are a *real* movie star, you know that? Nobody can take their eyes off you, even with all that shit going on around you."

"I don't get it, but maybe I'm not supposed to."

Ben smiled. "Yeah, maybe it's better you don't. Just stay the way you are."

"What I'd like is for you to stay the way you are, right here."

"I wish I could, but I have to get back."

"Today?"

He nodded.

I reached for his cock. It was hard again.

He lifted me up and slid it into me. As I bounced up and down on it, I felt incredibly silly. I began giggling. I was suddenly the most famous young actor in the world. And here I was sitting in Ben's lap, his mammoth cock filling me, in my little bedroom at Bird's Eye, with my lover, really the brightest star in the world, in his own bed, passed out again.

As Ben was finishing, Kyle walked into the bedroom. He stood there, not saying anything, for the longest time.
I didn't say anything either, just watched him watching us, stroking his cock. Ben had wanted to finish with me on my back, so he rolled me over and was slamming his cock into me, my legs wrapped around his upper torso, locked in his embrace.
After a while I closed my eyes; I couldn't look at Kyle any longer, at what I sensed was sadness in his eyes, even as he was getting off watching us. I want him to accept the fact that I love sex as much as he does, but I am beginning to doubt he ever will.

Now Kyle says he has to go back to New York right away and he has decided to go back on the same plane with Ben.
"I want to give you some space, to work things out with Logan," he says slamming shut his suitcase.
"There's nothing to work out," I say. "It's over." I try to embrace him. He moves away, lugging his suitcase and his guitar.
"That's what you said before. It's always over and then it begins again."
"He was just helping me out. I passed out." I am following at his heels like an obedient dog. I want him to listen to me. Just once.
"Yeah, I know. It was pretty embarrassing."
"More to me than anybody. I just can't drink."
"Well, I gotta go."
Kyle sends for a limo to take them to L.A.X. I would rather not see them off so I make my goodbyes at the front door.
Ben wishes me good luck, gives me a little kiss, leaves me alone with Kyle. Kyle takes me in his arms and hugs me to him. We kiss. A short kiss. He tries to pull away but I won't let him. I hug him and say, "Don't stay too long." But he isn't listening.

° . .

Slowly I make my way back to my bedroom. The late afternoon sun shimmers on the pool as I pass it and I decide to take a swim. Entering the bedroom, I step over the litter of newspapers, close my eyes to the mess on the bed, the filth and stench of Ben and me fucking, the smell of spent sperm. I start to tug off my jeans and look at myself reflected in the mirror. Once I am naked, I step closer to the mirror, my cock in my hand. I have had more sex over the past few hours than I have ever had yet I'm still hungry. I am starved for sex! But my lover has gone off with Ben, Bud is at home with his wife, Sam and Jay are both home with their wives, and Mac is home with Kevin. Martin has his chauffeur. Steve Sommers has his boys in the bathroom. Ned's probably on his treadmill. Everybody I know is occupied. I am alone.

I stroke my cock, rising as it always does. I turn to look at my profile. I'm not so bad. Little, but okay-looking. My eyes drift down, to the newspapers reflected in the mirror. They all have my picture in them, as part of the biggest grossing movie of the year (maybe, somebody said, of all time). They are going to do a poster of me. I'm on the cover of every teenage fan magazine. I am about to jump naked in the pool at Bird's Eye, in Malibu. My red Porsche is waiting for me in the garage, ready to take me wherever I want to go. Yeah, I'm alone, but I'm not doing too badly. I let go of my cock and step back, to look at myself again. And I am cute. I really am. Even my ass is getting to look good. Maybe from so much exercise.

No, I tell myself, I won't jack-off now. I'll take a swim and then go shopping – shopping for sex.

. . .

"Hi, Kyle," the hustler says, bending over, looking into the interior of the car. I liked his jeans with the bulging crotch and when I slowed down he waved. I'm in the Corvette. I wanted to have the top down, to feel the wind in my hair, and I can't afford another ticket driving the Porsche. This is much less conspicuous, except, I now find, here on the boulevard of boys for rent. I smoked a joint, ate a big steak dinner, put on my new green Army fatigues I found in the children's department that fit really tight in the crotch. I wanted to be ready if I found any sex. Now, looking at the size of this kid's basket, I've found a gold mine, but it seems Kyle's been here before me.

"Oh," the kid says when he sees me. "I thought – "

"Kyle's out of town. I'm using his car."

He snickers. "Hey, man, you sure you didn't steal it from him?"

"Of course not."

"Been known to happen to him I hear. More'n once."

"I wouldn't know. I only just met him."

"And he gives you this car to drive?"

"Shows you how good I am at what I do."

He blinks, looks right, then left. "Hey, let's not stand here talkin'."

"Get in."

So now I know. I can't go cruising the boulevards but it's perfectly all right for Kyle. He can even get robbed, doesn't matter. He's entitled. I now decide he deserves whatever he gets. And obviously, one of the things he's been getting is this pimply-faced kid with the incredible basket. I would guess more than once. The stud knows the car, knows Kyle's name. His name his Howie. Mine's Richie, for the moment anyhow.

"We goin' to the apartment?" he asks, adjusting his jeans to show off what he's got.

"Yes."

"Kyle there?"

"No."

"He leave any pot there?"

"Of course. But just a little."

"Unless he has a party, man, and then there's more shit that you can shake a stick at."

My hand drops over his bulge. "I bet you did a lotta shakin" of *this* stick at his party."

He chuckles. "Yeah. Kyle really gets off on it."

"I'll bet." My fingers glide along the full extent of it, now I would guess fully erect. "How long have you been doing this?"

"Just a couple of months. I came in from Texas."

I rub the head of it. Huge head. He squirms a little. "Oh? Where in Texas?" I ask.

"Dallas. I was in Dallas awhile on my way here. I'm from Mississippi."

"If it's hurting you in those jeans, why don't you take it out."

"No, I'll wait till we get to the apartment. It's only a few more minutes."

I glance at his face as we pass a well-lit intersection. I guess he is only a couple of years older than me. Tall, skinny, homely really. But he knows how to advertise what is probably his only physical asset. As I massage the beast under the cloth, a spot of pre-cum forms on his pant leg.

So often in the past I had wanted to drive through the garage under the apartment building to see if the Corvette was parked there, but I feared Kyle would be either coming or going and it would upset him that I was checking up on him. Now I know things were even worse than I had imagined. Parties? This kid had been to one of Kyle's parties? A party without me?

The trip up to the apartment in the elevator is agonizing. I don't like this person at all. He is the worst of the street trash. In the harsh light, a vaguely criminal look hangs over him like a pall. He smells fowl. His clothes are filthy. Now I don't even care what he has between his legs, but when the elevator door opens and he gets out first and knows exactly which way to go, I decide I've come this far, I've got to go through with it. If Kyle can take it, I can.

"How did you meet Kyle?" I ask, unlocking the door.

"Oh, he was cruisin' one night and I was hangin' with a guy I know, Travis, and he pointed out the 'Vette. Travis told me who he was. I didn't believe him until Kyle slowed down and talked to us and then he invited us back here. After we'd been here awhile, he told Travis to call some more guys so it ended up we had at least ten here; maybe more, I lost count."

After switching on the lights, I see the place is a mess. It appears as if Kyle's been having a lot of parties of ten (or more) in here.

"Yeah," Howie goes on, "The party lasted two days. Two fuckin' days man! Kyle had to send Travis out to get more drugs. Shit, it could've gone on forever, but finally, just like that, he says, 'Everybody out!' He tells guys to stop fucking! 'Out! Get outta here!'"

"That doesn't sound like him – " I say, distracted now by the mess. I begin picking up ashtrays and glasses and empty beer bottles.

"Yeah, he said he had an important thing he had to do, as if we weren't important. But, shit, he'd never say that to you – " Howie says, grabbing me from behind when I bend over to pick up an empty bourbon bottle.

"Oh, why?"

He takes my asscheeks in both hands and squeezes them. "You know."

I pull away, go into the kitchen, which is disaster. I do some quick calculation. The cleaning people come here on Tuesdays. That means this party, this orgy, happened after that. Yes, Kyle had an important thing he had to do – he had to go to my premiere. He loves me after all. Otherwise, he'd probably still be here. Now I have an important thing to do: I've got to get rid of this kid named Howie. I turn and there he is, filling the doorway of the kitchen, pants unzipped, cock hanging out.

"Well?" he asks, stroking it.

I switch off the light. He is now silhouetted by the lights from the living room. He seems to glow; he actually looks rather good as long as the light is dim enough.

"Well what?" I ask, staring at his cock.

"Well, it's ready for ya – "

His accent isn't Southern, isn't north Texas, isn't anything. He, I decide, isn't anything. I can live without it.

"I've really gotta be going," I say.

"Going? We just got here."

"I just came here to check out the damage."

"What does that mean?" he asks, his voice rising in anger.

"Nothing personal. I just haven't been here for awhile. I wanted to see what needed to be done."

"This – " he strokes it. "This needs to be done. For starters."

"I don't think so."

He lurches forward, grabs me by the arms and pushes me to my knees on the floor. "You little shit, suck it!"

I shake my head. He moves closer, the cock in my face. It stinks of sweat, piss and cum.

"Get that outta my face."

"Open your goddam mouth – " He pushes my head forward and the cock careens off my cheek.

My nose in his balls, I begin to cough. "Maybe if you took a shower first - " I manage to gurgle.

"Shower shit. You take it. Take it now." he says, tugging at my hair, forcing my head back, then slamming it back into his crotch.

Still my lips remain closed, my eyes shut. He yanks me by the hair and I fall back, my head crashing against the tile. I scramble to get up and he pushes me down. He mounts me, straddling my chest, the huge penis still erect, more stinking than ever as pre-cum oozes from the head. He lifts my head up and slams the cock back at my mouth again. I shake my head and soon he is pounding my head against the floor. I am stunned. I haven't been attacked like this since I was very young. Instinctively I reach up and seize his arms, push him away, finding more strength than I thought I had because he falls away, crashing into the cabinets. But it is a momentary release because he is up and soon on top of me, pinning me to the floor with his knees, his hands again pulling my hair. His grip is sure and hurting. I cry out. Tears come.

"Suck it, goddam it!" he screams, bringing my mouth to the head of it.

There is no sense fighting it, I decide, opening my mouth, letting him shove it in. He lets go of my hair and lifts himself up. Palms flat on the floor, he starts doing push-ups over my face.

"Yeah, that's more like it. Suck it like Kyle did. Take it deep! Suck it!"

I had forgotten about Kyle. Kyle sucking this, like this? No, I don't even want to think about it. I reach up, grab his buttocks trying to maneuver to a better, less painful angle.

"Oh, yeah, ya love it. Ya love it," he cries, mistaking my participation for hunger. "I knew you'd love it!"

He fucks my face for what seems like an eternity, then finally pulls out and rolls over. "Yeah, you're hot, man," he says, "and now you want it up that little butt don't ya?"

"Is that what Kyle did?"

"Yeah. He had up there twice, one time with another dick along with it. Couldn't fucking believe it."

"Neither can I."

"Hey, what are you to him anyhow?"

"I'm sorta the janitor. I clean up his messes. Here and at the ocean."

"Hey, I'd love to see that place. Travis says Kyle never takes anybody there."

"No. Because I'm there. There's a lot of cleaning up to do there."

"Cool. But, shit, if I had you there, I wouldn't come here." He reaches over and rubs the saliva away from my chin. Suddenly he's gentle, kind. "You do suck a mean dick." He brings his hand to the back of my head and draws me into him. Our kiss is long and when he releases me he says, "That's more like it. Now I'm gonna fuck the shit outta ya."

He's cradling me in his arms and he lifts me up and carries me into the bedroom, kicking a few beer bottles away as he nears the doorway.

The bed has been stripped and I recognize some of Kyle's clothes strewn about.

"You get ready," he says, dropping me onto the bed. "I'll take that fuckin' shower." He strokes my leg, pats my ass.

"Okay," I say, practically speechless with the change in him. But one thing I don't need to do is get ready to be fucked. What I need is a rest from it. But then, why not?

"I want you to get your shittin' money's worth," he says, squeezing his cock.

"Okay." I'm glad now I packed some fifties in my sneakers, which I kick off and hide under the bed.

I find some pillows and toss them on the bed. When I'm naked, I lie on my stomach in the middle of the bed, hugging the pillows to my stomach. I am trying to imagine ten guys fucking in this room when Howie comes back into the room drying himself. Nude, he is nothing to speak of – he needs to spend some hours at a gym – but there can be no denying he is blessed with a cock from heaven. It is nearly as big as Ben's. Even limp it must measure eight inches. He presents it to my mouth again and now, fresh, long and hard, I think I could suck it all night. But he has other things in mind. He moves away, goes to the bathroom and returns with a jar of Vaseline. Slowly he coats the cock and then mounts me. I lift up to meet the thrust as it enters me. All the fucking over the past few days has prepared for it so it goes in without effort, all the way to base in one luxurious slide. Palms flat on the mattress, now he does push-ups over my ass, kissing the top of my head as he bangs me. I clutch the pillows and close my eyes. Yes, I decide, Kyle would have wanted this one. And more than once. Maybe next time we can have him together.

The fuck is quick and efficient, in a tough street whore's way, and I get off but he does not. When I go to the kitchen and dig the pot out of the secret place in the freezer, Howie is right behind me.
"Shit man," he says, "that's not even enough for one joint."
"I know. I think it's time we paid a visit to somebody."

We park in Frank's driveway and walk around the fence to the front door. I ring the bell. It takes several moments but finally a voice is saying, "Who's there?"
"Kyle's friend. Richards."
"Bring the money you owe me?"
"Yeah, sort of."
"How about the aliens, you bring them with you too?"
I chuckle. Frank has seen my movie, or at least seen the newspapers. Howie obviously has not and shrugs. "Only one," I say, looking at him.
There is much unlocking and sliding of dead bolts before he finally opens the door. Kyle was honest: he is ugly, and skinny. And I know Kyle wouldn't lie about the big dick. He's wearing his bathrobe. He grins.
"It's about time – but who's this?" he asks pointing to Howie.
"The alien: Howie."
"He's an alien, all right. I don't want him in my house." He starts shoving Howie back towards the door. Howie is stunned and doesn't react immediately.
"Wait, he's okay." I say.
"I don't want you in my house either," Frank says, grabbing me by the arm and shoving me towards Howie. "All this time Kyle kept tellin' me I couldn't meet you, that you had class, that you were different. Different shit, you're worse than he is. Bringing this piece of garbage in my house."
"Who you callin' garbage?" Howie says, a terrible wildness overtaking him.

Frank is as skinny as Howie but taller, older, and surprisingly swift. He blocks Howie's punch and lands one of his own into Howie's gut. I tug at Frank's arm. "Stop, he's okay, honest. He just needs a little cleaning up. And he's got a big dick."

He has Howie pushed against the door, restraining him. "Is that what you like too?" he asks me.

"I'm beginning to – " I rub his arm gently. "I know you have one, too. That's why I'm here."

Frank steps back. "Shit, I sure could use a good blowjob right now. Kyle hasn't been here for two weeks."

"I promised Howie a joint and Kyle didn't leave anything at the apartment. Can we have one first?"

"Cash first. I need some cash first."

I hand him two fifties from my back pocket. My other cash is still in my sneaker.

"That'll help." He puts the cash in the pocket of his robe. "I thought for a minute you were goin' to tell me to call Kyle's accountant. That fuckin' accountant! All he ever says is that I should get some fresh air and exercise. I tell him he can go fuck himself."

"I'll talk to him," I say, stepping towards him. Howie stays by the door. I motion to him to follow me.

"I think I'll just wait in the car. I ain't welcome here."

"It's okay, honest."

"Yeah," Frank says, "come over here, both of you." He moves over to the couch, upholstered in a putrid green in an otherwise fairly nondescript living room. On the coffee table is a oval mirror with a mound of cocaine on it. "Here," Frank goes on, "have a snort. On the house."

My agreeing to call Ned has altered Frank's mood – or maybe it was the offer of a blowjob, or both. I drop down on the couch next to him, take a straw and do a line. "Kyle doesn't let me do this," I say. "But I have sneaked some when he isn't looking."

"Careful, it's good shit," he says as I snort my way along a line that seems to run on forever.

Howie stands over the coffee table staring at the coke. I breath deeply and fall back into the cushions.

"Go ahead, help yourself," Frank says. "I'm sorry I got so carried away. I've had a hard night."

My hand slides across Frank's exposed thigh and between the folds of his robe. "How hard?" I ask as I lean into him.

"You don't waste any time. Just like Kyle. Always in a hurry."

He lets me part the robe and a cock to match Howie's is beginning to show some life. "Wow," I sigh, lifting it up as I lean over to take it between my lips. While Howie is cut and nearly white, Frank's is uncut and very dark. I slide my finger under the foreskin and nip it with my teeth. As I slide the foreskin back and begin sucking, I hear Howie snorting coke.

"Well," Frank says when I come up for air and am just nibbling on the head of it, "who's bigger, this kid or me?"

"I'm not sure."

"Let's measure."

Howie, kneeling on the other side of the coffee table, is still snorting; he smiles. "Okay, sure." He comes around to the other side of me and lets me take it out of his pants. Frank stands up so that I have them on the same level and I start to work Howie's up. It doesn't take much coaxing. Soon I've got both of them hard and they bring them together. Howie's is a bit longer, but Frank's this thicker. They are both incredible.

"Damn, I don't think I've ever seen a bigger one," Frank says, touching Howie. "Except once maybe in a porno flick."

"I'm going to do one of those," Howie says, smirking.

"Oh?" I say, looking up into his eyes. "A gay one?"

"I guess. Travis says they're the only ones that pay."

Frank laughs. "And they'll pay you a lot for that big dick. But I could never do all the other shit. I just like a blowjob. That's my thing."

He enjoys his *thing* as much as I do giving it to him. I suck both of them, going back and forth for awhile, then take both heads into my mouth at once. I'm going crazy with them.

"Well, my thing is fuckin'," Howie says. "C'mon, Richie, sit on it while you're suckin' Frank."

"Yeah!" Quickly out of my fatigues, I slowly squat over Howie, who is now seated on the couch. My ass is still moist from before so it isn't a difficult entry and I settle on top of him, letting it go in to the hilt, then I start bouncing up and down on it while I suck Frank, who is snorting more coke. We try other positions before we're done, ending up with Frank on his back on the couch, me over him, finishing him off while Howie fucks me to orgasm. If Kyle only knew what he was missing.

. . .

Months ago, Kyle's first disappearance lasted three days. When he finally returned, on a Sunday, I was floating on my raft in the pool, somehow thinking the sun's rays would heal my loneliness. He appeared at the edge of the pool, his hands on his hips, and just grinned at me.

My first thought was to ask him where he'd been but I had decided around the second day or so not to even acknowledge he'd been gone. I bit my lip and took off my sunglasses.

"Must be nice," he said.
"It could be nicer."
"Oh?"
"If you'd join me." I splashed water his way.

He did, stripping and jumping in nude, swimming over to where I was and grabbing me up in his arms. We kissed for a long time, at times violently. The fucking that followed that afternoon was more fun, more intense than any I could remember. I decided it wasn't such a bad thing after all if he stayed away for a couple of days; whatever he did, wherever he went, he was missing me – missing me so badly he couldn't get enough when he got home.

Later, as we had dinner, he brought it up himself: "I miss being on the road. I guess I just need to keep moving." He was trying to explain the absences, in his own way.

I nodded. "I understand." I did understand. Mac had explained it to me: "I have become superstitiously suspicious of the road," he said. "Look at what happened to this guy and that guy and how crazy they got. This is not a healthy thing. That was why the band that originally backed Kyle up stopped touring. They weren't learning from it, growing from it."

Now Kyle said, "I miss touring but I wouldn't want it all the time. Hell, I don't want anything *all* the time."

"I know." I looked away. I couldn't look at him when he was trying so hard to explain things to me. Things it seemed as if I could never understand if I had a million years to do it.

"I mean, you can analyze it to death."

"Then let's don't do that. Let's fuck. I want to fuck." Sex was something I *could* understand, that I didn't have to think about it. It made me feel good. All over. That's all I needed to know.

"That's my boy," he said, kissing me passionately. He was, I had to admit, the world's greatest kisser.

The fuck began in the dining room, on the floor, and continued into the music room and finally his bedroom. We took turns. He was, for once, matching me stroke for stroke, load for load. He missed me so terribly he kept saying all through it. And kissing me everywhere, even eating out my ass before he fucked it. It was so intense I thought he would end it all by eating me up, saving my penis for last. But he didn't: he came, in the wildest orgasm I could remember him having, sending spurt after spurt deep into my ass, and then, he fell asleep and I lay quietly for nearly an hour listening to him snore before I went to my bedroom. It was the best fuck we had since the beginning. I decided that if that was the kind of fuck we could have if he went away for a few days, then perhaps it wasn't so bad after all. And, for a time, Sundays lost their sadness.

FIFTEEN

The Next Day
    Bud has come for lunch. Actually, he came before lunch. Then it was my turn. He loves it when I bind him up with leather and fuck him from behind. He watches us in the mirror. He came again while I was doing it today, then finished by taking my cum in his mouth.
    Now we are lying in bed recovering. When he called he said his wife had let him back after the premiere. He had to promise never to see me again. Again. But he said when he made the promise he knew he couldn't keep it. I told him I was glad.

    And now, finally, over lunch, he breaks the news: he's starting a new movie, filming in Italy.
    "I don't want to do another hardware picture right now," he says. "This'll be a costume epic, lots of people running around in togas."
    "No part for a little boy?"
    "Maybe as an extra, in the crowd as the legions pass by."
    I chuckle. "No, I've done crowd scenes."
    Bud smiles. "But I do want you come with me to scout the locations. Just for a week. And we could stop off in London for the premiere of 'Space Travellers.' What do you say?"
    "Italy? I don't know the language. "
    "All you need is fifty words. That'll see you through. And I'll be there."
    "I don't know – "
    "It's in your contract you are to promote the picture. I'm going to sue you if you don't at least go to London for the premiere."
    I chuckle. "Okay. I don't want to be sued." I stand up, go over to him, kiss him. "No, I just want to be fucked."

We go back to bed and he fucks me again. He's happy I am going with him – after all, I did sign a contract. I think. When he's finished, I snuggle into the crook of his arm. "Okay, I'll go to Italy." I take his big cock, now lying limp against his thigh, in my hand and squeeze it. "Provided I can have this every night."

"And in the morning too, if you want it."

"I'll take it whenever I can get it."

He squeezes my cock. "But I want this, too, you know. I can't seem to get enough of it."

I take his cock in my mouth again, as deep as I can, massaging his thighs as I suck. He won't come again, he just did, but this will give him something to remember until Italy.

And he gets into the sixty-nine position and we stay like that, sucking, and licking and kissing, until I come again. He goes crazy when I come, moaning and groaning, not wanting to give it up. But he has to. His wife will wonder. "God you taste good," he says, trying to arouse me again.

But now my mind is on travel. Air travel. Far, far away. "Would I have to change planes in New York?" I ask.

He draws back, looks into my eyes. "Can't forget him?"

I look away and shake my head. No matter what, there is always Kyle. Always.

"If you want to fly to New York first, that's okay with me."

"No. Afterward." I hug Bud. "I think on the way back."

Two Weeks Later

When you travel with Bud Logan you may travel first class but you also don't get a moment to catch your breath. He's been everywhere, done everything, so all he did was point out the sights, so that I could go there and take tours when I came to the city again. London was just a blur: "There's Buckingham Palace. There's Westminster Abbey. There's Harrods."

At Harrods I made him stop the limousine. I *was* going shopping whether he liked it or not. I would take a cab back to the hotel. "But we have to travel light," he protested. So I had everything sent back to Bird's Eye.

Bud helped me through my the press conference. We did it together, the star of the movie and the director, facing the news cameras, fielding the questions. Jay's publicist in London, Harry

Spencer, made everything go smoothly, including the sleeping arrangements. We had a two-bedroom suite at the Dorchester; Jay must have told him we wouldn't mind sharing the accommodations.

Publicity means having to be interviewed and mostly all I had to deal with was the teen magazine editors, who want to believe everything. I have developed a technique, answering most questions with a spaced-out, "Wow! Yeah?" "Cleverly managed," one editor wrote after sitting with me for twenty minutes in a coffee shop in Beverly Hills.

Harry had lined up a series of interviews in a suite at the Hilton. Everybody was obsessive about my dreams. Each time I considered the question as though I never had thought about it before.

The first interview was recorded, for radio, to be played later. The interviewer was a fat, funny-looking man with red hair. At one point, I interrupted him: "Wow! You have great socks." He was so flustered, he looked down at his feet, to see if perhaps he made a mistake when he got dressed that morning. "It's nice to see red socks with a blue suit and a white tie," I said. "Did you wear that in our honor." He just grinned. At the end of the interview, they asked me to do a promotion for the interview that will appear on the station. But Bud said he'd do it, introducing me to the British public as "the world's biggest new star," high praise from the world's biggest director, in more ways than one.

The second interview was for a teen fan magazine in America that had done countless stories on me before. It was planned before we left Hollywood that having me in London would be a good angle for a new story. They set up their cameras and wanted me to pose in a cap with the magazine's logo on it. I put on the cap and the interviewer, a pretty girl, got in the picture with me. They gave me a T-shirt with the logo on it, in case I wanted to wear it some time, and have my picture taken in it. "Thanks." They asked me if they could follow me around London and take my picture at some landmarks. "Okay," I said. At last, I figured, I could actually see something of the city.

The girl asked, "Who is your favorite film actor?"

"Kyle Cartwright." Not Brando, not De Niro. Harry shook his head.

"He hasn't made a movie in so long," the girl said. "I wonder what he's doing."

"So do I."

The inevitable came up: "Who are you dating?"

"It's like people think you have more choices when you're famous, but actually it really limits you.

"I'm a natural loner. But it's something I'm working on. I think my ultimate lover will be like being alone. It will be so comfortable, I won't have a problem sleeping or feel I have to entertain them or worry about them understanding me. I hope. My biggest insecurity is my body; being little, I have a complex. But I do have a big love." That, she said, would be her headline: "The Boy With the Big Love." And they took my picture with Big Ben behind me.

The third interview was for a newspaper. The reporter, a slim guy who did the entertainment column, couldn't keep his eyes off my crotch. Where do I live, what do I do when I'm not working, what do I eat?

"I hike in the hills, go to the beach. I drive my Porsche. I go to the health food store. I cook."

"And at night?"

"I don't party much. Mostly, I watch TV just like anybody else. I love TV."

On our way out, Harry took us to the coffee shop. He wanted to talk to me a minute.

"You can't keep bringing Kyle up."

"Why not?"

"It's just not smart. There's so much talk already. Your favorite actor! Jesus Christ!"

"They didn't ask me who my favorite singer was – "

"You have to stop being so honest. One of these days – "

We were interrupted by a man with gray hair and too much of a suntan, wearing a strangely-colored leather jacket featuring flags of the world. His name was Roger and he had missed the press conference. He wanted to talk to me about being on his radio show. He kept on and on, sweat breaking out on his brow, that he wanted to have his picture taken with me, if he could just find a photographer.

"Okay," I said.

As he wandered off, Harry said, "When he started to perspire, I thought he was going to pull a knife."

The man returned with a tourist in tow, had her take the picture, bought the film from her. I smiled. "Where *did* you get that jacket?"

"In America. San Francisco," he said, running his hand across a sleeve. "Do you like it? I'll get you one – "

"Thanks. Send it to Harry. He'll see that I get it."

The man left, promising to meet us outside the restaurant, in the lobby, in five minutes. I asked the waiter, "Is there a back way outta here?"

. . .

The frantic pace continued in Rome, until the second day, when Bud announced he was going with some of the production people into the Northern part of Italy to scout locations. He thought it best if I just stayed in Rome. He would be gone two nights. He said he was going to miss me terribly.

I didn't have the heart to tell him I was glad he was going; it would give my ass a chance to rest. I had never been with Bud every single night and it seemed as if he wanted sex even more than I did. I suddenly realized how it was possible that he could leave my bed and go home and fuck his wife. And I thought *I* was horny all the time.

I was alone in Rome. I couldn't believe it. It was a warm, bright day. I wandered around shopping, cruising, thoroughly enjoying myself. After dinner, I found myself in the Villa Borghese when a fog rolled in. I was tempted by a few of the hustlers, imagined sucking every one of them, but, with the fog closing in, I decided to return to the hotel. I thought I knew the way but I ended up in a deserted alley. I suddenly became aware that someone else was there. In the yellow light of the street lamps I saw a tall figure standing next to a garden gate. As the figure moved toward me, I could see it was a youth, perhaps even younger than me. He hesitated, then came up to me. "*Buona sera*," he said softly.

I now remembered him, passing time with other pretty kids in the gardens of the Villa Borghese. He had enormous eyes but that was not what attracted me. His white cotton sailor pants clung to a basket that was beyond belief. I looked down to check it out once again. It was a bulge begging to be touched and as I reached out to do just that, he turned his back and hurried away. I followed him. As he walked, his buns swayed from side to side and it was so tempting, so mesmerizing, that I quickened my pace and ended up only two steps behind him.

He stopped suddenly and went into another alley. I stood still, watching him. His hand fell and began to slide down his leg. He traced the outline of the bulge, then opened his fingers and slid his hand back up his body, stopping at his chest. He squeezed his tits as if he was offering them to me. I stepped toward him but, when I was within two feet of him, he brushed by me and returned to the street. I followed him again. He stopped under a lamppost and waited for me. Again when I was close, he continued on his way. As I followed, he turned and nodded, continuing to keep my interest. We walked along the Via Marguta, keeping our distance. When he arrived at a pizzeria, he knew some boys there and greeted them noisily. I passed the place but waited just beyond. Finally, he left his noisy friends and crossed the street, with me in hot pursuit. Soon he was opening a gate and slipping inside. When I got to the gate, he peeked out, looked both ways, and then grabbed my hand and pulled me into the yard. He led me to a large open room and up some white stone steps to a door. He pulled a key from his pocket and opened it. He let me in, then locked the door behind us. We had not said a single word to each other since his first greeting to me. I started to say something but he put his fingers to my lips. "*Sh-h-h. Silenzo!*" he whispered.

A lamp from the street was our only light. As my eyes adjusted to the dimness, I could make out a large bed standing against the wall opposite the window, a long wardrobe with heavy doors against another wall, and a wash stand. When I sat on the bed, the mattress creaked. He leaned over and brought his lips to mine. We kept our eyes open as we kissed. His mouth was on mine – full, soft, sweet beyond description. I was astounded that his mouth alone could bring me to such a state of excitement. I melted against him. His eyes were breathtaking, dark pools, reflecting the yellow light. He kissed me all over my face and kept on kissing me, even as he undressed me. When I was naked, he began sliding his tongue across every inch of my skin, ending at my cock. I was so excited I came the moment he brought his mouth to it. He held my cock and kissed it for a few minutes and then stood up. I lay on the bed watching as he undid the buttons of his tight cotton pants and stepped from them. He tossed his T-shirt away and stood before me stroking his cock. I guessed it was at least as long as Bud's, but slender, snake-like. As hurting as I was back there, I wanted it in my ass in the worst way. He pulled the foreskin all the way back to expose the head and pre-cum dripped from it. I got to my knees on the bed and reached for it, but he stepped back, teasing me. He kept stroking it and when it was finally stiff it was longer than Bud's. It wasn't as long as Ben's but still it was in the running. I nearly fell off the end of the bed trying to get to it. He stifled his laughter and brought my mouth and his cock together. On his face was a slight smile but his eyes were wide and full with desire.

In bed, my feet wound up at his neck and I tried not to come too quickly as he began his vigorous thrusting.

His expert sucking and fucking of me made me feel inexperienced. How could a boy, a boy younger than me, be so talented. Then I realized that maybe there were many boys like me who had been exposed to sex early. I met men at the hotel; perhaps he met his in the streets of Rome. Perhaps he was a hustler after all, and the reason he played such a game with me was because I was not just another number but somebody he sensed was somehow kin. We kissed and he was like no one else I had ever kissed. I couldn't figure out exactly what it was. It was as if he had fallen from another planet where they never did it and here he was doing it with this little American kid. My jaw ached after awhile, he just didn't want to stop. Even after he'd come, he kept on kissing me.

As the hours passed, we lay entwined, shifting slightly occasionally drowsing, waking and drowsing again. Our lips brushed and clung in countless kisses. Our tongues touched, then flickered over eyelids, earlobes, over warm flesh. Toes caressed toes. Our hands cupped and fondled, our greedy mouths sucked. I brought my fingertips to stroke his erection and he came again. My fingers clutching his cock, wet with his cum, I fell asleep at once.

At dawn, I watched his angelic face sleeping. In the fresh light he appeared to be barely a teenager, I thought, yet a man in every way. Cuddling close to him, I returned to sleep again, only to awake to find him watching me. Suddenly, he was kissing me again, then lifting my legs over his shoulders, entering me. I gasped with the pain as he slid it all the way in. As my mind raced in circles, he pulled me to him and his eyes danced with playfulness as he fucked me. After awhile, he began moving in slow motion, to prolong it, the silence broken only by my whispered gasps as each thrust hit the mark, and then his groaning as he quickened his pace and came again. He collapsed next to me, kissing my shoulder. Once more the room was still.

I wanted to talk to him, to tell him how much I had enjoyed the night, but he put his finger to my lips. "Sh-h-h." He raised himself on one elbow and looked down at my face, tracing his finger along my cheek and across my lips. "*Tesoro,*" he said.

Having no idea what he was saying, I nodded. "*Tesoro.*"

Suddenly, there was a light knock on the door.

"*Vene, Mamma, vene!*" he called out.

I pulled the sheet over my nakedness and pretended to be asleep. The door opened and closed. I opened my eyes slightly to see his dark-haired mother, wearing a pink bathrobe, come into the room carrying a breakfast tray. "*Buon giorno, Giorgio,*" she whispered, setting the tray on an oblong table near the bed. Her son looked remarkably like her. She was a lovely woman of perhaps 35. She kissed her son on both cheeks, then poured two cups of coffee. I heard her whispering to Giorgio and leave the room.

I pretended I was startled awake by the click of the door shutting and when I turned to look at my young lover I found him sitting on the edge of the bed sipping his coffee. I rose up and put my arms around him and kissed him sloppily on the back of the neck.

"*Buon giorno, caro,*" he said. His voice was deep, seductive for someone so very young.

"*Buon giorno, Giorgio,*" I said, attempting the language.

I went over to the table and put some sugar in the coffee that had been poured and took one of the round rolls from a basket on the tray. I sat on a heavy wooden straight chair next to the table and ate my breakfast. I could not take my eyes off of him. With his black curls and big, beautiful eyes, he was an angel. He smiled as he finished his coffee and tossed back the sheet. His cock was erect again and he stroked it casually, stretching the foreskin.

I gazed at the splendid thin penis and grinned. I thought about the Italian words Bud had taught me and I cried out the only one that fit: "*Belissimo!*"

. . .

Bud came back from his trip looking tired and a bit sad. He met with the people financing the toga picture and told them they would have to increase the budget by at least five million. They said they'd have to go back to the banks. The project was put on hold. "It's okay," Bud says. "This always happens with these international projects. It's just as well. Jay called and said the people at 20th are so excited about the grosses for 'Space Travellers' they want me to start the sequel right away so it'll be in theaters by Christmas after next."

"*Right away?*"

"But we won't need you until after New Year's."

But *he* needs me right this minute. Although he is weary from his trip, he still can't wait to get me in bed. The man is invincible. So we begin in the living room of the suite, on the couch. When he enters me, his eagerness coupled with the rawness from being fucked so often by Giorgio causes me to cry out. He doesn't want to hurt me; I tell him to keep on. I know it won't be long before he's getting rid of two days' worth of not seeing me. When he does, it's probably the biggest orgasm of our trip. "Oh, Bobby, I love you," he cries as he slams it into me. He holds me in his arms, his cock still inside of me, and kisses me on the forehead..

"What does *tesoro* mean?" I ask.

Still panting, he thinks a moment. "Why?"

"I just heard it yesterday and I'm trying to, well, you know, get better acquainted with the Italians."

"Fast," he says. "*Too* fast."

Little does he know *how* fast.

SIXTEEN

A Week Later

I have stopped off in Manhattan on my way back from Rome to see Kyle but Jay hasn't seen him for several days. "I threw him out," Jay said. He started talking about it and ended up ranting and raving. I could tell he was miserable. Kyle – his "boy" Kyle – had truly disappointed him for the first time. "He trashed the place. I couldn't believe it. If my wife saw this mess, she'd die. It took a week to clean out the garbage." He shook his head sadly. "It's never going to be the same."

What also isn't the same is Ben's apartment. He's in the process of moving, he tells me over the phone, and everything is a mess; I can't come over there, but he'll stop by here later.

I tell him Jay's taking me to the Russian Tea Room for dinner but we'll be back by eleven.

Ben promises to be here.

"That's good," I tell him. "I have only tonight. I have to get back to California. They're doing a big photo spread on me in *Teen Dream* magazine. All I seem to do these days is pose for pictures."

"I wish I was shooting it."

"I do too. But you can do some shooting tonight – and I don't mean pool, either."

"I know what you mean. And I promise I'll be there by midnight at the latest."

I sigh. "Oh, I almost forgot," I lie. I have saved this for last. "Have you seen Kyle?"

"No. Not in a while," he says. Then he abruptly changes the subject. "Do you have your own room there?" he asks.

"Yes, of course."

But now it isn't as simple as I made it sound. Ben is waiting outside the building as Jay's limousine rolls up. Jay sees him and chuckles, "I've heard of groupies but this is a bit much."

"He is a bit much," I say, my eyes fixed on Ben's crotch.

Upstairs, Jay fixes us brandies and, after complaining that the cost of dinner was outrageous, that everything is up – oil prices, interest rates, inflation – everything except the grosses of his movies and his dick, he excuses himself. I try to explain to Ben that Jay is a very special person to both Kyle and me and he may wander into the library later.

"Kyle told me all about him when I was in Hollywood," Ben says.

"Then you won't mind if he just watches us?"

"It would be weird," he holds me close, kisses me on the tip of my nose. "But I've thought about you so much, I don't think *anything* could interfere with it."

And it doesn't. Jay is sitting across the room in the winged-back chair by the windows. We have turned on the radio to a classical station for Jay and put the lights out; there are only the lights from the surrounding skyscrapers to illuminate our sex. I thought for a while that Jay wouldn't come in, but he was only giving us time to be together, to get so far into it that it wouldn't really matter what happened around us. And he was right. I have missed Ben more than I thought. The bed has become a river of sweat. I am rocking with him, pushing my hips up to meet his, taking all of him and barely letting him go before moving back up for more, digging my fingers into his back. He groans in that deep, throaty voice of his, concentrating, moving his hips against me in his usual forceful way. I cannot get enough of this, the biggest cock I have ever known. After several days with Bud, one beautiful evening with Giorgio, and now this, I am on an incredible high. The only thing that would make it better would to have Kyle here.

As Jay approaches, we are fucking like a well-oiled machine, steady and strong. Our purpose is not orgasm, simply the pleasure of making love, of being together again. Jay sits on the edge of the bed and leans in to stroke my arm, caress my legs as they are wrapped around Ben. I reach out and touch Jay's penis, now as hard as it ever gets, and I jerk it gently until I hear him taking familiar short, wheezy breaths. Then his hand goes over mine and brings it back to Ben's shoulder. He kisses my hand just as Ben is coming. It is a strong orgasm; Ben grabs my buttocks, sending me higher on the bed and rises up to finish perched over me. He keeps it in me and jacks me off. When I am close, I call out for Jay, to tell him he can take it, take it all down his throat, but he has left the room.

SEVENTEEN

Two Days Later
There are phones all over Sommers' house in Bel-Air. One in the Jacuzzi, one floating on a raft in the middle of the pool, another under a waterproof cover in the shower, and one by every chaise. The pavilion has a seating area with speakers set into the floor, a changing area, powder room and outdoor shower. Steve says it was designed to resemble a Thai temple, all in a periwinkle color with salmon and turquoise. "I don't call this a pool house. It's my sanctuary. It's a very spiritual place."

"I can see that. I'll bet you spend a lot of time on your knees here," I say.

He smiles, but he's largely ignoring me, conducting much business by the pool. To his secretary, a small, skinny old woman, elegantly dressed, he waves, gestures, shouts, indicates by means of quick thumbs up or down which call he takes next, who should be put on hold, who he will call back. Finally he tells her to go home after she serves me a Coke and makes him another scotch and soda.

As much as I wanted to stay in New York, be fucked again (and maybe again and again) by Ben, and look for Kyle, I had to get back to Los Angeles. There was the *Teen Dream* layout and Mac called saying Sommers wanted to see me. He had a part for me in his new picture. "I can just imagine," I said to Mac, who told me to get my ass over here.

Now after taking a long swallow of this drink, he says while Kyle is "ebbing," I am "flowing."

"Girls get these crushes on pretty boys and they run riot, but as quickly as the hormones flow, they can ebb. The clock is ticking for both of you, but you're an actor, you can do other things. Kyle is a singer. There are a lot of singers."

"There are a lot of actors, too."

"Yes. But this business is a simple matter of timing, nothing more. Look at Travolta and 'Saturday Night Fever.' "

"Travolta?"

"'Grease,' boy, 'Grease.' And this new one, it's called 'Saturday Night Fever' and it's already in the can for Christmas. This will be big. B-I-G. And we're going to sail right along with it. It's like you and this space thing. You're timing is perfect too. You're hot." Draining his glass, he goes on, "But there is a price for everything. *Everything*."

He removes his fat wallet from a pocket in his terry cloth robe (he doesn't wear a caftan by the pool) and lays it on the table in front of me. "But I don't want you to think you have to do anything to get this part. Parts in my movies are not for sale." He taps his fingers, pudgy like sausages, on his wallet, which is roughly about where I think his heart is, and says, "But I *do* want you. I've wanted you from the first time I saw you. Now I insist on paying for it."

I chuckle. "I'm not for sale. You know that."

"Everything has a price."

"I don't know what mine is."

"That's what I figured. You know, when I can't buy something, I become obsessed by it. I want you more than I've ever wanted anyone. Do you believe me?"

"No."

He chuckles again, this time more guttural. "You're a smart little shit, I must say that. I didn't think you'd believe that, but it's true. From that first moment, in the pool house at Bird's Eye, I knew I would have to have you. One day."

"Why me? You can have anybody you want. Bigger, better than me, all of 'em."

"They may be bigger but they're not better. There's something about you that men like me just go crazy over."

"I'm sorry."

"No, I'm the one that's sorry. I guess I repulse you."

"Yes, you do," I say, pushing away from the table, standing up.

"Oh, yes, be mean to me, I love it." He reaches out for me as

I pass him.

I turn and look down at him. "I know you do. I met a man like you once back in Texas, same kind of man."

"And what did you do for him?"

"I didn't do anything. I couldn't then. I didn't know how."

I let him take my hands in his. "And now you do?" he asks.

"I'm Kyle's lover, remember. I've had to learn a lot of stuff."

He kisses my fingers, one by one. "I'll bet."

I try pulling my hand away but he holds it. "You and Logan, is it still on?"

"I see him sometimes."

"That's another thing. When I heard about it, it made it even more imperative I get you here. I was asking myself, besides your obvious charms, what do you have that could cause a happily married man to go through hell for you?"

"I guess he wasn't as happily married as people thought." Am I to be sentenced to being the Boy Who Stole Mrs. Logan's husband for the rest of my career?

"And then I heard from Martin. He said the three of you had quite an afternoon."

"I guess they had fun."

"Then what's the secret?"

"I guess you could say I give a good massage."

He chuckles. "Well, then, can I buy a *massage*?"

"No."

He lets go of one of my hands and raises his arm, as if he's going to strike me. "You little shit!"

I smile. "Be mean to me, I love it."

"I knew I'd find something that'd please you." He grabs my hands and squeezes them.

"What would please me is if you'd just leave me alone." I struggle to pull my hands away but his grip is strong.

"No, I know what would please you even more is a part in my new movie."

"Oh? So now it's back to that again. There really *is* a new movie?"

"That's why I asked you here. Not to suck your dick but to give you the role of a lifetime."

"Oh?" I stop pulling away, relax. "I didn't think you made pictures any more."

"I don't, but I'm producing it for a friend of mine, he'll be directing. We need somebody who'll get the kids to the box office and you're it."

"I am?"

"You know you're *it*."

His nibbling begins with the fingers and before he is through he gets what he wanted. How could I refuse him after he'd given me "the role of a lifetime?"

What makes his blowjob so great is that he loves doing it, maybe even more than Kyle. Maybe even more than I do, given the right cock. He gets me so hot I'm ready to burst and then he keeps me hanging. We go to the Jacuzzi and he continues. Finally he lets me come. My heavy load flows into his mouth but he can't stop sucking. When I am hard again, he goes back at it with a vengeance. Then, suddenly, he glances at his watch, a huge gold one that looks like a coin. "Oh," he says, looking up, seeing the puzzlement in my face. "I'm sorry. I don't want you to think I am timing it. I'm so used to paying by the hour, it's become a natural reflex."

"Have you gotten your hour's worth yet?"

"It is your hour. This isn't costing me a thing. You'll be in the movie whether you let me do this or not. But you know that."

What I *do* know there's got to be a catch and, as we are washing ourselves in his extravagantly mirrored powder room inside the pavilion, I find out what it is.

"We're filming right now in Fort Lauderdale," he says. "I'm going there in two weeks and I want you to go with me."

"Have you discussed this with Mac?" I ask.

"He's all for it. He thinks it would be a good change of pace for you after being in outer space."

"What is this picture?"

"A musical."

The Next Day

"Dance? I can't dance," I tell Mac over the phone. "Kyle is the one who can dance. When we go out, I just watch him, really, just watch him."

"You're an actor," Mac says. "You can fake it."

For Steve's disco movie, "Movin' On," I need to learn how to dance, at least *fake it*, in a hurry. I go back to the guy who had

296

thrown Kyle out of his studio when he hired him to teach me how to dance once before – Alexander Tenney.

Tenney has become more and more outspoken about gays in Hollywood. He told Kyle it was important for people to come out so others can gain acceptability. But coming out was the last thing Kyle would ever want to do and they argued about it. It ended up that I never did get dance lessons. Now he's choreographing the movie.

Now I'm sitting in Tenney's studio, sipping a Coke while he drinks coffee.

He can't seem to stop talking about coming out: "I always thought I was out," he says. "I presented myself as myself. I didn't try to be anyone else. I didn't take girlfriends to award shows the way you guys do. I didn't do anything to cover it up. I just lived my life. There was a part of me that really didn't think it was important to make an announcement. But to the gay community, I say 'I'm gay.' But I pride myself on being 100 percent man."

"You're that all right." Beautifully muscular, there is nothing feminine about him. I would expect to find him in jeans and a cowboy shirt but he's in white leotards and when he stretches his legs before me, exposing the bulge at his crotch, I sigh. I always like looking at ballet stars' baskets, always very generous.

Tenney sees where I'm staring and rubs it. "We'd better get busy."

"Yes."

He puts on "Love Hangover," one of my favorites. "Now," he says, "think of dancing as making love set to music. You can do that, I know."

I follow his feet and pretty soon I've got it. But I work up a sweat trying to keep up with him.

"You have to *feel* the beat, not just hear it," he says.

He repeats "Love Hangover," then puts some other stuff on. By the end of the hour, I'm drenched with perspiration but I feel good about myself. I was almost able to keep up with him.

"You can take a shower if you want to."

I'm in the shower when he comes into the bathroom.

I pull the curtain back, covering myself with it, and ask, "Anything wrong?"

"No," he says, pulling off his leotards. "Everything's right."

His cock is big, not as big as Bud's but big enough to hurt. It is semi-hard as he strokes it. "Is there room for me in there?"

I smile and push the curtain away. He can now see my dick is hard.

He smiles. "I guess so."

I bend to adjust the temperature of the water and gasp as his single, slim finger probes my ass. He soaps it, then slides it deeply into my hole. He withdraws, only to plunge in again, and again, and again. Two fingers, then three, and finally his cock. I force myself upright and Tenney bends over, pressing his chest against my back while he fucks me wildly. He pulls out for a moment. The warm water slicks us quickly and his fingers rove over my body, finding every crevice, every orifice, followed by his mouth and tongue. He soaps and then plucks at my nipples. He turns me around and slides his erection into me again. I moan, cry out encouragement to him, jacking myself off. His hands take over and he brings me to climax. His quivering slows. He withdraws and takes me into his arms, kissing me with unrestrained passion, his erection pressed between us. He moves his soap-slippery hand to my ass and presses. His other hand goes to my nipples. Finding them hard, he plucks them, plays with them, sucks on them. His fingers now vibrate again in my ass. He lifts me up so that he can set me down again on his cock and, now, with my shoulders pressed hard against the tile, my legs slung over his shoulders, he launches into his final assault on my ass. We kiss as he comes. He has given new meaning to the expression, "Get down."

Now I'm glad I finally went to Sommers' house.

EIGHTEEN

Five Days Later

My mother's new husband Vinnie, an old friend of Kyle's, has just flown in from Texas. Mom stayed home to take care of the Colonel.

It was three days ago when Vinnie buzzed the gate at Bird's Eye and I let him in. When he got out of the rented Ford, he swept off his broad-brimmed Stetson, revealing a thin layer of heavily greased gray hair. In a deep voice, with a Texas accent that he had somehow acquired since marrying my mother, he said, "Howdy," grinned, then put his hat back on and ambled into the house. It doesn't take long to become a cowboy.

He was pleasant as I showed him around the house. "I've been invited here before, you know," he said. "But I always refused."

"Well, you finally made it."

His expression turned grave. "I wish it could be under better circumstances, son."

"Why *did* you come?"

"Where is Kyle? Where is that bastard?"

"I think he's in New York. With him, I'm never sure. He comes back. I don't mind."

"But your mother and I mind. She's sick about the way he's treated you. And I found those documents she signed."

"What documents?"

"Agreements Kyle had Mac and his accountant draw up through their attorneys. Kyle gets 50% of everything - did you know that?"

"No."

"Half! He's got half of you!"

"He has *all* of me."

"It's insane. Kate said she didn't even read the damn thing!"

I was speechless. I had been brought up to believe life was simple. "All you have to do," the colonel would tell me, over and over, "is live up to a cowpoke's standards. Always say 'Howdy' when you see someone; trust everybody unless you have good reason not to; help people in need, even if they're strangers; play hard; don't brag; and, most important of all, tell the truth."

"Half!" Vinnie, now living by the cowpoke's code, went on raving. "Half! You know what that'll mean now, now that you're who you are?"

"And who *am* I anyway?"

"You were on TV for chrissakes!"

"Yeah, I was."

"You're a movie star now. Your picture's on enough lunch pails to fill a thousand school cafeterias, girls are writing you a thousand letters a week, you will be doing the sequel now for a huge salary plus a percentage."

"So?"

"So now we're going to get you out of here."

"Out of here? To where? Where do I go?"

"I don't know. Anywhere but here. I know this guy. I won't let you stay here any longer."

"But this is my *home*. I live here."

"Your home is in Texas."

I started to cry. I couldn't believe this was happening. "No. This is my home. I'm never going back to Texas. I can't."

Vinnie stood over me, started shaking. He had never seen me break down. I was doing a good scene, as if the cameras were rolling. He started running his fingers through my hair. "Now, now. I'm sorry." He took a deep breath. "Okay. I'll stay here till the bastard gets back. Your mother and I will protect your interests."

"I don't need any protection, don't you see? Kyle's my lover. I am *in love* with him. Nothing else matters. He can have every penny I make. I don't care as long as I'm here, with him."

"But he's not here! I bet right this minute – right this very minute – he's getting fucked silly in New York. I know what he does. I used to be part of all this shit. I *know* what goes on. You apparently don't know or don't want to believe it."

My tears kept flowing. I couldn't stop them. "I know more than you think."

He shook his head. "Oh, you're smart all right, but you're still just a kid. You weren't even legal in this state when he brought you here. There's such a thing as the Mann Act. Kyle could be in a lot of trouble."

"He's already in a lot of trouble. Just leave him alone. Leave me alone!" I ran out of the main house and into my room, slamming the door behind me.

I thought he would be pounding on the door, demanding to be let in, but he had picked up one of the pool phones just outside my bedroom and I could hear him talking. I listened hard but couldn't make out what he was saying.

In a couple of minutes, he came to my door. "Okay. I've got your mother on the line. You tell her just what you told me."

He had played what Grandpa would say was the trump card. It was a long conversation, mostly Mom talking and me saying yes or no. That's the only way I can talk with my mother: just listen, agree with what she says, then hang up.

"So?"

"So you can stay here and tomorrow we'll have a meeting with Mac and Ned and Jay Julian and work this out."

"Shit, I want a meeting with Kyle Cartwright, that's who I want a meeting with."

"I don't know where he is. Nobody does."

"I hope I never do see him again. I'd take him and – "

"And what?"

"Never mind. You wouldn't understand."

But I *did* understand. I was there when "El Dorado" was being filmed. I knew what Vinnie would do to Kyle. And Kyle would love every minute of it.

Jay was busy all of the next day but suggested we meet for dinner at a little out-of-the-way French restaurant he knew. It was a splendid dinner but I had trouble keeping it down when I found out just what Kyle had done. Ned was late and when he did arrive he came armed with a big black book and a dour expression. Very withdrawn, unsmiling. All he said to me was, "I miss you."

I said, "I'll call you."

"Kyle's a thief," Vinnie blurted before Ned even sat down. Mac shook his head and tried to make light of it. "After all," he chuckled, "I discovered him shoplifting in Beverly Hills. What could you expect?"

"You all were party to this," Vinnie said.

"No," Ned said, clearing his throat. "It's all my fault. At the time, I wanted to give Kyle what he wanted. I tried to warn Bobby. Now I don't care what happens. We'll amend the contract any way you see fit. But Kyle owes money all over town and it'll take me awhile to sort it all out and get a handle on the extent of the damage."

This was news to Jay, who was growing more and more angry. "After I kicked him out of the apartment, I tried to reach him," he said. "I've called the people who look after my apartment. They haven't seen him. I don't know where he is. It's not like him to be acting like this."

"He's not the Kyle I found in 1968," Mac agreed, his eyes misting over. "He's turned into somebody else."

They were acting as if I wasn't there, which was fine with me because I was taking it all in, trying to understand what was really happening. Mac wished to avoid a lawsuit from my mother and Vinnie. "And," he said, glaring at Vinnie, "anything else you might try."

"We could do plenty, I don't need to remind you. This is just a kid we're talking about. A little boy a grown man has taken advantage of it every way possible."

"No, it's *me* you're talking about," I finally interrupted. "And I don't want anything to happen to Kyle."

"But fair is fair, Bobby," Jay said to me.

"Yes, all we want is this to be worked out fairly," Vinnie said.

"What's the bottom line, Ned?" Jay asked, lighting another big cigar.

Ned grimaced as the smoke drifted towards him. He swallowed hard, then said he had been thinking a lot about it and the easiest way out was to draw up a new contract that would have Kyle turning over all of his property to the company Mac and Jay had set up for me, BR Productions, in lieu of repayment of the money that had been paid to Kyle unfairly and the funds withdrawn from my bank account.

Then came the news that astounded me the most. Jay had

engineered a contract that I had signed but never read. My share of the profits of the most popular movie of the year would earn me $5 million. Plus the merchandising, the guarantee for the sequel, the other revenue and invested capital came to another $5 million. I wasn't even able to vote and I was a millionaire. But somehow, none of it mattered. None of us knew where Kyle was.

"We've lost him," Jay kept saying. "We've lost him."

Ned cleared his throat again and said, "He's not *Kyle* any more; he's somebody else, somebody none of us wants to know."

"Speak for yourself," I muttered.

. . .

"Slow down, Bobby," Ben said as I tried to explain it all to him the next day. I wanted him to come out to California as soon as he could.

"I'm sorry. It's just that I miss you and I'm so lonely here."

"I still don't understand. *You* now own Bird's Eye?"

"Not me; the company Mac set up for me, I'm sort of a corporation all by myself."

"This changes things, Bobby."

"Why?"

I could hear him clearing this throat, taking a deep breath. "I've got a confession to make. Kyle's here. He's been here for a month now."

"He was there when you came to see me at Jay's?"

"Yes."

"And you didn't tell me? You lied?"

"I'm sorry. He told me to. He didn't want you to see him like this. He's still in pretty bad shape but he's doing better now. He's off the coke. But he's still drinking. I've done the best I can with him – "

I hung up the phone before he could finish the sentence.

I had no sooner returned the phone to the cradle when it was ringing. It was Mac. I told him where Kyle was, gave him the number. Then he told me I could pack up everything that was Kyle's and send it to him. "No, as far as I'm concerned, this is still his house. He is still my lover."

What happened next is vague. They say smoking pot affects your memory and I guess it's true because I don't remember much about it. I *do* remember I took a sedative the doctor had prescribed and then smoked a joint and was terribly hungry. Vinnie said we'd go out for ice cream. The idea of it intrigued me. Having my stepfather buy me ice cream. He drove his rental car. I got to giggling, putting the window up and down and thinking it was really neat that even rental cars in California have power windows.

Vinnie said I was acting silly, that he'd never seen anyone get so silly smoking dope. I remember watching him watching me as he was crunching on his cone and I was still licking my ice cream. I was getting really into it, licking around and around like a circle with no beginning and no end. Vinnie said it was just like life, going around and around, with no end to it. I thought he was very wise at that moment. But he couldn't watch me licking for very long; he must have known I was fantasizing it was his cock I was licking. I began to fantasize what he would be like more and more and by the time we got back to Bird's Eye I had finished with my ice cream and leaning against him. At first it didn't bother him but eventually the closeness began to get to him. He pushed me away and I'd lean right back into him again.

After we pulled into the drive and I got out to open the front door, I fumbled with my keys. When I finally found the right one and put it into the lock and entered the password, or what I thought was the password, the bells went off and I thought my head would burst with the shrieking. Vinnie was laughing hysterically. He ran to the phone to tell the police I had set the damn alarm off accidentally.

He stood at the sink washing the ice cream off his hands and I stood behind him, wanting to touch him but afraid.

"Is it true?" I asked finally. He turned the water off and was drying his hands. "Is what true?"

"That you and Kyle were – you know?"

"Look, I was hired to keep an eye on him. He's had a lot of problems for a long time that kid. But that seems like ages ago now. Everything has changed since then."

"You mean you don't still – ?"

"Still what?" He had a strange expression on his face, as if he was challenging me, challenging me to call him a queer because he'd fucked Kyle.

I touched his arm. "Fool around?"

Shaking his head, he moved away.

"Kyle was the only man I've ever been with more than once. And now that I'm with your mother, well, she keeps me satisfied. No woman has ever satisfied me the way your mother has."

"I'm glad to hear it."

"You're a lot like her. When you love, you love with all your heart." He walked past me into the music room.

I followed him, stripping off my clothes as I did. "I'm more like her than you know. God, I feel so silly right now – "

"You are silly. Would it help to lie down? I mean, I'm an alcoholic not a drug addict. I don't know about these things." He turned and saw I was naked. He shook his head.

"I'm not a drug addict."

"No, you're crazy. Put your clothes back on."

"No. I'm always naked here, unless Anna May's here cleaning."

He shook his head and turned away, started going through the TV magazine. "Have it your way."

"I always have it my way." I found another joint and lit it.

"So I've noticed. But some day you're gonna have to grow up and learn that it doesn't always go your way."

"I hope I never grow up then."

He switched on the television, sat down in the armchair facing it directly. "Don't you get bored out here all by yourself?"

I sat down across from him and sucked on the joint. Then I said, "No. I enjoy it. I spend months and months on a picture, surrounded by people, so it's nice to have some time to be alone, not to have to take direction all the time."

"You could use a little direction. Look at you, puffing away like an idiot."

I was incredibly horny. I hated Vinnie, in a way, but, in another sense, I was terribly attracted to a man who was now married to my mother but who had fucked my lover. To have sex with Vinnie would make it a package deal. I got an erection but didn't touch it.

Vinnie was having none of it. He stood up. "I'm going out. I can't be around you when you're like this."

Just as Vinnie stood up, the buzzer at the gate sounded. Vinnie went to the box. It was Ned, he had worked all night and had driven all the way out here with the papers. He must be very worried about what he had permitted Kyle to do. Although he denied it, he probably loved Kyle. Everybody loved Kyle. Lusted after Kyle. That was Kyle's problem, I had begun to understand. Everybody loved him and he really didn't love anybody.

Vinnie led Ned into the music room and apologized for my condition.

"There's not many kids that would be sitting around naked, smoking a joint in front of their stepfather," Ned laughed, "especially with a hard-on." Ned reached down and squeezed my cock.

Vinnie took the papers and said, "I'll leave you two lovebirds alone while I look this over."

Ned watched him leave the room and when he heard the door of Kyle's bedroom slam, he said, "What's eating him?"

"He misses my mother."

"And I've been missing you. I think I'll make you come over to get your allowance from now on. This direct deposit shit isn't working."

And it wasn't long before Ned was making a direct deposit up my ass. I decided I didn't need a new accountant after all. He had made me a millionaire, what did it matter that he had tried to help Kyle. I would have tried to help Kyle all I could if I had been him. And besides, I was terribly horny. Ned had me on the leather couch, on my stomach, pumping away when Vinnie walked back into the room.

Ned was close and didn't care what Vinnie thought, he was going to come.

"God, I can't leave my little boy alone for a minute," Vinnie said, chuckling.

"It's all in the family," Ned said as he was pulling out. "You want to jump in?"

"Hell no. I had a chance at that over two years ago when it was illegal, now it'd just be immoral."

"But it's the tightest one I've ever had. And the boy loves it so much."

Men were talking about me as if I wasn't there again. But now it mattered. "Don't I have a say in this?" I rolled over, my eyes flashing. "What am I, just a piece of ass?"

"It's not so bad being the best damn piece of ass in Hollywood," Ned said, still stroking his dick.

"Not if it means what I think it does. Let me see the papers Vinnie – "

"So *now* he's the businessman. My kid, the millionaire, the fuckin' corporation."

"I've got a pen in my brief case. You can be a witness to his signature," Ned said.

"This is so fucking bizarre I can't stand it. My kid's going to sign all these documents just after his accountant has fucked him senseless? I tell ya, you've got style Schuyler."

"I'm *not* your kid, Vinnie," I reminded him, not looking up from all the legal mumbo-jumbo. "Like you say, you had your chance."

Vinnie said it all looked in order. BR Productions had, in effect, bought KC Company. But I told them I liked to think of it as a merger. Kyle and I had finally merged, legally at least.

After Ned got dressed and left, I lit another joint. I was dizzy with all the excitement. And I hadn't come yet. My hard-on wouldn't die.

Vinnie stood over me, straightening his pants and saying he'd had enough of California and was leaving right then. His job was done. I told him he was just scared to stay another night at Bird's Eye. "Yeah," he said, "I might end up killing you."

"I'd be willing to risk it," I said, rolling over, exposing my ass to him again.

"It is tempting, I've got to admit," he said, staring at it. "But somehow I don't think I can handle it right now."

"I think you could. If anybody could handle it, you could." I reached up and felt the stiffness at his crotch, the bulge I had noticed slowly appearing while he was standing there watching Ned finish hadn't gone away. "Look at the way you handled this whole messy business." He didn't push me away.

"This could get a whole lot messier – "

"Yeah, real messy." I dropped to my knees before him and slowly unzipped his pants. He continued to protest as I slowly lowered his underwear; he tried pulling away but I gripped his cock. When it was fully revealed, it quickly became stiff and I stared at it, my eyes bulging. I couldn't believe it – Vinnie's cock was even bigger than Ben's. I could barely get my hands around it. I was too shocked to speak. No wonder Kyle was so happy in Texas. He had this – and me!

"Don't do it, Bobby. Let's don't do something we'll always regret."

I looked up at him, still clutching the incredible cock. "I don't think we'll ever regret it. It will be our little secret."

"I've heard of stepfathers having little secrets with their stepchildren but this is really a switch."

I was too busy to respond. I was going to give him the blowjob of his life but I wouldn't go all the way. Not this time. It would be asking too much. Just to make him come in my mouth would be enough. For now. He tilted his head back and closed his eyes, probably trying to blot out who it was that was doing this to him. But when it was over, he would always remember. And I knew he would never regret it.

I tried to take it all the way down to his pubic hairs at least once and it took some doing. I gagged at first but finally I managed it. It was more fun just to suck on the head of it, massaging the thick, dark shaft with my hands as I did. I let the saliva dribble down and used it to get some good action going even though I had to let go of it with my right hand because I just had to come; my desire had been building up incredibly. It must have been building up in Vinnie too because when he realized I was coming, out it came – a gusher worthy of the size of his penis. I let it splash into my face and then, finished myself, I could bring both hands back to it and cup the balls while I slid it back into my mouth about half way. That left at least five inches to look at. He pushed it deeper into my throat. "Kyle deserves this. I'm doing this for him." Whatever reason he gave made no difference to me as long as he was doing it. Whatever made him feel better about it. He began a fucking action that went on until all the cum was released. I swallowed it but I didn't want to give it up. I kept tugging on it. Vinnie came down from his high and reached for his trousers, which had now fallen down around his ankles. "Up!" he ordered. "Get up now."

My hands left the cock and I hugged him to me. I knew better than to call him "Daddy."

Now as I watch Vinnie waving goodbye to me and driving away in the rental car I suddenly envy my mother. He isn't such a bad guy after all. And then there's that cock –

Three Days Later

Kyle, suffering from jet lag and God knows what else, is sleeping it off in his bedroom. It is still *his* bedroom. We agreed to that last night after his plane landed.

Mac had reached him in New York and told him what had happened with KC Company. He told him he'd better come back to Los Angles right away and arranged to have a ticket waiting for him at the airport.

"I thought you might want to pick him up," Mac said when he called me.

"Thanks," was all I could say.

I was waiting for Kyle outside, near the luggage carousel where I always met him when he returned to L.A.X. I was driving the Corvette, which seemed to upset him. "Why are you driving my car?"

"I like it better than mine. I can put the top down." I didn't mention the traffic tickets. Ever.

"Oh."

He was silent for a few moments. Then he said, "Oh, but it's not mine any more, is it? I keep forgettin'. Funny ain't it?"

"I don't think it's a bit funny. And look at you."

"What's wrong with me?"

"You're a mess. I didn't even recognize you."

He unzipped his pants. "This. Do you recognize this?"

I took my eyes off the road to glance down at his penis. "It hasn't changed. Maybe a little worse for wear though."

He stroked it. "God, how it missed you. Missed your pretty

mouth on it."

"Then why'd *it* stay away so long?"

"Lost it's mind I guess. Just lost it's fuckin' mind."

I reached over and stroked it. "I love it, Kyle. I'll always love it."

"That's what I was hopin'. That you still loved it. That's why I came right back when Mac called. You had him call, didn't you?"

"No, I didn't have him call."

"Oh. Well, I guess you don't love me anymore but at least you remember it and still love *it*. "

"I *still* love it – all of it, and that includes all of you, you asshole."

"Then why - " he hesitated, pointed to a grocery store we were passing.

"Hey, stop, I wanna get a Coke. You like one?"

"Yeah, sure."

He got out of the car. "Hey, you got some change? I'm short right now."

I pulled a fifty out of my wallet and handed it to him.

"Hey, I don't need that much."

"Take it, so you'll have some money on you. I don't want to be doing this all the time."

"A loan. A loan until after I do the fourth album."

"Right."

I watched him as he went into the grocery. There was still a spring to his walk, and from behind there was no mistaking the Cartwright ass. As much as I hated to admit it, I missed fucking him more than I missed sucking his cock.

He returned to the car carrying the Cokes and when he got in he spilled his on the seat.

"Goddam," I swore. "Be careful, Kyle. That's leather and it'll stain."

"Sorry. Don't mean to mess up *your* car."

A few moments later, he said, "Mac said it was Vinnie's fault, that Vinnie'd come here, caused all the trouble."

"Mom is only looking out for my interests."

"Vinnie stay at Bird's Eye?"

"Yes."

"That's fuckin' great! I could never get Vinnie to Bird's Eye and now he's sleeping my bed, fuckin' my lover!"

"You're disgusting."

"That's what Vinnie used to say! Do you know that? That's just what Vinnie used to say, 'You're disgusting!' That's what he'd say, sonofabitch if he wouldn't."

"You are. You are disgusting."

He sipped his Coke. Some of it dribbled on his jeans.

I accelerated and the wind blew his hair across his eyes. Brushing the strands away, he asked, "Well, did he?"

"What do you think?"

"I don't know what to think any more."

"Neither do I. But at least I know you still consider me your lover."

"You'll always be my lover. Will I always be *your* lover?"

"You're just saying that 'cause you want a blowjob."

"That and a fuck. I don't know why but I've missed you."

. . .

"I don't know why but I've missed you," I say as I enter him. I got him in the shower by agreeing to take one with him. Now we're in bed. The blowjobs are over. Now the fun begins.

"Then show me," he says, raising his butt up to meet my cock. I slide it all the way in.

"God what a beautiful ass," I say, taking it in my hands as I begin banging away.

"Fuck it," he cries, bending all the way over. "Dammit, fuck it."

NINETEEN

The Next Day
    The poster. The Bobby Richards poster. Mac had taken Kyle's down and put mine up in his office. I insisted he put them both up. Side by side. Now Mac is displaying them proudly, saying, "The face and the ass, together."
    My face. That's all they wanted on the poster, just my face. With Kyle, of course, it had to be the face *and* the ass.
    "I hear Charles Adams has some other photos of you that he says I should see. What did you do over there anyway?" he says. This is the subject of the meeting. My nude shots.
    "I was high. I was *very* high. He took advantage of me."
    "You wanted him to take advantage of you. That's the only way you'll do it, if you want to."
    "Yes, I wanted him. But I also wanted the photographs. They're not so bad. There's no cock, if that's what worries you."
    "But plenty of ass I'll bet. Did he take 'em before or after he fucked it?"
    "You're in one of your moods again."
    "I guess I'm the only one left that hasn't enjoyed your company."
    "You're my manager."
    "That means I get nothing."
    "It means you get a percentage. A *big* percentage."
    "It means I get nothing and you know it. Ned, Steve, the list is endless. Even Kevin. My lover, you couldn't even leave him alone - " He comes around his desk and stands in front of me, runs his fingers through my hair.
    "Mac, stop."
    "Hey, I've done it here before. Just hold the calls, lock the doors - " He takes off his rimless glasses. He is handsome

without them. I could, if I really put my mind to it, enjoy it.

He puts his hands on my head and tilts my face up to meet his kiss. It is a polite kiss. Then he steps back.

"At first, I thought you were just cute. But I like you more and more. And this is the high I like to see you having, high on Kyle, not pot."

"Me too." I stand up. "Look, I have a lunch date."

"With whom?" He holds my arm.

"I'll tell you later." I pull away.

"No, I don't want to know. The thought of yet another guy fucking you and you turning me away – "

"Go home for lunch, Mac," I say. "Suck Kevin's dick. It'll do you good. It's a much nicer dick than mine. And he loves you."

. . .

Charles Adams' photographs didn't worry me but the ones taken by Jim Donner, the self-styled king of sleaze journalism, did. Jim wanted to interview me over lunch at the Brown Derby and the man Kyle called the most loathed, feared journalist in Hollywood was greeted warmly by everybody. In fact, after we sit down, I comment about how nice everyone is.

"Yeah," he says, "it's easy to make fun of Hollywood. But we have the kindest people here I've ever met. Underneath, they're warm, affectionate, longing for somebody to like it here, to share it with 'em. If somebody does then they're reassured."

"I love it here but Jay Julian says it's all wrong, all fake. All like a movie, that we have to go to New York to see reality."

"He can have that kind of reality."

When I told Kyle I was going to meet Donner for lunch he was furious, refusing to let me go. I told him he had nothing to do with it, this was my career I was talking about. Then he reminded me I had met Donner in Texas and I began to worry. I put things together, things I had forgotten about. I had given so many massages at the hotel they all began to run together in my memory, but Donner I did remember. Not the name, but the things in his room, the fancy cameras and recording devices. I was a little afraid of all that hardware, wondering if he was recording me giving him a massage. When he rolled over, his cock was erect, throbbing. When that happened, I normally just put a towel over it and went on. If the man said anything or did anything, such as accidentally on purpose push the towel away, I would take it as a cue to apply oil to it and jack him off. Once in a while I was moved to kiss it and suck it if it was a nice one and Donner's was nice. He managed during the course of the blowjob to get his camera and take a picture of me with his cock in my mouth. I didn't think too much about it at the time because I was not fully aware of who he was or what he was doing there.

Now I have a pretty good idea what he wants.

A blond, slender waiter stands before us, swaying slightly. Singing under his breath, he clears the first course.

"Cute kid," Donner says as the waiter moves away. "I'll have to remember his name, ask for him next time."

"He could be fun."

"That's the whole point," he says as we begin eating our chopped sirloin. "Fun. I want to have fun before I'm too old to enjoy it, you know?"

I nod and go on chewing.

"Kids in this town'll do anything to get a fix, just anything you want as long as you pay. And I pay good. But I'm sick of that. For once I'd like to just have fun, without having to pay, you know?"

"You want somebody to pay you?"

"In a way. To pay me for a small favor."

"A favor?"

"Like the favor of destroying some old negatives of some embarrassing photographs."

"That favor would be worth a lot. An awful lot, I would think."

"I have taken so many pictures, I had forgotten about a couple I took of you until I saw that spread on you in *Interview*. I realized I had better pictures of you than that."

"But you couldn't publish them."

"No, but just the peace of mind that would come from knowing that they no longer existed, that would have to be worth something, wouldn't it?"

"Something. I'm not sure quite what."

"Oh, I think you know."

"No, I don't."

"I always say that competition in this town isn't just business, it's bed."

"Right now I don't feel like going to bed with anybody."

"I hear it's been rough with Kyle. I hear all kinds of things."

I shrug. "Right now, Kyle's back with me at Bird's Eye. It doesn't matter what happens, we're still lovers."

We continue to eat and as we are finishing, Donner says, "Okay. So what do you want me to do with the negatives?"

I smile. "Keep 'em safe for me. Maybe you and I will get together some day and look at 'em, for old times' sake."

"You're a sweet kid. Likable, like they said in *Interview*."

"I like you too."

Blackmail is a scary thing to think about but that's all I'd been thinking about for two days since Donner's invitation to lunch. Now I could go on, clear my head, move on. But I left the door open for Donner to come in some time. I have learned that people need open doors.

Two Days Later

Now Jay's on the phone, having a fit: "Have you seen *The Hollywood Reporter?*"

"No."

"You'd better. Donner's got an article in here about you and Kyle."

"What did he say?"

"He somehow found out about the contracts, now he's calling it a swindle. It's all in there."

"Oh shit."

"I'd better come out."

"All right. And it would be good for Kyle to see you."

Kyle tries to be on his best behavior for Jay but it is impossible. He'd seen Donner's column a couple hours ago and began drinking. Now he's whipped again. Jay is appalled. He leaves right after dinner. I get Kyle to bed. He begs me to fuck him. It seems as if a wind is blowing in the bedroom, a wind that blows the cares away, and I fuck Kyle. In spite of everything.

TWENTY

Two Days Later
When Kyle went to Mac's office to meet with the Capitol people and discuss a fourth album, Mac told him that I was going to Fort Lauderdale to play a part in "Movin' On." Mac said he was trying to get Sommers to let Kyle do a song in the movie. Kyle said he hated disco music and wouldn't do it. Mac called me and warned me Kyle might be trouble when he got back to Bird's Eye. I am packing my suitcases when he comes into my bedroom. He has a tumbler full of vodka in his hand.

"Going somewhere?" he asks.

"To Fort Lauderdale."

"Why didn't *you* tell me?"

"I was afraid to."

"So now you're afraid of me! What the hell is going on?"

"I'm sorry. I was going to tell you – "

"What, on your way out the door?"

I leave the packing and go to him, take him by the arm and pull him over to the bed. "I know how you feel about me – "

"You do? Do you really? I don't think you have a fuckin' clue. Do you know how bad I'm hurting? I wish I could die."

"Don't ever say that. It's just that it's all happening so fast."

"It sure is," he jumps up, spilling vodka all over the bedspread. "One day I'm the star in the family and the next thing I know, you're this big star and I haven't got a pot to piss in. You've got it all, everything except my fuckin' guitar! Talk about fuckin' fast! I wish I were dead. Gone! Outta here!"

He darts from the room with me in hot pursuit. "Please, Kyle. Don't do this. Not now. Please!"

He doesn't stop. He races into his bedroom and slams the door before I can reach him. The sound of the lock turning reverberates in my ears.

. . .

I have only two scenes in the part of the movie that is being filmed in Fort Lauderdale. What should easily be accomplished in a day will take a week. The rest of my scenes will be done at the studio in Hollywood. I don't have to dance in the location scenes so I relax. Sort of. I find I'm sharing a suite with Steve. At least I have my own bedroom. I will keep the door locked.

I spend all day on the set. It's a movie about spring break, a "Where the Boys Are" for the Seventies. The real stars of the movie are the girls. I fit right in with this bunch, giggling and carrying on. It's as if I was back in high school. The casting director has recruited a bunch of local guys to be in the beach scenes and I wouldn't mind going to bed with each of them. Of course, Steve has reviewed them all, in some way or another, by now and it could be some may show up at the hotel. The fun is guessing which ones.

Steve takes me to the Down Under for dinner, with several of the girls and the director, Paul Kraft. While we are eating, a suntanned blond god arrives with a package for Steve. Earlier, Steve had told me he loves Fort Lauderdale for the service he gets: the good coke and the studly prostitutes. The young man is given some cash and told when to be at the hotel. I admire the hustler and Steve says we can share him.

When we arrive back at the Pier 66, Steve says he's really tired, he's had ten numbers so far today and that's why he ran out of coke. "Tell you what, I'll just watch."

I smile. "I can handle that."

And handle it I do. I don't recognize the six-foot-three blond from the set. But he should have been there. The hair is long and silky. The face is okay. The body is perfection. And the cock is truly beautiful. At least eight inches, well-formed and cut. Steve loves it. He changes his mind. He has to suck it. He snorts some coke, offers me some. I do a line and suddenly I can't get enough of the hustler. Steve says for me to slow down, save some for him. "There's plenty," I say, licking and nibbling. I run my tongue around the rim of the dick and suck furiously. I slide it further into my mouth, making spirals with my tongue around the shaft, feeling the pressure at the back of my throat, nearly gagging, then moving my tongue back up the full length of it, nipping gently with my teeth as Steve works on the balls. I gently caress the head, then let Steve on it. I stand up, suck the sun god's nipples, run my hands over his warm, smooth stomach. Steve, greedily slurping below me, moans when he senses the stud is ready. And Steve hasn't had his hour's worth. The cum erupts from it and splashes in Steve's face. He wraps his arms around our bodies and hugs us to him, taking the cock back in his mouth and nursing it. I look up into the stud's face. He's breathing deeply and smiling. He asks, "Can I fuck you?"

I look down at Steve, still sucking. "Do we have time?"

Steve lets go of the cock and says, "I'll pay overtime to watch that."

We're all snorting like fools and the stud has me bending over, my face in the powder while he's plowing into me. Steve sits in an armchair next to us and it is the first time I have seen his cock. He is jacking off watching us. I am so turned on, I move over to Steve and drop my head in his lap. His cock is puny, like some of the men had in Texas that I would visit in their rooms when I was growing up. They were always the ones who seemed to appreciate me the most, always buying me the nicest presents afterward. Steve can't believe I'm doing him and he runs his fingers through my hair and kisses me on top of the head. He cuddles me to him and runs his hands along my back, watching the stud's cock slide back and forth in my ass at a leisurely pace. He has come once and is in no hurry now. After all, he's getting paid overtime.

The Next Day

I arrive on the set to find a new scene has been added; my screen time has been increased. Somebody must like me. I can't imagine who.

TWENTY-ONE

A Week Later

When we land at L.A.X., Steve's limousine is waiting for him and he offers to take me to Bird's Eye. It is late afternoon when we pull up to the gate. There are six cars in the driveway.

"Kyle must be having a party," I sigh.

"I better go in with you," Steve says, patting the back of my hand gently. "This should be good."

I don't try to stop him. I might need all the bulk I can get. But I have begun to look upon Steve's chubbiness as generosity rather than bulk.

All the doors of the house seem to be open. The kitchen is piled with unwashed glasses and dishes. As we walk into the living room, a girl in a yellow robe like a Buddhist monk's is lying on one of the couches, her mouth wide open. A light-skinned Negro is lying on the floor in front of her. He is naked and I sneak a peek at his cock. Quite formidable, even lying limp on his thigh. It is uncut and appears to be covered with dried sperm.

"You're late," Jake says, coming in from the pool, laughing.

"Late?"

"Party started two days ago. People coming and going. But it's over now." He is dressed only in rumpled shorts.

"Where's your wife?"

"Went home. Yesterday. Had enough."

We stroll out to the pool. In the near twilight, the purple

azaleas and golden hibiscus stand out brilliantly. Bougainvillea leaves float in the pool along with a naked woman on my raft.

"Who is that?" I ask.

"Baby somebody-or-other. I never catch the last names."

"Fan of yours I take it?" Steve says, greatly amused at the whole scene.

Jake's eyes twinkle. "They're all fans of mine."

Another girl steps out through Kyle's bedroom door. She's dressed, ready to leave.

Jake goes over to her, they talk, she leaves and Jake comes back to us. "That's Natalie. She's going to take me home."

"What about Baby?" I ask.

"She's your problem."

I have a hunch my problems are just beginning.

Baby pushes her big sunglasses down her nose and peers over them. A look of recognition comes to her face. "Don't I know you?" she asks.

"I doubt it," Steve says, thinking she is talking to him.

"No, not you, him," she points a shaking finger at me.

"No, I'm just here to clean up the mess."

"Oh," she says, sliding her sunglasses back up her nose.

"The party's over," I tell her, and lead Steve back into the living room, where we find the Negro and the girl dressed like a Monk have already gotten the message. We see them fleetingly as they go out the open front door.

The girl climbs out of the pool and goes to where her clothes have been tossed on a chaise.

"Well, you don't need my help after all," Steve says, taking me in his arms and kissing me on the forehead. "I'll call you tomorrow."

In the music room, I find two more girls and wake them up, tell them to leave and then go to my bedroom. There I find two more girls, in my bed. I hold my temper and suggest they leave as soon as they can. Bewildered, they obey.

I don't want to go to Kyle's bedroom until everyone has gone. I stand at the door and say, "Nice to have seen you," as they depart.

Now a sense of emptiness fills the house; it is relatively back to normal. As I pass them, I straighten a few chairs before I get to the poolside door to Kyle's bedroom; the door that was locked to me when I left is now open. Kyle has passed out in the rumpled bed. He is naked and empty bottles of vodka litter the floor. I step over to the bed and pull a sheet over him, then, as I go to turn out the lights that had been left on in the bathroom, I see a faintly recognizable face. When I step over to the tub, it becomes clear: Howie has come to another party; he finally made it to Bird's Eye.

It takes a few minutes to sober Howie up enough to get him out of Kyle's bathroom and into my bedroom. But when he lands on my bed, he promptly passes out again. I let him sleep while I start cleaning up the house. When I return to my room two hours later, Howie is awake but he appears to be dazed, confused. The room is not familiar. He barely remembers me.

"Oh, yeah," he finally says.
"Did you tell Kyle you met me?"
He nods. "He was surprised, sort of. He didn't think you were down working the streets. That was all he said. I didn't expect to see you here, though."
"I told you, I come to clean up the mess."
"This your room?"
"Yes. I stay here sometimes. There are a lot of messes these days."
"What a party!" he suddenly is alive, remembering it. "You shoulda been here, man. I never fucked so much pussy in one night!"
"I think the party lasted two nights. Anyhow, are you ready to go?"
"Go? You mean you wanna get fucked?"
"No, I mean, I'll take you back downtown. When you're ready."
"I thought you liked this."
"I do. I like it very much. But it looks like it's all worn out."
He strokes it. It doesn't seem to be responding. I have some coke left from my week with Steve; I hate to waste it on this guy but I can always get more. "Here," I say, "maybe a snort of this'll help things."
I pull the bag from my suitcase and pour the powder on the mirror, make a couple of lines for him. He snorts it, I finish it.

After I've stripped, I climb in bed with him, spread his thighs, go to work. It is a masterpiece of a penis, I must say. Steve just has to see this one.

When he climbs on the bed and parts my thighs, I can't forget he has just been with Kyle. I keep seeing Kyle, stretched out under him, longing for him, waiting to be fucked by him. When he enters me, I become Kyle, and my asshole throbs greedily against his cock. It is touching me where it had touched Kyle, where Kyle himself had so often been, and I think of Dugan, Nico and Ben, all the ones we have shared. I take my cock in my hand and begin jacking off. Slowly, rhythmically he begins the deep thrusting that soon brings on an orgasm that jolts my body. A smug expression on his face, he gently eases the gigantic cock out of my asshole and stands up. "See, it wasn't worn out." He shakes it at me. "Yeah, it still has a lot of life in it."

I roll over and perch on the edge of the bed. "I want to suck every ounce of life that's still left in it." I reach for it.

"That'll cost ya."

"You can have the rest of the coke."

"Okay," he says, lifting the cock to meet my open mouth.

On the way downtown, I ask, "Have you made any porn movies yet?"

"No. Full of shit that's what these guys are. Full of bull-shit." He spits the words.

"I know someone who could arrange it with a single phone call." I stroke the bulge in his jeans. I can't help it. I love his cock.

"Oh?"

"Yes. He knows everybody who is anybody. But you'd have to let him suck you off."

He nods. "When do I meet him?"

"How do people reach you?" All my rubbing has given him another erection. He is truly incredible.

"I got a girlfriend, sort of, you know. She takes messages for me. He could call her."

After I deposit him, like an empty Coke bottle, at the street corner where I found him before, I lean over to take one last look at the bulge.

When I return to Bird's Eye, the pool lights are on and Kyle is floating on my raft. He is nude. In this light, he is so beautiful it brings tears to my eyes.

"Nice place you got here," he says.

This is the wrong script. This is the moment when I'm supposed to be indignant. I'm supposed to cuss him out for throwing a party without me, messing up the house. But he is gazing at me with that look of love and possession and pride I have grown accustomed to.

I tug off my clothes and jump in the water. I swim up to him. "I just took your big boyfriend back to his street corner."

"That's what you get for drivin' around pretending you're me. You know, you'll never get away with it. You're just too little."

I tip his raft and he splashes into the water. I love him more than anything.

Three Days Later

"What the hell is this?" Steve says to me over the phone.

"What the hell is what?"

"This kid Howie's dick. I've never seen anything quite like it."

"C'mon, Steve."

"I'm serious. You sure know how to pick 'em."

"No, it was Kyle. Kyle's the one."

He chuckles. "Yeah, Kyle sure can pick 'em all right."

TWENTY-TWO

Monday, September 19
The phone rings; it is the middle of the night.
It is Kyle. "Hey, boy, what are you doing?"
"Nothing."
"Did you just get up?"
"No. I just went to bed."
"Hell, I haven't been to bed yet. What time is it?"
"*Here* it's three a.m."
We go on talking but long silences are blurred by his slurring to begin a word, like someone waking out of drugged sleep and slipping off again between syllables. He's on tour promoting the new album. Record stores, nightclubs, wherever Martin could book him. Martin sent Joe with him, to keep him out of trouble.
"How's Joe?" I ask.
"He's out. We're in Dallas. He likes Dallas. I hate Dallas. I hate Texas."
"I know."
"Bad things happen when I go to Texas."
Every time this happens, I have the terrible feeling that I have failed him. But I think that one could not escape failing him no matter what. Nevertheless, I am sad. It is hopeless. I cannot go back and start over.
Four hours later and the phone is ringing. It is Kyle again. Now he sounds perfectly natural. "Hi ya, boy."
"Hi ya, Kyle."
"I want you to fuck me."
"I'm busy."
"Are you busy Friday night?"

"Friday?"

"I open Friday night at Max's Kansas City."

"Max's *Kansas City*?"

"It's a little place in New York. It's the end of this tour. Joe'll be gone. Thank god. Bastard watches me like a hawk. I can't get away with anything."

"Oh."

"Hey, what can I say? I go where they want me. I'm not a big fuckin' movie star anymore like you."

Nor is he the teenybopper's darling any longer. They've moved on to Shaun Cassidy and Andy Gibb, but he's better than both of them put together, I think.

"Mac said you have Friday off," he goes on.

"I have lots of time. Steve's little movie wrapped last week. I don't start the sequel until after New Year's."

"Oh, yeah. The sequel. You and Bud Logan."

I don't respond. It doesn't deserve a response.

"Well, okay. See you Friday."

"Well, maybe."

And he hangs up. I hold the receiver a moment before I slowly drop it back into the cradle and stare at it. It is my reaction shot.

. . .

Sales of Kyle's third album for Capitol, while not spectacular, are holding up rather well. One reviewer said, "Dreamy 'Hush Sweet Lover' is an erotic cascade of gliding notes in which Cartwright's voice dips and shimmers like a waterfall of desire. Cartwright's is a focused and utterly captivating performance - it's hard to resist his breathy, seductive phrasing - displays all the joy and pain of love, and an artist who can wrap it all up in style and presence. An old-fashioned song cycle of unrequited love, at once traditional and *sui generis*."

I keep listening to it, jacking off to it. I can't help it.

The little nightclub tour, hastily-arranged by Martin to take advantage of the good reviews, is making money. But Mac said Joe told him every time Kyle hits the stage he is hurting. I told Mac if Joe were around I'd be hurting too; I don't think he appreciated my humor.

But Kyle doesn't appear to be hurting tonight in New York as he comes onto the little round stage in the middle of the room and begins with Billy Joel's "New York State of Mind." By the time he's singing "Comes down to reality/and it's fine with me/Cause I've let it slide . . . " he's made the song his own, at least for tonight, with me.

Finally, he gets to it: "Hear my voice through the din/Feel the waves/On your skin/Like a fall from within/Come back to me/What on earth must I do?/Scream and yell until I am blue?/Curse your soul/When will you/come back to me?"

He's singing these lyrics directly to me. I am sitting at the back of the room, at the bar, alone, but he found me. I blush. He smiles and goes on for the big finish: "...Ride the rail/Come by mail/C.O.D.

"Leave a sign on your door/Out to lunch/Evermore

"In a Rolls or a van/Wrapped in mink/Or Saran/Any way that you can/Come back to me."

It's a wonderful show. Kyle's in good voice and his back-up is strong: a young Negro playing the piano, whom he introduces to the crowd as "C.C." I think there's a spark of something more there but don't want to dwell on it, just have fun. Andy Warhol and his pals, at a ringside table, go backstage first and I wait until they leave.

"Come back to me?" Kyle asks as he lets me into his dressing room and locks the door behind us. He is wearing only his pants.

"It seems as if I've never been away."

Our kiss lasts several moments. Finally, he asks, "Did I move 'em tonight?"

"You moved 'em."

"But mostly I think I moved *you*."

"Yeah."

"Good. It was all for you tonight, boy," he says, patting my ass. "All for my *little* boy."

He takes me in his arms and as he sucks my ear lobe, desire churns within my body at his nearness. He runs his fingers through my hair. "I love you, Bobby."

"Fuck me, Kyle. Please, fuck me." With his body straining against mine, I know we are kindred spirits, that there would never be a love as great for me, and maybe not for him. He steps back and unzips his pants. Holding me tightly in his arms from behind, he slips his hand down the front of my pants. I am hard.

There is no couch or rug to lie down on so I lift myself onto the edge of a road case that holds some leftover sound equipment. He tugs off my jeans and throws them in a heap on the cold cement floor. Grabbing my ass, he spits on his cock and thrusts it deeply inside of me. I go blind from the searing pain of him rushing it so, of being so demanding. But I asked for it. He pounds in again and again. Then his dick slides out so that only the head of it remains and wet strands of his hair cling to my face. I wrap my arms around his neck and draw my legs close up around his waist. I want him back in me completely again so badly I begin to shout and scream.

He muzzles me by kissing me.

Soon I become aware of a loud, banging noise, like hammering. It becomes deafening: the road case is being flung repeatedly into the wall by the force of our thrashing bodies.

"Let's go back to my hotel, okay?" I say.

"Hotel? I thought you'd be staying on Park Avenue."

"Jay's wife is at the apartment."

"Oh." He hugs me close, not looking at me. His movements have slowed. He's taking his time. It feels so good.

"Okay, but you didn't have to go to a hotel. I'm staying with C.C., you know."

"No, I didn't know," I hold him tightly. "I thought you were still with Ben."

"No, that's been over a long time." He jabs me, very hard, picks up a momentum now.

"Oh." I gulp. "Well, whatever, but my hotel would be easier."

"It is easy, isn't it?" he pulls back, watches it going into me. Now it's sliding in to the hilt. "Like this, us?"

I nod. "You want to come now?"

"No. Let's wait till we get to the hotel. We'll get thrown outta here any minute. They're ready to close."

I nod and he pulls out. I lie still for a moment, getting used to being without his weight, then slowly I lower my legs and start to get dressed.

As he zips up his pants he says, "You know, I've been playing this set for weeks but tonight I suddenly knew I was moving them. It was havin' you here. That's what it was. And it's like the tides come in, and we're on that tide. Wow, what a night!"

Now he's into stillness. It's quiet except for the street noise far below us. In bed, there's a wonderful feeling of familiarity as his tongue enters my asshole. He tastes his own cum, tickles the soft sensitive lips of my ass, then pierces it as hard and deeply as he can. He withdraws it, then starts again.
The sound of his groin and belly slapping my ass now fills the room. He takes his cock almost out, then with little short thrusts, renews his fucking, then rams it in all the way down to the pubic hair. I come when he comes and we lie still, his arms wrapped around my stomach.
"Wow, what a night," he says, softer now, with feeling, caressing my ass.
"You can say that again."
"Okay," he says, "what a night! What a boy. *My* boy. I just love my little boy."
This is the Kyle Cartwright fuck of long ago, the fuck I have missed so terribly, the fuck from someone I love and someone I know loves me, even if sometimes he doesn't act like it. At one point he says he never wants me to give up on him. "I need somebody to crawl home to." We never realize what we've lost until later, then we discover it. But yet even as he's hard again and enters me and starts fucking me again, the music doesn't seem to sound like it used to.

I check out of the hotel. We're going to C.C.'s after all. He says I have to meet C.C., who, he admits, is more than just his accompanist. My heart sinks. "Hey, you always wanted a big black one. Now's your chance."

We arrive at C.C.'s and the pianist is out. "He has his friends. I don't ask," Kyle says.
We aren't in the cramped apartment in the Village ten minutes before we're in the bedroom, necking. It's not even noon. He pulls away from me. "I've treated you like shit. Now I want you to treat me like shit! Please!" He gets on the bed, nude, begging me. I roll him over and start swatting his ass. I

reach between his legs, caress his asshole. His ass twitches. How many have been there who didn't seem to care how it felt to him? I ask myself. But I care. I will hurt him, but I will be nice about it. I slap his ass, spanking hard, soft, and in between, until both sides are warm, red.

The black dildo he brings out is unbelievable. He says he found it in a shop down the street. It is the biggest one he's ever seen. "Is C.C. as big as this?" I ask.

"It's not that he's big, it's just that he's – well, you'll see."

Years of trouble between us let go as I fuck him with the dildo. I have never really hurt him but I am hurting him now. He's howling as I sink it into him, pull it out nearly all the way, sink it in again.

My fingers go in next. He's crying out, groaning, loving every minute of it. He blows me while I continue giving him what he wants.

. . .

C.C. finally arrives. He is very pleasant to me and we go to dinner at David's Pot Belly. We sit in the window, as if we were on a stage, but the performers are in the street, walking by. We laugh at the passing parade on Christopher Street. It feels good to be able to go out in public with Kyle.

I ask Kyle if he's going back to Los Angeles with me.

"No," he says. "C.C.'s got some friends here that want to record me at a club for the fourth album. It'd be 'Kyle Live!'"

"I'd love it," I say. He's enthusiastic for the first time in months. I'm happy for him. But he's with someone else now, someone he cares about, who cares about him. I feel left out.

When we return to the apartment, Kyle goes into the bedroom and closes the door, leaving C.C. and me in the living room. C.C. puts on Kyle's first album.

"He really is good," C.C. says, sitting across from me on the couch, kicking off his shoes. He stands up, takes off his shirt.

"When he works at it," I say. "What's he doing in there?"

"Doing some lines, getting ready." He rubs his crotch, stares at me, his large dark eyes glistening in the moody light of the single table lamp. God, I want him. I want to suck him and fuck me senseless, but I don't want to share him with Kyle.

I look at my suitcases, still by the front door. "I think I'd better go."

"Oh?"

"It's got nothing to do with you. I find you very nice and, well – "

"I understand."

"At another time, another place, I'd be all over you in a minute."

"I would like that."

"I know I would like it, but not like this."

He nods. "Do you have a place to go?"

"Yes. I'll just go back to the hotel." I stand and step towards the door.

"You're sure?" he asks, following me.

"Yes." I turn and he takes me in his long arms. He is six feet tall and all muscle. I hug him to me, lay my head on his chest. His heart is beating very fast.

"*Tesoro*," I say.

"What?"

"Oh, it all happened so quickly. Sometimes I don't think I can deal with it. This is one of those times." I look up into his handsome, smiling face. "Please understand."

He nods. "Another time, another place," he says, putting his finger under my chin and tilting my head back.

We kiss. It is a short, friendly kiss.

"Kiss him goodbye for me," I say, pulling away from him.

"I will. He loves you, you know. You're his little boy."

"I know. I'll always be his little boy."

TWENTY-THREE

Monday, November 21

I am back in New York with Jay. He has meetings to attend and I hitched a ride with him on the Gulfstream. Kyle hadn't called and I couldn't find any record of C.C.'s phone number. I decided if I went with Jay to Manhattan, I could find my lover. But when I got here Mac called to say he had at last heard from Kyle. It seems he had gone with C.C. to California. The Negro went to Berkeley to see his family and Kyle went to San Francisco, and was now back at Bird's Eye. I was furious. I decided to go shopping.

When I came back to the apartment, Jay had the television blaring in the library. He was puffing on his big cigar and drinking brandy. I knew something had happened. He told me I'd better sit down.

We watched transfixed as a brushfire that started inland was moving across the mountains towards the ocean. Malibu, they said, could be turned into a pile of ashes. The fire would move swiftly, Jay said, because everything was very dry after two years of drought. He had been trying to reach Bird's Eye all afternoon but there was no answer. He'd been in touch with Mac, who knew nothing except that Kyle was not at the apartment and must be at the house.

I couldn't stop crying. I felt powerless. I couldn't sleep and when I took a sedative and finally dozed off, images of the house going up in flames woke me up again.

Jay was up most of the night on the phone to his secretary, to everybody he knew, trying desperately to get more information. Finally, he couldn't stand it any more and cancelled all of his meetings and ordered his pilots to get the jet ready, we were going back to California.

It was a sad flight. Jay stayed on the phone, arranging things that didn't need to be arranged, just to keep busy, try to get his mind off of it.

I was a basket-case. Jay let me smoke a joint and I finally passed out.

Mac met us at the airport. By this time, the fire had been contained and rescue workers had given him the news: Kyle had made his way to the pool but it was too late. I broke down completely. Jay hugged me and told Mac to take me home with him. Jay lit another cigar and, in shock himself, got into the limousine without saying goodbye.

Mac and I rode to his place in silence. I was numb. All I wanted to do was get there and then I could really let go. Mac was solid, not a tear, but I could see the hurt in his eyes. Kevin was waiting and I broke down in his arms. He held me and then we shared a joint while Mac made busy on the phone. I had to be protected, he said. Somehow. He hadn't had a chance to really think things through but he did his best.

Kyle's death brought Ned to Mac's and we cried together. That would be last time I would cry. Crying wouldn't bring him back. I had lost him, perhaps lost everything that was at Bird's Eye.

The following day, they were permitting property owners into the hills. Mac went with me. When I first saw the damage I couldn't believe there would be anything left but there was. The fire-retardant plants that Kyle's gardeners had put around most of the property had helped. The worst damage was at the end of the house where Kyle's bedroom was. The firemen had been able to extinguish the blaze quickly but that part of the place would have to be completely rebuilt.

The image of Kyle trying to get to the pool stayed with me. He really didn't want to die after all. As often as he said he wished he could, he didn't want to.

"There's one thing that wasn't made public, to protect you." Mac said as we drove back into town.

"Oh?"

"He had traces of semen in his stomach. He'd taken

somebody's load just a few hours before it happened."

I smiled. "That's good. That first day here, he told me he wanted to die with a cock in his mouth. At least one of his wishes came true."

TWENTY-FOUR

A Week Later

I'm singing to myself the same old song, the one he sang on that grassy Texas slope so long ago: "Don't Let Me Be Lonesome Tonight." I am eating M&M's like we did on that joyous day. And I am crying.

Kyle doesn't belong to me anymore, as if he ever did, but the land does. I walk a lot and the neighbors will see me and give me disapproving looks because only from time to time have I ever ventured down these roads on foot. But I will walk around Bird's Eye until I'm exhausted, until I accept that he is somehow still here and that we are still here together, the two of us, hopelessly, madly, desperately, together. And in love.

Tenney saw me at the memorial service yesterday and said, "Life is not a gift but an option, Bobby. What matters is that you be true to yourself. Kyle could never do that. He had to be what others wanted him to be."

I nodded. Tenney's words will always live with me as I continue to lie about who I really am and what I really want. But I am an actor, after all.

TWENTY-FIVE

Four Days Later
   I'm in New York again; it's beginning to grow on me. Finally. Jay told me I needed to come here, to let the workers do their job at Bird's Eye and get back in touch with reality. I don't know that one gets in touch with reality in a beautiful apartment on Park Avenue but I'm working on it.
   We've just gotten back from Montana. We buried Kyle there, next to his brother, Kale. It was very sad. Just me and Jay and a preacher. Mac was going to go but, as usual with him, something came up at the last minute.
   "It's a shame about Kyle. In those last years, he was everywhere, trying to please everybody," Jay said on the Gulfstream on the way here after the funeral.
   "I know. At one point he was even fucking pussy."
   Jay shook his head in dismay. "He was so caught up in being Kyle Cartwright that the boy from Montana got lost and he *became* Kyle Cartwright, the cowboy character from 'Silver City.' But that was not a good thing to be. He didn't know who Kyle Cartwright was. Cary Grant told me once that's what happened to him, that good old Archie Leach just ceased to exist. So far you've been able to avoid all that, Bobby. I'm proud of you." He patted my knee, then handed me a key.
   "What's this?"
   "The key to the apartment. It's *your* apartment now. I was going to leave it to Kyle."
   "But your wife?"
   "She won't set foot in it again. After that last trip, when she

was finally done redecorating it, she said Kyle had killed any desire to ever stay here again. Knowing what he may have done there, the kind of people he was with, what he did to it – " He shook his head sadly.

"I don't know what to say."

"You deserve it. And there'll be more when I'm no longer here, you know. Much more. I had my attorneys set up a trust fund for you. You can make your own pictures some day, do anything you want."

I was speechless. I just kept running the key through my fingers. Then I laid my head on his shoulder. "I love you, Jay."

"You're a good boy."

"But I will disappoint you, just as he did."

"No. Not in my lifetime. You're different; you're a good boy."

Now he comes into the bedroom from the bathroom, naked, fresh from his morning shower.

"You look beautiful this morning," he says softly.

I put down my pen and notebook and reach out to him. "I feel beautiful here, in this beautiful place."

"It's your place now. It's beautiful just because it's your place." He takes my hand and strokes the back of it gently. "I thought I'd never love another man and then I met Kyle. And I never thought I'd ever love anyone more than Kyle, and then I met you. Isn't it funny how life is?"

"I love you, too, Jay. More than you'll ever know."

I throw back the sheet, roll over and lift my ass up to meet his hands. He rubs the cheeks and says, "You are *such* a good boy."

TWENTY-SIX

The Following Night
". . . You'd have more fun if I let everybody know who you are."

I turn my attention away from a photograph of me hanging on the wall of the gallery. It's Ben, saying the same line he used at the first party we ever attended together. I'm at his opening, a show of his photographs.

"Don't you dare," I say, rolling the program with my hands, threatening to hit him with it.

He looks wonderful. I want to suck his dick right now.

"Your secret's safe with me," he says. "Always has been."

I take a deep breath. I'd planned this, in a way. I'd seen the advertisement, knew the artist would be at the opening. I ducked in quietly, not bothering to sign the guest book. It took him only three minutes to come over to me.

I look at the picture again, of me at Bird's Eye. He took it before we left for the premiere of "Space Travellers." I am wearing my tuxedo, looking very grown-up and un-Bobby Richards, yet I have my hands in my pockets, trying mightily to be casual.

"Like it?" he asks.

I nod. I'd forgotten he'd taken it. "I like it so much I'm going to buy it."

"No, I'm giving it to you, just as soon as the show's over."

I grin. "I have to wait until the show's over?"

He smiles. "For the photograph."

The Following Morning
Ben's cock always seems to be bigger than I remember it. I

curse the day I let my jealousy over Kyle staying here get to me.

"I couldn't understand," Ben said on the way over to his apartment in the cab. "I was just trying to help him, not take him away from you."

"I know. I know that now. At the time, I was so naive about things. I still am, in a lot of ways, but I'll try to make it up to you."

We held hands and he said, "It's me that has the making up to do. I should have called you, should have told you how sorry I was about Kyle."

"I still have nightmares – "

He looked past me, out the window, then gazed back into my eyes again. "What can I do?"

I smiled. "You know what you can do. You've always known."

Now he begins to rock back and forth, sliding his hard cock in and out with that incredible rhythmic motion he has, his thighs smacking against my ass, and the pain has become unbearable. I haven't been fucked like this in so long and this is the third time in just a few hours. He grips my asscheeks with both hands and pushes hard, running his hands up my back and moaning. I try to ignore the pain. I look up, into the mirror. He wanted it this way so each of us could watch in the mirrored headboard but now he is hovering over me, obscuring my view of the penis, the cock of my wildest dreams. Soon he is pulling out, letting the cum splash on my back. I witness once again his fabulous orgasm and how beautiful he is when he's enjoying it like this. And nobody comes so hard, so often. I have met my match.

We lie together kissing and then I lay my head on his chest, feel his heart thumping wildly. I idly stroke his cock, reflecting again on the intensity of the fucks.

He asks, "How long are you staying this time?"

"Until after New Year's. And then I have to start the sequel."

"Oh, yeah," he says, "the sequel."

Reprise: Come Back to Me

Hear my voice
Where you are
Take a train
Steal a car
Hop a freight
Grab a star
Come back to me

Catch a plane
Catch a breeze
On your hands
On your knees
Swim or fly
Only please
Come back to me

Have you gone to the moon?
Or a corner saloon?
Or to rack and to ruin?
I don't care
This is where you should be
From the hills
From the shore
Ride the wind
To my door
Turn the highway to dust
Break the law if you must
Only please just
Come back to me

Hear my voice through the din
Feel the waves
On your skin
Like a fall from within

Come back to me
What on earth must I do?
Scream and yell until I am blue?
Curse your soul?
When will you
come back to me?

...Ride the rail
Come by mail
C.O.D.
Leave a sign on your door
Out to lunch
Evermore
In a Rolls or a van
Wrapped in mink
Or Saran
Any way that you can
Come back to me

Song by Burton Lane and Alan Jay Lerner
(Copyright Chappell & Co., Inc./ASCAP)

HOORAY FOR HOLLYWOOD

*"Strip the phony tinsel off Hollywood
and you'll find the real tinsel underneath."
– Oscar Levant*

THE DREAM PALACE

As a little boy growing up, I did the same things week after week and Saturdays had a special place in my life: I got to go to the Palace. My afternoon at the movies. And I lived by the movies – not just by them, either, but for them and in them. Serials, cartoons and the feature film. The features I loved most were the ones about cowboys and starring cowboys: Hopalong Cassidy, Gene Autry, Roy Rogers and, most of all, Harry Hunter.

Harry didn't achieve the great popularity of the other stars because he went to serve his country in the Second World War and, after the war, it seemed he could only get supporting roles in other types of features. But eventually he returned to leading man roles. Star-struck, I followed his progress through movie magazines. Harry was, to my mind, the perfect man. I had no idea in those days what this *really* meant. All I knew was, I wanted to be with him.

Later on, after my older brother initiated me in the pleasures of gay sex, I began fantasizing that it was Harry who was making me feel so good. In his early westerns, Harry was a nimble rider and had a trick of throwing his right leg across the horse's neck in his comic dismounting scenes. I began to picture Harry pulling that same stunt with me. When Harry was shooting somebody, he had a grim deadpan expression and after the Daisy Company put a BB replica of his gun called the "Harry Hunter Special" I just had to have one. In his westerns, Harry wore a white hat and an air of lethal calm. When he took his hat off, his black hair was slicked to a part as precise as a razor slash. Of course, that was the way I had to wear mine. His chiseled face was handsomer than any of the other actors of the era and, as I grew older, and Harry's fame increased, I would often have people comment that I looked like him. By that time, I was almost as tall as he was and, as he always did, I tried to maintain a year-round suntan.

In 1956, I went to Hollywood myself and began working in television. A couple of years later, I never expected to be in the cast of a film starring my boyhood idol but that's what happened.

After reading for a director on the Universal lot, I was leaving the office when I saw a handsome man, just ambling along, wearing a tailored white suit, white Stetson, cowboy boots. I did a double-take; it was Harry. He looked at me, too, and smiled. I introduced myself and just started walking along the street with him as if I was really going in the same direction. I told him I was one of the kids on the "Sweethearts" series on CBS. I also told him they were now even letting me write some of the script. "But not the funny stuff."

"Don't watch much TV," he said, shaking his head. "No actor in pictures does TV, let alone watch it."

"Oh."

He stopped, turned and looked at me curiously. "Damn! You know, you look and act amazingly like I did when I was your age. It's almost as if I had found a long-lost twin brother."

It was almost as if *I* had found nirvana. Harry Hunter was taking *me* to the commissary. Buying me coffee and a cookie if I wanted it. I did, a chocolate chip.

He had only coffee, which he slurped while smoking a Pall Mall. I went on and on about my passion for his *films*, recounting my favorite scenes in every one of them. Finally he stopped me and said, "Hey, some of those I don't even remember. I was drunk a lot of the time, you know."

"No, I didn't know." He looked terrific. Whatever drinking he had done must have agreed with him. At just past forty, he was more distinguished looking but carried himself with the same swagger he did in the early westerns.

"Well, you're somethin' else, kid," he said, blowing a smoke ring. "I oughta get you to ghost write my autobiography."

I didn't want to write anything, I just wanted to go on talking to him, but he had an appointment with the production people for his new movie, "Life Sentence." He grinned. "You look like me and you're on TV, right?"

"Yes."

"Maybe you'd like to audition for the part of my son in this epic. There's only a couple of scenes – "

"Tell me when."

The next thing I knew, I was on a plane to Pittsburgh. Pittsburgh? I asked. That was the setting of the movie and my scenes with Harry were to be filmed on location. Harry had already been there a week.

In Pittsburgh, Harry took my arrival as his opportunity to escape the company filming at a prison and, as he put it, "coach me on my scenes." The night I arrived, after I had checked into my room at the Holiday Inn, Harry took me to a striptease joint in his rented Oldsmobile. Harry had two martinis and ended up with the lead stripper, Kitten, on his lap. "You're very nice," he said to her. But when she told him, "I also act," we left there in a hurry.

"Look at those kids," he said as we passed some teenaged boys leaning against a building, their hands in their pockets, provocatively showing themselves off. "Youngsters standin' on street corners in the middle of the night."

It wasn't even midnight, but to Harry maybe it seemed much later than it was – all the time – because in the bar in the motel, he proceeded to down another two martinis and I heard the full, sad story of his life. About the women he had been involved with and the ones he'd turned down, and all the children he wished he'd fathered.

"There's still time," I said.

He nodded and stared into his empty martini glass. The more he drank, the more affectionate he became. I was astounded by the affectionate pats on my ass, the hugs, the fact when we sat on bar stools our legs would press together and neither of us would move them. At midnight, I saw Harry to his room and then went to bed myself, dreaming of what it would be like to be in the room two floors up with Harry. He had noticed the boys on the corner before I had. There was still hope.

The next morning I went to Harry's room only to find him still in bed. He had ordered extra ice from room service along with his orange juice and danish roll and had already started drinking. As he walked about the room, lighting cigarettes, pouring drinks, explaining the scenes we would have together, he was dressed only in his boxer shorts. I gazed adoringly at his physique, something beautiful that had never been fully displayed in a photograph or in a film. I was amazed at how fit he looked considering all he drank. I longed to run my hands over his hairy chest, suck on his nipples, work my down to his navel, and then to –

He was ranting and raving about how bad the film was, how the director stunk, how awful the location was, and so on and I begin to think what a shame it was he couldn't appreciate everything he had. Here he was *starring* in a new movie at Universal. He wasn't a star of the top rank, but his name was always above the title. He had a beautiful home in the Hollywood Hills, nice cars, money in the bank; seemingly every material need was met. I began to wonder what needs were *not* being met. Why the hasty retreat from the strip joint? Why the casual touching of my body? Why this "coaching" business? Maybe all he needed was a push. That was all *I* needed, and it had to come from my brother; no one else could have done in at that time. But here was a film star who had been kind enough to get me a role in his movie, one that involved getting me to the location – suddenly it all clicked in. Yes, he did need a push. He had pushed me about as far he could; now *he* needed a push. I began to feel special. It was all coming together.

"Hey, let's get some lunch," I said, jumping up, interrupting his harangue.

"Oh, I'm sorry. I get so worked up. I was ignoring you."

I stepped over to him. "I'd never let you do that for long. " I stood before him as the adoring fan I was, yet I was bold enough to stroke the back of his hand as he brought the glass to his lips.

He held me in his gaze over the rim of the glass as he finished the drink. Slowly he put the glass down on the table next to the bed and took my hand in his. "You're on to me, aren't you?"

"Are you *on* to me?"

"From the first moment."

"I didn't mean it that way."

"But it was nice that I took it that way, wasn't it?"

I had never kissed a man before but he had kissed women so often for the camera and for real that he knew just what to do so I gave myself up to him. I felt as if I was being swallowed up by the most incredible force I had ever known. As our mouths locked, his arms crushed me to his chest and his hands squeezed my buttocks. This was not what I had expected. In my fantasies, I thought he would take me as my brother had, without any preliminaries. Just, "Here, suck it, and okay, roll over on your stomach and spread 'em." Harry was making love to me, to every inch of my body, and sucking *my* cock. I couldn't believe it – and I couldn't keep from coming. The wonder of it was, he loved it. Took every drop.

Now I wanted to adore him in the many ways I had in countless dreams. At first he was reluctant to surrender completely to me but I would accept nothing less. He lay on the bed on his back, watching me as I gorged on his beefy body. I got him so worked up that he begged me either to let him come or to let him fuck me.

I had never been fucked by my brother. He had only showed me how to jack-off, how to suck a dick. Anal sex was something I had learned about in high school, and then it was me doing the fucking. And then only once, one warm afternoon in my bedroom with door locked. My partner, Jeffrey, a screaming faggot from the seventh grade, couldn't take it for more than five minutes.

Harry was massively hung and just looking at his penis standing straight up from his belly, I didn't see how it would be possible. But it was worth trying.

He was gentle with me, sucking at my hole for several minutes, tonguing it, then greasing his finger for a gentle probing. I came again while he was doing that. He couldn't believe it and asked if I wanted to continue.

"Oh, yes," I sighed. "Please."

Two fingers were next, still massaging gently. My cock was soon erect again and he sucked on it while he continued a slow finger-fucking of my ass. Before long I was begging for it.

"You have to get it ready first," he said, straddling my head with his thighs, his cock semi-hard and dangling lewdly before me. I licked the head for a while and then opened my mouth wide. He slid the cock in and began fucking my mouth, a pleasure so intense I didn't want it to stop. But after a few moments, he said, "God, I better do it now or I'll come sure as hell."

Lifting me up by the ankles, he brought the bulbous head of his cock to the well-prepared opening. I could not see how it would ever fit. The rigid shaft of what appeared to be purple-veined marble glistened with my spit as Harry began inserting it. He knew how to rub, and probe, and slowly stretch so that it suddenly slid in without the pain I had expected. There was pain, yes, but it quickly was forgotten as Harry, totally in control of his fabulous instrument of pleasure, began his thrusting. I surrendered completely, locking him to me by crossing my ankles, and he scooped me up in his strong arms and held me, rocking me back and forth, hardly moving his cock, settling in for a long fuck. We kissed, tentatively at first, and then with real passion, as if we were being filmed. My hands went to his head and I was holding him tightly when he came. He lifted up so that he could slam it in to the hilt as he filled me with his jism.

I dozed, lying close to him, feeling his incredible warmth. At one point I opened my eyes to find him sitting up, just staring at me. "What's wrong?" I asked.

"Nothing. Nothing at all," he said, taking me in his arms again. I reached down to guide him into me again. "Hey, I'm all fucked out," he said.

"Doesn't feel like it."

This time, being "all fucked out," he didn't come, but I did, and then it really was time for lunch.

The next morning, it was raining and the wipers beat back and forth against the windshield. "Jesus, what a crummy day," Harry said.

"Do you know the way? Do we need a map?" I said as we passed a gas station.

"No. I know the way. Hell, I was out there all last week. Bastards, picking locations in hell and gone. And for a black and white picture. They told me that Otto Preminger is filming 'Anatomy of a Murder' in Michigan in black and white so we guess we can do this thing in black and white and go to Pennsylvania, so I said, 'What do I know?' and they said, 'Right.'"

"It'll be fine," I said, patting his knee.

But it wasn't. Not really. "Look there," I said, pointing at the sign. It read "Steubenville, Ohio."

"Jesus, we're on the airport road. This isn't right. We're going in the wrong direction."

"I thought you said you always wanted to make a picture in Ohio."

This got him laughing, laughing so hard he had to stop the car. "You're the funniest little sonofabitch I've ever met."

"Maybe the littlest."

"Hey, that's big enough for me, boy. Big enough for me. Any bigger and I'd feel inferior."

"We'd never want that to happen."

What did happen was that he pulled into a gas station and we asked directions to the Allegheny County Workhouse. The guy at the pump looked at us as if we were planning on breaking someone out.

"The *what?*" he asked, scratching his head.

Harry repeated our destination, emphasizing every vowel.

"Well, buster, you're real lost."

"I know that," Harry said, shaking his head.

"Tell ya what, you turn around here and go right back to downtown. Then ask them there. Ask at any gas station. Yeah, you're thirty or forty miles from there."

"Jesus, I better call 'em," Harry said, getting out of the car.

In a few moments he was back and telling me that we could have the day off. It was raining anyway and they'd work around us, but we had better be there tomorrow, first thing. In fact, they were sending someone to pick us up.

"You know, they're not such bad guys. It could have been worse. I had an offer to do this thing about a jazz musician in Harlem. Now *that* would have been something."

In a few minutes we were going into a tunnel, then out onto a cloverleaf and, as the rain started coming down in torrents, he just pulled over and started laughing again.

"Baby," he said finally, "I'm lost."

"No," I said, curling up to him. "You're found."

Our kiss lasted a good five minutes. I was ready to go down on him when there was a rapping on the window. It was the police!

Harry rolled down the window. "What's the problem?" the

cop in the black rain gear asked.

"Hey, chief! Am I glad to see you. We're lost! We've been forty miles out in the country and now we're headed back that way again. "

The cop smiled. "Where are you headed?"

"We were going to the Allegheny County Workhouse but now all we want to do is get to the Holiday Inn."

"The Workhouse? Oh, yeah, aren't you that actor fella, Harry Hunter? Doin' that movie down there aren't ya?"

"Yes, if we can ever get there."

"Any other time I'd lead you outta here, but not in this rain."

"Well, all I want is to get to the Holiday Inn."

The officer pointed to the tallest building in town and said, "Just go there. The Inn's right next door."

"Thanks, chief." Rolling up the window, Harry said, "This is what happens when you go on location. Nothing but a pain in the ass."

"That's for sure," I laughed, rubbing an asscheek.

"You shut up!"

As we were driving back to the hotel after dinner, we passed the Strand theater and I noticed "White Rapids" was on a double bill, starring none other than Harry Hunter. "Stop!" I screamed.

Harry slammed on the brakes. "Whoa! Now what?"

"C'mon," I said, "we're going to the movies." I pointed to the marquee.

"We can go to the movies at home. Here we can go to bed."

"We'll be going to bed a lot from now on."

"Promise?" he asked, groping me.

"Promise. Now, let's find a place to park. This is one of my favorite Harry Hunter pictures."

"Lord almighty! It's one of the worst pieces of shit ever made!"

"That's why I like it."

"You're crazy."

Crazy, yes. About Harry. And sitting in the dark with his image flickering on the screen and his one hand in mine and the other stroking my erection. Suddenly, I was back at the Palace, and I wasn't dreaming any more.

AT A PARTY IN HOLLYWOOD

As this stud I could never love moves ahead of me, our drinks in hand, eyes flicking a path to the atrium, the sun bounces off the pool, blinding us.

Blissfully naked, we embrace by the doors leading to the pool. He twists a cooling patina of sweat on his upper lip into a question mark of a kiss on my neck and his hand goes to my crotch. As he gropes the firmness he finds, his mouth opens on my open mouth, and once again I am beguiled by this big black stud. Terrifying blackness in a field of dazzling white.

I had not expected to find him at this party in Hollywood. The last time I saw him it was in New York, in the dead of winter. I was on the subway, going to the Village and I sat next to him. His leg was soon pressing against mine. I returned the pressure. He pressed harder and smiled. He got off at Christopher Street and I followed him through the snow. He made me pursue him two blocks before he turned and introduced himself: Matthew.

It was a tiny apartment with white walls, very little art. An old sofa which had once been white almost filled the living room.

There was little time for pleasantries. He knew what I wanted. Soon I was lying between his legs, sucking him. It was an enormous penis, the kind I have grown to prefer: huge, black, erect. Why this obsession? Why not? I've had everything else. Now only this will do.

He got up after a few minutes and had me lie on the sofa on my stomach. I closed my eyes. He moistened his long dark fingers with lube and worked them into my anus. I reached under me and began stroking my own cock. His fingering of me was enough. I could come just like that, but, no, he stopped, swung my leg off the cushion and climbed over me. Slowly, confidently he began. His fucking of me took on its own enchanting rhythm, a luxurious movement black men have perfected. I came first, of course, but he kept on, insistent, and just before he came, he pulled out and the jism warmed my back.

After washing ourselves, we strolled through the park, and I bought us cappuccinos at a small bakery he knew.

I told him I had to get back to my hotel. He said he wanted to do it again. "Okay," I said, but this time I wanted to watch him. I sat on the sofa and leaned back. He lifted my legs and, holding me by my ankles, he guided the glorious, cut thing into me again, slowly. Now I watched as inch after absurd inch slid into me, effortlessly. Even though I've taken so many of these big black ones I've lost count, each one is a sweet new sensation and this one was sweeter than most.

With every thrust, I grew more enamored with his extraordinary prowess. Before long, he was spreading my legs as wide apart as he could and stepping up his rhythm. His sweat dropped onto my belly as he slammed into me, more demanding now than before, as if this is truly going to be the last time.

"I only come to Los Angeles if I'm paid for it," he says now, as we come out of our embrace.

"Everybody has to come, though, sometime. Just to see it," I said. Hollywood is a place where dreams can come true and growing up is optional, but it is not a town for losers, so it is not entirely a surprise to find Matthew here, but it did give me a start. He was big-league sex and what had begun as just another JO party had now become quite something else.

Sonny Griffin had called me a week earlier, saying he had invited some new faces, kids in from New York to make yet another fuck flick. Sonny is forever remaking the great films of our time, adding sex scenes that would have made the original even better. His latest project is a parody of "All About Eve." He thought I'd be great in the George Sanders part. I laughed, "Who's doing the part Marilyn Monroe played?" He said it hadn't been cast. I never expected a black man to be in the cast, but then Sonny likes dark meat almost as much as I do and he finds any excuse to use them.

"I had no idea you were in Sonny's videos," I said to

Matthew earlier.

"This is the first one for him. But I've made others in New York. I was afraid you wouldn't come home with me if you knew what I did."

I smiled. "Hardly. In fact, I've met a lot of the studs, thanks to Sonny and these parties."

Now he is looking right, then left. "Where'd everybody go?"

"They're still around. We just came out here. Few of 'em will be as public about it as this, strange as that may seem. Most of these guys are quite shy."

He grins. "Afraid's more like it." He pressed my hand to his cock, now semi-hard. "But you weren't a bit afraid of it, were you?"

Such a question deserves no answer. I drop to my knees before him to show him just how fearless I am.

It may be a jack-off party but I had prepared myself just in case. Matthew's finger finds the slickness and he grabs my thighs and pulls me over him, bringing my asshole in line with his cock. He lifts up, sending the huge cock into me with one jolt. I gasp, try to adjust to it as he continues bouncing me up and down on it. I rise up so that I can wrap my arms around him and I begin riding the prick, my thighs tight against his sides. Suddenly I am aware of others in the room. Someone is closing the curtains and soon the room is softly lit. Rock music is coming from one of the other rooms, now opened. We are surrounded by men, dicks being stroked, as I continue to bounce. A fat prick is put to the right of our heads. A thin, long cock, very hard, is brought to the left of us. Each is left to vibrate, urging us to touch them. I reach for the one on the left, Matthew the one on the right. We play with them for a few moments before we begin sucking them. After they come, others are presented, but I fall back onto the carpet, Matthew begins his final thrusting and the others close in, jerking off and spewing their spunk on my body just as Matthew is getting close. He pulls his cock from me and takes both of our erections in his hand and jerks us together. Two men kneel and, as we come, they take the jism and spread it with their own on my belly. Exhausted, Matthew falls forward and takes me in his arms. We lie here together, alone now, and he kisses me.

A few minutes later, Sonny himself comes into the room. He had not been one of those who surrounded us; I would recognize his prick anywhere, fat, dark, uncut, about nine inches of succulent, prize-winning dick. He is covered with sweat and his cock was flaccid, swinging back and forth as he approaches us, still lying in each other's arms on the floor.

"How 'bout a swim, guys?" Sonny asks, going over to the curtain.

"Great," I say, as Matthew lifts himself off of me.

As the curtain opens, I look out to the pool to see six guys I had not been introduced to earlier. "Who are *they*?" I ask.

"They're going to be in the *next* video."

"The *next* video?"

"Yeah," he laughs, pointing toward the one-way glass wall opposite us. "You and Matthew sure were the stars of the first one."

AT A PARTY IN MIAMI BEACH

"He'll pick you up at the airport," Manny told Todd over the phone.

"How will I know him?" Todd asked.

"He'll know you. He's seen all your videos."

"But does he tip?"

"Hey, for you, my number one boy, more than a tip. Look, he's loaded and he's been left with nobody to leave it all to. His sister was killed in a car accident. He just needs somebody to make him feel good."

"He's come to the right place."

"Like, I said, my numero uno. But be careful, he's liable to try to sell you one of his condos at half price."

Todd chuckled. "No, he'll *give* it to me."

"*Numero uno!*" Chortling, Manny hung up the phone.

Todd was waiting for his luggage at Miami International when a tiny man in pink sport coat, yellow shirt, green trousers and white shoes with gilt buckles approached him.

Todd snickered, thinking 'Piece of cake.'

What hair remained around the man's bald pate was the color of silver. The round face reminded Todd of a red apple. A long cigar was thrust out of the tiny mouth. The man held out a small, damp palm, pressed Todd's hand once, twice, three times, then said, "This is a pleasure. I am Max."

The smiling brown eyes that were studying him were, Todd felt, too big for Max's size. They were, Todd decided, a woman's eyes.

At the curb, the trunk of a huge white Cadillac was gaping open. Todd tossed his suitcase into it and slammed it shut. Max opened the passenger door for his young visitor and Todd got in. As Todd sunk down into the seat upholstered in red plush and soft as a pillow, Max slid in behind the wheel. He pressed the button and the window rolled down. He spat out his cigar, pressed the button again, and the window closed. "I'm allowed to smoke about as much as I'm allowed to eat pork on Yom Kippur, but habit is a powerful force. It says somewhere that a habit is second nature. I don't remember where it says that. I'll have to remember to look it up. Trouble is, I can never find the book I'm looking for. I have three homes - one here, one in New York, one in Tel Aviv - and it seems like I can never find anything."

"Well, you found me," Todd said, running his hand along his thigh.

"On the phone. I love the phone. Yeah, I had no trouble finding you. You know, it's easier to call Hollywood or Tel Aviv than a number right here in Miami Beach. Goes through a - " he paused, as if struggling to find the right word.

"Satellite?" Todd ventured, continuing to massage his thighs.

"Yeah, a satellite. I forget words. I put things down and don't remember where."

"I hope you don't do that to me," Todd said, a grin spreading across his sun-kissed face as he brought his left arm across the back of the seat.

Max groped the boy's bulging crotch. "I don't think I'll be able to put that down. Hmmmm."

"Yeah, we'll have fun, I can tell."

"Fun, that's what it's all about. Yeah, each day I live is like a miracle from heaven. The doctor allows me a nip of whiskey, but just that, but he didn't say anything about sex. And I didn't ask him!"

Max's hand finally left Todd's crotch and he pulled the Cadillac up to a huge condominium building glistening in the sun on the Beach. A parking attendant took over. Todd walked into a lobby that reminded him of a colossal movie set, with ornate rugs, mirrors, lamps, and paintings. Max's condo was just like the lobby, the rugs as red and plush as the Cadillac's upholstery.

Once in the apartment, Max hugged the porn star. "Oh, I'm glad to have your company. I'm in such a state I can't be alone for a moment. This fine apartment turns into a funeral parlor."

Todd dropped his suitcase in the hall. "Do you have a

bathroom in this place?"

"Hey, more than one, more than two, more than three," Max answered, leading Todd to the guest bedroom. They passed a giant picture of a little boy urinating in an arc while a little girl looked on approvingly. In the bathroom, the toilet seat's lid was transparent, with a two dollar bill implanted in the center. Todd lifted the seat and "Over the Rainbow" began playing.

Max stood at the door, his eyes studying the stud as he unzipped his pants and pulled out one of the biggest and surely one of the most photographed dicks in the world. Todd was used to people staring at it. He revelled in the pleasure it gave them just to look at it. Todd closed his eyes and began pissing.

Max continued to stare. "Excuse me," he said, "you don't mind if I stay?"

"No," Todd smiled. The mighty stream had dwindled to a trickle. Todd shook the last drops from the head of the monstrous organ. "I enjoy it."

"You are quite a performer. I have every video, you know, every one."

Todd turned and the long, fleshy cylinder dangled provocatively between his legs. He slid his hand along the full measure of it, reputed to be eight inches soft.

"Is it really ten and a half inches?" Max asked. "That's what they called one of your videos, '10 1/2'"

"When it's hard. Really hard. It takes me a while to get it hard all the way."

"Well, we have a while," Max said, kneeling down on the white bathroom rug.

Todd unbuttoned his trousers and spread open the crotch. Max touched the glistening pale pink knob and gently ran his nimble fingers up the thick shaft until he reached the thick patch of light brown pubic hair. The cock was as white as alabaster and richly veined. Max reached into the trousers and seized the balls. They were lightly furred and full. The cock began to throb in Max's face, as if it was beckoning him. He leaned forward, rubbing the shaft against his cheek. Todd stripped off his shirt and tossed it on the floor. Max slowly lowered the boy's trousers down his legs and, as Todd kicked off his shoes and stepped from his pants, his cock careened across Max's lips. Max opened his mouth and tried to catch it but Todd stepped back, tantalizing him with it. He tweaked it and it began to harden a bit.

Max took a deep breath and slowly began inserting the cock into his mouth. Before long, he had five inches of it in and Todd began bucking his slender hips. Max braced his hands on the smooth asscheeks as Todd took over, lunging in and out of Max's mouth as if he really meant to come. Harder and harder Todd pressed into the older man's tiny mouth, the manhood swelling to truly epic proportions. Max clenched the boy's hips and hung on as the boy slowly pushed him back until he was lying flat on his back on the carpet, the cock never leaving Max's mouth. Todd straddled Max's chest and held his head while he continued to plunge into his throat. When the orgasm began, he jerked the cock from Max's mouth. The cock pulsated and jets of cum hit Max in the face. Rising from Max's body, Todd saw Max stick fingers into the puddle of sperm and bring them to his mouth, licking them, sucking on them.

"Hey!" Todd said. "Don't do that."
"I wanted you to come in my mouth. I wanted to taste it."
"But you don't do that these days."
"Why not?"
"It could be dangerous. You never know."
"I have lived a long time. I can afford to be dangerous."

Later they stepped out onto the balcony, which overlooked the Atlantic Ocean. Far off in the distance, a ship swayed on the edge of the horizon. From sixteen floors up, the people Todd spotted on the beach seemed to be insects.

Max brought glasses of wine out to the balcony. They toasted each other. "It is good to have you here. I feel so very alone now with my dear Goldie gone. My sister was my only living relative and she was crazy. She had every complex you can find in Freud, Jung, and Adler. She married a Gentile, a truck driver, drunk like a fish. They were visiting me, right here in Miami, then decided to go to Disney World." His eyes misted over. "He was driving."

"Nobody should drink and drive."
"Tonight we walk."
"Walk?"
"To the party."

In a few minutes, Max re-appeared on the balcony with a white tie with gold flecks on it. "We're going to my old friend Reuben's. He bought one of my condos when he moved here from New York."

"Am I dressed okay?"

"No, you shouldn't wear anything. It's a shame to cover all that up." He slid his hand across Todd's ass. "But nudity isn't allowed in Miami Beach so, yeah, you're fine."

. . .

The door to the living room opened and Reuben greeted them as if he hadn't seen Max in weeks but they had played golf the day before and couldn't stop kidding each other about their lost balls.

The apartment was smaller than Max's but still huge to Todd. Todd toured the apartment. Spotlights illuminated every painting. A piano concerto was blasting from the stereo. In all the commotion, Todd could scarcely hear what Reuben was saying to him when he brought him a glass of wine. "I'm glad Max invited you. Isn't Max a nice guy?"

"Nice 'n rich," Todd said with a sly smile.

"Yes, he has a way of making money. He's dealt in everything: buildings, lots, stocks, diamonds. He took care of his little sister as if she was the daughter he never had. Pampered her. She was a brat. He wanted her to marry a rabbi but she ended up with a truck driver with a big dick." His eyes fell to Todd's crotch. "There's just something about a big dick, isn't there?"

"Yup," Todd grinned.

Before long, the compliments started, the handshakes, pressing of the flesh. A stout man seized him and held him around the waist. "I'm Jerry. I loved you in 'Long Haul.' I'm in the freight business. I wish stuff like that went on in my trucks!"

Another man, white-haired, short with an enormous belly, with a square head that sat directly on his broad shoulders, brought Todd a fresh glass of wine. He ran the fabric of Todd's shirt through his fingers. "Nice goods. Calvin Klein?"

"Yeah, I guess. It was a gift."

"I'm in the garment business. Sam." He held out a heavy, sweaty hand. He smelled of alcohol and hair tonic.

Todd brought the glass to his lips. "Hi, Sam."

"Dinner!" Max cried, pulling Todd away. "Everybody follow us."

They trooped across the street to a hotel resplendent with multi-colored lights and a gushing fountain in front. Two uniformed attendants bowed as the men moved through the huge glass doors that shushed open for them. The lobby of the hotel was even more colossal than Max's condominium, with tropical plants, vases, sculptures, and a parrot in a cage.

They went down a long hallway and entered the dimly lit restaurant. The head waiter greeted them effusively, bowing and scraping to Max as if he was overcome with joy that the man had made it there safely.

"Yes, that walk across Collins can be a killer," Max joked.

Two waiters attended to the table. Max knew both of them by name. They appeared to be twins, Jack and Jim. Max whispered to Todd, "It's really Jack and Jill but we humor them." Both wore tuxedos, patent-leather shoes, bow ties, and ruffled shirts. Jack took the orders, Jim wrote them down. They both affected French accents. Max said they were French Canadians.

When Todd said he was a vegetarian, Jack assured him he would be served the best dish a vegetarian ever tasted. This got a guffaw from Max. Max gave Jack precise instructions on how his fish was to be roasted and specified the spices and seasonings for his vegetables.

"There are times if you would have told me I'd be sitting in such a place eating such food with Todd Torrance, I would have considered it a joke. I had one fantasy in my life, one time before I died to get enough bread to fill my stomach. Now," he said, rubbing his belly, "look at me!"

A man with a camera materialized. "Let's have pictures taken," Max said.

"Smile!" the photographer ordered. The men leaned into Todd, Max on one side, Reuben on the other. They smiled. The camera clicked.

Max told Todd to go around the table, lean over and have his picture taken with the others. Sam held Todd's cheek against

his. Jerry stroked Todd's leg as the camera flashed.
The photographer said he'd have them developed and be back in half an hour.

"Ah, what fun. So many here, they are rich but they just sit. They have no one to dress for. Outside of the financial page in the newspaper, they read nothing. After breakfast, they start playing cards. Can you play cards forever?"

Reuben said, "They have to, or die of boredom. But there is one consolation for them - the mail. An hour before the postman arrives, the lobby is filled. They stand with their keys, as if waiting for the Messiah. Pity the postman if he's late! And the poor bastard who opens his box and it is empty, he starts to grope and burrow inside, still hoping."

Max laughed. "And if the Social Security check doesn't arrive, they worry about it more than the people who have no bread. In my way, I'm every bit as silly as they are but at least I follow my doctor's orders. He wants me to walk, I walk. He wants me to eat right, I eat right. He wants me to stop drinking, only have a nip, I will. He wants me to give up smoking, so I only suck my cigars."

"What about sucking dick?" Jerry asked.

"I can do all of that I want to! Why is it taking so long for my fish?"

"It's probably still swimming in the ocean," Jerry said.

"And the fruit in Todd's salad has yet to be planted," Reuben said, patting the stud's knee.

"Ah," Max cried, "here is the photographer! A fast worker! Let's have a look!"

The photographer handed all the prints to Max, who gave him a fifty dollar bill. Max passed the photos out after glancing at each one admiringly. He held up the one he was in with Todd and Reuben.

"Ah, Todd is so young. So handsome. He has his whole life before him."

"He's had a pretty full life for one so young," Reuben said.

"Yes, he's full of life. So full!" Max said, smacking his lips.

"And now they say you shouldn't swallow all that life - " Reuben said.

"Oh, but just a taste can't hurt," Jerry chimed in.

"Here they come with our food," Max said. The door opened

and the headwaiter entered leading three men pushing carts.

As they ate, Max talked about the changes in Miami Beach. "It used to be that seeing the plaque they put up on the oldest tree was the highlight of your trip. Now, there is South Beach and all those gay clubs. The gay boys know how to have a good time. They make the place fabulous. They should give them a medal. Instead they want to put them in jail. When I was a boy and studying about Sodom, I couldn't understand how a whole country could become corrupt, but now I know. Like here, Sodom had a constitution and all their lawyers reworked it so that right became wrong and wrong right."

"Yeah," Jerry said, "that area below Fourteenth was dangerous in the old days. Now it's all the swish and fish crowd."

"Too much attitude for me. More attitude than there is in L.A. for sure."

"Yes, in New York and L.A., people are all business. No time for attitude, eh, Todd?"

"Just business as usual."

"Is business good?"

"Are you kidding?" Max said. "For a kid like that, business is always booming."

"Here you just have people sitting by the phone waiting for someone to call." Jerry said.

"Yeah," Max said, "with so little time, you want to snatch pleasure where you can."

"To Todd - " Jerry said, raising his glass in a toast.

Each clinked glasses with the other and Todd, as if he knew something no one else did, had the biggest grin of anyone at the table.

On the way back across the street, Max drew his arm around Todd's slim waist. "If we go back up to Reuben's, will you entertain my friends a bit?"

"I don't know. That could get expensive."

"I'll take care of it."

Todd beamed. "In that case, the more the merrier."

When they were in Reuben's apartment, Max said, "Reuben, why don't you show Todd your new Jacuzzi?"

Reuben nodded. "Love to."

Max turned to Todd. "Reuben took out a bedroom just to make room for it. Some people think it's a swimming pool."

"Big enough for five?" Todd asked, grinning.

"Well, no, you might have to stand!" Max chortled.

While Reuben took Todd into the bathroom, Jerry and Sam joined Max in the kitchen where he was pouring brandies.

As Todd went into the separate room that housed the toilet, Reuben turned off the lights. The enlarged bathroom had a panoramic view of the wall of neighboring condos up the beach and the light from the building next door gave the room a warm, seductive glow.

When Todd emerged from the bathroom he was naked. Reuben was also naked and already seated in the swirling waters. As Todd stepped over to the pool, his cock swung enticingly from side to side. A sigh came from deep down Reuben's throat. Todd climbed into the water and stood before Reuben. The older man's hand reached up and gently stroked the semi-flaccid cock. As many times as Todd had played this scene, he still found it fascinating: how men could spend hours worshiping his cock. It was a gift, he thought. He had nothing to do with it. It was nature having fun, creating something unusual. He felt it was only right he take advantage of it.

Before long, the slurping and smacking sounds filled the room. One by one the others entered the room, stripped and climbed into the pool. Every few moments, Todd felt new hands stroke his skin. Strong, aggressive fingers glided over his body, pinching, kneading, rubbing. Lips touched his skin, on his buttocks, his thighs, his balls, his nipples. He just stood in the center of the Jacuzzi, his head back, his eyes closed, and allowed himself to be adored. At times, there were three on his cock at once, then there were only two, then just one, all the while someone sucking his ass. When the last one had orgasmed, there remained only the one at his ass. As Todd began to turn, the sucking stopped. Todd saw it was Max. Now Max made love to Todd's penis even more ardently than he had in the afternoon. At one point, Todd opened his eyes and noticed they were alone. "Let's go back to your place," Todd whispered.

"Okay," Max said, before taking one last lick.

. . .

"It is late," Max told Todd after they returned to his apartment. "If you don't mind, I will retire to my room. You have a TV in your room, there is food in the kitchen. Be comfortable. I will see you in the morning." He kissed Todd lightly on the cheek.

"Goodnight," Todd said, heading for the kitchen.

Todd slept late and, after a shower, he joined Max in the kitchen for breakfast.

"You pleased my friends. I thank you."

Todd nodded, his mouth stuffed with a bagel with cream cheese and strawberry jam.

"Today you will please me before I take you to the airport, okay?"

"Sure."

In a few minutes, Max was naked, lying on his stomach in the middle of the king-size bed in his bedroom. After watching some videos, as Max sucked him, Todd had gotten almost completely hard. He excused himself and went to the guest bedroom. When he returned, he had sheathed his cock in latex.

"Why are you wearing that?" Max asked.

"I always do."

"Not today. I hate those things."

"But - "

"I have so little time, let me enjoy it."

"So little time, bullshit. You got another twenty years."

"No, I don't need another twenty years. Sixty is plenty."

Todd sat on the bed, stroking his cock. "You don't want to risk that. I've seen guys die that way. It is a lousy way to die."

"You take care of me, I take care of you."

"No, I couldn't."

"You are okay, I am okay. There is no harm."

Todd pulled the rubber off his dick and plunged his throbbing erection into Max's butthole. The old man cried out with the pain but Todd did not slow down. He knew if he did, he would go limp and he would not be giving the trick what he was paying for. And Todd wasn't Manny's number one boy for nothing.

THE COVERBOY

Something happened when I kissed him. I didn't mean it to happen; neither did he. It was just something that clicked within each of us. Needs being met. Dreams becoming reality.

I had no business kissing him. We were parked in front of a busy restaurant, people walking by. But I did it anyway. I put my hand on his and held it. He left it there, let me stroke his soft skin. We kissed again and I pushed his hand into my groin. When he felt the evidence of what his kisses were doing to me, he sighed, "Oh, my god."

"What's wrong?" I asked.

"Nothing. *Nothing* at all," he said, grinding his hand into my crotch.

From then on, I knew, some time, I would be in bed with him. It was not to be that first night. That would have been rushing it. He said he could have, but first he wanted to see if I was on the level. And I wanted to see if *he* was on the level. We danced around that one for a long time.

I had agreed to meet the kid against my better judgment. Morris called me from New York: "Look, the boss met this kid in Miami. He's adorable. He wants him for the cover on the story we're doing on Florida models. He wants you to interview him."

"Me? Why me? Who is doing the story?"

"Well, nobody actually. I'm pasting it together from bits and pieces. Tell you what, I'll send everything down Federal Express and you do it all."

"I used to do that, remember. Used to. I'm retired now."

"You'll never retire."

"Not at this rate."

"Besides, he's not even twenty-one."

"Who?"

"This kid. Eduardo, his name is. And he's from Spain."

"Oh? But I like blonds."

"At your age – "

"I know, I should be grateful for anything I get. Well, I'll see."

What I *was* seeing was beautiful. Looking at Eduardo across the table in the restaurant, I could see why he had charmed Alfred Stern, the publisher of *High Fashion* magazine. It didn't matter that the kid was only five nine, short for a fashion model, he had "potential." Not only did the kid travel all the way to Miami at his own expense to enter *HF's* contest, he was brazen enough to send his head shot to Alfred ahead of time, with a little note, saying he'd see him at the show. Eduardo was already a winner before he landed in Miami. And he was winning me over as he talked about his short career as a model. After coming from Spain four years before, knowing no English, he set about to live the American Dream. He graduated from high school and began modeling, catching the eye of a couple of women who ran an agency in Tampa. He appeared as a caddie in a bank commercial, did print ads, was busy enough to afford to buy a new car.

I put dinner on my credit card. He wanted to contribute, pulled out a rolled up twenty, but I told him to put it away. We finally agreed he could leave two dollars of the tip. Next time, he said, it was his turn. Then he would "share" the magazine with me, and perhaps more.

It was in this car we sat and kissed, held hands. We talked about the books I had written, about movie stars and porn stars and other celebrities. He said he was fascinated by porn stars.

"The only problem is, when they go to Southern California, they can easily fall into the fast lane and not want to go home. Vince Cobretti told me once that he would be fine if he could just stay out of Hollywood. It takes a certain type of guy to go there, do it and then return to a more-or-less-normal life."

"I have seen a few of them and I would like that, to do that, maybe just once. Just to see."

"You would be exotic, I'll have to admit that."

"Maybe if modeling doesn't work out, maybe then."

"You'll be too old by that time. You have the perfect look right now. You're 21 but you could pass for 16. That's ideal."

"You would get me an appointment?"

"I could. Once you're on the cover of *HF* I'll send it out to my friend Sonny Griffin. He's one of the top directors. He likes dark-skinned guys. He'll love you. And I'm sure he'll use you – at least once." The thought of how Sonny might *abuse* Eduardo also crossed my mind, but I was confident, now, seeing how tenacious the Spaniard was, he could handle whatever Sonny dished out. And probably beg for more.

After an hour of sitting in the car, we promised to see each other again when the magazine came out. He wanted more than anything to be on the cover of *High Fashion* and I had to warn him a girl would be the larger figure but we were doing a feature on both male and female models in Florida so it would be appropriate that a male be represented.

In Miami, *HF*'s contract photographer, Billy Lomax, had shot some terrific stuff of the contest as it was in progress and then, when Alfred suggested it, took Eduardo to the beach and got some stunning shots of him coming out of the water, his white bikini clinging to his crotch, showing off an admirable endowment. And it was one of those that I picked as my choice for the cover shot, with another from the series to be used inside. When I showed the pictures to Eduardo, he asked if he could have them. "Later," I said, "when the project is finished."

. . .

Eduardo called nearly every day until the magazine finally came out. It got so I would simply let the answering machine pick up. I really had nothing more to say to him until I actually had the issue. When the samples arrived, I called him and we made a date for dinner. He had bought a copy on the newsstand so the one I presented him with didn't consume his attention the way I thought it would. Rather, he spent the hour at the restaurant talking about Hollywood and the possibility of doing porn flicks. I again attempted to dissuade him by telling him stories about how bad things had happened to good boys who went into that business, but he seemed as intent on my making arrangements with Griffin as he was on being on the cover of *High Fashion*. "But," I confessed, "I had no trouble with the cover. It is obvious you have great beauty.

What must be confirmed before I make any phone calls is whether you have talent for – " I hesitated, smacked my lips, went on, "How shall we put it – performing?"

His long lashes fluttering, he said, "Why don't we go now?"

As I normally do when I go to Tampa, I had booked a room at the Golden Palms, at the far end of the building, with easy parking directly in front of the room. No marching through lobbies for me. We had held hands on the way to the motel and he continued to ask questions about the porn biz. I continued to warn him about all the pitfalls but he was determined.

Once in the room, he kissed me, our tongues meeting and dancing. The fingers of his right hand rubbed gently round and round the head of my cock. My hands slithered down his back and squeezed his firm buttocks. He dashed to the john. After a few moments, the toilet was flushing and he was out, unbuttoning his silk shirt. He did have good taste in clothes, I thought, a model's sense. His chest was what I had expected, flat, hairless, a little boy's chest. What came as a surprise was the horse cock that came flopping out of his underwear. I had gotten on the bed fully clothed, my back against the headboard and was fiddling with the controls for the radio and television while he undressed. I set the radio on the same rock station he had put on in the car and tossed the remote control onto the table just as he was slipping off his white CK briefs. He stood before me nude, running one hand across his chest, another tugging on the foreskin of his flaccid penis. He didn't say anything, just looked at me anxiously, as if seeking my approval.

"Here," I said, "let me do that." I leaned over, putting my head level with his crotch and took his cock in my hand. Sliding the foreskin back, I drew it up to my lips and began kissing it. The more I kissed it, the harder it became until, finally, it was fully erect. I guessed it was easily eight inches of thick, unspoiled, satiny meat, nothing spectacular but adequate for porn. Besides, it looked enormous in proportion to the rest of him. As I slid the cock into my mouth, he brought his hands to my head and began running his fingers through my hair. I go long periods between sex these days so I wanted to savor this magnificent cock, but after just a few minutes of my sucking, licking and otherwise admiring it, he pulled out of my hands and pounced down on the bed. He grappled with my belt and managed to undo my pants and reveal my erection. "Oh, yeah," he said, positioning himself between my thighs on his stomach. His sucking of me was much more expert than my own and I feared I would come, but when he felt I was ready, he would draw back, play with it a while, then resume.

I watched him carefully. If the cameras were rolling, he'd be terrific, I thought, as he took me all the way down to my pubic hairs, then drew it out again to manipulate it with his fingers.

He pulled my pants and underwear off of me and then unbuttoned my shirt. He kissed my neck, sucked on my skin, nibbled his way to my nipples. His fingers teased one nipple while his mouth sucked the other, back and forth, then making exciting patterns of spit on my skin as he tracked down to my navel. Eagerly he ran his fingernails up and down my chest as his tongue massaged my navel and worked its way down to my cock again. He lifted my legs over his shoulders and spit into my gaping asshole. I handed him a rubber from the package of them on the bedside table. He sliced it open with his teeth and then slid the lubed condom over his humongous erection. He was in me in an instant, almost all of him. "No, no," I pleaded, "slow, please, slower."

But it was no use. He was in me fully, fucking grandly before I could say another word. And soon I was into the heated rhythm of his fucking. He had pulled me down on the bed so that he could lift himself up and, bracing himself, increase his tempo. As he leaned over, sending it in all the way, I sucked air through clenched teeth. He parted my teeth with his tongue and kissed me. His spasms mounted, one on top of the next like waves, until he finally came. I reached for my cock but he pushed my hand away from it. When he was finished, he rolled over, bringing me with him. He parted his thighs and said, "Now it's your turn."

He was, I was to find, as good a bottom as a top; better, in fact, because, having come, he was in no hurry and I could leisurely explore his body with my tongue as I teased him with my condom-sheathed prick, well-lubricated, gliding up and down in the groove of his ass. I tweaked his nipples harder and harder as my mouth got down to his cock. Finally, as I plowed into him, he sucked a lot of air and started going, "Oooooo, yeah," with every thrust. Just like in the movies, I thought; this kid'll be a natural.

Eduardo had, as far as I was concerned, passed the test. If he wanted to go to Hollywood to try his luck, I would do everything I could to help. Sonny liked what he heard and wanted me to send him some photos. "Oh, he'll be fine," I said. "In fact, he'll pester you to do death until you put him on the box-cover."

About six months later, I received copy of Sonny's long-awaited gayporn parody of "All About Eve." Sure enough, there was Eduardo, smiling at me from the box-cover in vivid color. Sonny himself had played the George Sanders part and Eduardo did his best in the role Marilyn Monroe had played in the original. Sonny's note accompanying the tape read, "Kid's great. In fact, he's moved in. Come see us when you're in town." Come indeed.

THE STALLION

He is long-haired, rangy, with about as much sense of the outdoors about him as the garden of the Hotel Bel-Air allows. The magnolia tree looms large, the insects buzz, the birds chirp, and his hips, encased in tight jeans, sway seductively as he makes his way to my bungalow.

I sit on my chaise longue watching him as he taps on the door, looks to the right, then the left, resting his weight on one foot, then the other. I let him wait for a few moments. After all, he's kept me waiting for two days. "Off on a shoot," he told me. "Back on Thursday."

When I first visited Southern California, it seemed very familiar. Like most people, I'd seen it all before, in flickering images in films and on television. It appeared to be exactly as I imagined it, tempting me to participate in the illusion. Here, more so than anywhere else it seems, anything is possible. All one needs is a break. And that desperate hope is shared by millions of hopefuls. They wait on tables, they valet park cars and limos, they hustle. And part of the hustler game can easily be films. Fuck films. And it is from those casts I draw my most memorable tricks.

Now this stud is probably drained of every ounce of cum, but what the hell, I have to go home tomorrow and, for me, he's the only game in town. I had seen the pictorials and masturbated to them. Then I read an interview he gave to a magazine:

In his first video, they named him Rock Hardin and he says he doesn't regret it. "It suits me," he says...

Then Rock came to Tampa to dance at one of the bars. I drove an hour to get there. I was early and Hal, the owner of the bar, told me that he could arrange a private meeting for me at Rock's hotel but I decided to wait and see the show. As the show ended, Hal came over and said he'd booked Rock for two sessions that night and if I wanted to see the boy, I'd have to come back the following afternoon. "I'm sorry," I shrugged. "I can't."

"That's the way it goes – " Hal said. "Win some, lose some."

In his interview, Rock said: "When I was nine, my brother, who was 13, showed me how to feel good. I couldn't come yet, but I was fascinated by the white stuff comin' out of his dick. I touched it, smelled it, tasted it. I can't explain it but I liked it."

Sex has become my religion and the pursuit of it has consumed me as it can the worst religious zealots. And, these days, I cannot afford anything but a sure thing. That is why I made this booking. After all, these performers make their living fucking.

"Within two years," Rock went on in his interview, "I was fucking my brother. I mean, fucking runs in the family. There were ten of us kids, for chrissakes. I wanted him to fuck me but I didn't think I could take it. But by the time I was 17, he was fucking me."

I come up behind him, introduce myself, unlock the bungalow and usher him in.

He appears flighty and laconic, the way he did in the bar. Then after a drink, the mask falls away and he has a certain sweetness. Porn flicks have hardened him but not beyond repair. He seems to relax. Kicks off his shoes. Perhaps he sees me as a moment of respite from a hectic shooting schedule. "Off on a shoot" indeed. I tick off the number of his "shoots" I have collected. I lose count at about twenty. The names of the movies no longer register but the sight of his partners fucking him are unforgettable.

"How was Cougar to work with?" I ask, recalling the scene where four boys are getting it on. Rock never even flinched when Cougar's famous dick, currently called the biggest in porndom, slid into his ass. Perhaps he had been doped up.

"Nice guy," Rock says. "But I wouldn't want to live with 'im."

"I mean, did it hurt?"

"Yeah. You know, when they're that big, they never get really hard. But he's very gentle and you just relax. Everybody wants to get fucked by him so he's learned how to do it without hurting anybody."

My curiosity is so great that I tend for forget what Rock is here for.

"I never jack off any more. I hold it for the shoots or for guys I meet. It's opened up a new dimension of sex for me."

I stroke the bulge in his jeans. He accommodates me by unbuttoning them, letting me pull the sizable meat from its captivity. It smells freshly scrubbed. I nibble on the fine head, work my way down the nicely cut shaft to the balls. The cock is even more beautiful than it appears in videos. The balls are massive. The hair has been neatly trimmed.

"They couldn't keep their hands off this in Tampa," I tell him between licks.

"You were there?"

"Right at the bar."

"Yeah, I love that place. Everybody's so friendly. If they ever closed the doors, everybody would get naked and we could have a good ole orgy."

"Is there any place better to dance?"

"Orlando's good, too, and the Show Palace in New York. The guys really get off on it there."

Getting off on it is precisely what I have in mind. I strip the rest of his clothes off of him and get naked myself. I pull him on top of me, draw up my knees, the soles of my feet resting on his chest to control him as he enters me. Soon he has slung my legs over his shoulders and he is fucking me wildly like a stallion...

"I had a dream once about a horse that fucked me and then unzipped himself to reveal he was man with a dick as big as a horse's. His dick was filling me completely, so completely that when he came, it filled my mouth."

As he thrusts and grinds into me, I tighten my hold on him. He takes my erection in his hand. When he senses I'm nearly ready to come, he bunches my balls in one hand and, with the other, presses the flesh near the base of my cock.

"There's a spot near the base of the cock you can press and it shuts the tube off. The semen that's building up goes right back into the balls. You get a tingling sensation but don't come. It's like going over the edge but getting snatched back in midair."

"Oh, god," I cry, shaking uncontrollably. He smiles mischievously. And keeps pressing. And keeps fucking. He seems genuinely interested in earning a generous tip.

"...I met this guy in the park. He was only 19 and we sixty-nined and fist-fucked each other at the same time. We laid side-by-side, with our dicks against each other's chests. When I came it was the most fulfilling feeling that I've ever had in my life..."

Like the stallion of his dreams, he bucks and heaves into me as he comes. This is the most fulfilling feeling I've ever had in *my* life. God, his cum fills the rubber when it should be filling me, jetting up into me so far I can almost taste it. He withdraws, slowly, gently. He stands up. I reach over and peel the rubber away, letting it drop to the floor. I hug him to me and place the now semi-flaccid cock into my mouth. It no longer smells scrubbed. I lick it. One drop won't kill me. I roll over onto my back and hang my head over the edge of the bed. I begin stroking my cock, intent now on my own orgasm. He bends his hard prick so that it slides easily into my mouth and down my throat. As he begins to fuck my face, I close my eyes and breath in the marvelous musky scent of his sweaty, heavy ballsac.

I begin to come; he cannot stop me now. My pleasure is so intense I begin to choke on his flesh deep inside my throat. Oh, he tastes delicious. I will be generous with this boy. Very generous. I will remember him in my will.

Adam Hart

THE HEARTTHROBS: BEEFCAKE, CHICKENCAKE

"Sex is the root of it all."
– Walt Whitman

PREFACE

For these *Best of* collections, we seek to bring into better focus the celebrities whose ups and downs (and ins and outs) we have been chronicling over the years. These are but a few of our favorite sex icons, very special celebrities who have uniquely defined themselves and then set to work elaborating upon their image. Keeping track of their achievements is always a fascinating experience because it is, as Neal Gabler of the *New York Times* says, an incontrovertible fact that "the lives of celebrities today are themselves performance art, works-in-progress that compete with their work on screen, stage, stadium or CD." The writer Anne Rice says that rock stars especially live up to our Romantic concept of the artist: "We want them to surprise us, we want them to go out on a limb, and the more they do, the more we pay them."

Madonna, Gabler says, is the most obvious example: "Having early on established herself as wild and wanton, she has continued to operate at the frontiers of her image, easily incorporating our shock at her behavior into her role. Even petting with a young boy in one of her videos might shock, but still not surprise. Nothing she could do would seem to violate her persona."

If celebrities *do* defy their image, we punish them. And we expect them to remain relevant: the "life movie" continually needs new episodes. In order to stay in the headlines, it helps, sometimes, to bask in some reflected glory of fame and no one seems immune to it. Frank Rich, also of the *Times*, points to Michael Jackson's spending New Year's hanging out with Michael Milken, the star felon of the '80s, in Las Vegas watching Barbra Streisand and avoiding photographers. In 1991, Madonna showed up with Jackson, who was described as her "comrade-in-bizarreness," at the Academy Awards ceremonies. Besides sitting together in the front row during the show, the then pop sovereigns attended the party at Spago afterwards, where Warren Beatty found them seats at his table. (On the show, Madonna sang a song from Warren's "Dick Tracy" and it won the Oscar.)

"Taken together, the lives of the celebrities create a sort of psychic energy field that surrounds us and penetrates us, binding our universe together," the critic Richard Schickel says. But the danger comes when we become obsessively focused on a single celebrated individual. Thus, a fan becomes, as the derivation of the word implies, a fanatic, and therefore potentially dangerous.

I must confess I have become obsessed to some degree with a few of these heartthrobs. Marky, Corey Haim, Jeff Stryker, and Ryan Idol, for instance. The root of this obsession is, of course, sexual. I purely and simply want to have sex with them. While I wouldn't mind having sex with *any* celebrity, it is these few that have become the objects of my passion in a concentrated way. And I'm not alone. In the profile of Ryan Idol, for instance, I report about the guy who writes *Advocate Men* that just looking at pictures of the handsome hunk causes him to spring a boner and, if they don't stop printing pictures of him, he is in danger of whacking his whanger until it falls off. My own compulsion is to keep a fuck flick set on a scene that I find exceptionally arousing. Matt Gunther's scenes in "Buttbusters," for instance, or, for a while, *any* scene with Cody James. It is to porn that we turn, of course, for the ultimate turn-ons because they simply give us for bang for our buck.

I haven't quite made the leap to fantasizing about having sex with a celebrity. Having *had* sex with a few porn studs has given me the distance I need. No one, however splendid, can live up to one's expectations, there are just too many factors involved: how I'm feeling that night, how *he's* feeling that night, even the weather. But by *not* actually having sex with them, I can keep the promise alive, letting them surprise me with every twist and turn of their lives. And, yes, how very comforting it is to have Marky or Keanu say, when asked if they'd ever have gay sex, answer, "You never know." And how reassuring to have Adam or Ryan say, when asked if they'd ever take it up the ass, to respond, "You never know."

Leonardo DiCaprio,
in a recent publicity photography

LOVING LEONARDO (DICAPRIO)

When one considers Leonardo DiCaprio, one tends to think of the song by Cole Porter, "Easy to Love" ("You'd be so easy to love..."). Not only is this one cute guy, he is also supremely talented. No actor in recent memory has come from sitcom television, ("Growing Pains"), to prominence in film in such a short time. He was named Best Supporting Actor by the National Board of Review and his Oscar nomination as Best Supporting Actor (for "What's Eating Gilbert Grape") was the icing on the cake for the young star.

Now all Hollywood is scrambling to hire him. Sharon Stone, co-producing as well as starring in the western "The Quick and the Dead" with Gene Hackman, said they had topped out financially on the project but they wanted Leonardo so badly they found more money. Hopefully, this move will pay off. "It better," Sharon said, "or I'm going to beat the living shit out of him: 'Hey, you little punk, I want my money back!'"

Beating the "living shit" out of Leonardo is not *quite* what we would have on our minds if we ever got him alone. Consider the evidence in so far: Interviewer Kathryn Harris for *Detour* magazine, describes the scene as he enters the restaurant for their business lunch: "A fly buzzes too close to my ear. Leonardo DiCaprio glides in. And what follows is the discovery that there are quite clearly no flies on him. He's a six-footer, which only emphasizes his slight frame and perfectly youthful face of 18 years. Tranquil light-blue eyes and a shock of blonde hair, cut in a preppie style. Blue jeans, T-shirt, and his customary short-sleeved shirt over the top. A pair of sharply-defined, almost demonic eyebrows." I keep hearing: "You'd be so easy to..."

The "demonic" Leonardo ("Leo" to his pals), says he wanted to be an actor to gain acceptance: "I didn't fit in with the people at school. So I thought, I'm going to at least act. I thought actors get what they want, you see. It was my total insecurity phase. I had a lot to learn back then. Later I realized that acting was an opportunity, was something that I enjoyed, and had a talent for – and that I had a need to create, be with people, communicate and make things happen." (Wow: "You'd be so easy to...")

In the film "This Boy's Life," DiCaprio's character accepts the homosexuality of his chum, played by Jonah Blechman. Based on Tobias Wolff's memoir about a boy growing up in the emotionally abused '50s, the film had fine acting all around but, as critic Peter Biskind said, "the big surprise is newcomer DiCaprio, who steals the movie from Robert De Niro and Ellen Barkin (in a) coming-of-age story that refuses sentimentality and stock responses."

That sounds like Leonardo himself, who relished playing Arnie, Johnny Depp's dimwitted brother in his latest film, "What's Eating Gilbert Grape," directed by Lasse Halstrom of "My Life As A Dog" fame. "He's the most honest character in the whole movie, that's why I like him," DiCaprio says. "But he's always blubbering or drooling or jumping up and down he's pretty damn out there."

Halstrom says, "I thought we needed someone who wasn't as good-looking, but Leonardo's abilities were there in the first audition. All the actors who were auditioning for the role had watched the same tape of a retarded boy. Leonardo was the only one who had picked up on the essentials, the body mannerisms, and integrated them. He was the most observant. Then, on the shoot, Leonardo was able to switch on and off very quickly."

"And," film critic Jeffrey Wells comments, "there was the added pleasure, savored only by good-looking, in-demand actors, of looking like the most disgusting kid on earth."

"I had a chili-bowl haircut," DiCaprio says, "I looked so vile, it was great."

It is astounding that this beauty could look so vile, but it was worth it. "The gifted young actor Leonardo DiCaprio has won justified raves for his tour de force as Arnie Grape," *New York* magazine said. But we agree with *Premiere*, who said: "DiCaprio plays Johnny's retarded younger brother and his performance is so uncanny and touching and inspiring that you want to give him ten Best Supporting Oscars just so he'll stop and promise never to do it again."

Tall, narrow and pale, Leo has a focus about him, Wells asserts, "an air of quiet consideration. And there's a lot to consider. The actor received raves for his career-making work in 'This Boy's Life.' Now, building on the momentum of signing with the top-dog agency CAA, Leo's main order of business is to avoid "making big dumb, shitty movies."

"Leonardo DiCaprio is 18 and not 18 all at once," says film critic Erin Culley. "Though he's got the wit and frankness of someone twice his age, he's still a kid who slouches around in saggy, baggy pants and loves Led Zeppelin and rap. Leo says he got his name as a result of a trip his folks took to Italy while his mother was pregnant. They were looking at a painting by DaVinci when I kicked for the first time, he explains. She took that as a sign."

Leo's been kicking ever since. In fact, when Aljean Harmetz met the boy in Hollywood to interview him for *The New York Times*, she said he managed to sit still for 23 minutes, and that may be a record: "Sitting in the Revival Cafe with his long legs and size-11 feet stretched out . . . he fidgets and squirms, leans on the table to pick slices of eggplant out of his panini, twirls his lemonade glass, drums on his collarbone, drinks his caffe latte with a straw. His straw-colored hair dances against his forehead as he twists and turns.

"His first clear memory is of wearing yellow-and-red tap shoes and being lifted onto a stage by his father to entertain people waiting for a concert. At 14, he told his parents who separated years ago but live near each other that he wanted to be an actor. 'I knew I didn't want to be one of the set things they said I should be at school doctor, lawyer, blah blah blah,' he says. After 50 auditions, he won a role in a Matchbox car commercial. His first thought: 'I'm getting paid for something I enjoy doing and I get to miss two days of school.' After playing 'your average, no-depth, standard kid with blond hair,' in 'Critters III', he had a role in the short-lived television series, 'Parenthood,' and played a homeless boy for the last season for 'Growing Pains.' ('Never again!' says Leo.) Then came 'This Boy's Life.'"

About appearing with Robert DeNiro, Leo says: "I knew when I took on the part of Toby that I'd have to forget the guy playing opposite me was Robert DeNiro. I'd have been in shock at his acting, and I would have looked like this kid who really envies Dwight (his nightmare dad) which in fact is quite the opposite; Toby thinks Dwight's a total loser idiot. I think Toby is really universal. There are so many elements for people to identify with because he's like a real person. A lot of people identify with the abusive part because they've been abused in some way, but people also see the emotions he has and identify with them. I've been through all that stuff myself. I feel much the same way."

Once DeNiro agreed to do the film, cameras rolled. "If DeNiro made it happen," Peter Haldeman said, "DiCaprio makes it work. In a movie about how people behave, Toby's behavior is undoubtedly the most complex; his surface adaptability conceals an anarchy of heart and hormones. The actor was required to age from 12 to 16, a process complicated by DiCaprio's own unexpected voice change and two-inch growth spurt during the five months of shooting." *Entertainment Weekly* found his performance to be "eloquent "and *Interview's* reviewer said it was a "fearlessly honest portrayal."

In the film, Toby, confused, becomes a Boy Scout, affecting a brutal indifference to everything; yet at the same time he's drawn to Arthur (Blechman), an effeminate intellectual boy who recognizes Toby as a soul mate, both fluid boys out of place in Concrete. In one of what will now be one our all-time favorite film scenes, Toby gets his first kiss from Arthur. Arthur, who has a little white dog, is a poseur, too, playing at being fey and then running in anguish when the boys call him a homo. Blechman, David Denby says, gives a lovely performance delicate but proud, with a fierce independence that can only be called manly.

US magazine touted Leo as a dark horse for best supporting actor honors: "The Academy loves newcomers and he is brimming over with both talent and potential." The New York Film Critics' Circle voted Leo runner-up in the best supporting actor category. And he was nominated for a Golden Globe for Grape. *Entertainment Weekly* named him one of its Rookies of the Year: "This year, Leonardo DiCaprio had the crap beaten out of him and emerged victorious . . . and (he) lost out to Christian Slater as the late River Phoenix's replacement in 'Interview With the Vampire' because he looked too young."

"DiCaprio gives a fresh, sharply intuitive performance . . . this 18-year-old is a genuine find," raved Peter Travers. Another critic, Steven Rea, agreed, saying: ". . . the picture has an absolutely convincing, charismatic star." The director, Scotsman Michael Caton-Jones, said: "His character is in every scene. We needed someone who could convey the emotional subtext of what's going on and not be intimated by two heavy-weights. When Leonardo read for me, it was simple: he was it. But when someone reads for you that early, you don't believe it. So we tried loads and loads of people, but we came right back to him."

Jim McClellan commented, "DeNiro plays a character who starts out like a putz (he has a silly haircut) but turns out to be a psycho (he dons a scout uniform, flashes the cracked grin and beats the shit out of cute juvenile delinquent Leonardo DiCaprio. DeNiro's character , incidentally, forces him to get a buzz cut, the same kind of haircut that got Leo rejected when he was ten: Before I got my first job I went in to talk to some agents and they didn't like my haircut. I got discouraged."

Leo was even more discouraged about school: "I was frustrated I wasn't happily learning things. I know it's up to you, to a degree, but a lot of times school is just so dull and boring, it's hard for a kid to learn in that environment. You go to school, you go to this class, go to that class, study this, study that, get your homework, go home. There's hardly ever any vibrancy there. I needed to go to a place where I was excited about what I was learning. For me, it's all about getting a person interested in a subject by linking a lot of happiness to it, a lot of joy in doing it."

Early on the talk was that Leo was going to be the next River Phoenix or Johnny Depp, and that the girls would be falling over him. But he doesn't want that. He says he wants to take only roles he can relate to: "You lose a little in the paycheck but I don't need to pay a chauffeur. I can work for the art and try to be a young actor with a mind of his own, doing different things. In the long run, it's the best way to survive." He says he's pretty settled with the attention he's getting: "I know people will recognize me, but, hey, there are much worse things."

Leo, an only child, still lives at home. "A lot of times,

teenagers are in a rush to move out and assert their independence. I am independent and free; I don't have a big reason to move out right now other than to have a different place to sleep. I like having their guidance around me."

He is, he told Harris, not "too keen" on his own generation right now. "There are too many people trying to be cool, living their lives in stereotypical fashion, considering how they are perceived rather than how it is they perceive themselves. A bunch of leather jackets in nightclubs with all those girls around them. I would abolish stereotypes, put them in a little closet and let them think about things. Put them in a different environment. So much depends on what you have experienced in your life."

Leo doesn't believe in heavy make up or flashy cool clothes like those of his generation prefer. "I do have a sense of style of my own, but lately I really haven't cared. I don't make a gigantic effort to look good. It's something that comes naturally. The last time I did press photographs they didn't say no to what they wanted me to wear and then I felt like a fool for wearing it. It was something really tight."

When it comes to girls, Leo says he doesn't have a girlfriend. "I think I need an older girlfriend. Because from my experiences there haven't been any my age that I can really communicate with." (Oh Leo, "You'd be so easy to...")

Madonna, in publicity still from her book, *Sex*, with Boy Pussy Joey Stefano and friends

Madonna protege Nick Scotti in publicity photo from his album

MADONNA'S MEN

"I feel like a million tonight," Mae West said, "but one at a time." At one point, before the sizzle began to fizzle, we were beginning to think of Madonna as the Mae West of the '90s. Indeed, it was the filmmaker Pedro Almodovar who said, "Madonna's much funnier than she usually appears. She was like Mae West. She said she wanted to meet me because she would very much like to work with me someday. I asked her why she couldn't be funny like this in the movies. She said, 'Well, why don't you find out?' I admire her because her ability to be such a strong rip-off artists is very original."

Like Mae West, Madonna emerged as a true Bitch-Diva-Goddess, with an enormous ego, and tons of chutzpa. Mark Pritchard of *Frighten the Horses* magazine says: "We got taken in by Madonna. Lots of queers, as well as FTH, celebrated Madonna in recent years because she provided visibility to queer sexuality. Ooooo, we all went, look at that! Madonna honors queer sexuality! We exist!

"But with her book *Sex* Madonna crossed the line from celebration to exploitation. With its blandly homophobic text, its questionable use of racial and sexual minorities, and its reluctance to show its heroine in any situation which was truly compromising, *Sex* showed us how little respect Madonna really has for the people whose images and culture she uses."

Through the controversy and clamor, Madonna maintains she's not finished with us yet, as Michael Szymanski reported in *Genre*: "The mystery isn't gone. The saturation level isn't even close."

Case in point: the Girlie Show, her 1993 concert series, which *US* magazine characterized as "Studio 54 meets Las Vegas in which Madonna did a bad Marlene Dietrich imitation and wore a silly fright wig." Wig notwithstanding, many Mexicans didn't want her at all; 30,000 of them sent letters to their congressmen saying that her onstage simulations of same-sex intercourse made her the "pornographic queen of rock."

Madonna said, "Don't they know I'm a gay man trapped in

a woman's body?"

Playboy noted that critics say she's losing it, but 72,000 fans packed London's Wembley Stadium for her show and in Toronto, where they once busted her for obscenity, the police said this time they'd pass. "Nothing's obscene there anymore, it seems," *Playboy* said.

When the show reached Madison Square Garden, Peter Galvin, writing for the *Advocate*, was back on her band wagon: "For two nonstop hours, her tour may not be shocking, but it'll sure knock your socks off. Madonna wowed the screaming couldn't get enough crowd with a thrilling blend of circus panache, disco fever, bathetic baladry, German cabaret, MGM-style choreography, Dolce and Gabbana costumes and, best of all, a new sense of sincerity and playfulness." Peter was all for giving her own variety hour on TV. MTV we presume.

Time said: "The fascinating thing about Madonna is that she is all-real and all-fake – in other words, all show-biz. Madonna, once the Harlow harlot and now a perky harlequin, is the greatest show-off on earth."

Even the august *New Yorker* magazine was raving: "Madonna may have failed at other things, but her stage presence – her fluent and daring dancer's imagination, her genius for iconographic playfulness, her libertine expansiveness – is a wonder of our times."

The writer Anne Rice says, "We really are so used to Madonna that we don't see how incredible she is. In years to come, I think that we'll look back on her as a real revolutionary."

Still, Szymanski says that familiarity breeds contempt and since we're so familiar with her, we're allowed to pick on her. "The magic of Madonna," he maintains, "is that she's just like everybody else."

Yes, but few dames are this tough. She moved from Bay City, Michigan to New York in 1978 with only $37 and local legend has it she clawed, slept, and climbed her way to the top. People with that kind of single-minded determination are fascinating, even if one doesn't agree with their points of view.

A typical Madonna point-of-view: "I wouldn't want a penis. It would be like having a third leg. It would seem like a contraption that would get in the way. I think I have a dick in my brain. I don't need to have one between my legs."

Dick in the brain, on the brain. Anywhere you can get it. Rumor had it that the Melodic Erotic actually did have oral sex with a male model while photographer Steven Meisel snapped away for *Sex*, her book inspired by the 1933 photo book, *Paris de Nuit*, by Brassai (a.k.a. Gyula Halasz), which celebrated the seedy side of Paris life. Madonna's longtime publicist Liz Rosenberg would only say: "Let's put it this way, if she did have sex, I'm sure it was safe sex."

But Rosenberg denied that Madonna just sits down and thinks about how to blow people's minds. "She's only interested in exploring the boundaries of her creative life."

Those "explorations" have involved her with many men, some famous, some not-so-famous, but all of them interesting.

Here are just a few:

Rodrigo Freire

We start off with the very latest (at least at this writing in early 1994), and perhaps the most scandalous. He's a studly 15-year-old who first said they did it, then said they really didn't. (We suppose to admit it would get Madonna in real trouble somewhere.) Anyhow, this gorgeous number is now on the cover of *Interview* magazine, photographed by Bruce Weber and up for a role on "Beverly Hills 90210."

Said Madonna's pal Liz Smith: "Madonna – her love – even a hint of her love – is like a fever. And when you catch it, you're made!"

Rocky and Tony

One of Madonna's most startling confessions in her book *Sex* is that she's really not a sex maniac, that she would rather read a book. As Quentin Crisp said, "Perhaps she as thinking of her bank book."

We can't imagine her wanting to read a book, any book, even her bank book, when she's in the company of one of her tastiest flavors of the month, Rocky. A spread of him in *Sex* screams out: "Who is that dude?"

"Rocky of the Mediterranean smile and Sistine Chapel torso," said New York writer Otis Stuart. "Madonna saw him at Tatou late one night, found out he was a top banana on the Manhattan male-stripper circuit and the rest, thanks to 'Sex' and its sister video, is history. As always, La Ciccone lines up behind distinguished company. A native New Yorker, Rocky appeared in 'People magazine's '50 Most beautiful People in the World' issue and has lit up *New York Newsday* as a 'Man of the '90s.'"

To all this, Rocky simply replied, "Why not?"

"Why not?" is apparently her one-time beau Tony Ward's credo. According to the *Star's* Janet Charlton, Tony will sleep with anything that's put before him. He's been both engaged and married to other women, but he supposedly often dressed as Madonna and fantasized about the star watching him having sex. When they first combusted at a party (he'd been in her 'Like A Prayer' video but she hadn't noticed him, she put a cigarette out on him and it was love at first burn. She quickly found that the publicity he generated as a gay porn magazine model created even more steam that a high-priced publicist could dream up. Michael Musto calls Tony "the ultimate pansexual plaything. The ideal human brooch for Madonna, who apparently enjoys having a love slave. We sit and wonder endlessly who straps on what and does what to whom."

Musto says, "While most stars would have tried to suppress such a boyfriend's gay/drag associations or dumped him, Madonna just basks in the bad-mouthing."

Rocky and Tony may be gorgeous but, according to Madonna in *Sex*, neither one's provided her with the greatest sex she's ever had (She hadn't met Rodrigo as yet, remember.) Listen to this: "Sex with the young can be fun if you're in the mood. One of the best experiences I ever had was with a teenage boy. He was Puerto Rican. He was uncircumcised...it was really awesome because he was so young and so in wonderment of it all. He was fearless. He would do anything. He wasn't very big. He was just a baby. See, I'm not a size queen. But it was excellent."

Ah, yes, the "wonderment of it all!"

Madonna's "Babies"

And speaking of wonderment, in her documentary "Truth or Dare," Madonna is seen watching her male dancers kiss. She yelps, "Oh God! I'm getting a hard on!" She said it was her favorite scene in the movie. "I love that people are going to watch that and go home and talk about it all night long. I live for things like that."

In the same movie, sitting backstage and picking petals off a daisy, she muses, "He loves me. He loves me not. He just wants to fuck me." In bed with her troupe of male dancers, she asks, "Do we want to be accepted by Hollywood?"

"No!" they chorus.

"Do we care what people think?" she prompts.

"No!" they reply.

"Do we want people to kiss our ass?"

"Yes!" they yell.

During the making of the film, one of the dancers, Oliver Sidney Crumes, 21, a heterosexual, felt taunted by some of the gay dancers, especially Luis Camacho. "Oliver was Mr. Macho Man," Camacho admits.

According to Slam Gauwloos, 22, another dancer, "Oliver was a toy for Madonna. He was dumped and he gagged, and we laughed because we knew it would happen." Madonna says that she was "carrying on an Oedipal relationship, a mother and son. It wasn't fully realized. He played 'Little Boy' to my 'Mother.' I took him under my wing and wanted to educate him. I'd give him books. He got attached." Another dancer, Kevin Stea, 21, says that at the end of the tour Madonna confessed she had a crush on him when they first started. "And I thought she hated me because she treated me in a very businesslike manner."

"Dream on!" Madonna says now. "He can say anything he wants. I kept my distance because he didn't bathe!"

Distance or no distance, by the end of the tour, all the guys were calling her "Ma." As Stea says now, "She was very maternal. She was always worried about us. There were always condoms in our per diem."

Tom Hanks

But then Madonna has this "thing" about gay boys. Film star and now author (*Hello Darling, Are You Working?*) Rupert Everett told her, "The way you are with men is just like a queen." In fact, she feels very comfortable among the "queens." You might say she *is* the queen among queens.

When Madonna was making the film "A League of Their Own," with Tom Hanks in Evansville, Indiana, Madonna said she hated the place, that she might as well have "been in Prague." Co-star Lori Petty recalls: "We worked six days a week. On Saturday night, we would go out, no matter how tired, how dirty, how filthy we were. There were a couple of dance bars that we would go to and just dance and dance and kind of let it all hang out." Hanks says: "There was only one gay bar in town and Madonna found it. It kinda became her hangout."

Warren Beatty (And Kevin Costner)

Hanging out is what Madonna did for a time with Warren Beatty, a world-class womanizer for two decades. Indeed, Woody Allen once said he would love to be reincarnated as "Warren Beatty's fingertips." Hollywood's most celebrated lothario is, of course, now much-married to Annette Bening and with child, but when he was still single Madonna featured him in "Truth or Dare" and he featured her in "Dick Tracy." Off-screen, they featured each other. At the time, Warren said she "was more fun than a barrel of monkeys." Madonna, at the time, worried about being compared to former Beatty lays such as Bardot, Natalie Wood, Joan Collins, Leslie Caron, Diane Keaton and the hundreds of others. Then she decided she was "better than all of them."

Recently, when asked if she still talked to Warren, Madonna laughed, "No. I wish. I mean, I wouldn't say we're enemies or anything like that. He's married and has a family and I just feel like he's in another country. But he's a great guy. He really is, and I learned a lot from him." But you wouldn't know it from the footage in "Truth or Dare." At one point, when the aging stud visits her dressing room, she orders him, "Don't hide back there Warren, get over here." Appearing very uncomfortable, he complies and when she calls him a "pussy," he turns white.

At least that's better treatment than she accorded Kevin Costner when he appeared backstage to compliment her on the show. "I thought it was neat," he says. Madonna waits until he turns his back, then sticks a finger down her throat and pretends to gag. "Anybody who says my show is 'neat' has to go."

Christopher Ciccone

A painter and designer living in New York, Chris Ciccone, Madonna's baby brother, decorated the star's new house in Coconut Grove. "She didn't want to be on the beach," Chris says, "It's too crazy over there. She just wanted a place to hide. The approach to famous people is a little different down here. It must be the heat." The star used the Mediterranean-style house as a backdrop in *Sex* and liked it immediately, but the people that were living in it didn't want to sell. Money talks, however, and eventually they let her have it, moving across the street. Chris says, "Madonna wanted a beach house even though it's not on the beach, so that's what I did. It's what I call shabby chic. And she said she had to have a boat. It's the one thing I haven't done yet. Buy that boat."

Chris did the stage design for the Blond Ambition tour (which was filmed as "Truth or Dare"). He did the star's house in California. Now the contractor in Miami he hired to refurbish the Grove house has hired him to re-do their offices. But mainly, he says, he paints pictures.

Boy Pussy Joey Stefano & Nick the Dick

Yes, wherever she is, Miami, L.A., or elsewhere, as columnist Michael Musto said, "The best place of all to be a fly on the wall continues to be anywhere where there's Madonna." He duly reported on what quickly became known as "The Book

Party" when Madonna's book *Sex* was released: "The invitation was a laced-up, bodice-like black card with a caricature of a bound, but not gagged, Madonna beckoning us inside. And what lurked at Industrial Superstudio, where the remove-your-material girl chose to stage this orgiastic feast of autoerotic publicity? Softcore Madonna videos and other uncut goods. Chocolate-covered bananas and other dangerous sweets. People faux-nailing each other, photo blowups of guess who hitchhiking wearing guess what. All that was missing, in fact, was the book (there was one copy in a glass case, guarded by goons) and Madonna behind a glory hole, the proceeds going toward AIDS research.

"But she was there in all her glory, at least appearing when we all looked in a mirror and said her name five times. Sporting breast-shaped braids and braid-shaped breasts a la' Heidi cum Eva Braun, a beaming Madonna, told reporters about her quest for 'perfection' and 'more genius' as crowds clamored. Madonna was in a roped-off section that even Christian Slater had to force-weasel his way into. We came, we saw, we came again. 'This is superb,' crowed David Lee Roth. 'She's peaking,' other, nastier guests contended. When did I hear that before? Oh yeah, in '83."

Madonna told everyone the book was supposed to be a $49.95 joke. According to book critic Calvin Tomkins, writing in *The New Yorker* magazine, it was far from laughable. He called it "a real downer. Not because the humor is as hard to find as the shocks but because Madonna ought to know by now that when you have to tell your audience that something is a joke it is time to get off the stage." We do agree with Tomkins, however, that the photographs are not only non-erotic, "they are just plain bad." When you consider Meisel shot all those frames, you can't help but wonder what they threw away. As Tomkins says, "image after image is dead on the page - lifeless, derivative, imaginatively limp."

Limp indeed. There's only one memorable male member, that of Nick the Dick, one of the Gaiety's favorite strippers, large and uncut. Yummy! Even the greatest exhibitionist we've ever met, Joey Stefano, covered his private parts! As Madonna commented, "The only guys who would take their clothes off were the guys at the Gaiety. Most of the men that were in the pictures were very shy."

We rather enjoyed the text more than the photos, except of course the spread on the boys at the Gaiety, to which we could easily relate because we've been there so often. Vince Aletti agreed: "...the dark, heady spirit of the photographer Brassai hovers over the most sustained and successful sequence -- Madonna and two tuxedoed friends slumming at the Gaiety boy burlesque."

The *Advocate's* columnist Callicott wrote: "In a fit of self-indulgent frenzy, Madonna dragged her willing accomplice, photographer Steve Meisel, to the Gaiety Theater in New York along with renowned professional art fag Udo Kier to snap a few pictures of Mr. Stefano writhing around the floor with the club's house 'hos' while Madonna sat on the floor in a formal gown, attempting to look affected. Art? Nah, but who gives a fuck? Joey looks better than ever with a lock of floppy hair in front of his eyes, and his world-famous booty hole is exposed for all to see and justly worship. I must say, Joey just might be the only boy I've ever seen who solicits a knee-jerk response to throw a Jeff Stryker dildo up his ass every time he bends over. More power to La Stefano's boy-pussy mystique, and Madonna, dearest, get a life."

The screen tests were conducted in Meisel's studio and Madonna presided over a mock casting couch. She asked two key questions, "Are you afraid of nudity?" and "Would you mind kissing me?" Not surprisingly, most were game. One doorman hunk for the Manhattan club Live Bait conducted his entire interview with his fly open. Madonna chuckled, "That's a good start."

Willem Dafoe

Speaking of having your fly open, in "Body of Evidence," released in January of 1993 and a quick bomb, Willem Dafoe gets tied up by Madonna and then she drops hot wax on his torso. Some of this scene and others ended up on the cutting room floor. "NC 17 films are just harder to market," said an spokesperson at MGM. So, again, Europeans get to see a hard version while we get an "R." "None of the sex scenes has been totally removed," said executive producer Stephen Deutsch. Madonna was happy with the R-rated version, but not Dafoe. He says he was initially attracted to the project because "the erotic scenes would be explicit...I've performed without clothes before. It taps into my narcissistic and exhibitionistic sides."

Michael Szymanski says Dafoe "is known for a large asset that didn't appear on screen – not even in the NC-17 version. As he sits down for an interview before Madonna walks in, he seems awkwardly aware of his reputation and crosses his legs for the whole chat. His mother saw Joan Rivers talking with The Holywood Kids about Dafoe's outstanding part because he has done prolonged nude scenes on stage, but he didn't think it was appropriate to reveal all for film."

"People aren't used to male genitalia and if you put it in a movie, then I think people fall out of a movie. I don't know if you've noticed, but there's more baggage with a man's than a woman's. There are more stories attached with one than the other because one's essentially internal and one's external.

"For me, for men, when I've seen men's genitals on stage, there's too much societal stuff with it. What's it look like? Is he circumcised? Is it big? How does he feel about the size of it? Is it erect? Is it not erect? Frankly, I think you see as much of me as Madonna in this movie."

Madonna said: "The rating game is hypocritical and ridiculous. The board allowed more of Dafoe's butt but only if they could cut the close-ups of cunnilingus." Now you're talking!

Nick Scotti

"He comes highly recommended," George Kalogerakis said in an article about Nick Scotti in *Vanity Fair* magazine. "And he photographs well partially submerged in water." And anywhere else, judging by the photo layout. This is one hot hunk who has his debut album, "Nick Scotti" now in stores thanks to Madonna. Nick was a model from Queens who happened to meet Madonna at a party at Herb Ritts' house. What happened after that is left to one's imagination but one thing we do know, Nick sent a demo tape to Madonna and she liked it and hooked him up with Reprise. But Scotti doesn't want to overplay the protege stuff: "Madonna opened the door and my foot was in and the rest was up to me."

When the album was released in April of 1993, *Entertainment Weekly's* James Earl Hardy wrote that Nick came straight from the Michael Bolton school of singing and that he has one thing going for him: his looks. "It doesn't help him at all on this empty album. He tries hard to be hip with dance and R&B - flavored pop, but the results are only blah." Hardy thought only the funky "Get Over," which Madonna co-wrote and joins him in singing, rises above mediocrity. "Stick to modeling, Nick," was the reviewer's advice.

Teen Machine, however, loved it. "Brilliant!" they raved. The interviewer sent by *Detour* to get the background on Scotti in his New York apartment said the Italian suffers from the dreaded white-boy-sounds-black Rick Astley Syndrome, but otherwise she celebrated the takes four, five and nine. "He goes 'Hmmmm' and you are his." When Nick answered the door in jeans and a T-shirt that fit a little too well, she said, "He is right, there is no justice."

Scotti left high school at 16 and started modeling at 17. He gave up that lucrative career for recording when he was 22. It took him two years to come out with the album. He admitted "manipulating Madonna" beyond belief. He made a string of gestures in describing this, from kneading dough to twisting string around his finger. "Seriously though, she wasn't like, 'Get this kid off my back.' She was serious about listening to my tape because we had such a significant, and good conversation that night. You know, when you are in a situation that is just special? Not that it was sexual." Oh?

Robert Plunket

And speaking of things special, our homeboy Robert Plunket, author of the delightful book *Love Junkie*, has had his own dealings with Madonna and just how special they become is up in the air at the moment.

"I had intended to write a totally light, frothy book about sex," Plunket says about the book. "But then AIDS hit. I kept waiting for it to go away so sex would be funny again. Then I realized sex would never be funny again. But I also realized I'd stumbled into more profound material. I was forced to become a philosopher rather than a comic.

"I think the book explains why AIDS happened in the gay community. It freezes a period of time just before something unimaginable was about to occur. You know, it bothers me that gay people who got AIDS at that time are viewed as wild, hedonistic people. If there's a message in the book, I think it's that so many of them were desperately lonely people who only wanted to be loved, and wanted it so badly that they did things that were foolish in retrospect."

In 1992, Plunket went to New York and signed to make the novel into a movie. His deal was with Madonna's production company, Maverick Pictures. "Madonna said she wouldn't star in the movie but you never know. The part would be perfect for her," Plunket says. Can't you just picture Madonna as Mimi Smithers, a bored upper middle-class housewife who has a strange relationship with a gay porn star modeled after Casey Donovan and starring Brad Pitt? The time is 1981 and Mimi discovers how witty gay men are how well they party and what great shoppers they can be.

Critic Dale Reynolds has compared Plunket to Joseph Keenan and Patrick Dennis, equally funny gay writers. Reynolds said: "Plunket creates the proper amount of ridiculous situations and enough exaggerated emotions to fill the QEII (one of the settings). Until the focus of the book goes somewhat awry in the second half, his screamingly funny observations and dialogue will keep you disturbing your neighbors for hours."

James Marcus, reviewing the book for the *Village Voice*, praised Plunket for strapping "a paragon of unconsciousness into the driver's seat," his narrator Mimi. "Plunket pushes his mouthpiece to such lofty and comical levels of unreliability that he may have succeeded in creating a whole new rhetorical category - the Oblivious Narrator."

Not a thought crosses Mimi's mind that isn't related to shopping, brand names, or small-time social climbing. Her breathless, blow-by-blow descriptions of her living room decor sums up her sensibility to perfection.

She goes for fifty pages before it dawns on her that a man at her pr office, Tom Potts, is gay. "I plead guilty to being obtuse," she says in a rare moment of clarity. But, as Reynolds says, for Mimi there's always another delusion around the corner. Drawn into the gay scene, she finds herself attracted to a porn star, Joel, whom she describes as the "most perfect proportioned human being I'd ever seen."

Mimi starts by answering the star's fan mail. Then she finds out that his modeling fee was $250 an hour. "I'm not quite sure what he modeled during these modeling sessions, but he was always running off to one, clutching a gym bag and saying, 'Well, I've got to go model. Make sure you turn on the answering machine when you leave."

"And then there was his acting career. True, it was limited, so far, anyway, to films that are usually thought of pornography. But don't forget that in their day D. H. Lawrence and Ezra Pound and even Donatello all had this charge leveled at them."

Answering mail includes sending out photo sets. The one set that sells the most is the one showing Joel with nothing on at all. "Now, I'm not a connoisseur of such things but I did know this - his penis was not of a particularly large size. Compared with his magnificent body it seemed a little out of scale, like an elaborate cocktail ring with just one tiny diamond. In only one photograph did you get a good look at it - Joe standing in a doorway, arms akimbo, a sneer on his lips and his penis hanging there, small, red, defiant, a little raw from overuse, like dishpan hands."

Eventually, Joe is filming at her home. Writes Mimi: "On the off chance you ever have a pornographic movie filmed in your home, here is a list of tips you might want to clip and save. I certainly wish I had such a list." And, having had many occasions to meet such performers, we liked the fifth tip best: "Don't be frightened of porn stars. True, they are a little intimidating at first. After all, what kind of person would do this for a living. One thing was certain - they were not the sort who could be counted on to make an eight AM train."

If there's anything Mimi got out of reading the letters it's that "men constantly lie about their sex lives, even to themselves. Especially to themselves. They can rationalize anything."

Finally, she gets Joel to take her to bed: "'Suck,'" he says, pushing her to her knees. Mimi: "I stared at his penis. It was smaller than I remembered, and not at all hard." Eventually, Joel does manage to get it hard, by looking at himself in a mirror. Shades of Ryan Idol.

Robert himself admits: "The book wallows in sex, but it's the kind of sex that happens in real life - frustrating, humiliating, ridiculous. The 'right' scene isn't there."

Although he finds fault with Plunket's sidestepping of the enormity of the AIDS issue, Reynolds admires the author's talent: "Plunket is so deft, so surgical in his comic precision, that I'd love to see what he could do if he sobered up, bore down, and got (perish the thought) reliable."

Born in Texas, like Mimi, Robert grew up in Bronxville, N.Y, and earned his bachelor's degree at Williams College and his master's degree in film and theater at Sarah Lawrence (he was the 10th male student to enroll). He also has an MBA from UCLA where he worked in arts management before turning to writing. Plunket has even worked in movies as an actor. But his scene in "White Palace" was cut. "James Spader did it," he says, "because he hates me. A real jerk. Everybody in show business hates him. The most hated man in Hollywood."

And perhaps now Plunket thinks Madonna is the most hated *woman* in Hollywood. After he finished the script for Madonna, he reported she was stunned for several days: "Indeed, she was so overwhelmed that she inadvertently tried to stop payment on the check. And the reaction from directors who have read it has been even more ecstatic. My dear friend Martin Scorsese said he had never come across a script that more deserved to be 'in the can' but that after 'Age of Innocence' he was not attempting any more 'classics.' And darling Jane Campion, whose sweet little movie 'The Piano' is such a surprise hit, said that while she had never read quite like it, she, as a relative beginner, felt she should stick with films in which the characters have motivations. Oh, well. To be perfectly honest, I don't think 'The Piano' and my film are in the same class at all. At least my heroine can talk ('That's the problem,' said Jane.) Anyway, I'll keep you posted. We're still waiting to hear from Fellini."

Sean Penn

We leave the last word on Madonna and her men to her ex, Sean Penn, who, when he was married to her, frequently tied her to a chair.

Says Madonna of Sean: "We did make a really good couple, didn't we? But we had our problems. Even if it doesn't work out, there's that person that you love. I did have a real connection with Sean and I still do. I feel close to him even though we're not physically close. There was a lot of pressure. I mean, it really is amazing we didn't kill each other. But I don't feel it was a waste of time. I still love him." But, when Newsweek asked, she said, "Straight men need to be emasculated. I'm sorry. They all need to be slapped around. Every straight guy should have a man's tongue in his mouth at least once."

To that, ex-convict Sean replied: "It's her wit. Yeah. But look, I'm not a better expert on her than anybody else. I don't know her any better from having been with her. I was drunk most of the time, anyway.

"But whatever anybody thinks about what she does, she serves as a brilliant reflection of what people respond to and what they want to see – on every level.

"I like her, yeah. I just don't want her living at my house."

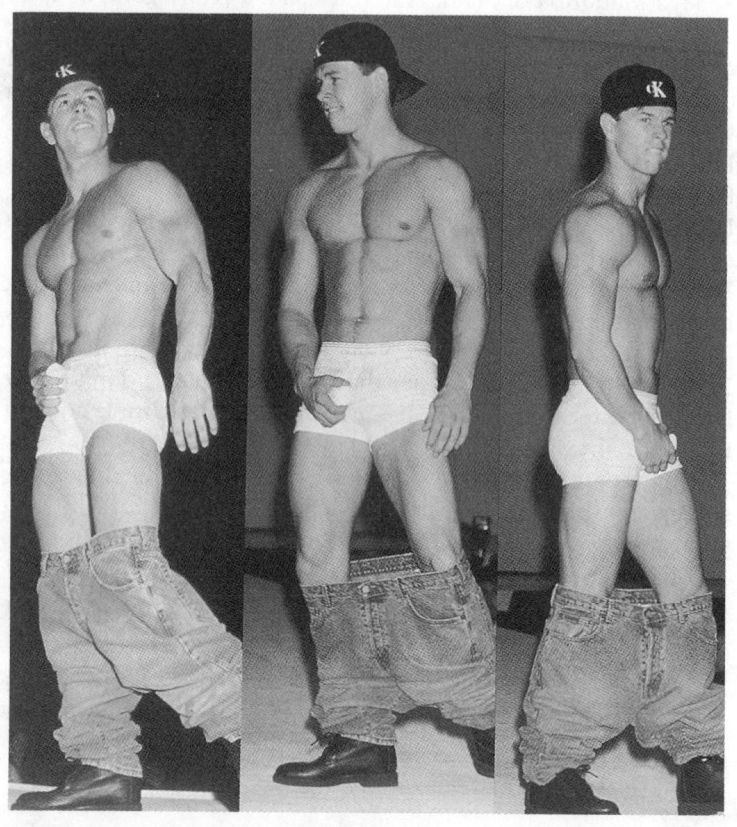

Rapper/model Marky Mark takes matters in hand in widely circulated news photos

GOING DOWN WITH MARKY MARK

Not every man who meets her is thrilled by Madonna. The Great Underpants Boy circa 1992-93, Marky Mark, told an English magazine that he thought Madonna was great until he actually met her! Now you would have thought that might have been the *meat*-ing of the Century. The headlines alone would tend to turn you on, all those MM's! But no, Marky was not impressed: "I seen (sic) Madonna in person and before that I thought she was kind of cute but she looked like somebody out of 'Beetlejuice,' man! Seriously!"

Those remarks (and please note, we quote Marky exactly as he speaks, as above, without changing his use – or rather, abuse – of the English language) led to what became known as the "M & M War." The end result of this battle had Marky suffering the put-foot-in-mouth fate of Donna Summer as far as many gays were concerned. The "tremendous set-to" between Marky and Madonna reached a climax (of sorts) at a birthday party in Hollywood for "Truth or Dare" director Alek Keshishian. Marky says he went to the party by himself and was only there ten minutes when Madonna came after him. "I was like, 'What's up?' And she was like, 'Don't fucking say hi to me. You know what the fuck you fucking did. You dished me. You're a fucking asshole, a fucking fake.'" They exchanged more heated words until Madonna said she was going to find someone to "kick" Marky's ass.

Marky tried blowing it off when a Maverick records executive, Guy Oseary, travelling with Madonna, jumped in. At first, they simply sassed each other and left but then Oseary came back and threatened Marky a second time, telling him he'd settle things outside. "I know you don't want to fight me," he said. "I knew you was a pussy."

Marky said, "All right. Whatever."

But soon Marky saw there were two others joining Oseary. That's when he started swinging, landed a punch, and brought Oseary to the floor and they began wrestling. The other two

Maverick records people started banging and kicking Marky until other guests broke up the melee. A guest at the party told New York gossip columnist Liz Smith that this incident did not happen the way Madonna says it did. Her version goes like this: "Marky is not a bad kid, but he and Madonna are both dopes and have too much attitude. Marky pinched Madonna when she went by him. She turned on him and said something like, 'Don't try to be friendly, considering your rap lyrics about me.' Marky did NOT make any homophobic remark."

Michael Szymanski, in *Genre*, claimed to have the *true* scoop as well: ". . . The *real* story about Madonna and Marky Mark (and this is from someone who was there) is that the boy-toy rebuffed her persistent advances, and that's why she started the rumor about the anti-gay remark – knowing it would cost him a Donna Summer-like avalanche of hate from his homo fans. Leave it to M to take being evil to a whole new level. Anyway, Marky likes younger, virginal girls whom he wants to touch for the very first time."

Whatever really did happen, the hostess of the party, Angela Janklow Harrington was grateful: "Thank God that happened. It was such a *bad* party!"

At the peak of the hype, Jim Mullen, in *Entertainment Weekly*, said "the whole country was talking about it," and "Madonna vs. Marky Mark. They were really fighting over who has bigger breasts."

And speaking of Marky's breasts, are among the most exposed of all time. Early in 1992, he was the first celebrity to be honored with a pullout centerfold in *People* magazine's "Teen Idol" issue. Even the venerable columnist Liz Smith made note of it: "Don't you all just love the issue with its amazing pull-out of bare-chested Marky Mark? I understand that many People staffers were laughed to scorn by their friends from other publications over this little addition. (Just jealous they didn't think of it first!?)" And, for once, Mark Robert Wahlberg's briefs weren't showing. But he was photographed with his hands in the pockets of his jeans, pulling them up so that the crotch is magnificently displayed. And then there's that dumb-boy face, genuinely open, so pleasant that you find yourself saying, "such a kid," and imagining what fun he'd be, especially in bed! Even Madonna thought so at the time: "I turn on MTV and there's a boy in his underwear for 20 minutes. And I thought I was bad!"

Marky said his pants-dropping began in L.A., at Magic Mountain, right after his first record, "'Good Vibrations," came out: "It was just one of those things, man. I was doing something kinda berserk and I just dropped my pants. And I remember I saw 50 million flashes and I was like 'Oh, shit!' I was like 'This might be something.' Then it started getting a little out of hand. Now my fans tend to demand it."

Because his fans demanded to know, Marky revealed that he lost his virginity over a course of five encounters with the same girl. We mean, this is a stud who takes his sweet time! Heaven! He was 16 and it was the first time for each of them. And just in case you get to meet him and manage to steer him to your bed, be aware his condom of choice is: "Trojans, ribbed, in the gold box." It's good to be prepared.

Celeb watchers called Marky a "hip-hop hunk" and he did admit at the time that he worked out "about two hours every morning. I usually do it in the gym of whatever hotel I'm at. If I don't work out in the morning, I don't feel too good for the rest of the day. Weight lifting is the only time to let my frustrations out. And the cuties love it." Indeed, the "cutie" readers of *Teen* magazine named him "the hottest hunk" in music.

The star got into body-building when he stopped smoking. He began eating like a pig and gained thirty pounds so he started going to the gym. Soon Marky's muscles looked as if they were topped with more muscles. The 5'8", 160 pound stud said, "I enjoy doing push ups." (You can do push-ups over me anytime, honey.) The stud puppy has a 31-inch waist and 16-and-a-quarter-inch biceps. One can only fantasize about the *other* measurements. The heaviest weight he has lifted is 300 pounds. Besides the obvious benefits, Mark said the regimen has made him "feel good."

What gay men were doing at this point was just trying to cope. Steve Saylor said: "God forbid you should turn to MTV, where Marky Mark is eternally stripping down to his jockey shorts and fondling his sweet sensation over and over and over again." This "sweet sensation" was duly noted by the teen magazine *Sassy*, whose stories are all written in the voice of a teenage girl: "Marky Mark...disrobed, sporting boxers over a pair of those groovy Calvin Klein undershorts," said one piece, "and well, all I can say about what happened next is, I hope Marky respected himself in the morning."

Of course, there were some fans who didn't groove on his sexiness. One said, "Actually, I don't like the way he pulls his pants down and grabs onto...(she laughs). Well, anyway, that's my opinion. What was the question again?" When asked if he weren't famous, would they still love him, one fan replied, "Be serious. He's cute!" Another: "If I saw him walking down the block, I swear to God I'd go up to him and I'd go, 'Excuse me. What's your name?' Just like any other guy." But Marky's not just like any other guy. In fact, he's got that rarity, a third nipple. He says: "It's cool, it's unique. Not too many people have them, and it's not hazardous to my health or anything. It's not something to be ashamed about. It's dope. And bitches like to suck it."

And then there's the tattoo on Marky's ankle. "It's Sylvester the cat with Tweety Bird in his mouth. I went to the tattoo store and said, 'Give me that tattoo!' I only picked it because I wanted to cover up what was there before, which was a playing card, a club. I did it on my own. I made the club out of India ink. But it's corny. I regret getting it because it marks up my body for life. And if I ever do anything bad they can identify me by it."

To further assist his fans in identifying him, Marky exposed himself to Lynn Goldsmith's camera to create *Marky Mark*, a $15 photo book liberally spiced with Marky quotes. Quite appropriately, the stud puppy dedicated the book to his *dick*.

Indeed, his dick was supremely exposed by Calvin Klein for about two years, gently tucked into white briefs, of course. Marky's assets were not only gracing the pages of almost every magazine in the country, they were also on display on every bus and/or shelter, first in New York, then San Francisco. Indeed, the crotch of Marky Mark must be the most photographed one of recent times. It all started when Bruce Weber shot hundreds of feet of film of it for a spread in *Interview* magazine. As Vince Aletti commented in *The Village Voice*, "Marky Mark crunches up his face, drops his pants and squeezes the bulge in his Calvin Klein briefs."

Marky talked about his relationship with CK: "You know, he's just been so la-arge. I mean, even in the neighborhoods, if you had a pair of Calvin Kleins, you was the man. So I went to his house and I met him, hooked up. We had one set deal. They gave me $100,000 to do the commercials and the photos."

Seeing the first underwear ads, Susan Orlean, writing in *The New Yorker*, said: "Of all the guys who are standing around bus shelters in Manhattan dressed in nothing but their underpants, Marky is the most polite. For instance, even though he is very busy getting ready to go to Japan for a promotional tour, he took the time to call from Los Angeles the other day just to chat about his new role as the Calvin Klein Underpants Boy.

"Underwear has always figured prominently in his performances but it is only in the last weeks (as the CK model) that Marky has ascended to the status of lingerie luminary. He actually was a little late in calling me but said he was at the gym doing some upper-body work. Who could begrudge him that? After all, if photographs of you nearly naked were plastered everywhere, then upper-body work is exactly the sort of thing you would be wise not to neglect. Nonetheless, Marky was apologetic. 'I'm sorry, really sorry,' he said. 'I hope I didn't screw up your day, or anything.'

"In the ads, which were photographed by the master Herb Ritts, Marky looks like a horny and impudent sixteen-year-old pleased with his pecs, his abs, and his underwear.

"Now, about his *thing*. Since he was a little kid, Marky has favored gigantic pants riding very low on his hips. 'I can't move around in tight pants,' he says. 'I've always been into the baggy thing.' But he has always favored Calvin Klein underwear. 'It's some crazy shit seeing the posters of me in my underwear all over the place,' he says. 'But the pictures are really me, you know? But I've pulled my pants down in front of people millions of times. It's not that big a thing for me.'"

Not a *big* thing? Come now. And those posters became a hot item on the black market, fetching hundreds of dollars apiece on the deprived West Coast. Musto spotted The Underpants Boy on a typical night out in New York: "Marky Mark showed up to discuss his Calvins with David Lee Roth, who boasted of wearing Fruit of the Looms. 'Twas truly a meeting of remarkable behinds. Earlier, at the Palladium, Marky had politely refused to strip for a public access cable show, saying, 'I have to get permission from my label and my manager before I do anything.' You mean the guy has to notify them when every time he drops his drawers? They must comprise the busiest communications center on the entire planet."

When Marky first came upon the New York scene he was much less inhibited. Musto reported he spotted the star at the Ritz in the Big Apple, that quickly turned into something from the gay strip joint Show Palace: "Shedding his jacket and strutting around bare-chested, later dropping his pants to reveal briefs tightly encasing what could only be described as a baseball bat. A waifish urchin no longer, he grabbed his crotch repeatedly and quipped, 'How's everybody in the motherfuckin' house doin' tonight?' Dancing and rapping like a demon, he barely remembered to pull the pants back up before stumbling offstage and hurting his knee. This guy makes Madonna's masturbation shtick look like an Anita Bryant orange juice commercial. The girls in the crowd went berserk, the guys booed."

But it was not just the crotch of Marky that captivated his fans at this point. His glorious chest left everybody breathless. George Wayne, writing in QW, recalled Marky's showing up at the "Boathouse Rock" party to aid AmFAR: "Marky Mark (I just want to eat his tits) was there too, but had only leers. Marky didn't like the idea of me shouting, 'Show us your tits!' as he butched it up for the paparazzi."

When promoting the Klein line, Marky sometimes had the clothes designer himself, now much married and drug-free, in tow, beaming delightedly as Marky scrawled his name on anything and everything that had the CK logo.

A spy on the scene in San Francisco at Macy's department store reported the rapper was "flirting outrageously with all of the guys." When someone asked him if he'd ever wear Fruit of the Looms, Marky said, "Well, I ain't gonna say while I'm sitting here next to Calvin Klein." Calvin just smiled. (I mean, if you were Calvin, wouldn't you be smiling?)

At the beefcake boy's San Francisco appearance, kids started lining up at 8 a.m., but it seemed no coincidence, Jim Provenzano reported, that the first in line was an older gay man, Tony Bruno, who had actually seen Marky at a concert at the Warfield Theater. "He's great," Bruno said. "He shows he's non-judgmental, no matter what you are, your race, your sexuality." Bruno confided that he was not going to wear his Marky-autographed briefs, he was going to "frame it." Provenzano said that a small herd of gay men showed up about an hour before Marky's appearance. "We're devoted but not demented," one fan said. Another fan reported that Marky's bus shelter posters were a hot item in S.F. "The one at Castro and Market was broken into twice." Then the fan revealed, "It's an Allen wrench that you need."

Another fan called Marky "homo-positive. For somebody that's such a street tough, he's sending a really good image." At the signing, Provenzano reported, Marky pulled up his shirt to show the trim of his Calvin Klein undies under his baggy pants, and spoke semi-intelligible phrases about the "good people comin' to support the Funky Bunch." (His other band members were cordoned off to one side.) Marky obliging signed the packages of underwear presented by the first 200 people in line, who, Provenzano joked, were rushed by like political deportees. A gang of hired goons kept the photographers at bay.

After the signing, Marky and Calvin were rushed to a waiting stretch limo and, as they sped away, Marky leaped up through the sun roof, ripped off his shirt and hat, and exposed his torso "like a beefy young Pop Tart." A young gay fan was assaulted by a bunch of girls when he managed to catch Marky's cap.

Meanwhile, back in New York, the heroic billboard of the buff boy on Times Square could not be ignored. One day, two men are standing at a light on Third Avenue in Manhattan, Guy Trebay reported, when Marky Mark glided past.

"I'm getting fed up with Marky Mark," Man One griped, only semi-exasperated. "Every time you turn around, there he is, with his pants down and his arms in the air. I can't take it!" 'I know," said Man Two.

"I was talking to a friend the other day," Man One went on, "and he was saying he wondered how straight men deal with it, Marky Mark on the bus, 50-foot Marky Mark in Times Square, all these queer images. Does it scare them, or do they find it empowering?"

"Are there any straight men?" Man Two replied, and Trebay

said the wisecrack seems to contain a truth central to the Marky Mark ad campaign: "The whole country's horny for teen male flesh, and Marky's the proof. What his records can't do for his career, his briefs might. And in the process, decades of cornball homoerotic imagery – from Von Gloeden to Mapplethorpe – have gone mainstream. America is being outed by Calvin Klein."

"So I called X," said a note from Trebay's pal Vince. Vince is a "veryclosefriend" of Calvin and his wife Kelly. Vince contacted X to see if she could get him a copy of the Marky Mark bus shelter poster. "Anyway, she calls me today and says the company has had so many requests they've practically established a desk to deal with them. The bus shelter posters are available at $500 each, she says. She says she might be able to get me smaller ones for free. Where would I put the big one anyway? Under my pillow? On the ceiling over my bed?"

The billboard on Times Square generates much comment, even among the trendy: "The other night, a couple staggered out of the Thierry Mugler opening party at USA, shaking the smoke funk from their clothes. Shivering, they headed toward Broadway and there, high above them, loomed Marky. 'Whoa,' said the woman, a toiler in the fields of journalism. 'I never saw that before.'

"'I know,' said her companion, a fellow media slut, 'pretty amazing, right?'

"'You know, we tried to get him to pose for the magazine but he blew us off.'

"'Why?'

"'He's too-too.'

"'Too what?'

"'Too *big*.'

"'But his records are in the toilet.'

"'Yeah, but his pecs are a major event.'"

Columnist Lisa Jones disagreed, saying Marky was "way off the mark. The mantra 'expropriation' is as overused as the act itself, and when you're reading America, it's a muddy term with a muddy payoff. But, as Marky Mark marches on, allow us this: If he ain't the Rocky of the early '90s, let us eat our Vanilla Ice dolls. And does America and New York City in particular, a city that's 60 per cent color, really need another great-white-hope fantasy, imagined by Calvin Klein, oozing down on us from billboards in Times Square?

"Some celebrate Marky Mark, whiter and larger than King Kong, as the mainstreaming of the homoerotic. More obvious is the bite that Marky takes from black male style culture from be-bop to hip hop, from Joe Lewis to Naughty by Nature's Treach. The straddle, the dance moves, the baggy pants, the drawers showing, the jay larger than yours, we've seen it all before. Show a crew-cut Irish-American youth like Marky noodling his jay and it's guilt-free teen fun. Put up a 'Harlem Brown' via Newark, like Treach, and the *Times* might run an editorial on billboards that will promote urban violence. "More bile-inducing than the Marky spread is sponsor Calvin Klein himself, whose ads do run a whites-only shop. With the Marky campaign, we've caught Calvin serving up black male panache, but, in keeping with the designer's usual racial codes, doing so by trussing it up in Marky's mediocre white-rap face. Those concerned about images might think of passing on the Klein label until the designer enlarges his camera lens to include a world that ain't just a day at Aryan gym.

"In some version of an ideal world (possibly 'In Living Color's Black World'), chocolate-for-days Treach gets to play Calvin Klein's 40-foot plus Times Square demigod. Ask black girls in the know about hip hop's young gun and they get moist over his classic 'hard' looks. Put Treach up there and you wouldn't have to waste the extra 10 feet to get his jay in the shot. You'd see the brother's face, and quite simply, that's all the information you'd need."

While every black male we know says he'd rather be loved for his mind than his jay, the obvious cannot be ignored. Seriously, how on earth can you ignore something so big and black and long? And that's just the penis! Add the balls and it's simply overwhelming.

At the end of 1992, the teen fan magazine *Tutti* was offering up "Marky Mark's Undies" in what it is heralding as the "Contest of the Century: We See London, We See France, We See Marky's Underpants! It's Completely Gross! Yes, we here in Tuttiland are known for being on the edge of everything. And it is for this reason that we are proud to announce that for the first time ever, this magazine is giving you the chance to win a pair of Marky's underwear! That's right, a pair of actual MM undershorts! Just think how cool it would be to own an actual pair of these in-demand undergarments. You'd be the envy of all your friends and relatives. People will want to know you. They'll want to be your friend. It'll be great! Even filling out this coupon will put some zest in your life." But, in a note, the magazine's editors were compelled to assure their young, impressionable readers that: "Marky owned and touched the underwear we're giving away but he never actually WORE them. So all you hygiene freaks out there can relax." Well, shucks, that did it for us! We wouldn't want the undies UNLESS Marky had worn them! And, even better, if he'd spilled a little of his cum on 'em. Or, at the very least, sweated in them! Indeed, the sweat off Marky's balls should be bottled and sold.

On New Year's 1993, dish diva Musto journeyed to Marky's first concert in a gay venue (at the Boys' Bump Night at USA in New York City) and reported: "Looking petrified of the crowd, the rapper, wearing long sleeves and surrounding himself with the Funky Bunch, avoided the edges of the stage and didn't take a single thing off (he only dropped his pants for a millisecond. His agency claimed he had a third degree burn on his back. If he's that uptight in future gay engagements, he'll really get burned."

Marky didn't have many more gay engagements, but he got burned anyway. He had told an interviewer that he had never even "dabbled in homo-ism" during puberty. "You think about everything," he admitted, "but I never did think, Would I like to do him? But a large part of the gay community has shown an interest in Marky Mark. Like I said many a time, it's cool for men to find me interesting, and to show a liking to me. Like I said, I prefer women, and I always have, but if that's what they're into, then great. I work out, I train hard, I'm happy with the shape that I am in. It attract girls – obviously it also attracts men, which is cool, if it's their thing."

Despite the mounting criticism, Klein went on with the second phase of the Marky campaign. John Seabrook attended the festivities when Marky posed for his new series of ads and reported back to the tony *New Yorker* magazine, of all places: "In planning the photographs, some people at Calvin Klein had argued that the existing campaign – which includes images of Marky Mark with his pants down, grinning – had reached the end of its life span, and a different approach altogether was necessary. Artistic director Fabien, however, believed that the images could be 'worked' a little further, as he likes to say, and Calvin had decided to follow Fabien's advice: 'Fabien and I are on the same wavelength,' Calvin said.

"The shot was at Sun Studios, which is on the top floor of a building on lower Broadway . . . Marky Mark arrived, removed his street clothes, and put on a new pair of Calvin Klein underwear and CK jeans, with the jeans pulled down below the waistband of his underwear and over his feet, so that he was walking on the ends of his pant legs. He went forward and posed for (photographer) David Sims so that Sims could shoot a few Polaroids. He sawed his finger under his nose, then sneered. Sims Polaroided the sneer. He sawed his finger under his nose again. He stuck his finger into his nose and said, 'You, take picture of this. Yo, the booger shot.' Sims Polaroided the booger shot.

"While Sims was shooting a couple of rolls of Marky in the low-slung jeans, Fabien consulted with Neil Kraft, who handles in-house advertising for Calvin Klein, about the next shot. On a small yellow pad Fabien quickly sketched for Neil the image he had in mind. It showed Marky with his underwear down around his ankles, covering himself with his hands.

"'I like it,' Neil said after studying the drawing.

"'Fabien shaded around Marky's hands and said, 'What about his . . . '

'Neil said, 'His zuzu? What's the word for zuzu in French?'

"The two men chatted in lowered voices so that Marky, still posing in front of Sims, could not hear. Marky said, 'Yo, some lady shaved my face off in like three different places, made me feel like a dawg. Shaved me like a dawg.'

"Neil, still pondering Fabien's drawing, said, 'Who shaved you like a dawg, Marky?'

"'Do we need to show what the underwear looks like?' Fabien asked Neil.

"'I think people know what a pair of Calvin Klein underwear looks like by now.'

"Fabien shrugged. 'That's it, then.'

"When Sims was finished, Neil went over and informed Marky of Fabien's plan.

"'Yo, you want me to what? *What?*Yo, man, you want me to take dwauuuughs off, man?' Marky stalked around the room in a cartoonish side-to-side hip-hop swagger, saying, 'My drawers! Yo, man, my drawers! Man wants me to take my drawers off!'

"A young man named Miguel, who had come with Marky, walked over and said, 'Yo man. Don't do it, man. Don't take your underwears down. Yo man, even if you covers yourself with your hand, man, some hair can still show out of there.'

"Neil said, 'Well, it's not as though he'd never grabbed his dick before in a national magazine.'

"Marky did some fingertip pushups while he thought about the idea. Bands of muscle swelled in his shoulders as he smoothly lowered himself off the floor. Then he got on the phone, possibly to negotiate a change order. Finally, it was decided that Marky would wear his underwear down around his ankles but would cover himself with a black CK baseball cap, not his hand. Fabien received this news with a shrug and did another pencil sketch for the stylist, who rummaged around among the clothes racks and came up with a black hat. Marky walked up in front of Sims, said 'Ready?' and pulled his underwear down around his ankles while Miguel and Sims' assistant held a board up in front of his middle. When the hat was in place, they lowered the board. Marky's underwear was crooked around his ankles, so that you couldn't quite read the 'Calvin Klein' on the waistband, and Neil started to kneel before Marky to fix it but got embarrassed, and Miguel had to come to the rescue.

"Sims shot a Polaroid, then quickly shot a roll . . . Marky, his underwear up around his middle again, swaggered over and looked at the Polaroid. 'Awww, man,' he said when he saw it. 'You're goin' to have to pay me like three billion bucks for that picture. First of all, my hat is my trademark, man, and now I can't even wear my hat, 'cause I got my balls in my fucking hat. Second of all, my mother's going to be pissed at me. Yo, my mother said, 'I don't care what you do, just keep your drawers on.' He shook his head. 'And now this happens. Yo , man, where am I going to love?'

"Fabien studied the Polaroid. 'That's it,' he said, with another shrug. 'That's the eee-maj. It is a scoop, yes? It is mega. Can you imagine what a sensation it will cause?

"I looked at the Polaroid. Now, remembering how it looked, I feel as though I have already seen the image all over Manhattan – on bus shelters, going by on buses, plastered in a long sequence along scaffolding.

"I said, 'What are you going to do next time? Remove the hat?

"'Bing!' said Fabien. 'There's the copy.' He made a little block of his type in space with his fingers. 'Next year we remove the hat.'"

Well, enterprising retouchers went ahead and removed the hat. They found an appropriate photo of Marky and added his *zuzu*. Soon fax machines were working overtime sending the nude Marky with hard-on out all over the world. And the enterprising editors at *Inches* magazine even printed it in their December, 1993 issue. Although the Marky *zuzu* looks suspiciously like the one adorning Eddie Perez of "Cholo!" fame, the porn performer that met Marky at the Electronics Show in Vegas, where Marky was plugging his exercise video, we still find it thrilling. It'll do till we can see the real one in color, maybe in *Playgirl*? As Marky would say, "Awww, man."

But the stud puppy was exposing himself for GoodTimes Video in "The Marky Mark Workout: Form, Focus, Fitness." *Premiere's* Tom Russo: "This is a fun tape. Marky yells 'Pow!' a couple of times, works out with incredible babes whom he ogles liberally, and says motivating things like, 'Everybody's beautiful, man. Go out and get yours.' Unfortunately, I can't imagine Marky got to looking the way he does because of this workout, which consists of some weight-lifting exercises and push-ups on chairs. Marky spends half of the tape at the gym, where he races through the machines. The best part comes at the end, when he has a hilarious, Abbott-and-Costello dialogue with a nutritionist and then jumps into a Jacuzzi with a bunch of babes. Pow!" The best part for us was the beginning, when Marky is awakened by his trainer. He rubs his eyes, lets the sheet drop, revealing that remarkable chest, and then sits up. As the sheet falls, we were hoping to see this stud, as one would expect, sleeps in the nude. But, alas, he wears his Calvin Klein briefs to bed, and it can't really be morning because he doesn't have a good ol' stud puppy hard-on.

In June of 1993, Marky was at the video convention in Las Vegas promoting his exercise video, which came out for Christmas. For fans of the buff boy, it made quite a stocking stuffer. One of our spies at the big video convention had his picture taken with the rapper and said, "Marky has the most kissable lips I've ever seen." His lips? (God, I never noticed his lips. Time to look again, folks. No, don't keep looking at that chest...the lips! Well, as far as I'm concerned, he's kissable EVERYWHERE!) The Hollywood rag *Spunk*, also at the convention, spotted Marky and have now christened him "crater face." They asked if it was steroids or acne. We know, we read his book (the one he dedicated to his dick), it was acne. And as long as he brings his makeup along on our date, who cares? Besides, we'd be too busy to count the zits on his cheeks.

Zits aside, Marky's up-from-the-ghetto success is truly remarkable. After their parents' divorce, Mark and his eight brothers and sisters remained with their mom, Alma, in Dorchester, Mass. In this predominantly black neighborhood, he had to learn some smooth moves just to stay alive. He and Donnie learned the moves and joined break-dance groups.

Eventually they came to the attention of Mary Alford, a music manager on the Boston scene (whose biggest client was Rick James). Her dream was to put together a group of kids along the lines of the Jackson 5 or Menudo. Then one day Mary happened to meet an old friend, Maurice Starr, manager of the New Edition (Bobby Brown, Johnny Gill) and explained what she was doing. He said he was trying to do the same thing; they decided to pool their efforts. The result was a group called New Kids on the Block. Mark was only 13 and Maurice and Mary liked Mark and Donnie and added them to the act.

But after six months, when the group gave their first concert they were booed off the stage. The chemistry was wrong and Marky, who couldn't sing, could only rap, was dropped from the group. It was a tough time for the youngster. Donnie, his best buddy, his brother, was becoming a phenomenal success with the most popular singing group in the world at that time and Marky was stuck at home. Marky went back to the streets, got arrested five or six times. "I was on the verge of ruining my life," he admits. "I used to chill, smoke weed, I quit school." But finally he was able to get it under control. He started spending time at the Dorchester Youth Collaborative, a youth center where kids like me hang out to get away from trouble. "They just tell you, 'You screwed up once. Look at your life.' So what I discovered was that I was into rapping and performing and that's what I truly loved. Hip hop, street rap was close to my soul."

Marky's mom recalls: "One of the family jokes is that when Marky was about three he would get in front of anything where he could see his reflection. It could be the toaster or the oven and he would climb up on top of the counter and sit in front of us and, you know, trying to flex his muscles when all there was was little bones." One day, in the flush of the New Kids success, Donnie came home and the brothers began rapping together, just like in the old days. Donnie suggested they write some of the stuff down and before long Donnie decided he'd invest some of his New Kids bucks in his little brother. Donnie put together the Funky Bunch, his posse of six dancers and rappers. "They sing dance and act crazy like me," Marky says. On the Kids' 1900-91 tour, Marky's group was the opening act. That did it. Marky was becoming a hit. With a handful of rap demos, Mark approached the record companies and on July 23, 1991, his first album, "Music for the People," was unleashed on the public. Donnie was the producer and co-wrote most of the tracks. MC Spice, a Boston rapper, co-wrote and co-produced a couple of tracks. The album was a smash, helped, without doubt, by the videos on MTV.

"You know man," Marky reflected at the time, "we could've taken a pretty face and made a hardcore kid. But this is me. This my way to express myself, to tell the whole world how I feel and maybe do some good. Music has that effect on people. I will not do anything to make myself feel uncomfortable. Not put on a cute smile, not get pretty-boyed up. The most important thing to me is that I do it my way, without hiding myself.

"Music is my life. The last job I had, I was a bricklayer's apprentice. And I was happy with that job, too, because it was something that made me feel good. To build a wall for the side of a building felt really good to me."

Many critics feel only a black person can rap but Marky said he was the "real deal. Hip-hop, street rap was close to my soul. I had always done freestyle raps. The first raps I did with Donnie were real down-and-dirty. People who understand rap aren't going to say anything about my being white. Hip-hop was almost whitewashed and turned into Vanilla Ice." Marky says Vanilla Ice claimed a right to rap because he went to a tough school in Miami. But it turns out he was mostly from an all-white, upper-middle-class suburb in Texas. Hip-hop isn't black music, it's street music."

The Advocate's Lance Loud called him "Hip-hop's answer to the Venus de Milo." Lance watched him filming a video in L.A., driving the damsels dizzy, and announced that to the world that cute Marky was queer-friendly. Between takes Marky joked with girls and lots of gay guys assembled on the edge of the parking lot. He performed several unscripted crotch grabs, winked at the swooning audience and generally showed himself to be a unisexual cockteaser of major proportions. At one point he grappled the chain-link fence between him and his now-flaccid followers and pretended that it was a – how would you say? – glory hole. Then, with breathtaking aplomb, he proceeded to demonstrate something that looked an awful lot like fellatio on an imaginary member with such zeal, eyewitnesses swear Linda Lovelace would have found it educational."

"I hate to admit it," said R. Couri Hay, "but I went to the Off-white Party at Limelight with about 600 other dedicated party boys. I stayed until Marky Mark was 'depantsed' on stage by three boys with a plan. It was a beautiful sight and night to behold."

At an autograph-signing session, girls were screaming, shouting, crying, and asking if they could rub their photos on his chest. He agreed to everything, except when one girl wanted his cap. There was no way he would ever give up his cap. He said he only takes it off when he's in church, but we have seen him in concerts without it. Must have been his hair that day. The music critic Adam Block said Marky was "an Irish Catholic who threatens to give the church a good name. The buffed pud-boy is getting as famous for flashing his underwear as he is for his endearing musical chops."

"Although he's hetero, he's quick to say he's comfortable around queers and is even flattered that they find him attractive. It's rare," Block asserted, "for a male pop star with teen appeal to be so plainspoken and supportive about queers. It's rarer still in the world of rap, where Mark has at least one foot tapping." Among brown-haired, hazel-eyed Marky's nicknames - I kid you not: "Mizo," "Miz."

"When dissecting Mark's mode, the obvious feature is more substance than style," the author of a biography about the star, Randi Reisfeld, wrote. "He has worked to create an almost perfectly sculpted chest, with bulging biceps and, as one reviewer put it, 'a stomach as rippled as a potato chip.' His close-to-exhibitionistic display of his upper body is a large part of what sets him apart from the other young rappers and performers. He has marketed himself as a hunk, a studly package few can resist. His effect isn't limited to prepubescent princesses. It knows no age boundaries. The older women leave him love notes, with their phone numbers attached to very personal items. They come right out and (even on hand-painted banners) say exactly what it is that Marky does for them (and what they'd like to do for him.)"

With all these fans wanting him, what about this boy's love life? How about a girlfriend? everyone wanted to know. In the video version of "Music for the People," Marky has a rap that goes, "I try to show 'em the joint, so maybe I can get a little bit of juice back at the hotel." But, if you can believe his comments to the press he isn't getting any "back at the hotel" or anywhere else. "Sure," he admitted, "I'd date a fan but mostly I'm in and out of town too quick and nothing comes of anything." (Nothing comes? Come on!) Marky laughed, "I need one bad. Donnie still gets all the girls. I haven't done anything really romantic so far. I've been in Boston too long and nothing romantic ever happens here. They say romantic things happen in Europe." (Look out Paris.) "My preference is for females," Marky insists, "but I respect anybody for their sexual preferences. And gay people are probably the most harmless people and would never try to do anything to hurt you, you know what I mean? Which is good. I feel very comfortable around gay people."

Gay publisher Casey Klinger commented, "Take a number.

Marky ain't puttin' out for no nellies, but we can dream can't we?" (In his picture book, he at least admits to kissing his brother Donnie.)

To ingratiate himself with the gay community, the star lent his presence to celebrity affairs held to raise money to benefit AIDS research and appeared on the AIDS awareness video, "Red Hot + Dance," dressed completely in black. "I'm glad that gay people are so free with their words," he said, "and they're not hiding. If I were gay, I wouldn't want to have to hide it."

Hiding it certainly is hardly Marky's style but he swears showing it all began as an accident: "It was a funny thing about dropping my pants. I was performing in L.A. and I loosened my top button. The pants were loose anyway and they slipped while I was doing some moves. Rather than stop and pull my pants up, I waited till I finished the move. By then, my pants were around my ankles! The crowd went crazy. Actually, I don't do it in my show any more.

"Although, when I come out for my slow song at the end of the show, I come out with just my boxer shorts and a robe and do this big safe sex thing, just to let people know that if you engage in sexual activity that you are protected and that your partner is as well. There are a lot of people dying over something that is so pleasurable. So we have this big condom thing and this big talk at the end." (It would have to be BIG.) By this time, journalists were saying that Marky had the baddest mouth they'd ever heard. Said one: "He talks constantly, about anything that comes into his head: muscles, food, his rise to fame, his friends, cars, girls, and more girls. And there's not a single sentence that doesn't contain a four-letter word. And when he's not talking, he's making up risque raps."

Some of those raps ended up on Marky's follow-up to his million-selling "Music For the People," "You Gotta Believe," which opened to mixed reviews. One critic said: "Dismiss him as a trouser-dropping bubble gum beefcake if you want but Marky Mark and his brother and producer Donnie Wahlberg make fine pop rap records and here they've toughened things up a bit, more to fine effect." Donnie and Mark teamed for the cut, "Loungin'". *Entertainment Weekly*'s critic found that although Marky "has a body of death and he has sold tons of records, all he wants is respect. 'You Gotta Believe' is filled with bleating pleas to be taken seriously. But Marky is sorely deficient in the two key hip-hop disciplines: He can't rhyme and he can't rap. And when he decides to make statements (as on the acoustic 'American Dream'), he's more dopey than dope."

Details' reviewer agreed: "Calvin Klein underwear model Marky Mark may have undeniable flex appeal, but he is not strong enough to lift the enormous chip off his shoulder. His second LP opens with a radio interview ('Intro: The Crisis') in which poor Mark is dished by critics in the street and ends with Marky's riposte ('The Solution'): 'Yeah, I have somethin' I'd like to say to them... F-F-F-FUCK!' In between, his defense is equally eloquent. On 'Don't Ya Sleep' and the title track, an old-time rap filled with funk guitar, diva whoops and scratching, he makes a case for his relevance 'stomping into the '90s' and begs not to be judged by his color. He makes it difficult, however, with his increasingly vanilla taste." The single, "You Gotta Believe," stalled at No. 49 on the charts and the album dropped dead at No. 67. "Has he lost his musical audience?" Musto asked. "Maybe, but those pecs still sing a tune all their own." "People loved it," said the star, "wow, this kid's running around on TV in his underwear. But now that I got them interested, I want to make a good musical impression." But whatever you do, kid, don't lose your attitude. As *New York Times* noted, "(He) has all the requisites for being a teen-age idol: a handsome face, bulging biceps and a shameless attitude." Other guys have the other two but it's the third that makes Marky "a true icon of the cultural moment."

In the 4th edition of the *Movie Buff Checklist,* Campfire Video's bible that lists all the stars and the films in which they expose the most skin. The latest issue sports a wonderful picture of the moment in Marky's video when Donnie Wahlberg pulls the kid's pants down. That butt is as gorgeous as the rest of him.

In the fall of 1993, Marky appeared in his first movie. He was cast, to quote the publicity copy, as "a high school wise-guy with a reputation! He learns a deadly lesson the hard way" in "The Substitute," a made-for-USA-network movie. The lesson was given by a psycho teacher to her one of her most playful students, Marky. She ends up shooting him dead half way into the picture. But Wahlberg played himself very well (he's had lots of practice being obnoxious in a classroom, of course) and looked heavenly even with all his clothes on.

Late in 1993, Marky was signed to play a recruit in Penny Marshall's production of "Renaissance Man," a comedy starring Danny DeVito. Marky was worried about getting the part because the Madonna set-to occurred just before he was to go to his interview with Marshall. "Penny had already heard from Madonna," Marky says. "She asked me, 'What happened?' I had to defend myself. I told her about the press thing, and she told me, 'Yeah, well, Madonna's real sensitive to that stuff.' But it really hurt me too. As much as I try to go out and promote, 'do your own thing,' I can't believe people would listen to that. You'd think people who know me would know I wasn't a gay basher."

Early on, many gays were troubled by a continuous stream of Marky "outlaw" quotes, such as the ones he supposedly made on a London tabloid show. "They were totally disrespecting me," the stud says now. "The show is known for that. They were going crazy on me. So I was just sitting there in my own world." While he was sitting there, Shabba Ranks was being interviewed separately. When Marky heard Shabba quote the Bible and say that gays should be crucified, Marky said, "Well, wait a second here." And then they wanted Marky to perform with Ranks. Marky didn't want to do it, but pushed him on stage and they did a little rap together before Marky had had enough and said, "Fuck you! Fuck *The Word!* Fuck everybody! I can say whatever the hell I want. Shabba can say whatever he wants. And you can say whatever the hell you want." At that point, Marky walked off and threw the microphone down: "I stole from my mother, stole from my father, stole from my brother, stole from my neighbors. I stole a lot, stealing was hot. I stole from stores, houses, people, stole cars." Perhaps now that he's in the money, he'll return everything? Back up the truck.

Marky often discussed his troubled past, admitting arrests for "shoplifting, drinking in public, assault and battery, fighting, drunken disorder. Stupid stuff," he told George Wayne of *Vanity Fair*, "but no bank robberies." But the stud has made a point of never discussing two incidents that led a judge to throw the stud in the slammer. When he was a kid, he lived with his mother in "a very racially mixed neighborhood," Marky revealed to Shuan Assael of the *Village Voice*, a reporter who was determined to make public the singer's dirty laundry now, that he was internationally famous for his fresh laundry, namely his CK briefs. In 1986, Marky was one of a gang of ten whites who terrorized a class of young black children by throwing rocks at them. Wahlberg, 15 at the time, escaped prosecution by signing a restraining order. But that didn't keep him off the streets.

By 1988, he had dropped out of school and had been arrested twice, for a juvenile larceny offense and for shoplifting. Then he was again caught in a racially-motivated drunken brawl, this time with a Vietnamese named Thanh Lam taking the beating. Court records show that Marky called the man "Vietnam fucking shit" as he hit him with a five-foot-long, three-inch-thick stick. Later that night, when Marky was arrested, he admitted hitting "the gook in the head with a stick." Though charged with three counts of civil rights violations, Marky was allowed to plead guilty to just two counts of contempt for running afoul of his 1986 restraining order. Now Marky says, "We were all out getting drunk, getting high, and the guy had some beer and we wanted to take some of it. But I was the one who was the most drunk and didn't try to run and I caught the bag for a lot of people." But he denies it was racially motivated. "I don't look at it as me having a war with the Vietnamese people. I was also injured in the fight. But the officers weren't taking any explanation. Everybody was just pointing fingers." Marky ended up serving 45 days of a two-year sentence. As a condition of his parole, he was ordered to undergo alcohol treatment. "I'm not gonna blame it on my father not being there, or my older brother being in prison. I'm not gonna blame it on anything but myself. I know it's fucked up that people will prejudge me. Nobody talks about how I was on parole for three years and never did a thing. What's fucked up now is that I've been trying to stay out of trouble and this shit just seems to surround me."

"This shit" includes an incident in December of 1990 when Marky was arrested for attacking a youth with a baseball bat who had criticized his singing in a bar. The youth managed to escape, but Marky smashed all his car windows with the bat.

The arresting officer recalls, "I was afraid he was going to kill someone. I ran up to him and yelled, 'Stop! Police!' and then he turned on me with the bat. Seeing my uniform and the fact I had a gun drawn on him, he realized it was a good idea to drop the bat." No charges were filed. In May of 1992, Marky was suspected of beating a South Boston man and in July he invited two men leaving a gym to "come over here, so my boy can slap you around a bit." In this case, his "boy" was his bodyguard, the big black Derek McCall. McCall was at the center of the episode. Crehan's friend came up to Marky and his bodyguard and said, "Why do you keep bringing these niggers with you?" Marky admitted shoving Crehan's friend but he denied hitting Crehan and breaking his jaw. When the case finally came to trial, Marky was found not guilty.

And then there was the *Advocate* in June 1993 exposing Marky's mentor Calvin Klein in living color, with the stud standing behind him, as he received his award from the AIDS Project Los Angeles. The magazine said that the award to Calvin for a "Lifetime of Achievement" was considered "obscene" by many in the gay community because Calvin has been noted for his uncaring attitude. Said Rodger McFarlane, executive director of Broadway Cares/Equity Fights AIDS: "It makes my skin crawl. Calvin is one of the first people we asked for support and he was bitterly ungenerous, vicious and unresponsive."

AIDS activist and playwright Larry Kramer was equally appalled: "It's totally gross. It just makes me puke. Here we have a man who's done so little to fight AIDS but is being given a major award, solely - I would imagine - because he is David (the billionaire record producer and "bi-sexual") Geffen's close friend. It's like the Jews honoring David Duke!"

APLA events manager Diane Connors said that prior AIDS advocacy has never been a consideration in the selection of an honoree for the fashion event. "This isnot a noble thing, but these events are fund raisers and maybe not everybody is as deserving as somebody else, but if someone more deserving can't afford to do this event for us and can't sell tickets, then they can be deserving all they want. If we're not raising money, then we've missed the boat."

For his part, Calvin donated two hundred grand, which

McFarlane called "pocket change," for the wealthy fashion designer and marketer. There was no comment about how much Marky gave, other than simply exposing his best assets.

And those assets have had an effect on gay men that is astounding. Erstwhile photographer (and lustful fan) Stuart Bailey recounted, for *Better Homos and Gardens*, his "opportunity of a lifetime" to accompany his friend Holly, a teen fan magazine writer, to a Marky Mark concert in California: "Most of the audience was your standard gum-chewing, wide-eyed-fuck-me-now-Marky!!!!-because-I-haven't-had-my-first-period-yet teenage girl, but my eagle eye spotted a few boys in the crowd.

"When Marky slammed onto the stage, the crowd went wild. He performed all of his greatest hits and towards the middle of his set, he crooned 'Sugar Cool Mack Daddy.' I couldn't quite make out the lyrics but I'm sure it was something about spotting a hot 30-year-old male photographer in the audience and falling madly in love with him and how they would spend eternity together living off Marky's earnings.

"So I could record this momentous occasion, a friend had loaned me his camera, complete with a huge zoom lens that would put Jeff Stryker to shame. I conserved film wisely at first, knowing Marky would be near naked on stage before the concert was over. Sure enough, during the last few songs, Marky did his trademark strip tease, removing his jacket, his cap, his shirt, and finally pulling his shorts down to reveal the top half of his underoos. My camera was as overactive as my libido. His pecs! Click! That washboard tummy! Click! He flexes his biceps! Click! He shows his armpit! Click! He grabs his cock! Click! Click! Click!

"Backstage, Holly and I were the only VIP's over 20. Marky sauntered over to us, his stud boy torso covered by a 'Censorship is Unamerican' T-shirt. 'Hi, Holly,' he said, recognizing her from previous interviews for her magazine.

"Holly introduced me. 'Hi Stuart!' Marky said. 'It's nice to meet you!' Marky offered his hand, giving me one of those funky 3-part handshakes. My hand didn't respond, making a repetitive jerking motion on his hand instead. I couldn't speak. I wanted to tell him how zesty he was. I wanted to ask if it was all steroids. I wanted to offer to lick the sweat off his chest. I wanted to be his backstage sex slave for the rest of the tour.

"Suddenly, Holly had an idea that we should have our picture taken together with our bellies exposed. We both peeled our shirts up. Marky sneered for the camera. My tongue fell out. Click! Marky shook my hand again and we exchanged goodbyes. Somehow, this time I felt his touch was warmer, his eyes friendlier now that our belly buttons had been formally introduced.

"The next day, after waiting 60 breathless minutes at the photo developer, I was told my entire roll of film was overexposed. I hadn't set the flash properly. Outside on the sidewalk, I dissolved into a puddle of tears. Ironically, the only thing that was visible on the roll of negatives was a strip revealing our bellies.

"In the '70s, I cut out David Cassidy photos from *16* and *Tiger Beat* magazines, taping them to my bedroom wall. Each night before sleep, I dutifully kissed my Davids goodnight.

"At college, my dorm room was plastered with a mural of Menudo. Now, Marky adorns my West Hollywood refrigerator. As for the future? Let's just say you can be sure I'll be first in line when Macaulay Culkin records his first record album."

In January 1993, Liz Langley reported, Marky showed up at Dwyer High School in West Palm Beach to strut his stuff to help raise money for band uniforms. The director of the band said Marky was "very positive, well-mannered. He did a little bit of that dropping his pants thing but he had three pairs of pants on. He had pants on top of boxers on top of briefs and he didn't drop his pants, they just sort of slid down. He personally made $3,500 that night. " A student said, "He was a nice guy. Not at all like 2 Live Crew. He talked about staying in school, how he's sorry he didn't finish school and he's determined to go back." Marky still is insisting he *will* someday get his G.E.D.

At the end of 1993, while *Rolling Stone* was crying, "Pecs ahoy!" and had reduced Marky to a "lite rapper underpants shill," Woody Harrelson was taking Marky's place on Times Square in CK underwear – but not in many big gay hearts.

"In today's world, Peter Pan is a pervert," noted Fenton Bailey. "On the one hand, the idea of the pervy Peter Pan is a very hot concept. Marky Mark, the essential all-American boy, has been milked to sell underwear. Sure, he's old enough to have sex (the kid even dedicated his book to his dick), but the whole concept stinks of teen spirit. His cherubic face toys with the idea of the underage – Lolita with muscles. But we all know that when he grows up, his ability to sell y-fronts will fall off a cliff."

Well, in 1993, sales didn't actually fall off a cliff (Calvin's doing quite well, thank you), but because of all the tabloid talk, Marky might as well have taken a jump as far as many gays were concerned. *Entertainment Weekly's* Jim Mullen cracked a joke about it: "Gays won't buy Calvin Klein's underwear until he drops Marky Mark; some straights won't buy it until he drops his prices."

As 1993 ended, Marky tried to make amends with his loyal gay fans. In an interview with the *Advocate*, the stud puppy said that he goes to gay clubs with a gay writer who is a friend of his. "Whenever I see him, we always go to a club or something and hang out," Marky revealed. "He said that he thinks that I'm gay and I just won't come out with it. I think it's just because I am comfortable around him and around the situation." And then came out with the shocker, which was not widely reported: The interviewer, Judy Wieder, asked Marky if he had ever had a *relationship* with a man, he said, "Nah." When she asked, "And you don't ever see that happening?" Marky replied, "Uh, not now. But you never know. You *never* know."

And speaking of never knowing, Marky says he and David Geffen are "real cool." "I talk to him all the time. I call him up for business advice. It's very rare that you will find somebody who will not only give you advice but good advice. I met him the first time at Calvin's house. They were like, 'The only reason we want you is because you were doing your own thing, and that's what we want you to do for us. We think it's cool.' So I was like, 'Cool.'" Marky went to Calvin's and Geffen was just hanging out there. They talked, they laughed, they notice Marky's pants were hanging down. They had him try on some stuff and then they talked again. Calvin said he would like to have Herb Ritts take the pictures for the ads. "Well," Marky recalls, "you can get me to do the pictures if Herb is going to take them! 'Cause Herb Ritts is the man!"

In the same interview, Marky revealed his stepfather's brother, who lived with the family for four years, is gay. "He makes the best chocolate-chip cookies ever! He's very much like an uncle. He still spends Christmas with us. He buys us the best Christmas gifts. Fly shirts and sweaters! I'm talking fashion! But I don't feel that I should have to say all this for people to believe me." Marky says he's somewhat of a drifter; he has sneakers "in New Jersey and at my mom's house in Braintree, Mass." which his brother Donnie bought for her.

Advocate readers seemed to be delighted with the interview. One fan from Utah wrote: "I'm tired of the criticism Marky Mark has received. How many of us at 22 didn't say stupid things or could have survived the scrutiny of the media?" Another fan said, "Thank you, *Advocate*, for renewing my faith in (as well as my crush on) Marky Mark." Another said: "Granted Marky did not stand up tall and proud (with Shabba Ranks) and defend gay sexuality, but when we can't even get our own closeted film and TV stars to do it, why should we expect a straight boy to do any better? GLAAD has bigger fish to fry, and maybe it should direct its energies in that direction. Have they ever heard of the pope?"

All was not sweetness and light, however. One reader said, "I cannot believe our community is without interests other than pecs and abs." Another: "You devoted 13 pages and the cover to this fluff!" And yet another: "Bullshit! Marky Mark has played the gay community like a fiddle while laughing all the way to the bank." Our answer to this is, Marky can play with our fiddle any time, as long as we get to play with his!

And speaking of fiddling around, at the end of 1993, *Vanity Fair* named Marky to its Hall of Fame: "Because he has proved Dorothy Parker right, in demonstrating that brevity is indeed the soul of underwear. Because he can grab his crotch for fashion's brief encounters and make us want to cry, 'Down, boy!' Nothing can stop the upward curve of the bulletheaded rapper with the boxer's physique. Marky Mark can tan while the rest of us burn, and we should bless the day M.M. went starky stark." This accolade irritated some readers: "Hall of Fame deserves much better. Marky Mark is a desperately soulless media fabrication who cannot rap to save his pecs and will undoubtedly go the way of Vanilla Ice, Gerardo, and, uh, the dinosaur?"

Dinosaur or not, at the beginning of 1994, Marky was preparing a new album and the teen fanzines were still singing the rapper's praises. "When we think of Marky Mark," *Tutti* was saying, "all we can say is 'WOW!' This dude has gone from a shy, skinny, chain-smoking kid to a massively muscular, outgoing, intelligent, talented rapper/model/actor in just a couple of short years. Way back when big bro Donnie decided it was time to take some of the spotlight and produced his 'Good Vibrations' (*the* record of 1991) and Marky was suddenly in demand."

As far as we're concerned, there'll always be a demand for Marky, or someone like him. As *Esquire* revealed in a poll in early 1994, when women were asked who they would rather date, Marky or Bill Clinton aide George Stephanopoulos, 60% said Marky, 35% opted for George. Yes, for gals or gays, there's just something irresistible about a "massively muscular" stud puppy who just can't stop dropping his pants.

Before and After: Corey Haim in 1987's "Lost Boys" and as seen recently in a publicity photo making a fashion statement

THE SHAME OF COREY HAIM

I became obsessed with the 5'-4", 113 pound, blond, blue-eyed actor named Corey Haim after seeing him in 1986's "Lucas," in which he played a 15-year-old nerd and which has, as one of its many enjoyments, a realistic shower sequence in a high school gym. Then came the stylish vampire comedy "Lost Boys," in which the actor took a bath. I mean, this kid had to be the *cleanest* actor in Hollywood. Little did we know.

By 1989 he was getting rave reviews for his fine thesping. About "Dream a Little Dream," one reviewer raved: "Goofy Corey Haim lends his light and silly charm to provide the few laughs in this film." During the filming of "Lost Boys," Corey became involved with the handsome young actor Brooke McCarter and Brooke gave up his career to become Corey's "personal manager" as well as "best pal." Things were looking up – in more ways than one.

And, by then, Corey had became a darling of the teenybopper set. What the fan magazines were heralding as "Haimster-mania" set in. There was even a calendar featuring the adorable lad in scenes from the horrible horror movie "The Watchers."

But suddenly it seemed Corey was overcome by it all; he started hanging out in Hollywood's infamous fast lane. The reports were discouraging. Like me, New York photographer Larry Clark had become enamored of the star and fretted about his survival.

Said Larry: "But then he came back and got a 900 number. I was curious so I called and he went into this incredible rap about how he was all fucked up on cocaine. He was saying things like 'You just wouldn't believe how everyone in L.A. does cocaine and I was doing so much cocaine I got down to about ninety pounds and my mother put me in rehab.' He must have just got out because he sounded like a reformed drunk: 'I'd rather cut off my arm and throw it out on the expressway than ever do coke again.' He was freaking out. And then I read some articles about it. Now he's probably trying to forget he ever said those things, trying to rehabilitate his image."

During 1990, his sometime-pal Corey Feldman was arrested on drug charges. The story was that when Feldman found out his girl friend was also screwing both Charlie Sheen and Haim, he "tried heroin to forget." Later Feldman said: "Haim turned his back on me all during the drug problems."

In 1991, Corey appeared in his own video, "Me, Myself and I." His publicist was saying the star wanted to clear the air, to counter rumors that had been flying about him: "We did it to let people know what's really happening in my life. I just wanted people not to still have the wrong impression of me after everything that went down. Things are back to normal now." The 45-minute video includes Corey talking about his life, what it was like before he became an actor, scenes of him playing hockey and baseball (and the one we loved, floating on a raft in a swimming pool), driving his new sports car and his thoughts on the perfect date. Corey's sage advice: "Take the hurdles in life that come to you. Everybody has lots of obstacles to overcome. Just go through them, be patient and everything will happen." I sent a friend a copy of this wonderful video and he called me several days later to say that I had shattered his illusion about the tyke. Now he was saying Corey was a "brat."

"Exactly the point," I said, "can't you just imagine the scenario when you got him alone? Can't you just see what would happen if you tied him to the bed?" My friend, possessing an imagination every bit as wild as my own, quickly saw my point.

Tying Corey down, or being tied down by Haim, was not only my wish but that of many a young girl, even during Corey's extended rehab period. So great was Corey's popularity he was voted "Male Movie Star of the Year" by *Teen Beat* readers while still in rehab. When he got out, Corey appeared in *Teen Beat's* first video format magazine, talking about the movies and taking questions from an audience of screaming young girls. He handled it well, although he appeared to be more "out-of-it" than "with-it."

It was reported that he was back in the fast lane again, hanging out with other stud puppies such as Josh Evans, the handsome young son of producer Robert Evans, and Balthazar Getty, at Hollywood's fashionable Sunset Social Club, presumably drinking Perrier.

In 1991, in 20-year-old Corey's "comeback" movie, CineTel Films' "Fast Getaway," he played the 16-year-old son of a bank robber. After testing poorly with preview audiences, the film went directly to video stores, where his gay fans could rent it and enjoy his scenes in tight jeans and drag in the privacy of their own homes.

Then came "Dream Machine," which also went directly to video. *Entertainment Weekly* commented: "Reformed party animal Haim plays a clean-up piano tuner who inherits a Porsche with a corpse in the trunk and is pursued by a killer. If this is meant to be a teen action comedy, just where are the laughs?"

Next Corey was on rollerskates for "Prayer of the Rollerboys," still billed over-the-title and co-starring with Patricia Arquette. This bomb also went directly to video. Now, if it had only been called "Prayer of the Gayboys..."

Early in 1993, Corey made the news again. This time he was shooting at targets with his BB gun in the backyard of the home he and his mother share with his manager, Michael Bass. When Corey threatened Bass, he phoned police and had Corey arrested. The charge was reduced to a misdemeanor.

When he isn't in trouble with his handlers, Corey is making movies at a rapid rate. In "Oh! What A Night!" Corey plays a 17-year-old who falls in lust for an older, much married woman. Their tryst in a hayloft could have been a spectacular episode, but it is filmed in deep blue and Corey appears to have worn his boxer shorts through the whole thing. *Entertainment Weekly* duly noted: "The post-Lucas Haim has aged nicely."

Our patience waiting for Haim to become "an adult" on screen was rewarded with the 1993 release of "Blown Away," first telecast on HBO and then released on video. Here Corey bares all at last; well, practically all: his butt is as wonderful as we assumed all along it had to be.

Corey was also patching things up with Feldman. The two are appearing together in "National Lampoon's Last Resort" which goes direct to video on April 13. This frolic will be followed by two other Lampoon films, "Flying School" and "Stunt School."

Corey also appears in "Just One of the Girls," just out on video. This dopey made-for-TV movie in which he cross-dresses to avoid a high-school bully, only to have the bully fall in love with him. The bully, a handsome young stud, takes Corey, as a girl, home and kisses him passionately on the lips. Aghast, Corey bolts from the car and runs into the house, dashes upstairs and washes his mouth out with Listerine. Of course, then they cut to another scene and we didn't see what Corey did about his erection. *New York* magazine said the movie would be "remembered long after 'Tootsie' is forgotten - but not until then."

Reflecting on Corey's frequent cross-dressing brings to mind this recent, bizarre real-life-imitating-reel-life story: Handsome young Brandon Teena moved into the quiet town of Humboldt, Nebraska, and began dating Lana Tisdel and other girls. "He was my dream guy," said one of the girls. "He knew just how to treat a girl. He brought us flowers and candy. He had the most gorgeous blue eyes and he never pressured us into having sex. We just kissed, that was all."

Well, the "he" turned out to be, in reality, Teena Brandon, and it was soon after she was exposed that John Lotter and Tom Nissen, both of Falls City, Nebraska, murdered her. A week earlier, she accused them of raping her. The young men had read the story about Teena in the local newspaper and when they met her at a party still couldn't believe it. They forced her into the bathroom to prove it. After she was naked, they raped her. Brandon reported the rape but the cops did nothing. The Sheriff said, "You just can't arrest somebody for rape. We had to be sure she was telling the truth. After finding out about her masquerade, we would find anything she said difficult to believe."

To our mind, Chad Lowe was much more fetching – and much easier to believe – as a girl in a similar movie, "Nobody's Perfect," but Corey was at least a bit more convincing here than in "Fast Getaway." And you know what they say, once they've done drag, can a gay character be far behind?

News photo of Billy Idol with Dennis Hopper at the Grammy Awards

Porn Stud Ryan Idol, in publicity photo by D/X Co.

FRESH IDOLS:
RYAN & BILLY IDOL

*"Do not lie down (have sex)
with a man, as (if) with a woman.
It is idol worship."*
- Leviticus 17:22

Billy Idol

"How can I tell you about Billy Idol?" Sandra Bernhard asks. "It's so deep. He was, essentially, the one who saved me when I was in the abyss. I'll never forget the night I tracked him down at the Sunset Marquis. My world was coming apart at the seams. I was binging, I was purging. I felt like all my friends were saying horrible things behind my back. My paranoia was at an all-time high. I was out of control, hysterical, a recovering drama queen.

"The minute I saw him I started to get a grip on myself. Billy laid some Tough Love on me. He took me by the shoulders and dragged me to the mirror.

"'Take a good look at yourself, lady,' he demanded. 'You have it all. Beauty. Success. Admiration. Me. Stop being so self-indulgent. Count your blessings.'

"'He shamed me. But suddenly I was surprised. My world really was spectacular; it just took someone with Billy's vision to snap me back to reality.

"'My God,' he said. 'Life is so precious, so fragile. Ever since I fell off the bike I'm grateful for every moment. I even love my scars, Sandy.'

"What a kindred spirit!

"As if all he'd done for me wasn't enough, I noticed him heating up some pikake-ginger massage oil. Sadly, most people aren't aware of Billy's healing powers. They think he's just another snarling lip. I know better."

The snarling lip is basic to his appeal, plus, Sandra says: "He always looks like he's thinking something erotic. Billy goes a long way on the 'bad boy mama warned you about' image.'"

Idol *is* thinking something erotic – and what thoughts! We always say, when thinking erotic, go *totally* erotic. When Billy was injured on his motorcycle, his mother sent the priest to his room to give him Communion; then she went to England and told the papers that he took Communion. So when Idol had a press conference, the first question was, "Now, about this born-again question..." Idol said, "Look, you've got it all wrong. It wasn't 'born again,' it was 'porn-again.'"

And again and again. Porn star Savannah, for instance, is one with first-hand knowledge of how erotic Idol can be. Gay porn producer/director Chi Chi LaRue said, "Miss Savannah is a really cool chick. We dished and she told me about how fond rocker Billy Idol is of her.

It also seems Mr. Idol loves our biz and *all* the girls in it." And then there's the case of Vaginal Cream Davis, the mistress of illusion. As *Monk* puts it, Vag has taken the fine art of drag, the gay man's masquerade, to a boisterous conclusion: "I graduated from Columbia with a degree in Slavic Languages and I majored in Macedonian. I was an interpreter for the UN for a year and half. And I used to be a prostitute. I still am. I just charge more money now." She lists among her clients, Billy Idol, as well as Eddie Murphy, Arsenio Hall, and Donald Trump. He (she) was even exposed in the *National Enquirer* as having done the nasty with John F. Kennedy Jr. She says that black people have a name for people like her: "In the life, we black homos like to say we are *in the life*." Billy Idol, we would take it, likes life in any form he can get it. Consider what computer analyst Neil Strauss (writing in *Village Voice*) recalls: "I remember the first time I saw Billy Idol's floppy disk. It was a warm spring evening in 1984, and Idol had brought his 'Rebel Yell' tour to Chicago's Aragon Ballroom. After the concert, the tow-headed singer stepped onto his dressing-room balcony to appease a handful of fans chanting 'more, more, more' outside. Idol's lip curled upwards as he lowered his leather suspenders to his knees and started dancing with himself, waving his long, flaccid, and very pale member at the crowd below.

"The next time I saw Idol's floppy disk was a month ago on

MTV. The former William Broad was sitting serenely in front of his computer and responding to electronic mail. Jacking to cyberspace via the two-finger hunt-and-peck method. Idol typed his message slowly: 'Smile, Your (*sic*) on MTV.' It wasn't just Idol's bad grammar, but his cumbersome relationship to the keyboard that indicated he hadn't been taking any smart drugs lately."

Smart or not so smart, at least Idol knows when to leave. As part of the Rock in Rio II Concert (with other stars such as George Michael and Prince), he commented, "The audience stood each day from two in the afternoon until three in the morning. Thank God I left the hotel when New Kids on the Block arrived and all the girls started screaming, 'Donnie!' It was time to get out."

Billy admitted to *Details* interviewer David A. Keeps that he was into Ecstasy. In fact, he said, "I've taken everything, heh-heh-heh...There's an element to life where you feel they've got you by the balls, and how the fuck do you get away? I've tried everything: music, sex, drugs, you name it. In the '80s I got ruled by things like drugs. And it really wasn't much in the end. You just turn into this horror of a person. You bore yourself to death. But when you're young you've got this boundless energy, so you can torture yourself."

Now he's into fighting, fighting on all fronts and not just wearing a ribbon, to explain why he didn't wear one to the Grammy ceremonies. "Rebellion," he says, "is never unacceptable."

Critics condemned his latest album "Cyberpunk" and fans didn't respond. It peaked at No. 48 on the Billboard chart. *People* magazine picked it as one of its Worst of Song for 1993 and said: "Glam-punker goes out on a limb then saws it off. The usually antic rocker takes a sobering trip into the high-tech future, which he discovers to be soulless and, apparently, hookless." Strauss said that Idol must have thought it was easy to metamorphosize from glam-punk to *cyber*punk and perpetuate his image into the '90s. "But *cyber* is more than a prefix. Few cyber-punks were ever glam-punks; this is a domain of the mind, not the haircut. Idol's mistaking progress for style when he calls computers 'the new cool tool' and lets his record company place pandering ads in Mondo 2000 that read: 'Jack into Billy Idol's 'Cyberpunk' where the digital datastorms of steel and silicon fuse with the wild, beating pulse of rock 'n' roll.' There's nothing more offensive than being patronized, and that's why the loudest screams following the release of 'Cyberpunk' were heard in cyberspace, specifically on the 'alt.cyberpunk' news group in the Usenet, where a heated debate over Idol's computer skills and financial motives took an odd twist when Idol himself got on line."

Strauss says that the response to computer kids was downbeat. They scoffed that Cyberpunk was "'a desperate attempt to salvage a career headed for the gutter' and that he was "bastardizing (the) movement...for record sales. He makes lots of money producing meaningless noise. We have to bash him. It's the great American pastime."

Idol defended himself: "I've been cruising all through alt.cyberpunk and feel compelled to respond." Billy said he never exactly called himself a *cyberpunk*. "You're (sic) elitism is total bullshit. Anyone with a modem and a computer can get into cyberspace. That's why I got in here in the first place, to share ideas instead of shutting each other out. I ain't no rock star. I am an eager student...Basically, fuck all of you who question my motives."

Fucking, it would seem, is what Billy does best. After all, he says, it keeps him current. At the Billboard Music Awards ceremonies, Billy was the only presenter to swear on the air, saying he keeps his music, if not his sexual attitudes, up-to-date by "fucking a lot of young chicks." Yet, it's a vice. "It gets me in all sorts of trouble. Whatever I do, I always seem to get into some sort of mess. Song leads to women, that's how you make the wine. Then *they* start to whine." Hey, we know the remedy.

Ryan Idol

Billy Idol once said, "I figured I can be an idol just by calling myself one." Ryan Idol, whose real name is Marc Anthony Donais, followed the same logic and it seems to have worked. After all, if we were to idolize anyone, it would have to be the porn industry's own Ryan Idol. This would be phallic worship taken to the ultimate extreme because, unlike Jeff Stryker, Ryan's a funny, friendly guy whose heart (and usually his hard-on) is in the right place. "Sex is a real important thing to me," he says. "I like to do it really well, like I try to do everything else. I'm glad I've been able to make sex a big part of my life. I like the idea that there are men all over the world who think of me when they're being sexual. I get off on it. I'm proud of it, but I know it's not just my doing."

No, God had a lot to do with it, but Ryan had to be willing to sacrifice, to work, and to stretch. And stretch he did, with each new video until, finally, in late 1993, he sucked Tom Katt's dick on video, in "Idol Thoughts." Now he says it's his favorite movie, unlike the next one.

The first time I saw Ryan was in 1992, and on our way to The Party of the Year in Tampa, Ryan held centerstage. Every inch the superstar he was groomed to become, he kidded Kris Lord (with whom he later admitted he had had a fling) that he'd let him fuck him in the ass for a quarter of a million dollars. Whether that offer was open to someone with less endowment than Lord we were not certain, but with Ryan, in true trademeat fashion, you feel anything is possible. In fact, he asked the chauffeur, "You a doctor? You look like a doctor."

"No, but thank you," the chauffeur beamed, checking out the handsome Ryan in the rearview mirror.

Idol smiled. "Well, you can inspect my ass anytime."

Savoring that prospect, the driver almost ran a stoplight.

Forever the tease, Idol said, "I like girls and I like guys. I like any place I can put my dick." Talk about trade!

Ryan was a star with his first video, "Idol Eyes," and shrewd management has created a gay icon who seldom fails to impress. On stage, magnificently costumed, he's got an act that provides many highlights, not the least of which is his faux humping of a member of the audience who has been seated in a chair on stage. This monkey business is forever preserved on his video "A Very Personal View," featuring the entire act as performed at Studio One in L.A.

On the second night of the Party of the Year, things got off to a bad start for Ryan when, as the stars were climbing out of the car, one fan mistook Lex for him. Ryan found this inconceivable considering that at 6'-1" he towered over the others, especially Lex. Then Ryan had to abort his first performance when he became dizzy, but he quickly recovered and was soon out signing autographs promoting his latest video effort, the appropriately titled, "Trade Off." This video was one of the biggest turn-offs in the history of gay video. Customers who rented this one came back into the store shaking their heads, slamming the video down and asking, "Can I trade this off?" Some renters demanded refunds. Some swear Jesse Helms was behind the production of the video! Some complain the characters are either debased or ashamed of what they are. If this had come from any other producer and starring any other performers than Idol and cute newcomer Axel Garrett it could easily be dismissed, but this was one big disappointment.

Early on, Dave Kinnick called Ryan a "problematic porn star" who was robbed of his best feature, talking dirty, in "Trade Off," since he never opens his mouth. As it is, he's playing himself: "...a confused young straight man interested in experimentation, but only if it is to be with like-minded, big-dicked muddleheads. We lose interest in this `to be or not to be' queer analysis."

But by design or not, Idol has managed to keep our interest because it seems every video he appears in has created controversy. One fan wrote that he fast-forwarded through Idol's "Score 10" except for the final scene. Says the fan: "He's one of the best straight, gay for-pay guys. He has a sense of mischief and fun. The funniest thing about the scene was the incredible lengths the cameramen went to verify Idol didn't need a stunt dick to do his penetrating for him." The reason for this care, obviously, was the brouhaha caused by rumors that porn veteran David Ashfield had stunt-dicked Idol in his first gay porn feature, "Idol Eyes," directed by Matt Sterling, wherein Ryan was asked to fuck Stefano. But Ryan insists that he didn't have any trouble with Joey. "I get off if the other person is really into me, really gaga. That's the way Joey was. He's a great kid, and I liked him a lot because he really dug me. We did things when the cameras weren't on; I wish we could have taped them." (Boy, so do we!) Ryan laments the outcome, or lack of same: "It was my first. I was petrified. I'll get better each time."

And he did. For "Score 10," Matt Sterling's friend and co-worker John Travis said that he didn't like to "break the illusion" by showing the mechanics of applying a rubber," but that they were very concerned about taking every precaution. The latex decisions on the video were left up to the performers. "In the scenes between Ryan and Dcota and between Mike Henson and Dolph Knight, it was their choice not to use rubbers. But we absolutely insist on spermicide."

In his review of "Score 10," Kinnick was now saying: "Idol locks in his screen persona as gay video's favorite beautiful, arrogant and superficial ass wipe." Kinnick objects to these hostile, straight-trade attitudes. "Idol is not the cause of this malaise, but merely a symptom of the affliction. "At the end of the video, we leave Idol smirking into the camera lens and telling us (and co-star Dcota) that he had 'a good time.' It is the very picture of a man absolutely dedicated to his own desperate specialness."

As one might expect, the video that shows Ryan off best is "Ryan Idol: A Very Personal View," produced by his onetime agent, Stuart Rosenberg (widely known as the physique photographer Troy Saxon). Although violating the first rule of stardom by introducing us to the man behind the image before creating one, this ego trip is worth the journey for the stud's playfulness during a photo shoot sequence. There are several endearing moments, including early on as Ryan sets the tone by saying he likes to hold off until he can't stand it any more...and that's how you feel waiting for something to happen. Eventually, it does, first at Studio One in L.A. where he shows off for the crowd in a loose black g string that leaves little to the imagination and then, totally naked, he shakes his pretty appendage and strokes it to the delight of the crowd. At one point, he gets a guy to sit in a chair on stage and proceeds to climb over him, shoving his ass in the guy's face.

"I love the power of performing," Ryan tells guest star Steve Hammond, another of Stuart's proteges, before retiring to the mirrored bedroom to talk to the camera as he jacks off. His dialogue is inspired: "You want some hard cock?" "Just picture it any way you want it." "Goddam that feels good." "I like someone who can bring me to the point and then stop, then bring it back again and again. I know you know what I'm talking about." "You wanna see this big cock come?" "Hey, you want me to come now?" After he shoots he says, "Such a pretty mess, eh?" "Ah, that was so incredible. Hmmm." Got that right,

Ryan.

Dish-diva Michael Musto recalls the time Ryan played in Manhattan: "Hundreds fell silent at the Mens' Room when porn star Ryan Idol - who looked as if he was covered in mayo or something-begging us to ask him personal questions as he ground his pelvis into the night. 'Andy Warhol said everyone will be in the spotlight for 15 minutes,' he told us, tauntingly. 'This is your chance.' You mean my big break was going to be in a dank, smoky nightclub interrogating a porn star about his oral/anal preferences? I'd hoped for something just a tad more glamorous, like sucking eyeballs out of fish heads on public access TV."

Early on, when asked if he was straight, gay or in-between, the stud replied, "None of the above. I really don't label myself. I feel I could fit in anywhere- no pun intended. There are people who would like me to be straight and people who would like me to be gay. If I say one or the other it ruins their fantasies."

Apparently one of Ryan's fantasies is to get fucked on screen. It's the event many have longed for ever since he gorged on Tom Katt's meat in "Idol Thoughts." With the release of this video, Kinnick's opinion of Ryan had mellowed: "The box calls it 'man-reciprocation.' You call it dick sucking. I call it money well spent. For this is something of a minor landmark in gay video - a straight-trade superstar coaxed into performing the unthinkable act of fellation for financial gain. How sordid. But before you think I'm gonna rip the video to shreds, you'd better adjust yourself in your chair. Ryan Idol gives the best performance of his career to date. He still manages to make faces during sex like a blowzy flatbacker finishing off her 30th trick of the day. But his dick, and yes, his throat, are in top form.

"Whether on the receiving end of winsome Chuck Hunter's deep-probing tongue or swinging on the tip of adorable Tom Katt's own ample appendage, Ryan appears to almost be having a good time, which is a lot more than anyone could say about La Stryker's own penis-sucking experiment on Alex Stone in his overblown 'Powerfull II' back in 1989. There's this fantastic moment when Ryan has swallowed Tom down to the base and a tear wells up in his eye and rolls down his face. He doesn't flinch. Now *that's a* real man!"

Luckily, "Idol Thoughts" was released prior to "Payne in the Ass" so that Ryan's co-star Katt had a chance to overcome negative reviews. We mean, if Ryan can get off the way he does sucking Tom's cock, how can there be *anything* wrong with this kid? Aaron Travis said, "The big publicity push for this video – brazenly announcing 'Ryan Sucks Cock!' – has got to be as tacky as any dress in Chi Chi LaRue's wardrobe. While most gay viewers will respond, 'So what?' (it's not like Idol's accomplished something his fans haven't), treating the star's big 'breakthrough' as a news flash apparently satisfies the split personality of gay Hollywood: A major gay porn star performs gay sex – this is news?

"Let's praise director Taylor Hudson (LaRue) for once again assembling a hot cast and capturing them at their best. The opening scene of Idol talking sexy and receiving oral worship from Chuck Hunter flash-starts the video, which comes to a boil with the next scene – Jon Vincent in peak physical form, chiseled and pumped, playing foul-mouthed daddy to Mitch Taylor. . . Idol gives up his oral virginity to Tom Katt, a doe-eyed hunk who finally gets the star grooming he deserves in this video. Ryan's mouth is stretched to such limits that a tear rolls down his face. It's classic! The build-up in this scene and the coy acting are overdone to the point of self-parody, but Idol's kinky cock-spanking fetish seems to come from the heart."

John Rowberry said, "It's not the cocksucking, it's the kiss that says everything in this closing episode. Ryan opens his mouth in anticipation for the first kiss, a sweet, exploring kind of kiss that makes heat radiate from the groin. The second kiss, a little later, after Tom has been sucking Ryan's cock, is even more telling. Ryan grabs Tom's hair and pulls him up for a passionate, desperate kiss, one where the tongues go so deep and the lips are covered with saliva. Tom has a nice cock and Ryan deep throats it with abandon, but unfortunately, Tom is a real bottom and real bottoms have a tough time looking convincing on top. Or maybe its too much attitude – regardless, he never sports a boner as stiff as Ryan's (Can you imagine having Ryan suck your cock? It gave me an instant throbber.) Unlike Stryker, Ryan doesn't make it look like a work for hire. His oral manipulations are thorough and very generous – it clearly looks like he wants to make Tom happy. (Nothing is going to make Tom happy short of Ryan's dick up his ass, which he finally gets.) I have to admit Ryan looks wonderful while he's sucking Tom's dick. The camera angles deliver the goods, often staying in close, but offering different perspectives of the much-touted oral workout. Ryan gives Tom a good fucking and then both deliver copious loads on each others' chests."

Phil Garrett said, "(Ryan's) thinking of doing something he's never done with a guy before. He's thinking about going down on Tom's juicy dick! And he does, and the rest is history. Although this is billed as Ryan's first time munching manmeat, he really knows how to work a guy's tool." Our reaction was, Ryan's been fooling us all along!

By being the one upon whom Ryan gave pleasure for the first time on screen, Tom became incredibly hot, travelling with Idol for personal appearances. When the two appeared in Tampa, Tom arrived early and we had a chance to chat. We found him a personable, likable performer, but then we had the same reaction the year before to Kris Lord, who has since gone the way of many high-flying porn studs: to oblivion.

At the end of 1993, it was rumored Idol was preparing to be fucked on screen. He had already picked out the hunk to do the deed, one who resembles Tom but has a bigger, thicker tool: Marco Rossi, seen as the bartender get a blowjob under the counter by a big blond jock in Falcon's "Mirage." Rossi is also magnificently displayed in John Travis' "Night Heat," as the hustler who goes into the wrong room at a motel. (But it mattered not because when the man saw the nude Rossi massaging his dick on the double bed – well, what would *you* have done?)

Falcon's ad whiz described the Rossi equipment thusly: "He's a dark bodybuilder with a long fat dick that's just made to be serviced...the blond under the bar gives him head - slowly working the giant dick from its fat mushroom head down to the cum laden ballsac." We shall see just how cum-laden it is if he gets to provide stud services to Ryan Idol!

Ryan, who stands 6'1" and weighs in at 190 lbs., spends a lot of time at the gym but he doesn't consider himself a bodybuilder. "I'm a body sculptor," he says. "I build everything that should be built to achieve the perfect physique."

Kinnick noted that Ryan has a pair of cherries tattooed above his dick, just inside his bikini tan line. "I wonder," he asked, "where the lemons and oranges are, let alone the jackpot?" The jackpot, it would seem, is Ryan's cock, a perfect cock that's 8 1/2" at full strength. Indeed, Ryan's groin, one reviewer commented, "looks as if it were cut by a master gemsmith."

The Idol groin (and mystique) certainly wows the ladies. Reviewer Pearl Chavez, reviewing the stud's "Letters from the Heart," a straight flick, says: "Idol gets his tired marriage sparked by his exotic teddy-clad wife Leilani. Although he struggles with rigidity at times, Idol is so gorgeous that this is easily forgotten." Well, maybe by her. But gay fans said Ryan's limpness in that movie proved he was "more gay than straight."

But everyone does agree Ryan is *gorgeous*. In 1993, when *Advocate Men* ran D/X Co.'s superb photo spread of Ryan, a fan (from Alabama) said that Ryan's name alone excited him so much his dick started oozing. "He could fuck me all day and all night long. I would give anything to fuck him and then make love to him. I have a video of him and I watch it so much, I'll soon have to get another copy. Most models are 'fucking gorgeous.' Ryan is 'super fucking gorgeous.'"

More to the point of porn, getting off, a fan in Utah called it "too much of a dream come true. I guess you guys want me to whack my cock till it falls off." What a way to go!

Late in 1993, Ryan told Robert W. Richards of *Manshots* that he's gone far beyond what he was supposed to achieve in life: "I come from a very poor, very unmotivated family – no one did anything with their lives." He grew up in Worcester, Mass., and was not putting his family down, just giving the facts. He was the only black sheep. Ryan said he was not a nerd, but he was very skinny and had a big attitude because of the person he was inside. "Not because of the body, because I didn't have it then. I got picked on a lot. I think that everything I've become is due to all the things I wasn't." Richards said that it was "very easy to just be trash in this business" and complimented Idol: "You've brought a whole different level of self-respect to it – you've presented yourself differently."

Idol thanked Richards for the compliment and revealed what

he considered the biggest compliment ever paid him. It occurred when a gay man came up to him in a bar and said that since the star had come into the business and become part of the family, he was proud to be gay.

"All of my dreams have already been surpassed," says Ryan, "other than being a *real* movie star. I've gotten great gratification out of being an adult film star, and maybe being a *real* movie star will be the only pinnacle I won't reach, but I will say, if I died tomorrow I would die with a smile on my face."

And, having known Ryan, so would we.

Adam Hart in one of our favorite poses,
from our private collection

Brian Heath, one of Adam Hart's strippers as well as a porn performer in his own right. (Photo: James Meckley)

Superstar Stripper Bryan, who also appears in the "Malerotic" dance video (Photo: James Meckley)

ADAM HART &
HIS HART-THROBBERS

We watch them on the stage and in the audience, the men pawing, kissing, fondling them. We watch them after the show, making the dates, passing out business cards, writing down beeper numbers. We may watch them week after week and never touch them, yet we are fascinated by them.

These are the strippers - male or female - gay or straight or bi - and, often, they are the objects of our most intense desire, because, unlike the sex bombs in the videos and the hunky things in magazine layouts spreading it wide, the flesh of these objects can be touched, and the price is really small to the reward we get. But what is the reward for the object of our desire? What makes them do this, night after night, week after week, some of them for years? We wanted to know.

Webster has two definitions for *exhibitionism*: "the act of behaving so as to attract attention to oneself;" the other is, "a perversion marked by a tendency to indecent exposure." So, we suppose, it is only a matter of degrees.

To help us understand the strippers, and ourselves, a bit better we decided to go to the source. As luck would have it, one of the hottest acts in this particular business just happens to be located in our backyard of Tampa Bay: Men of Structure, whose motto is "Dancers Who Will Rock Your Foundation." And the young man who runs this amazing enterprise is none other than one of our favorite rising young gay video stars, Adam Hart, known hereabouts for some time as the stripper Johnny Angel (not his real name either, but his real name is something intimate, at this point just about the only secret he retains). Johnny's so successful at what he's doing he needs two troupes of hunks (fourteen and growing) to satisfy the demand. This means that when you want to visit with the whole crew, you need a pretty big place to do it; plus the place has to be convenient for the guys and have, well, I guess you could say just the right atmosphere. My friend, and *Encounter* magazine's publisher, Art Mergen, said he knew just the place and called his longtime pals, Jeff Shama and Bill Sparks. When they said they wouldn't mind a bit if this bevy of beauties wanted to hang out around their pool for a few hours, all systems were go. So, on a sunny but cool and breezy day in January, Art and I met the dancers at a midtown bar where they were practicing their routines, then led them in a six-car caravan to the party house. We made several stops just to make sure everyone was staying with us on the expressways. When we reached our destination, one of the young men said to me, "Boy, you have a lead foot! We had trouble keeping up with you."

This got Art laughing. "Yeah, I've never seen John drive so damn fast. Usually he barely makes the speed limit!"

I shook my head in dismay. "But I never had Adam Hart and thirteen other studs following me before either! I guess I was just nervous."

But the dancers weren't a bit nervous as they stripped for the photographer and I managed to get a few questions in. My first question was always, Why do you do it? "I do it for the money," was the answer most often given, as one might expect. But aren't there easier ways of making a living? "Well, no not exactly. This sure beats working at McDonald's. Now that's hard work," said one. Another said, with delightful candor, "I'm just a lazy bitch."

And there were some in this troupe who were actually working their way through college. With their brains, brawn and beauty, more than a few of these would be guys you wouldn't mind taking home to meet Mom.

After all, Mom, like us, enjoys being entertained and these guys are entertainers to the core. Indeed, it seems the most famous stripper of 'em all, Gypsy Rose Lee, was right on target when she sang, "Let me entertain you . . . and we'll have a real good time."

But, of course, some are more ambitious than others when it comes to the "sideline" businesses associated with stripping. There were a few in this troupe who were entrepreneurs, not only making their fee plus tips but also doing "private" dancing on the side. Since we admire those dedicated to commerce, these are the hunks who interested us the most. But what would they do? Would they do anything? Well, almost. The prime, and we do mean prime, example of this is Kevin Storm, a longtime pal of Johnny's. As his name might suggest, this kid dances up a storm. He also appears in magazine layouts and gay sexvids under the name of Brian Heath for John Travis and others. ("Night Heat" is his latest.) Johnny introduced Kevin to Travis, which is only fair because Kevin taught Johnny how to dance. When asked why he stripped, Kevin (21, 5'-9", 155 pounds) said, "I love to dance." And he loves it so much he's willing to give private "shows," which may well include a nice massage if that's what the customer wants. Is he gay, straight, or bi? Kevin says, "I'm just myself."

Another dazzler on the dance floor is Christian (21, 5'-10", 180 pounds), who has been dancing for two years, first with Bare Assets and then with Florida Fantasy Night. He's one of the boys who's working his way through college, pre-med. Hailing from Chicago, he's been in Florida for four years but his goal would be to live in L.A., and if his medical studies don't work out, he'd love to be an actor in television. He says what he likes most about dancing is the "freedom of expression." He likes to dance in bars that play alternative music; one of his favorite tunes to strip by is "Bad English." Sexually, Christian says he's "open-minded" and, although he's never tried private dancing, he's open to it. He likes to entertain either a straight crowd or a gay crowd, it doesn't matter, and one of his favorite venues is Tracks in Tampa, where one night he suffered his most embarrassing moment when two of the guys pulled his T-back down just as they were getting off the stage after the final number. "The crowd really got off on it," Christian said with a sly smile.

"I'm the real man of the group," says Tucker (29, 6 foot, 175 pounds). And, as one might expect, he's not only the oldest, he's also the most experienced. Tucker's been dancing professionally for six years and has toured the world for the Chippendales agency and others in seven different tours. Germany was a highlight, where the crowds averaged 2,500. He's been on talk shows in the U.S. and on four shows in Brazil. The reason he does it? "To make money and have fun. These are people who need to be entertained." It doesn't matter if they're gay or straight. Dancing with the Hollandales got him started on the gay circuit and, through Johnny, he ended up posing for *Blueboy* and *Inches* magazines. He says he's into "personal investments: I've gotten past the point where a quick burn is going to get you ahead." And when he says, "I could sell anything," you believe him.

Tim (25, 5'-9", 170 pounds) is another older member of Johnny's troupe, and had only been dancing with the group for two days when we talked to him, having just come from an eight-month engagement with L.A. Hardbodies in New Orleans, playing straight clubs. The Baltimore native is another one who is "working his way through college," planning on becoming an interpreter for the deaf, which might come in handy because one gets the impression that with him around, you'd be speechless most of the time.

Blond, blue-eyed Shawn (20, 5'-11 1/2", 138 pounds) is eager to go back to college to continue his study of psychology. He had never considered dancing until one night he accompanied his friend Alex, who is also a dancer with the group, to a gay bar. The owner of the establishment came up to him and said, "I want you to dance tonight." "Who me?" "You."

"Well, I was really gettin' in to it," he says now. "Now I'm meeting people from everywhere." That is probably the greatest understatement so far this year.

Shawn's roommate Alex (21, 6'-6", 180 pounds) has been everywhere, or so it seems. He was born in Puerto Rico and his family travelled all over the U.S. before they settled in Florida in 1978. He too likes meeting people and will do private dancing. "I just want to make money," he says. And he's "opened-minded."

Also seemingly open for anything is Troy (22, 5'-9", 200 pounds), a beefy blond who considers himself bisexual and is also working his way through school (law school, no less). When we talked with him he had been dancing only three months. Another neophyte is blond, blue-eyed Hunter (22, 6', 175 pounds), who was a car salesman in Clearwater but got into dancing because "the money was better."

Mark Anthony (23, 5'-4", 180 pounds) is another of the musclebound hunks that every troupe such as this needs at least one of. He says he's been lifting weights since the ninth grade and now he has to do it every day: "I feel sick if I don't work out." His goal is to own his own gym some day, perhaps in Texas. He says he's "basically straight."

Another "basically straight" dancer with the Men of Structure originally came to Florida to "basically hang out." (These guys, you realize, always get down to the basics in more ways than one.) Cody (24, 5'-11", 176 pounds) had been laid off from his job in the archeological field in Canada and was getting a nice separation pay so he decided to spend the winter in Florida. Making the trip on his motorcycle he arrived in sunny Tampa without incident, but then he met Johnny, and now he's dancing the nights away. He says he's "loving every minute" of the attention he's getting – and getting paid for it besides.

We must admit whenever we are asked to "review" a bevy of beauty such as this, our personal tastes keep interfering with our conscientious reporting. All the while we were talking with the other guys, there was much activity: picture-taking, chowing down (the hosts ran out of sandwiches and snacks and had to send out for pizzas) and much drinking - but only sodas. From where we were seated, it was possible to survey everything, including the pool, and there was one long-haired youngster we just couldn't keep our eyes off of: Bryan (22, 5'-11", 175 pounds). Now this is a piece of work, we kept thinking as he kept coming in and out of the room in various degrees of undress, teasing the others with wisecracks or snapping them with a towel.

Such a tease, this one. And quick on the draw. Sensualist to the core, Bryan senses things and finally asked when he was going to be interviewed. When told, "Later," he smiled mischievously and said, "Okay, I'll wait my turn." Last, we thought, the end of the line.

Yes, we made the dishwater blond with the blue-green eyes, the deep, sexy voice, and the toothy smile, the last on the list for good reason: it was obvious that Bryan, as he told us eventually, "enjoys being sensual and sexy and enjoys pleasing other people." He's been in Florida since April and has danced for gay and straight audiences in Canada, New York and Pennsylvania when he had his own dance group, The Lover Boys, in upstate New York. He even caught the eye of *Playgirl* magazine and has done a dancing video for them. Very business-minded, he does private dancing, and he doesn't limit himself, saying "You never know what a boy might do."

His wildest night of "private dancing" was at a Valentine's Day soiree thrown by the son of a Congressman. "I was wrapped in Saran and told to lie down on this big table and then they laid the food out on me. I was the all-you-can-eat buffet." Although he didn't say who ended up with the tubesteak that night, the Clearwater resident did say he was "born straight, but I'm open-minded, in my own way."

Yes, stripping may not be the most important philosophical issue of our time, and indeed it may be less politically correct than ever, but sooner or later, every one of us must face the temptation of a beauty with undulating hips standing before us, begging, in his own way, for at least a tip. So remember, when this happens, c'mon, give, and give large because, as we've seen, the chances are good the boy is just putting himself through college – and you are a firm believer in higher education, aren't you?

. . .

The last time I saw Adam Hart he was sprawled out in a double bed with a white sheet barely hiding his private parts and the photographer was snapping away and Art, the publisher of *Encounter* magazine, was shaking his head in dismay and begging, "A little less pubic hair, please."

Decorum in a "family" magazine Art's should be maintained at all times, of course. But then I said, "Hey, these are for *me*. We've already taken yours."

With that, Adam Hart smiled and promptly rolled over, displaying what may arguably be the most beautiful butt in all of adult entertainment, and, of course, it belongs to a star who is always a top. My heart was beating so fast, I had to leave the room – but only temporarily.

I simply *had* to ask Adam if he would ever consider getting that beautiful butt plowed on screen. "One never knows," he said, with a twinkle in his eye. And I'm not the only one who wants to know about these things. "Where, where, where did you ever find Adam Hart?" a fan from Las Vegas asked *Advocate Men*. "I have never seen a more beautiful man in my life. That shot of his fine, smooth, muscular ass . . . oh, you can't imagine the orgasmic spasms my body went through the dozen or so times I got off to that one. And that was before I even turned the page to see the rest of the photos of him. It's not hard for me to imagine holding that warm, glowing skin next to me. But I'll be turning back to that shot of his ass for a long time to come and come and come."

Well, sir, *Advocate Men* didn't find him, John Travis did, after a Tampa bar owner sent a letter to the famous porn director in Hollywood. And Adam continued to get limited exposure during 1993. The idea was to make each Hart appearance an event – and that they were.

With one more film to go on his contract with Travis, Adam says the next "event" may be the popping of his cherry, at least on celluloid. We mean, this guy is ready.

As we learned, Adam's ready to do almost anything - if he doesn't have to fly, of course. Yes, the stud just loves the idea of "flying," but not on airplanes. So if you want to see him, if he can make it in his Jeep Wrangler, that's great, or, if you want to send your chauffeur to fetch him, that's even better!

What keeps Adam busy between those very occasional appearances on video is his dance group, the Men of Structure ("Dancers Who Will Rock Your Foundation"), which he has managed for over two years using the name Johnny Angel, not his real name either but, hey, that's about the only secret he retains. Born in Iowa ("I really am a farm boy," he says), Adam came to Florida three years ago with his parents.

Watching Adam work during the time we had with him and his boys to interview them and snap their portraits, it became increasingly evident this is a young man determined to go places. In fact, his venture into sexvids has become an educational experience and he's now talking seriously about directing, a la the successful star-turned-directors Gino Colbert, Angela Rivera, and Sam Abdul. "I find the adult entertainment industry very interesting," Hart says. "I'm a very organized person. I think I could do it."

"How does one create a superstar?" porn critic Ted Underwood asked. "In 'Take Down,' director Travis introduced Adam, a strikingly handsome dishwater blond with an admirable physique, impressive equipment, and a pleasant naturalness before the camera – clearly a young man with the potential to become a superstar of all-male films. In 'Take Down, Hart's sexual performance was tantalizingly limited. Although not an emotionless statue, he did function largely as trade, fucking his partners and allowing them to get him off. The only reciprocal action he performed was some rather heated kissing. Overall his demeanor suggested a youth in transition, in the process of discovering his true sexual identity. As such, he attracted not only those viewers who are drawn to 'straight-but-curious' types but viewers who are fascinated by watching someone 'come out' on film."

Film mogul ("Honorable Discharge") Jerry Douglas said, "Hart, an open-faced dishwater blond with a wonderfully expressive face that suggests depths yet to be plumbed, a rippling physique that seems more natural than gym-built, a bubblebutt that could have been the prototype for Michelangelo's David, and an impressively plum-headed dick that invariably shoots a single, stunning geyser of jism, is a very special find. Although he functions mostly as trade through the film, he does caress, jack off his partners, and kiss them – and one has the sense that his limitations are rapidly evaporating. This amazingly honest performance suggests again and again that Hart will deliver in subsequent films many things he only teasingly promises in this one."

In "Hart Throb," Adam's second effort, he stays the way he was in "Take Down," but he's no longer a college student. Now, film imitating life, he's a stripper, with everybody having sex all around him, and his roommate made for him. The opening scene shows the roommate, Claude Jordan (a Kristen Bjorn discovery from "Call of the Wild" who also appears in Travis' "Some Body Is Watching"), jacking off to images of Hart taking it off on stage. In the next scene, Hart stumbles into the dressing room while Phil Bradley and Yan Moreau (who Dave Kinnick says is "almost too coiffed to live but is lovely nevertheless) are fucking, with Bradley using two condoms. (This is truly a safe sex video - we have Brawn giving us a little lecture just moments before.) Turned on, but without a clue as to why, Hart allows himself to be picked up by Michael Brawn and, naturally, Brawn does all the work. Returning home, Hart hears noises coming from his roommate's bedroom and he becomes jealous, only to discover that the two occupying the room are Bo Summers and Ty Russell. This revelation culminates in Hart finally agreeing to let Jordan have his way with him. Underwood thought this scene impersonal and leaves the viewer hanging waiting for Hart to really get into it. It was as Kinnick said, "Adam Hart is making a career out of being confused. But there is no denying that Hart does a good job of convincing us that he needs convincing."

Underwood was hoping that director Travis "makes certain his protege's next screen appearance moves him off this plateau and a step closer to the superstardom he can achieve, should he so choose." Well, Travis did, by casting hunk Scott Russell to turn Adam on to the point of desperately wanting to reciprocate – to a degree. The occasion is "The Voyeur," an otherwise nondescript video wherein Adam plays The Exhibitionist, and does he ever! In his first scene with Bruce Spalding, there's some nipple biting and licking and a good deal of the kissing Hart gets off on but he just can't get that tongue down below the navel. Adam told me that the guy he was supposed to do the scene with didn't show so Spalding was pulled in at the last minute. Hart says he wasn't satisfied with the results but he was in no position to do anything about it.

For the finale, however, Russell enters Hart's life and mouth with an intensity that is matched only by Adam's assault on his ass a few moments later. The only thing wrong with this scene is the miraculous insertion – one moment they're doing oral, the next they're into anal and we don't see Hart's big thing sliding into Russell's greedy hole. Oh well, the sight of Hart pounding away missionary, that spectacular ass high in the air, is worth the price of the rental all by itself. But Adam explained this to me too: "What happened was, they had been filming other scenes all day and when we started it was very late and everybody was tired. We filmed the oral and then stopped. The next morning, around eleven, we got together again and did the last part." (Nothing like having Adam Hart for "brunch.") Adam said he was indeed turned-on by the hunky Russell: "He was a military man, older, about 34, and was down-to-earth, rather shy, easy to get along with. I felt comfortable doing it with him. It wasn't as if I had to reciprocate. It's wasn't as if John (Travis) just yelled at me, 'Do it!' I really did want to do it."

Someone Adam wasn't really comfortable with was Rick Bolton. As fans will recall, in "Take Down," Adam has sex with Bolton after Rick has been royally assaulted by the usually-bottom man Danny Sommers. This bottoming was accomplished, some say, after Rick had gotten hard off the set looking at girlie magazines for two hours. Adam says that he and Bolton were two 'take-charge' guys. "We really didn't click at all."

But according to Rick & Dave, the moral of this video is: "Be really good-looking and really confused about whether you're really gay, even though you shave your balls and wear International Male clothing. Join a frat and a wrestling team, don't have time to take an acting class, and you'll sleep with Rick Bolton."

"Sleeping" with Adam Hart would be about the last thing we'd want to do - we'd want stay awake every minute we were with him. Well, look, who could sleep?

And it's heartening to know that, unlike some other superstars of gay porn who say they are only "gay for pay," Adam says he's just into having "safe sex."

"Ultimate Porn Stud" Jeff Stryker,
courtesy Studio 2000

STRIKING OUT WITH JEFF STRYKER

"All day I've been thinkin' of fuckin' you with this big old fuckin' dick."
- Porn Stud Jeff Stryker in "Just You and Me"

Ever since Jeff Stryker came to prominence in 1983, there's been a new challenger to his title as Ultimate Porn Stud every year. But there's only one Stryker and the beguiling combination of a boyish face, perfect body, and long, fat, incredibly juicy cock that won't quit coming (he's usually good for two "money shots" per appearance) has sent sales of Stryker videos through the roof since he hit the screen

And to prove how important the penis really is, the world's best-selling dildo was molded from Jeff's magnificent one by Doc Johnson. But Jeff was miffed: "They added nothing in width but they added an inch in length. It insults me that they did that but they said that I wasn't 'fully motivated' when they were making the mold. But it's pretty wild. I always tell people I'm carrying around the master."

The fact that this "master" tantalizes while it repels gays is a dichotomy that fascinates. Director/magazine mogul Jerry ("More Than a Man") Douglas says: "Negative responses far outweigh the positive, yet the videos sell and rent like crazy, with swaggering Jeff Stryker remaining the ultimate example of the man we love to hate. If you're going to pay homage to a straight persona, you've gotta hate it. It's a phenomenon deeply rooted in the gay psyche. We hate these guys who seem to slide so easily through life, slipping between the thighs of men and women alike. How can they do this, some ask. Some of us who have been there just like guys more than girls and stick to it, opportunities aside. But with these guys, you never know. And that's the basis of their mystique."

Ric Bradshaw directed Ultimate Stud heir apparent Ryan Idol in "Idol Worship," an aptly named and imaginative AVG release, and Sid Mitchell commented: "Ryan's arrogant, almost parodic imitation of Jeff Stryker has never been put to better use than in the opening solo of this pseudo-military tale of life on a submarine patrol in the Indian Ocean. As the sub's commanding officer, Idol's arrogance seems not only believable but even appropriate, and for once, highly erotic. He j.o.'s while commanding his crew to keep their eyes on the radar screens.

But there's only one Stryker. In his solo video, "Just You and Me," which Idol also copied, Jeff stands before the mirror talks into it: "Do you want me to make love to you with this big fuckin' dick?" And out comes the cock, half-mast but still formidable. It's one of the most beautiful cocks you've ever laid your eyes on. It's long, thick, cut, perfectly shaped, very pink at the head and halfway back, topped by a small nest of light brown pubic hair. The body that comes with the cock matches it in every way. Perfectly defined, muscular without being absurd. The face looks as if it has been carved out of stone. It's pleasant in a midwestern farm boy kind of way. And when the stud smiles, the face becomes downright handsome. It is a smile that is so inveigling, so thoroughly compromising, as to almost render his partner to silly putty in his hands.

As he continues to stroke his mighty cock he snarls a bit and the contortions of his face add immeasurably to your enjoyment of his performance. Suddenly, the stud is in bed, slathering his body with champagne direct from the bottle. He orders us to lick it off and then, eventually, "Oh, look at that hot fuckin' cock! Get on it and ride me! Take it all the way, deep, deep inside of ya."

This raunchy monologue is also featured as a vignette in "On the Rocks" and is quintessential Stryker. In his book *The Arena of Masculinity*, Brian Pronger pays special attention to Jeff Stryker's verbal commentary: "After he has commented on his own masculine force, Stryker will draw attention to the joy of his partner by pointing out the rapture of the same: 'You like that big cock going up your ass don't you? Huh?' 'He likes that, don't he? See, he's got a big ole hard on.'"

Jeff said that in the beginning the directors just let him go crazy. "I wasn't guided," he said, "I wasn't pushed." And Matt Sterling confirmed this, saying the dirty talk was totally unrehearsed, undirected: "It came forth so willingly, so excitingly."

Appropriately, Jeff's first video was Matt Sterling's "Bigger Than Life" sequel to "Inch by Inch," after which he made several punchy flicks under the aegis of John Travis before striking out on his own. It is often said that good friends Travis and Sterling co-developed the Stryker persona, shaping him as well as his career. Stryker came to Hollywood from the midwest wanting to be a porn star but having no idea how to do it. Stryker succeeded because, as Travis puts it, "he was in tune with doing this. So many models today have the opportunity but are too busy doing other things. Stryker was dedicated to quality and building himself up." And, Sterling says, Jeff had that special gift great true film stars have: when the camera rolls, they exude charisma. Just hanging out with these pros, he learned from them and he took advantage of the knowledge they freely gave him.

The game plan was put into place and Jeff has followed it ever since: don't flood the market with product, keep people hungry, build up a distinct image and take control. Stryker's image early on was holding back, not reciprocating, creating, in Travis' words: "Illusion, a fantasy - that's basically what we're selling."

The Stryker mystique, then, was sex as punishment, fulfilling a fantasy, taking to the extreme the idea of the "straight" stud who doesn't mind giving a gay guy a thrill.

Mostly, Stryker gets praise from his bottoms. Erich Lange said: "He's a good fuck, a strong top."

And until "Stryker Force," in which he kissed a man twice, he never showed much affection for those willing men he assaulted. Typical of his method is the sequence in "A Portrait of Jeff Stryker," from 1987, which later was incorporated in the first episode of a 1989 Catalina release called "The Look." Herein, Jeff is running a garage and he takes two younger fellows, Ricky Turner and Kevin Wiles (at the time, two of the industry's workhorse bottoms) into his place of business, where Jeff disciplines them for breaking a windshield. He makes them suck his cock and then, after he fucks each of them and throws a copious load, he lets the boys overhear a phone conversation. It is then they realize he knew all along they didn't break the windshield and they stand gaping as he hangs up the phone and grins mischievously at them.

If one looks at these bouts as competition, on rare occasions, while letting Stryker think he's always "on top," "punishing" a boy's butthole to the best of his ability, a bottom may actually win the game. Consider the scene in "Stryker Force" with Robert Harris. Stryker offers himself and his huge cock up to the pliant Harris, who, from the looks on his face throughout the sequence, is having a helluva lot more fun than Jeff. And, by taking every inch of that meat, Harris is, in effect "castrating" the stud, bringing him down.

"You know," video pioneer William Higgins has said, "when you're in the business, you're always talking about the one that got away. Jeff Stryker was more or less like this because we always wanted to find somebody perfect to shoot with him. So he sat around waiting for a year and we didn't get nearly as much work done with him as we should."

Higgins told Jerry Douglas that Stryker's creators believe that the only person gays are really interested in viewing is "the quintessential top man who is essentially trade and is insulting to the gays. And you know I can play along with that when I feel like it, but I don't think it's a persona that I find attractive. I think that Stryker, more than any model I've ever known, generates more positive and more extremely negative comments than any other model. And you know, I don't find anything attractive or sexual about his screen persona."

Director Jeff Lawrence agrees: "Stryker is the ultimate effort in the thinking that the heterosexual is the epitome, stationed above us and forever unattainable. It pisses me off. Sex is, after all, sex, and I really do think that regardless of who is participating it brings us all down to a common level."

The first flick produced, directed and edited by Jeff was "Every Which Way," with Nick Elliot ably serving on camera. But it's the little "public service" message about condoms that he tacks on the end that we could have done without. It may be in keeping with his on-screen persona but blowing smoke rings and saying he needs a Glad bag instead of a condom, when added to the fact that one of the girls in the video says, "Take that rubber off and fuck me," is true theater of the absurd.

In his 1991 video, "Busted," art imitates life as Jeff

comments on his recent troubles with the Feds. (His studios have been busted frequently as part of the government's Project Post Porn.) *Frontiers* said: "Welcome to a world where the innocent pleasures of even way tame adult movies are forbidden by law. Porn producers are investigated, bugged and eventually hauled off by the strong biceps of the law...Jeff is still groggy from a long hard night of whatever it is he does at night (can't be sex; that's his day job) but Gino Colbert manages to give him a toe job, lick his butt and does various and sundry nasty things. Jeff lets him while a surveillance car lurks below his house. A couple of studs show up for an audition and Jeff invites them to join in the action. Basically everybody fucks everybody, except Jeff, of course, who never gets fucked by anybody. Meanwhile, back in the surveillance van, the FBI men start investigating each other. Off come the pants." This proves even FBI men can get turned on if Stryker leads the way.

Of all of the Stryker scenes, arguably the best from a gay perspective is found in "On the Rocks," directed by John Travis and featuring a climactic three-way with Joey Stefano and sexy Matt Gunther, who, as Stryker is plugging him, screams, "You're gonna make me come!" And he wasn't the only one.

Just when you think you've got ole countrified Jeff figured out, he surprises the hell out of you. He nibbled on Alex Stone's dick in "Powerfull 2" and kissed Joey Stefano on the mouth in "On the Rocks." God, fans were asking, can anal penetration be next? No way. Jeff was surprised by his fan mail after he nibbled on another guy's cock on-screen. "People like that dominant, aggressive image and I'll always keep that."

Yet, as Kinnick says: "More than perhaps any other star in the history of modern gay erotic, Stryker has manufactured and nurtured a screen persona calculated to capture the fancy of gay America. But that is only part of his success; the other part is that he is continually redefining his image, keeping his audience constantly poised for the unexpected, and providing them with surprise after surprise, every time out."

Speaking of surprises, in one interview Jeff revealed that he thought what he was doing was "morally wrong" who knows he's a "sinner" like everyone else but doesn't "choose to hide his sins." Yet, late in 1990, in his interview with *Interview* when asked whether he was happy in porn, he replied: "I don't think there's anything wrong with the movies I do. They're made to entertain people. I'd like to venture out of pornography. Maybe do a couple more videos, then go on to something with a wider audience. And just grow, basically. Because I got into pornography hoping it would be a stepping stone. If Traci Lords can do it, I can too. And I don't even think she can act. If I could get a major motion picture, I'd rely on my acting ability rather than my name. Because I do feel I can act. I've done a pretty good job of it so far, even though I've never taken acting lessons. I've been told that I'm a little like Brando or Dean. I don't know, though. I can't see that when I look in the mirror." One wonders what Jeff Stryker *does* see when he looks in a mirror.

Mostly, it seems, what Jeff can see in the mirror is that fabulous cock. The stud told Michael Musto that his cock has "a mind of its own. It's unisex. I like it and it likes me and we get along fine. It earns its own income. In fact, it supports me. Who's the smart one here?"

In 1993, Jeff sued the two companies that manufacture the dildo, charging they had infringed on the "intellectual property" rights he owns in his name and body; this caused his real name to appear in print for the first time: Charles Peyton. A judge said he would dismiss the case if the firms paid Jeff $25,000, but he questioned whether the case wasn't beneath the dignity of the court.

Fans questioned whether it wasn't beneath *Jeff's* dignity to promote a cock enlargement device, then make a video demonstrating its use. "Now look," one fan told me, "if anybody doesn't need such a thing it's Jeff." For sure:

Jeff says his cock is between nine and ten inches, "depending," and, in general, he likes to fuck with the lights on so he can watch it in action. But the first time he's with someone, he'll do it in the dark, "just so I don't get any rejection. It is quite intimidating. Gay men are obsessed with it until they have to deal with it, then it's a different story. But even in the dark, they say, 'What is that? Your leg?'"

Besides that infamous dildo, now available in the "realistic" and the "rotating" models, there's now a complete line of Stryker sex products, including lube, playing cards, the pump and the "How to Enlarge Your Penis" video at $19.95. He also has a nonsexual instructional video, "Strike Back Vol. 1," obviously aimed at gays who are sick of gay-bashing and want to learn about karate self-defense techniques. The muscular stud spends most of the hour-long running time topless so one critic doubted that the viewers of the tape would be practicing what Jeff was preaching. Rather, they would be opting for the "one handed chicken choking hold."

Vivid director Jim Steel, who seems to have kind words to say about everybody in the business, calls the stud "one of the smartest people and, as I'm sure you know, he is the nicest person as well. I first met him a long time ago when he was IT. Before they would release anything, there was just a picture of him month after month. And I could not believe anybody could be so charming. Completely charming. He would give you the shirt off his back, literally! He is square with you and this is the key thing. People who lie, I hate them, I can't deal with it."

During 1992, with the Feds raiding his offices (he's since moved his files into his home), Jeff released only "10 PLUS," a compilation of j/o scenes featuring his brother Rick, B. J. Slater, and Chance Caldwell, plus some scenes from previous Stryker productions. The fact that the star saw fit not to include any of his own scenes caused critic Dave Babbitt to say that it was unforgivable: "While the famous Stryker name and body is plastered all over the box cover, there's not one new frame of j/o footage of the celebrated Stryker ramrod. Would it have killed Mr. Stryker to jerk his cock for the cameras of his own production? Or does he care not one whit about the ever diminishing legion of fans patiently awaiting a product worthy of his star power? Why would any educated consumer purchase this collection of solos when he could witness enthusiastic sex in dozens of other productions? Don't aficionados of solo flicks deserve better?"

Lately, Jeff's been taking a breather from video and he's become known chiefly for being a party animal. In 1991 he garnered considerable press by attending the Love Ball 2, a surreal evening when over a million was raised for AIDS charities. The Roseland Ballroom in New York was packed with a glamorous eclectic group that included Jeff, David Geffen, Madonna, Calvin Klein and Sandra Bernhard. Musto reported that when club schmoozer Fred Rothbell-Mista told the star,

"You know how many times I've slept with you in my dreams?" Jeff had no reply, not even his usual *bon mot*, "Tighten that hole."

The New Yorker explained it all: "From the Kingdom of Sexual Disorientasia/Male Division: Certain members of the press realized that the guy in the bike-shorts-tight leather pants and open to the buckle white shirt was Jeff Stryker and proceeded to follow his every step across the celebrity waiting area, desperate for an interview but too tongue-tied to ask for one."

One who wasn't bashful was *The Advocate's* R. Couri Hay; he had the dubious distinction of getting the last word: "Jeff Stryker's got wrinkles, darlings, and I'm not talking about on his balls. The poor thing looked used, used, used. Well, there are always his early videos to cherish. So, now you know, I'm a bitch. Surprise, surprise. Jeff, wearing leather pants in 80-degree heat and two diamond rings he must have gotten from Liberace, left alone in a cab after telling me that 'love is as strong as your condom.'"

In 1992, he popped up at an AIDS Project Los Angeles benefit showcasing eccentric Parisian designer Thierry Mugler's summer collection at the Century Plaza Ballroom. Stud Stryker strutted his stuff with the likes of Michelle Phillips, Sandra Bernhard and Billy Zane.

Later, across the continent, in a rare strip appearance, Jeff got down and dirty at Webster Hall in New York for promoter Dallas and stayed on in the City to party with his friends, Boy George, Robin Byrd and Susan Barch. He took in Paul Rudnick's off-Broadway comedy, "Jeffrey," and posed with the cast.

In Paris, he was photographed by Pierre et Gilles, who put him in the tightest sequin trousers he could find and gave him satyr's horns, and did the Mugler catwalk in another fashion show. Gay fans went wild. The straights wanted to know who that "funny little man" was. (Jeff is five-eight.) "When the word got out," an observer said, "Jeff's hotel was besieged with men and women with only one thing on their minds."

In London, he appeared at Freak, at a series of themed monthly gay parties.

But before leaving for the U.K., Jeff agreed to take Jim

McClellan, from the British magazine *The Face*, on a tour of the headquarters of Stryker Productions in Hollywood (he works out of his home): "...an unassuming bungalow on a very swanky street in L.A. As soon as we arrive, Jeff insists on showing us round the warren of guyishly cluttered rooms. The things you might expect to find in a porn star's home – the kind of weird sex toys needed to stimulate a jaded sexual palate, the sad, soiled left-overs of last night's orgy – are nowhere to be seen. Instead there are telephones and TV's everywhere. In one of the bedrooms there's an arcade video game titled *Astron Belt*. In another there's a makeshift video edit suite. Across the hall is a nursery, piled high with toys for Jeff's three-year-old son, Little Joe. Out back, there's a pool and a set of weights (he works out for an hour every day.)

"At the center of the house is the living room, which is packed with kitschy stuff – two wooden horses from a merry-go-round, two mushroom dummies, a glass-topped coffee table whose base is a crouching black panther, some very bad abstract art, a life-size cardboard cut-out of Jeff doing karate (he's done an hour a day for the last eight years), a real zebra skin on the wall, a big-screen TV which plays daytime soaps continually while we're there. The stone wall is covered with flashing fairy lights. I ask Jeff if it's a deliberate design detail. He grins and says that he put them up three Christmases ago and it took so long he couldn't be bothered to take them down.

"Tanned, heavily pumped, sporting tight black jeans, white singlet and cowboy boots, Jeff looks almost too healthy. The boyish looks he had when he first started have mellowed into a kind of soap-opera handsomeness."

When asked what he'd do in his show in London, Jeff said: "I don't know. I usually wear some of the clothes (Thierry) Mugler made for me: cowhide chaps, leather pants, just beautiful stuff." When asked if, at some point in the evening, would he remove his clothes, Jeff said, "Well..."

"Perhaps he'll do his single," the reporter mused. For his visitors, Jeff played his demo tape, "a kind of funked-up twelve-bar over which Jeff delivers a rambling monologue on the subject of his main attraction (*"it's big and it's thick,"* *"it'll make you scream,"* etc.)"

Jeff said he wrote the words himself. "It's called 'Wild Buck.'

I wanted to call it 'Wild Fuck,' but we had to tone it down a little. I think it'll go over big in dance clubs."

When asked if his gay fans minded his appearances in straight videos, Jeff said: "I'm not sure. I hope not to offend anyone. My objective is that they be satisfied with what they see. I'm hoping to let people see that people are people, and to categorize and stereotype isn't so good."

To McClellan Jeff revealed publicly for the first time how he came to be a father. It seems a few years ago Jeff was pursued by a woman claiming to be an actress who was "desperate" to do a movie with him. He "met" with her for about three days and then she disappeared, only to turn up a few weeks later saying she was pregnant. "At first I said it couldn't be possible. But it was premeditated."

"When Little Joe was born," the reporter said, "Jeff was there with his attorney. "It was a nightmare," Jeff says. "The mother was trying to get outrageous sums of money from me to visit the child." The paternity was proved and after a court battle that dragged on for over a year, Jeff won custody. The mother is now in a drug rehabilitation center. "He's definitely a terrorist, but I love it," Jeff says of Little Joe. "It's like the ultimate dream – having a child, but not having to deal with that crazy woman."

"Crazy" is what some industryites say Jeff is. Kinnick calls Jeff one of the industry's "biggest spooks." "I've met him only once. It was January of 1990 at the Consumer Electronics Show in Las Vegas. (This was the year the Feds set up a sting to have companies send them product at fake stores in Mississippi and Oklahoma.) Stryker had been in a fist fight the night before and was showing some cuts and bruises on his face and I, like an idiot, swooped down on him with my journalist's note pad and pencil out. Actually, I just wanted to introduce myself and tell him I admired his work in the past. (The present is another story.) When he heard the word "press," he freaked. A very cordial facade became a stormy, muttering, bundle of nerves, and he suddenly spotted someone across the room that he absolutely had to talk to within five seconds. He was off, and I was left wondering what I had done wrong. The next year, he was at the show again, his face restored to its usual choirboy-gone-antisocial look, wearing a full length black leather trenchcoat. This time I didn't approach him. I say, if a legend wants his privacy, give it to him."

Thick-dicked Trey Tempest, star of "Takin' Care of Mike" and "Cool Hand Dick," among others, recalls making "Busted" with Stryker: "I was supposed to top in my scene, but the English guy - Matt Windsor - all of a sudden is telling everyone he can't get fucked. So, I was like, 'Okay, I want my $600 for this so I'll bend over and take it for five minutes, and we'll simulate the rest.' So we finished that scene and they said, 'You'll have an hour or two to rest now, and then we'll have another scene for you to do.' Well, ten hours went by, and they weren't ready to start taping my second scene. It was two o'clock in the morning, and I was really mad because I had been told I'd only be there a total of maybe six hours. I could have gone out and turned three or four tricks in the amount of time I was there. So I walked up to Gino (Colbert, assisting Jeff) and said, 'Look, I've been here for twelve hours. You're going to pay me $150 extra for staying so long and I'm not going to do the second scene.' When Jeff heard what was going on, he was really pissed. He said, 'No one has ever walked out on me before.' So it was like, I made history again."

Gino Colbert also figured in another history-making event when Jeff attended the *Gay Video Guide* awards show in Hollywood in December of 1993. To maintain at least a sense of decorum, the management had insisted that there be no frontal nudity, but La Stryker felt compelled to ignore the rules and, Dave Kinnick reported, had called Colbert to his limo shortly before he was to go on stage to receive a Hall of Fame Award. Colbert became, in essence, Jeff's "fluff" for the occasion. A fluff is a porn term for a person who gets a man excited off-camera so that he can walk on with a big ol' hard-on, which is what Jeff proceeded to do. But by that time in the evening, most of the celebrants had departed for less dreary climes, so Jeff played to a small but very appreciative house. Many in the industry took this as a sign that Jeff still regards his gay audience as important to his career and that he's willing to break a few silly house rules to communicate his message in the best way he can – wielding what was easily the Dick of the Decade ('80s) and may well go down as the Cock of the Century.

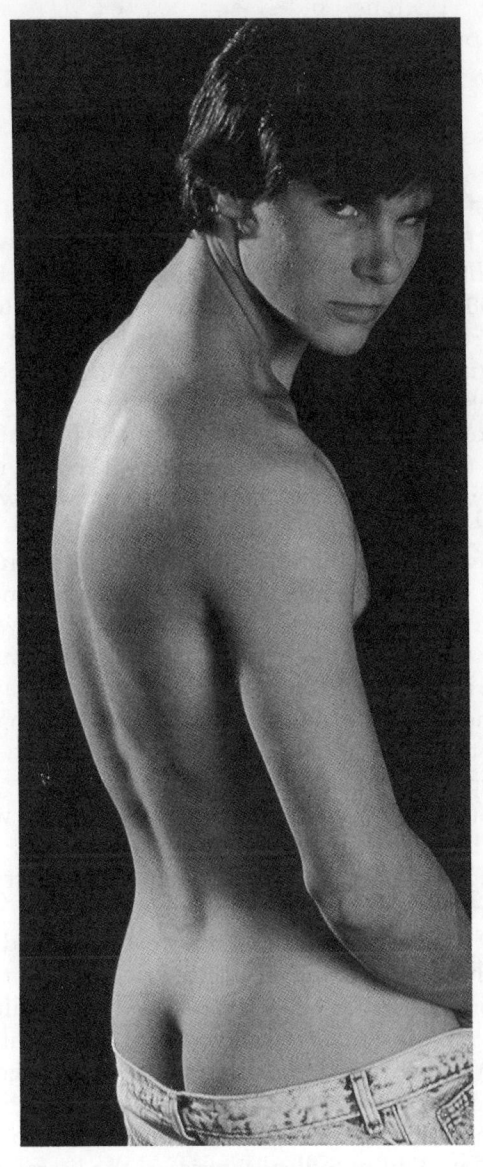

Porn Performer Tim Lowe

FOR THE LOVE OF LOWE: TIM LOWE

In the first volume of this *Best Erotica of* series, we excerpted a portion of the book *Lowe Down*, about Tim Lowe, bisexual star of over 30 adult videos. In a new Afterword to the latest edition, I revealed that Tim was arrested in January of 1993 for the strangulation murder of Allen Kinkead, 51, a San Francisco man. Kinkead's body was found bound and gagged in a bedroom of his apartment near Golden Gate Park after he failed to appear for work after several days. Police said robbery was apparently the motive for the killing. Tim was working as a dancer at the Campus Theater and had been living with Kinkead for several months. Tim and a girlfriend from San Francisco, Kimberley Stefanic, were apprehended in an Alamagordo, New Mexico, traffic block. They were driving Kinkead's stolen 1991 fire-engine red Pontiac Trans-Am.

When the story surfaced in the gay press in May, Jim Steel, who helmed "Rites of Summer" for Vivid starring Tim, said: "That's not the Tim I know. He was conscientious, caring, and showed up when he said he was going to."

It's not the Tim I knew either. Handsome Tim was talented - he had been chosen Best Actor of the Year by *Adult Video News* magazine for his performance in Jerry Douglas' "Fratrimony" - and seemed more than anything to want to live a "normal" life. The news of his arrest saddened me deeply because I had spent a long weekend with the performer in New Orleans preparing the book. He seemed a charming sort, the kind of boy you wouldn't need to hide your wallet from. A friend in Atlanta wrote me, "I didn't have Tim pegged as a killer by any means, but if you will recall even as far back as *Lowe Down's* publication, I told you he didn't appeal to me because he just seemed to be too egocentric, in the literal sense of the word, that only he mattered. I guess if you push that attitude far enough, violence is going to follow."

Things started going downhill for Tim at the time the book

was published. He stopped making films and was trying to find work as a security guard. Then, when he reported he was having trouble making ends meet what with the wife and kid to support, in July of 1991, I encouraged a bar owner in Tampa to invite him to dance at his establishment. The first night, I arrived to find Tim had missed his flight. I left, thinking I would catch him the next night, only to arrive to the news that when he did show up and found he couldn't do his usual jack-off sequence so popular at the Campus in San Francisco, he put on a plodding performance. He squabbled with the management over the extra fare because of the missed plane and was subsequently fired.

After I heard the news of Tim's arrest, I recalled that, in organizing the trip to New Orleans, I had occasion to talk with his wife in San Diego several times. The last time I spoke with her, as Tim was jetting to meet me, she said: "Take care of him. He gets into trouble when he goes out of town."

My headline for the story of Lowe's arrest in Florida's gay *Encounter* magazine was "How Lowe Can You Go?" The mail that came to us as a result of just using that headline was phenomenal. If I had ever doubted the great loyalty of fans to their favorite sex performers, this was enough to make me a true believer. Readers thought I was condemning the performer before he had even had his day in court. Upon reflection, I agreed. While the story was simply reportage, and an expression of my great agony over the grisly aspects of the case involving someone with whom I had spent some wonderful evenings, the headline, in true tabloid fashion, was a mistake.

An even greater injustice, however, was that wrought by the judicial system in California. Bear in mind, Tim has been rotting away in a jail cell for over a year when the news arrives that on January 10, a judge charged the ex-porn star not with murder but with involuntary manslaughter. "I've come to the conclusion that the evidence indicates the acts committed by the defendant amount to involuntary manslaughter," said Assistant District Attorney Bill Fazio. Fazio presented these findings to the judge, who subsequently reduced the charges. Fazio indicated that an autopsy revealed that Kinkead had high levels of methamphetamines and amyl nitrate in his body at the time of his death. According to San Francisco Medical Examiner

Body Stevens, Kinkead's medical condition and the drugs in his system made unclear whether he died of asphyxia or cardiac arrest. Lowe told investigators he had fought with Kinkead during a sexual encounter and he tied Kinkead up to incapacitate him and that when he put his arm around his neck and told him to calm down, Kinkead went limp and died. Fazio said that there was simply not enough evidence to say that the murder was premeditated. "Lowe could now receive probation instead of a prison sentence," said Dennis Conkin in *Frontiers* magazine. "A trial date has not been set."

This, we find, is typical of criminal cases where the accused does not have the resources to push his case through the courts. That Tim may well leave jail "on probation" with "time served" is great news. It would be even happier news if his time there has caused him to buff his bod and make a decision to return to what he does best, performing sex before an appreciative audience. While he does not present a good live sex show (unless he can jack-off on stage), he is capable on video and was always "up" for anything. Besides, a money shot from Lowe was always guaranteed.

Now that the facts are known, an avalanche of warm wishes will come from his fans – all over the world. We sometimes forget the impact American sex entertainment has overseas. Recently a portion of *Lowe Down* was featured in the popular British magazine *Rouge*, accompanying an article about bisexuality. With publicity like this, sex star Lowe could command megabucks for a return to the screen. Indeed, we suggested to Gino Colbert, Hollywood's King of Low-Budget Sleaze, he do just that. "The Return of Tim Lowe" would be a smash.

PHOTOGRAPHY

A substantial portion of the photography for this book has
been furnished courtesy of the Brown Bag Co.
For a catalogue of current products available,
you may send a self-addressed, stamped envelope to:
P. O. Box 1067, Los Angeles, CA 90078.
Please state over 21. Offer not valid in some states.

The photography of Adam Hart and his strippers was
provided courtesy of *Encounter* magazine and the
photographer James Meckley of Orlando.

BONUS BOOK

What Went Wrong?
When Boys Are Bad & Sex Goes Wrong
is included here complete and unabridged, as it
appeared in the original edition published by
STARbooks Press

Because reality is the greatest fantasy of all...

What went wrong...

WHEN BOYS ARE BAD & SEX GOES WRONG

A NON-FICTION NOVEL BY
JOHN PATRICK

And Special Praise for
"What Went Wrong?"
from William Barber, popular novelist and
poet, author of "Diary of New York Queen"
and "Marty:"

"'What Went Wrong?' is a
gripping, well-told story.
It's well-focused and works on many levels.
The growth and introspection of the ending
is exactly correct. I couldn't put the book
down, shivered in horror at the eruptions of
murder...I pictured every detail, the houses,
the wealth and the poverty, the sociopathic
behavior that I, too, know well.

"And now I'm cleaning up my
own act a little."

What went wrong...

When Boys Are Bad & Sex Goes Wrong

A Non-Fiction Novel by
JOHN PATRICK

STARbooks Press
Sarasota, FL

Books by John Patrick

Non-Fiction
The Best of the Superstars
A Charmed Life: Vince Cobretti
Lowe Down: Tim Lowe
The Best of the Superstars 1991
What Went Wrong? When Boys Are Bad
Legends: The World's Sexiest Men, Vol. 1

Fiction
Billy & David: A Deadly Minuet
The Bigger They Are...
The Younger They Are...
The Harder They Are...
Angel: The Complete Trilogy
Angel II: Stacy's Story
Angel: The Complete Quintet
*Angel: The Complete Quintet
(International Ed.)*
A Natural Beauty (Editor)
The Kid (with Joe Leslie)
Huge (Editor)
Strip: He Danced Alone

Entire Contents Copyrighted 1991 by STARbooks Press, Sarasota, FL. All rights reserved. No part of this book may be reproduced or transmitted in any form by any means, electronic or mechanical, including photocopying, recording, or any information storage and retrieval system, without expressed written consent from the publisher.

Every effort has been made to credit copyrighted material. The author and the publisher regret any omissions and will correct them in future editions. Note: While the words "boy," "girl," "young man," "youngster," "gal," "kid," "student," "guy," "son," "youth," "fella," and other such terms are occasionally used in text, this work is about persons who are at least 18 years of age, unless otherwise noted.
Photographs courtesy of St. Petersburg Times, St. Petersburg FL and the Atlanta Journal-Constitution, Atlanta, GA.

**Library of Congress Card Catalogue No. 91-065824
ISBN No. 1-877978-10-8**

The Rogues and the Lovers

A Gallery

Photo: Stephanie James

The Killer: Michael Gross

The Killer:
Henry Eugene Hodges

The Attacker:
Charles Stob

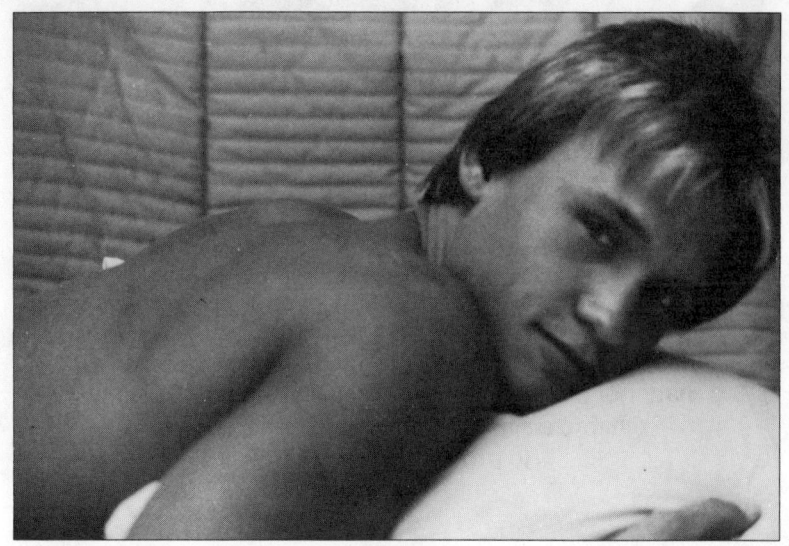

The Lover:
Tracy

The Lovers:
Brett & Ronnie

Note

While the names of the victims and their victimizers are a matter of public record, some of the names of the other characters in this book have been changed to protect their privacy.

Introduction

"Pity the nonfiction novel," Todd Kliman, wrote. "There is probably no more abused, misunderstood form in all of literature."

Writers, Kliman maintains, eager to exploit the possibilities of such a book, hoping to arrive at a truth more pungent and real than mere make-believe, have for years made terrible missteps in putting it together. On the one hand, the facts, a great accumulated mass of facts, cannot be toyed with. On the other hand, a heightened sense of imagination must come into play, to give shape and lift to the reportage. To allow one to overpower the other, or to employ one merely in the service of another, is to tip the precious balance the nonfiction novel requires. Because truth is elusive, life is messy, too filled with untidy little facts and odd, chance details, a nonfiction novel cannot rush to an inevitable, horrible truth at the end of it. Truth resists such streamlining and forcing.

In writing my romans a' clef, I have had the luxury to alter the facts to suit my dramatic purposes. However, for this book, I wanted to tell the whole truth and nothing but. The characters histories' are already in place, often on page one, so I had to avoid the tendency to be selective, only offering stories and incidents which would explain why what happened, happened. The facts, I quickly found, took over. It became a coup of facts, as it were, conspiring to dictate every decision. The compulsion to make sense of accumulated knowledge, to make it all fit somehow, nullified my attempt to make the book a voyage of discovery for the reader. After many revisions, I decided the best I could do with such material was to create layers, remain faithful to all the fringes of reality, letting the truth, whatever it is, after a web of details and colors and textures build up and finally reveal itself, as in the manner of time-lapse photography.

Someone once described the function of a journalist as holding up a mirror to the communities we serve, giving a view of the world as accurate and complete as he can. A journalist doesn't set out to offend and we're sorry when it happens. But it would be impossible to publish a book that everyone agrees with. Besides, it'd be boring to read.

What I offer you here is the story of men pushed over the edge and how their brutal acts impacted many lives, mine included. Because of this, some of what you are about to read may offend you and for that I apologize, but at least you've responded.

Prologue

Somewhere something went wrong.
I knew I was supposed to like girls and I did. I flirted with them outrageously. In fact, all my friends were girls. I even married one and stayed with her for ten years.
But early on I knew I wasn't like other guys. I loved books and movies and I wasn't interested in sports. My father thought I should be. My brother was such a jock that my father was always asking what the hell had happened with me. My brother became my idol. It seemed he did everything right in my father's eyes and I did everything wrong.
When I was twelve, my brother was seventeen and it started with petty thievery.
We would jump in his jeep and go to town. At the drugstore, he would engage the salesgirl in conversation while I slipped magazines under my coat and walked out. They weren't just any magazines, they were what my brother called "girlie magazines." Then, in the privacy of the bedroom we shared, he would spread them out on the bed, telling me I was supposed get an erection looking at pictures of tawdry women in naughty poses. It was obvious that he did but I didn't. Before long, I agreed to lie on the bed on my stomach, naked, with the magazines on the pillows on either side of my head. My brother would lie on top of me and rub his erection between my asscheeks. Soon, he wanted to insert his cock into my anus. I let him. I squirmed under the pressure. He took his time. Over a period of days, the pain gave way to pleasure and I began to play with myself as he screwed me. As he took his pleasure, he talked about the girls in the pictures, how hot their pussies would be, how they would love getting it from him and on and on. I identified with these cheap girls because my father had made me feel effeminate, inferior, disgraceful. But my brother, by lavishing a curious love on me in these moments, made me feel

wanted, needed, even desired. If this was the way to make my idol happy, I was willing to do it. It got to the point that I wanted my brother inside of me every waking moment. Before the sex between us had begun, my idol wanted nothing to do with me but afterward he was taking me to the movies and on the way home we would stop in a secluded spot and I would get to jump up and down on his cock. And he would take me out for ice cream and we would stop at the landfill and he would fuck me, then buy me another ice cream cone on the way back home. Nights when he said he didn't feel like it, I would threaten him with exposure so he would always come across. Not only had I made my idol a buddy, he was my secret lover besides. It was heaven.

Our idyll lasted two years. Then my brother went to college. When he returned, I was desperate for him, but he refused me, contemptuously yelling at me that he now had plenty of pussy and didn't need a "fake" one. Devastated, I set out in search of a new idol.

1

"What's up?" asked the scrawny young hustler with the bulging crotch as our eyes connected. He was one of several leaning against a brick wall near the intersection of Fifteenth and Spruce, the youths of the night, kids with nowhere to go, ever alert to opportunity.

"Nothing much," I replied, "it's Sunday." The bars are shut on the Sabbath in Philadelphia. I knew this from my several visits to the city on my public relations junkets for a Fortune 500 company with strong Bicentennial tie-ins. My client, like me, was a married man with children, and, I discovered, we shared a desire for exploring many forms of eros. He taught me where to find gay men. My first visit to a gay bar was in Philly, the Allegro. By this time, I had settled into a pattern. My attitudes had formed early on. Because it seemed I was being rewarded by my brother for the use of my body, I saw nothing wrong with paying for someone's company. My best encounters had been with those I had paid. I began to prefer it because I felt I was in control of the situation. As a married man, I sought a refuge from the emotional control of my wife. I felt it was unfair that sexuality be a slave to relationships. I sought the freedom to pursue eros where I could find it.

I had used services and met boys in bars in Philadelphia but on this particular night, with the bars shut and not having made any advance calls, I was attempting my first street pick up. Whatever I said to the scrawny youth over the next few moments seemed to have worked because we struck a deal. When we arrived at my room at the posh Latham Hotel, the kid ducked into the john. As I listened to him urinating, I stood in the middle of the room, on unfamiliar ground, wishing I hadn't gone through with it. Picking up street trash suddenly loomed as a dangerous new experience. Remembering my client's horror stories about how such boys beat and robbed their tricks, I stashed my wallet in the refrigerator.

When the kid came out of the bathroom, I was pouring myself a drink. I offered him one but he declined and quickly shed his clothes, bounced on the bed and started stroking himself. I blanched at his vile smell and I remembered what someone once said of French boys: "They should never remove their socks." My eyes roamed the rail thin body and settled on the pimply face. He wasn't ugly but he wasn't cute either. As he lackadasically played with himself, I made up my mind: I had done the wrong thing after all. There was no romance to this. It was commerce, pure and simple. Too quick. Too dirty, even in the splendor of the Latham suite. I wanted no part of it. "I'm afraid I've changed my mind," I said.

"Oh, no ya don't," he spat. "Ya give me my money or I'll call downstairs and tell 'em ya got a 16-year-old here in the room bare-ass naked."

I had only sipped my drink. I was stone cold sober. When I was under the influence, the innocent were as much at risk as the guilty. Calmly, evenly I tried to reason with the youth: "Oh, I intend to give you your money."

He snarled, "Then why'd ya stash your wallet in the refrigerator?"

I was dumbfounded. To this day I can't figure how he knew.

"No reason." I began stammering. "I, I, I really don't know. All I have is travellers' checks anyway."

"Don't trust me, eh?"

"I'm sorry."

"Ya, sure, asshole." He jumped up from the bed and tugged his jeans back on.

I was angered but I remained calm. "But, look, I wouldn't start making trouble if I were you." I swallowed hard. "My client's in the next room," I lied, "and all I have to do is start pounding on the wall."

"You look, asshole," he said, pulling his shirt on over his head, "just give me my money and I'm outta here."

I took my wallet from the refrigerator and handed him a fifty.

"Just fifty?"

"You wanted thirty. That's all I have. The rest is in travellers' cheques."

"Limme see - " he screamed, yanking the wallet from my hand.

The trembling seemed to start in my hands and knees, waves of quaking fear, too long suppressed, running uncontrollably through me. I lunged at him, wrestling for my wallet. He pushed me away, hard. I fell against the bureau, then lunged at him again as he made his way to the door. I grabbed at his shirt. He turned and hammered my face with his fist. Around the edges of my vision, I saw a door open and close. Then I saw black.

I awoke on the floor. Dazed, I struggled into the bathroom. The mirror reflected a ugly red welt on my cheek and a black eye but I was lucky to be alive.

*

Later that year, a few weeks after the big Bicentennial bash, reticent Teddy bear John Knight, heir to the Knight newspaper chain, had often walked the same street, passed the same corner, surveyed the same chorus line of cuties selling their wares that I had. But while I was a stranger in the so-called City of Brotherly Love, Knight was a known figure, had a luxurious penthouse on Rittenhouse Square and often cajoled boys into procuring for him, so it was not unusual they paid attention when John indicated that he was "horny as hell." One of the chorus line eagerly responded by telling John he had someone new to the street. "I can fix you up with 'im and if it works you pay me thirty," the kid told Knight. "Give nothin' to him. If it doesn't work out, pay me ten. No hassle."

"Sounds good," John said.

Slowly, the two men walked the four blocks, past the Allegro, and stopped at the Hasty-Tasty Deli. Signs on the outside window announced a gay dance, a dog lost, a roommate wanted. Inside, the cashier and grocery clerk talked in "get you, honey" lingo. The customers were friendly and the place was brightly lit. People can see what they are eating - and each other. The kid saw his friend at the table in the rear.

"Felix," he said. "This is John."

Felix offered his hand. It was a long hand and he dropped it into John's the way a haberdasher would slip a tie into a gift box.

John sat down. He asked Felix if he'd like another cup of coffee, then ordered three. Felix was quiet, the kid chatty. John sulked.

Felix whispered, "Is this guy drunk?"

The kid replied, "No, high. Always like that," then turned to John. "Do you like Felix?"

John nodded.

"Then it's a deal?"

"It's a deal," John answered, pulling a couple of twenties from his pocket. "Take care of it. And keep the change."

Five minutes later, Felix Melendez and John Knight left the deli for John's apartment on Rittenhouse Square.

Three months later, on Sunday morning, December 7, 1975, John Knight was dead.

"Murder victims are usually painted as saints and we read the gushy post mortem prose with a certain amount of cynicism," reporter Arthur Bell wrote about the case. There seemed to be a holding back in the copy, as if the newspapers were trying to soft-pedal the homosexuality of Knight, as if they didn't want to deal with it unless they had to, as if it weren't cricket to bring someone out of the closet after death, especially one of their own. Between the lines there were hints of gayness, allusions to a "secret life."

A week later, after an intense search that slashed through the gay community, during which anyone who remotely looked like the suspects was picked up and questioned, three suspects emerged:

Felix Melendez, 19, 5'9", 135 pounds, slender build, green eyes, shoulder-length hair, light complexion, birthmark on the outer right thigh and a scar on his abdomen.

Salvatore Soli, 37, 5'-4", 128 pounds, slender build, brown eyes, dark brown hair, dark complexion, track marks on both arms, tattoos on his right forearm of two hearts and a dove and the words "Mom and Dad." Tattoos on the left upper arms of a cross, a heart and a rose.

Steven Maleno, 25, 5'9", slender, muscular, dark hair, olive complexion, track marks, married.

It was said that all three were "dangerous" and they came from South Philadelphia.

As the investigation continued, the events of the murder night became clear: John and his houseguests, Dr. McKinnon, an old school chum, and his wife Rosemary returned to his Rittenhouse Square apartment after dinner. They had brandy in the library and reminisced about the old days. Rosemary fell asleep. About 1 a.m., the phone rang. Knight answered, spoke softly but with a hint of annoyance in his voice. The doctor overhead him tell the caller: "I can't see you tonight. I've got houseguests."

After he hung up the phone, Knight explained that the call was from a procurer who set him up with girls. Two hours later, there was another call and John was more abrupt with the caller. When he hung up, he suggested the McKinnons retire to the guest room. Dr. McKinnon speculated that John might be having a visit from a girl and they bade their host goodnight.

At 4 a.m., the doorbell rang and Knight answered. When John refused to let the visitor in, the McKinnons overhead a male voice say, "I love you, John. I must see you."

When Knight opened the door, Melendez entered the apartment, quickly followed by Maleno and Soli. They forced Knight to his bedroom, knocked him into a Ming vase and used belts and ropes and socks to tie his legs together and bind his hands behind his back. They gagged his mouth with one of his best silk neckties.

As they proceeded to ransack the apartment, they found the McKinnons. The doctor, drunk, was unbudgeable in slumber. The thugs made his wife, naked, help them pillage the apartment. She remembers that Soli had a handgun and that Felix roamed the place with a harpoon gun and a scuba-diving knife. After about ninety minutes, the doorman called to say neighbors were complaining about the noise. Felix told him he was Knight's brother and that they were practicing karate. The doorman told him to do it during the day. The call unnerved Soli and Maleno and they tied up Rosemary and left with what they had stolen. Felix stayed behind, nervous, muttering to himself. The doctor's wife pleaded with him to untie her. As soon as he did, she ran to the guest room, grabbed one of John's hunting rifles and woke her husband. Bell commented, "The explanation of what was going on was more sobering than forty cups of black coffee." The doctor rushed into Knight's bedroom and the heir appeared to be dead. Melendez stood on the bed shouting, "I didn't do it, I didn't do it!" McKinnon wrestled with him but he fled the apartment.

The coroner's report indicated there were four stab wounds in Knight's back. The stab wound in the chest, penetrating the heart, left a gaping hole. One of the wounds, police theorized, would not have been possible if Knight's hands were tied behind his back, indicating it was inflicted before the victim was bound. Bruises on the face and head were caused by the impact of blunt instruments. There were a minimum of seven blows.

Five days later, just an hour after Maleno was arraigned, Felix Melendez was found dead. "KNIGHT SUSPECT SHOT TO DEATH: BODY FOUND IN JERSEY" shouted the newspaper headline.

According to Dennis Rubini, a Philadelphian with gay liberation connections, Knight thought of himself as straight. "The 'gay' thing was that part of the psyche you kept in the closet along with three fur coats," he said. Another acquaintance said, "He compartmentalized himself. His life was like a long hallway with a lot of closets. None of the closets were connected and each time he would have to go back to the hallway to get from one to the other."

Homosexuality, Bell asserts, was a problem that gnawed at Knight. It bothered him because of his stature and the possibility that if his grandfather found out, he'd be cut off. "The men he dated were overaged children he wouldn't be caught dead with in a social situation. He'd find a poor waif and father him. Knight's own father died in the Battle of the Bulge a couple of weeks before he was born. He never had a father so some kind of reverse transference was a factor in his relationships with males. He looked for the baby face and the big blue eyes. If they didn't speak proper English and were poverty-stricken, they'd get points. Knight would take them to the Dorchester Hotel, give them food, let them fool around with his stereo and camera equipment, talk to them like a father, wrestle with them - and then came the nitty-gritty part where paternalism took the form of incest. Never would Knight seek out a male peer as a sexual partner. Affluent, intelligent homosexuals were avoided, even as friends. Knight knew that the sexual part of his life was strictly fly-by-night, destructive, impossible to reconcile even with the help of an analyst. The truth is, he acknowledged the hypocrisy of his life."

With Knight, sex was always a matter of cultural collision. "Diametrically opposed" was a figure of speech that could elicit a hard-on, Bell remembers. He could never sever the umbilical cord that bound him to a patriarchal society, a hierarchy who expected greatness from him. And greatness meant strength. Strength meant masculinity. Masculinity meant heterosexuality. And, for him, heterosexuality meant a facade. "Maintain a facade," Bell says, "for the world to see. Cheat in the dark abyss of the soul. Cheat in a dimly lighted backyard. The truth is, when you're rich and bothered and restless, a hustler is easier to cope with than a sit-down dinner for six. And with the help of gay publications, anyone can dial a whore."

But what John Knight was into could only be found on the street. He was the classic John.

And Felix was the classic street hustler. His brother said, "Girls would run after him. I'm sure boys did, too. The brown hair, the green eyes, he had kind of an innocent angel's face. His looks opened doors, but they were also his downfall. I can't tell you exactly when but he even caught a case of syphilis. He had to have an injection every day for a week before it went away.

"And he got into trouble for reckless driving. He got picked up once for having a knife on him. It was his protection, like rosary beads. He liked to pick a fight, but he'd usually run away.

"In 1972, Felix met Donna Leone, the daughter of a truck driver, and they started to date, but he didn't want to settle down. He was high-strung. He took a lot of pills. A couple of times the cops picked him up from the ground because they found him like he was having an epileptic fit. I think it was a nerve attack. I never knew how many drugs he took. He used to lie so much to me that I wouldn't believe him when he told me the truth. He loved to lie.

"Then Donna gave birth to Felix's baby in 1974. He wanted to marry her but she didn't want it. They stopped seeing each other for a while and he started hanging out in the City. I don't know whether he was gay. I never even thought about it. I was surprised when I heard he was. And I still can't believe it. You see, we were brought up in a Christian family where it isn't right to be homosexual. It must have hurt Felix's conscience. When he lived with me, I know many things were bothering him. I gave him a lot of advice to stay out of trouble. That last year, he couldn't seem to do anything he wanted to do. Then he moved in with Joe Paolucci, a baker. Suddenly, Felix had money. There were lots of flashy clothes. I knew he was still taking those pills because he looked glassy-eyed. He had to be on something.

"He never confided that his life was any different than it had been and he never mentioned John Knight. Never."

Homosexuality in South Philadelphia, Bell remarks, means drag queens. They're spottable, they wear their gayness on the outside, accepted as freaks of nature. The toughs protect them, banter with them. "Hey, sweetie, who's your date for tonight? Wanna give me a blow job?"

"It's not big enough. I want a real man."

A man who is homosexual but dresses like everyone else and passes is a threat.

If a member of a South Philadelphia gang is suddenly discovered hanging out with a homosexual for reasons other than hustling, procuring or beating the daylights out of him, his contemporaries most likely would rough him up and banish him forever from the paternal breast. Naturally, the church doesn't like fairies. They're an abomination. It's right there in the Bible, in Leviticus. In South Phialdelphia, machismo is all.

Philadelphia drug counselor Jim Kennedy put it this way: "You must understand class differences in order to understand the phenomenon of hustlers. The majority are working class. They come from broken homes and their feelings have been brutalized. They work out who they are sexually. Therefore, it becomes the leitmotif of their lives. In Philadelphia, they'll range from thirteen to about forty-one. The older hustlers go to parties and hang out in bars, looking for someone to keep them. If they can't succeed selling their bodies, they'll try to get a decent job. As they grow older, many of them end up picking up hustlers themselves.

"Until the Knight murder, the cops left the street hustlers alone. Their attitude was, if that's what these guys are doing, let them do it, as long as they don't hassle women on the street. Rarely was there harassment and rarely were arrests made along Spruce.

"Felix was typical of the gang who worked the street. He came from a Pentecostal background and the church is antigay. Felix had a multiple amount of oppressions working against him: religion, sexual orientation, class, and his Puerto Rican minority status."

Joe Paolucci explained how he originally met Felix: "I knew from a friend of mine, an older guy who works as a dry cleaner. You see, my wife and I had just separated and I needed a roommate to help pay the bills. Felix moved in and we lived together for about seven months.

"In the beginning he was working and going to school. Then he quit everything and got lazy and smoked a lot of grass. During the late summer he began to go down to Center City. I told him not to hang out there, that he'd get in trouble. But I could have been speaking to a deaf man. Almost every day he'd split to Spruce and Fifteenth Street, decked out, cleaned up, perfumed with that fucking cologne shit on him like he was going to meet Miss Universe.

"He didn't boast about hustling but I knew that's what he was doing because I saw him at that corner a couple of times. He met John there. I first heard about this rich guy from Felix maybe in

September. Then the telephone calls started. I never talked to John in person, only by phone. He'd call the house five or six times a week. If Felix wasn't home, he'd say, 'Tell him John phoned.' He'd never leave a last name or number.

"One night they were on the phone with each other for two hours. It got me fucking angry. I said to Felix, 'Look man, I don't mind you using the phone, but two hours of that goddam shit is too much.'

"A lot of times they would argue. I'd hear Felix say, 'Go screw yourself, John,' then he'd hang up. He'd feel real bad after and mope around. Then in ten minutes he'd call him back. It was like they had a romance going."

Paolucci had a history of petty theft and he boasted of rolling faggots. "A bunch of us would hang out downtown where Felix did. We'd lure these guys to the subway then punch 'em out and take their money."

Felix got Paolucci involved on the murder night because all of a sudden he wanted to be a tough guy. He had shot up with meth. "Man," Paolucci said, "meth does things to your brain cells." When he came home, Felix told Paolucci that he had to "cut the guy." He made a gesture as if he had knifed him.

Pint-sized drug dealer Soli was turned in by Linda Mary Wells, an eighteen-year-old "burlesque dancer" who ratted to protect herself. She told detectives she was with Soli in Philadelphia the night of the murder at Paolucci's. Maleno came in to cop some drugs from Sal. Then Felix came home and shot up methedrine with all of them. Soon, Felix was jetting in his own space. The talk turned to drugs and money and Sal said he was in need of some quick money. Felix left his private world to declare he had a rich friend. They agreed such a score would be easy and Felix dialed John.

With Felix dressed, in the words of Linda, "like a flaming faggot," the three left the house and went to Knights.

At 7 a.m., Joe's phone rang. Sal was frantic. "What the hell happened? What went wrong?"

Sal spat out that they were in a lot of trouble. "Felix cut up the guy."

Later, his companions asked Felix why he had killed Knight and he replied, "Just because."

Rosemary McKinnon testified that Felix had told her: "I was involved with John Knight and he fucked me over."

Linda knew the men killed Felix because they felt they were patsies, set up for Felix's lovers quarrel and Felix wanted to have them there to help in his fight with Knight. She felt she would be next if she didn't go to the police.

On the night of the murder, Soli was later to testify, Felix kept saying, "John, you shouldn't have did that to me."

"That's all he would say, over and over, "Soli said. "He was wired out, you understand. From the speed. And I guess all his emotions came out. I don't feel nothing about Melendex being dead. As far as I'm concerned, he deserved to die. But Knight, there was no reason in the world why that man should be dead. No reason at all."

On February 3, 1978, Salvatore Soli was found guilty of the murder of Felix Melendez and sentenced to life imprisonment.

A long-time friend of Knights explained: "John made a fatal error knowing the alley crowd. He thought he was bright, that he could cope with them when, in reality, he was a babe in the woods. That's why he was killed. He asked for it.

"It takes a long time to become what you are. What John became didn't happen overnight. He was away from home from the time he was young. First prep school, then college, England, the rich doting grandfather, everything one could want, except inward peace, which you can't inherit."

"He was a guy who could buy anything with class," a friend said, "but he didn't want that. He wanted people he could look down on with disdain. In his sober, lucid moments he didn't want to have anything to do with Felix. He was ashamed of him. That offended the kid."

An acquaintance of Knight's revealed: "In his diaries, John talked about homosexual experiences and how euphoric he had been in a particular encounter, but he would never come out and say homosexuality itself was terrific. It was a disease that one overcomes rather than accepts as part of one's makeup. For some people, it's fine but for John it was death."

Like most of us, Knight had been taught that homosexuality is bad, unacceptable. We hide in the closet, passing for straight, making fun of the obvious ones. And hating ourselves for it. And then, for some like John Knight, when your death is news, all of the camouflage is eroded on page one.

2

Fast-forward to 1979.

A clear, sunny day early in April. I answered a knock on the door of the townhouse on the edge of the Gulf of Mexico I was in the process of renovating. As I swung open the door, a paunchy man I guessed to be in his late 50's introduced himself: "I'm Ed, Ed Edman."

"John, John Patrick," I said, wincing at the stench of liquor on his breath.

His head bobbing wildly, his broad face broke into a huge grin. "I'm a friend of C.R.'s and I damn near bought this place myself. I was just drivin' by and I was curious what you've done to it."

C.R., the wealthy retired oilman I had purchased the condo from the month before, said there were several people interested in buying but they weren't the kind of people he wanted to sell it to. Now perhaps I understood.

"Not much yet, but you're welcome to look around," I said, letting him in. "My decorator and I were just discussing some of the details."

"Old Ed's harmless," the decorator, John Wolf, told me later. "He lives off his dividends from his General Motors stock and just drinks all day."

"Sad."

Four days later, I ventured down the coast to The Lighted Tree, an open-air bar on Pass-A-Grille Beach, a thirty minute drive from the townhouse. As I passed through the opening in the rickety wooden fence that serves as the bar's entrance, I was greeted by the sight of Ed, in baggy shorts and a Hawaiian print shirt, perching on one of the stools, talking with some friends. I went to the opposite side of the bar and ordered a beer and, as it was being served, Ed noticed me. An expression of enormous pleasure consumed his face. It was the look of "I never expected to find someone like you in a place like this." He slid off his stool and joined me. We shook hands warmly, both confessing we'd been great deceivers. Neither of us, it seemed, on first meeting, had suspected the other's sexual preferences. To be seen in a gay bar is a matter of consent. Rarely did one wander into such a place by accident, especially one as inconspicuous from the street as The Lighted Tree.

After a few moments of idle chatter, Ed, lightly touching my forearm to make sure he had my attention, told me there was somebody I had to meet and dragged me to a table under the enormous banyan tree that towered over the property.

There, Sterling Grace was holding court. While Ed may have been slavish to the point of repugnancy, his friend Sterling had a way that made your eyes follow him right from the start, a manner that was unusually confident, even bold.

"I know C.R.," Sterling said after we exchanged pleasantries, "you can't trust him. His tone sounded sincere, yet his face was teasing: turtle eyes that blinked slowly but did not look away, a wide grinning mouth. He started questioning me about my new property. My answers made his eyebrows rise up in the middle, in what I took to be a look of genuine concern. Finally, nodding resignedly, he suggested, "Let me review the documents. You never know."

I agreed and he instructed me to call him at his office at Flagship Bank. As he and Ed prepared to move on, there were other things I noticed about Sterling: he was elegant, a person one didn't look down on; his clothes fit him well, everything falling to the exact length of his arms and legs. He wore a madras shirt, open at the collar, and tailored trousers. His silver hair was full and shiny, his eyebrows thick and nicely tapered.

Sterling gave Ed a stern look as the older man began his waddle out of the courtyard. I smiled and nodded. Sterling shook his head and pinched my elbow as he passed me.

The next day I called the bank. Sterling was out, playing golf according to his secretary. I left my number but before I hung up I asked, "Oh, and what is Mr. Grace's title?"

"Chairman of the board."

I knew I not only had come to the right church, I was also in the right pew.

When we finally connected, Sterling told me that it would be much more comfortable discussing the documents at his home and, by coincidence, the next night, due to a last-minute cancellation, he was available.

Driving through Pinellas County on most any multilane road,

the view numbs your mind: a sprawl of mobile home parks, warehouses, car showrooms, hubcap shops, condo complexes, retail malls, motels, franchise restaurants, office parks, drainage ponds, billboards, and signs promising girlsgirlsgirls dancing at the nearest bar. Finally, I pulled off the highway, turning on 38th Avenue into the Broadwaters section where the streets are lined with palms and oaks, a quiet area of upper middle-class homes. I stopped at the one with the Chinese red double doors where Sterling and Dennis Corr lived together.

The chairman and I had cocktails by the pool and I marvelled at the beauty of the place. Orchids grew amid live oaks dripping with Spanish moss.

"This is Dennis' night with his mother. Every Thursday," Sterling said, dropping the documents I had brought with me on a table next to his chair. He sighed, "God, I hate being alone." He sipped his martini and asked me what I did for a living.

"I once said that I made giant plinths for little men to stand on," I said.

"And what does that mean?"

"Public relations. I've always had to live in a showy, extravagant, public way."

"In a closet?" he laughed.

"Exactly." I stretched my legs and sighed, "But now that I've moved to Florida I'm free."

"Oh, I understand more than you think. Ed said you were married once."

"Yes, and I have two wonderful children. A boy and a girl."

"You see!" he hooted, clapping his hands. "Every time I meet someone who has been married it simply reinforces my view that there's no such thing as a homosexual or heterosexual person. There are only homo or heterosexual acts. People are a mixture of impulses, if not practices."

"I couldn't agree more. And what somebody does with a willing partner shouldn't be anyone else's business."

"Damn right!" As he poured more martinis, he glanced at his watch. "Oh, I must watch the news!"

Sterling led me into his luxurious bedroom where, conveniently enough, one of the two TV's in the house was located. The other was in Dennis' room. We were perched on the edge of his king-sized bed watching the weather report when his wandering hand found its place on my knee, then worked its way up my thigh to my groin. I sat there dumbfounded, at once enjoying the pleasure his kneading of my crotch was giving me and wondering where this might lead. When it came to the point of unzipping my trousers, I decided I needed another drink and got up to fix it. I was determined Sterling would find me hard-to-get.

He made no further advances that night. We went to the Sand Dollar for dinner and, as we were climbing into our separate cars in the parking lot, he grinned: "You've got to meet Dennis."

"I'd like that."

"He'd like it, I'm sure," he winked. "Yes, when I get back from Pennsylvania, we'll all go out to dinner."

"That'll be great."

A week later, on Wednesday, June 6, 1979, while Sterling was still out of town, a naked Dennis Corr was found dead at the big house with the Chinese red double doors. He had been stabbed over thirty times.

*

In those first few weeks after I moved to Florida, things felt tricky. I had divorced, my clandestine lover of six years had moved to San Francisco to live an openly gay life, and was suddenly alone. I felt ungrounded, lost, even though my parents lived an hour and a half away, content in their sprawling retirement villa in Sarasota near Siesta Key.

And having had so much sex over such a long period, I felt sexually deprived. Sterling Grace's offer of friendship and perhaps more momentarily relieved my agony. His attention seemed genuine and I thought I'd have some fun with it. When I began to visit bars, I had been immensely flattered that older men would pay attention to me, send me drinks, stroke me in all the right places. I was in my late 20's and it made me feel like a teenager. Then I came to the realization that the men did what they did indescriminately, that if the prey looked interesting, even in a minor way, go for it. And the more they had to drink, the more interesting a younger man looked to them.

After our first meeting, I knew Sterling had chased every swimsuit in town but still I couldn't stop myself: I was curious to see just how far it would go, especially if Dennis were to be part of the equation. I figured that what Sterling couldn't get on his own, perhaps he got with Dennis in tow.

But, suddenly, the lover I was to meet was dead and Sterling wasn't even in town.

Sterling's maid, arriving at 10 a.m., found blood on the driveway and in the garage. Then she found the body in the living room. Policeman William Doniel said they had not identified the weapon or a motive for the stabbing. He said there were no signs of struggle in the house. Police were not able to determine if anything was stolen but they were looking for Sterling's silver Mercedes 280SL. Neighbors told news reporters they heard nothing unusual in the night.

The obituary ran a day later. Dennis was 39 at the time of his death. He had come to St. Petersburg in 1968 from his native White Plains, New York and was a tax consultant and accountant. Survivors included his mother, Isabelle, three brothers, and a sister.

In the same edition of the newspaper, it was reported that police were waiting for Sterling's return from Pennsylvania and that they were not sure how long he had been there. Asked if they had any suspects in the case, a detective curtly replied, "There are some possibilities." Asked if the slaying possibly could be connected with business, the detective said, "it's being kept in mind." Immediately, the house had been sealed. A yellow rope drooped across the front lawn and circular driveway and up the sides of the wide lot.

By Saturday, Sterling had finally returned from Pennsylvania and had gone to police headquarters to be questioned. Doniel continued to dodge most of the reporters' questions with, "We're not going to discuss that. We will make the decision on what will be released to you and you can quote me on that."

As late as 3 p.m. the day before, Doniel had been reporting the Mercedes was still missing when in fact two St. Petersburg detectives had gone to Orlando to get the car after police there had found it. A source close to the investigation said that the car "was really messed up inside."

Relentlessly, reporters badgered police about why they were withholding information on the Corr murder. Doniel denied any facts were being covered up.

At the same time, he repeatedly answered, "This is part of the investigation," in response to questions about motive, condition of the room where the body was found, and location of the stab wounds. Doniel would not say whether Corr's body had any identification on it but he said Lt. Lee Pierce knew Corr and identified his face, as did other officers on the scene that knew him. It seems Dennis had been an accountant for a flying firm where several policemen took lessons and bought or rented airplanes.

"Informed sources" told the media that a struggle had apparently started in a bedroom of the house and the bloody trail led through the garage and back inside the house where Corr collapsed and died lying on the floor near the telephone.

I sent flowers to the Corr family and kept my distance. I assumed Sterling had become consumed by the obsessive interest in the police search for the killers that usually supersedes all else in the wake of tragedy. He didn't have long to stew.

*

On Wednesday, June 13, when Michael Gross, 25, a parolee from the Attica State Prison in New York, attempted to cash a travelers check at an Orlando shopping center, the store clerk alerted police. Credit cards, travelers checks and jewelry belonging to Corr and Sterling Grace were found in Gross' possession.

Gross had been with Mark Hunter and 15-year-old Dawne Marie Rosenbaur, both of Orlando, when he was arrested. During intense interrogation, these companions told police that Gross said he had met Corr while hitchhiking in the early morning hours of June 6 and went with him to the house on 38th Way South with the intent of robbing him.

Before long, Gross was on his way back to St. Petersburg to be to be charged with first-degree murder. Police records showed that in 1975 Gross was sentenced from zero to four years for escaping from Oswego County Jail. Following his first parole, Gross was returned to prison for a parole violation. He had been again paroled on April 16. It was not known when he came to St. Petersburg but police said he had been in spotted in Orlando on June 4. Asked if this arrest had cleared Sterling of any complicity in the murder, Doniel said, "We cleared him several days ago as far as I'm concerned."

At an advisory hearing before County Judge Frank H. White,

Gross, whom reporters described variously as "burly," "muscular" and "blond-haired," appeared sullen. In a nearly inaudible voice, Gross told White he did not have an attorney "at this time" but said he would hire one.

It seems that everything that happens must happen on television or else it barely happens at all; without the remote from the jailhouse, the arrest might not have been official. The drama unfolded at six and eleven over the next few days, tantalizing the public.

I sought to relieve my anxiety over the tragedy in the company of boys. I called Jack Dodge, owner of the only escort service in St. Petersburg.

"Yeah, the whole thing's pretty awful," he said about the murder. "I've heard about Grace but he's never called me. I guess it'd be beneath him."

"Yes," I said, "There's lots of ways of buying what you want and Sterling has mastered it. Wine 'em, dine 'em and bed 'em. I guess I'm just not social enough to pull that off."

"It's all in what you're used to," Jack chuckled.

Because, over the years, my time was limited in every city I visited on business, I found the services of boys who advertise and call themselves models useful. They were not the runaway kind; some were actors or dancers between engagements, others had lovely bodies and loved sex, performing well and cashing in on their hobby. A good model was not bothered by age, weight, height or kinky demands and they seemed to be honest, veritable saints compared to the kids on the street. As a businessman, I honored the prostitute as a professional, assisting me in exploring my sexuality. I had paid for a psychiatrist for therapy why not a boy? Now alone in Florida, the fact that I was single and able to cruise the bars didn't alter a position I had grown comfortable with. To order up a boy was convenient as well as surer and safer than spending hours sitting on a bar stool or cruising the parks.

It was Jack who introduced me to Kevin Duncan. Even for sleepy St. Petersburg, Kevin wasn't much of a catch. He was short, rail-thin, and had a pock-marked face. But he was beautifully hung, something that turned me on to an incredible degree. On our first night together, Kevin proved himself a remarkable topman, attentive to my orgasm before his own, and I invited him back, but always through Jack.

Although I disdained making a routine of it, I was able to enjoy Kevin almost weekly. He was a cuddly companion, surprisingly forthcoming about some of the people he knew. He told me that he had met Sterling when he was in high school. Through Sterling and Dennis, he was able to meet other socially prominent gays in the city and developed special relationships with several of them.

"I met Dennis first," he explained, "at the park, and I've kept up a relationship with them. They don't know I hustle on the side."

"I won't tell."

His small confidences were appreciated because from what he said, and what I had heard from others, a picture of the Grace/Corr relationship emerged. It was a form of moral anarchy that held them together, a fearful shared hatred of everything that was restrictive and which they felt to be false in the society they lived in and against the grain of the majority. They loathed and dispised straight people and their existence was a neverending contest with the straights who have such a virulent rage at everything not in their book. But they did it in a silent manner. No one was to know about their relationship or their sexual orientation. For Sterling especially, such knowledge would surely mean financial ruin. Theirs was a secret which could only be shared with those who felt like they did. The media, with the police not talking and little to go on, didn't bother to probe into the relationship. Sterling left for Europe.

*

At the end of August, the Corr murder case was back on page one. Gross, held in Pinellas County jail since his arrest, was accused of sexually assaulting his 22-year-old cellmate twice in three days. The alleged victim, who had been arrested on narcotics charges, said he didn't tell guards about the assaults sooner because he couldn't get out of the cell. Sheriff's officials said the attacks allegedly occurred "very, very early in the morning." The cellmate was forced by Gross to shave his legs and make a dress and bonnet out of a bedsheet and parade around the cell. The last straw, apparently, was when Gross made the boy assault his anus with a broomstick while he watched.

Jailing a murder suspect with persons charged with lesser crimes is not unusual, a spokesman said. "They're grouped as unconvicted felons. There's only so many places to put people. You can't break it down too far or there wouldn't be enough room."

At the end of October, Gross was in the news again. He had helped to instigate a riot at the jail. After that incident, officials decided to have Gross examined by psychiatrists to see if he was competent to stand trial. Gross' attorney, Paul Scherer, said the young man had a history of psychiatric problems since the age of 9 and hospitalizations, including suicide attempts, one of which occurred at the jail. However, jail spokesman Merrill Stebbins said he could find no record of such an attempt at the jail.

*

When his young lover decided to move to California, Jack felt it was time for a complete change. He calculated there was more money to be made in Fort Lauderdale and his move left Kevin and another of his popular tricks, Brett Lumhagen, at loose ends. These boys appealled to me because they seemed to have their heads screwed on right, renting out their bodies as supplements to their income from other jobs. Suddenly, with no local service available and few boys advertising, I decided to solidify my relationship with Kevin, of whom I had grown especially fond, by securing him a position as an artist at a publishing firm I had invested in that produced a high-end real estate publication.

Brett, on the other hand, presented an entirely different problem. He had met and fallen in love with Ronnie, a 19-year old blond who lived in Sarasota. A few weeks before, on one of his rare evenings out, Jack met me at a club where Brett was dancing. Ronnie was there and I was instantly smitten. The lithe youth wore white jeans that bulged admirably at the crotch and wore his cowboy hat cocked at a jaunty angle. My chances of scoring seemed slim, however, because he appeared to be totally in awe of Brett.

"That's the point," Jack told me. "He's so stuck on Brett we're thinking he'll do anything Brett tells him to do." The reason Jack was at the bar was to cement a business relationship with the two of them and if everything went according to plan, they would be available as a duo. I told him I wanted first crack at that action.

I encouraged Brett to move quickly on Ronnie. Sex with Brett had become predictable. For $50, Brett wouldn't waste any time on preliminaries. He was barely in the door before he was groping me.

Once I was aroused, he'd rush to the bedroom and I would follow a few minutes later, knowing I would find him lying face down on the bed, naked, a porn flick playing on the VCR. When he heard me on the steps, he would lift himself up and start rolling his hips in time with the insipid soundtrack of the video. I would slip out of my shorts and mount him from behind, jamming myself into him. "Oh, yeah!" he would moan, and masturbate as I took my pleasure. Most of the time, he didn't come but after a while it didn't matter; I felt nothing for him and wanted nothing but a release from my own tensions.

"It won't be long," Brett kept telling me, tantalizing me. Finally, he gushed with the news: "I'm getting him to move up here and live with me." Brett said it was easier for Ronnie to find a new job than it was for him. Brett had been working at a bank as a teller for some time and couldn't get a transfer. Besides, he didn't want to live in Sarasota.

"I can hardly wait," Brett said, smacking his lips.

"Neither can I," I said, remembering the blond hair and the sexy body.

*

The trial of Michael Gross for the murder of Dennis T. Corr began in late November.

In his opening statements to the jury, Jack Hellinger, assistant state attorney, said Corr was stabbed a total of 35 times, in the neck, in the heart, and again in the back after he was lying face down on the living room floor. He said Corr was last seen at the Sand Dollar restaurant on 34th Street South shortly after midnight on June 6 and Gross was spotted the same night at the Holiday Inn-South less than two miles from the restaurant.

In a surprise move, attorneys representing Gross persuaded the judge to forcibly bring Dennis' brother James to court. They said James had refused to answer questions and may have tried to evade a supoena. When he heard about the move, James appeared volunatrily at the courthouse. He said he did not want to make any comment without his attorney being present. Gross' attorney Paul Scherer said that in a deposition, James acknowledged Dennis was his brother and he did not know Gross. Beyond that, he refused to answer any other questions, pleading protection of the Fifth

Amendment. The unanswered questions included queries about his criminal record, his knowledge of his brother's friends and whether he killed his brother or suspected someone else of the murder.

James, 41, was released from a federal prison camp at Eglin Air Force Base in October 1978 after serving a light sentence for perjury, wire and mail fraud, and making false statements to a bank. According to an article in the Washington Post, while he was in prison, James was suspected of masterminding a run on the stock of CHB Foods.

Finding this skeleton in the closet, the attorneys for the defense were claiming to reporters that Gross had been framed for the murder.

On the third day of the trial, Pinellas County Medical Examiner Joan Wood testified that the stabbing was "a sex crime," basing her opinion on the fact that Corr was nude, had been stabbed more than 30 times, and that there was an indication of semen in his mouth. Corr had an alcohol blood level of .119. According to Dr. Wood, to have a blood level that high, one would have to consume 5.2 ounces of liquor or 5.2 beers within an hour on an empty stomach.

The doctor indicated that Corr made a frantic effort to ward off his attacker. "His arms and hands had been sliced 10 times, leaving defense wounds." He had more defense wounds than any stabbing victim she had encountered. Corr died from multiple stab wounds that pierced his heart, liver, lungs and severed two main blood vessels in his neck. Wood believed Corr caught up with Gross in the garage as he was trying to escape with the loot and the car and Corr tried to stop him. After the initial attack, Corr ran into the house and was stabbed several more times while slumped on the living room floor. Corr's bloody palm print, found on a wall in the house, supported her theory.

During cross examination of Sterling, who was the state's first witness, Scherer questioned him about inheriting money from Corr's estate and his relationship with the dead man. Scherer asked for a mistrial when Circuit Judge Maynard Swanson stopped him from probing too deeply into the Grace-Corr relationship. Swanson refused the request and said the information was irrelevant and might inflame the jury.

Sterling denied he was the chief beneficiary of Corr's estate and said there would not be enough money in the estate to cover expenses. He said he returned a $25,000 note to Corr's mother and that she will also have the proceeds from a $50,000 life insurance policy on Corr's life. Sterling denied living with Corr on a permanent basis but acknowledged that Corr kept clothing and had a bedroom in the murder house.

Scherer was the third defense attorney appointed to represent Gross. Assistant Public Defender Robert Dillinger withdrew as Gross' lawyer in August. A week after the judge appointed Joseph Ciarciaglino to represent Gross, the counselor was held hostage in Gross' escape attempt which resulted in a riot at the jail.

In a sworn statement to St. Petersburg Police Sgt. Richard Evans, Gross claimed he met a man at The Sherwood Lounge in downtown St. Petersburg and they got to talking. The man asked him if he would "like to make some money" by robbing queers. Gross said sure. The man took him to Williams Park and pointed out Corr, who was cruising in his Cadillac. The man directed Gross to sit on a bench and look at Corr as he drove by. Gross told Evans that Corr picked him up, took him to the house and made sexual advances. The other man had followed them and was waiting outside, Gross claimed, and when he finished performing for Corr, he left and let the mystery man in. What happened in the house he claimed to have no knowledge of. Gross said he hitchhiked back to Williams Park and when the man returned he gave Gross a folder containing credit cards and travelers checks, a watch and some jewelry. Then the man drove Gross to Orlando in Sterling's Mercedes. However, during his testimony, Gross gave conflicting descriptions of what this mystery man looked like.

A man who asked not to be named said he picked up Gross a day or two before Dennis was murdered. "It shocked me," he said. "The whole thing. To think it could've been me! He is strictly a street person. He talks with a deep Eastern accent and sounds like a high-school dropout. By that I mean, he knows nothing about nothing. He's muscular, rough-hewn, and dresses casually, like somebody who had just walked off the beach. I wouldn't have thought him to be gay, just a hustler. He impressed me as a guy who knew a quick way to pick up fifty dollars."

The prosecution subpoenaed 67 witnesses for the trial. One of them testified only Gross' fingerprints were lifted from Sterling's Mercedes. Another, Gross' girlfriend, Marie Dawne, testified that in Orlando before his arrest, she and Gross had associated with a group that frequently used stolen credit cards and travelers' checks to get money. She said that Gross told her he had been hitchhiking when a homosexual picked him up and "was touching him." Dressed in jeans and a beige T-shirt, Gross sat quietly through the third day of the trial. But in the hallway during a recess, he acknowledged his former girlfriend. "Hi Michael," she said, waving. "I miss you."

When Gross waved, the girl turned to a friend, delighted. "Can you believe it," she squealed. "He actually waved."

*

"I didn't kill anybody," Michael Gross testified in a taped interview played at the trial.

A former cellmate disagreed. He testified that Gross had told him that he did kill someone. "He asked me if I had served in Vietnam," the inmate said. "I said, 'Yes,' and he said, 'Didn't you kill someone for the government? If anyone's a murderer, you are. I kill someone and they want to put me in the electric chair.'"

Thomas Davis, a county jailer, testified that when Gross had been moved to a private cell he asked why he was being isolated. After telling him that other inmates charged with similar crimes were not isolated, Davis said Gross told him: "Yeah, they haven't killed a rich banker like I have. You know, Mr. Davis, before they burn me for this one I don't want a special meal, just a good piece of ass."

*

Judge Swanson refused to allow Grace to be recalled as a witness. Acknowledging that Police detective Gary Hitchcox had testified that Grace admitted he and Corr had a homosexual relationship, Swanson felt there was no evidence that Sterling killed or hired someone to kill Dennis. He said that he would allow Sterling to be re-examined only on the grounds that he could see "how it could add to the search for the truth in some fashion and not just unncessarily tear down the reputation of a prominent businessman in this community."

But Scherer wasn't satisfied. "I've never seen a homicide case in which there is a person who has a close relationship like this one and is not an automatic suspect in the crime," he fumed. In his summation, he said "there is so much pressure to burn somebody in this case, I can't believe it. You think jealousy isn't a motive? Running around isn't a motive?" he asked jurors after speculating that Corr and Grace might have had an argument about their relationship. The prosecution countered that even if someone could prove Grace was not in Pennsylvania, the banker had no reason to want Corr dead and would not have picked "the worse way in the world to do it -at his home."

Scherer argued that prosecutors had failed to present any physical evidence placing Gross at the scene of the crime. He described his client as an "incompetent criminal" who couldn't use stolen traveler's checks and credit cards without getting caught, yet got charged with a murder that had "all the marks of a hit man."

The jury disagreed and, on Friday, November 30, after four and a half hours of deliberation, they found Michael Gross guilty of first degree murder. On the following Monday, the jury recommended life over death for Gross.

Roger Maas, one of Gross' attorneys, said that despite the conviction, there were too many unanswered questions in the case for the jury to recommend death.

As he stood before the judge for sentencing, Gross addressed the court for the first time. He said, "I just want to maintain my innocence."

"It is the opinion of this court that the evidence in this case would have amply supported a verdict in judgment of death," the judge told Gross, then sentenced him to a mandatory 25 years before he would be eligible for parole. "Someday I hope you will consider that your life was spared through an act of mercy by your fellow citizens and not because of an act on your part, because your acts do not justify any consideration as a human being in any way whatsoever."

*

In early January, while Sterling was once more vacationing in Europe, Gross was on trial again for trying to escape from the jail and instigating a riot.

The six-member jury heard two former inmates testify that Gross was an active participant in the riot and they saw him trying to pry open windows with the base of a fan.

One inmate revealed at one time he had been Gross' cellmate and that Gross had talked to him several times about escaping so that he could "take care of some business." That business, the cellmate charged, was to terminate witnesses against him.

Gross' former attorney, Joseph Ciarciaglino, held as a hostage with two jail guards, testified that Gross protected him while "crazies" talked about throwing the fingers of hostages out a window. He said Gross had armed himself with a broom handle and was planning to fight anyone who tried to harm him. The attorney acknowledged that his head had been covered when he was captured and that he was unable to see what Gross and others were doing.

The jury found Gross guilty of trying to escape but not rioting. Gross was sentenced to 15 years for attempted escape, to be served concurrent with his life sentence.

A month later, Gross' trial for assaulting the cellmate began. A breathless hush fell over the courtroom as the victim twice bowed his head and hesitated before describing the assaults to the six-member jury, two men and four women. He said that Gross ordered him to a shower in their cell, place a broomstick in his own rectum, and parade in front of other inmates. Gross told him that he had studied karate for 19 years and could kill him with one blow if he did not obey. The young man said Gross was angry because he had referred to Gross as a murderer. During the two days after the first assault, the young man said Gross beat him severely and forced him to sexually assault himself a second time. He said he didn't fight back for fear he would be killed.

While several other inmates testified to corroborate the victim's story, 125 wide-eyed students from Clearwater Central Catholic High School government classes, in attendance to observe, shot quick glances at one another as they listened to details of the assaults.

After being found guilty by the jury, Gross was asked if he wanted to speak before sentencing. He said, "I will say it the next time I come back."

"There won't be a next time," Judge Philip Federico said. "I'm going to sentence you now." And proceeded to add 75 years in jail to Gross' string of sentences.

*

On an unseasonably hot day near the end of June, Sterling was on my porch, peering through the screen into the living room.

My daughter, visiting me for the summer, was watching TV. Suddenly she cried, "Dad, somebody's looking for you."

I rushed to the sliding glass doors, opened them and went to the door of the screened porch.

"You're looking great," I told Sterling, but I was being kind. He had become a mass of wrinkles; the misery of his new life, a life without Dennis, had withered him.

"...I just wanted to make sure you knew Ed and I are building a place up the beach."

"Yes. I'd heard."

"They'll have construction finished in a couple of weeks."

"I've driven by several times but I never saw you."

"I've been traveling. I had to after the trial."

"Well, you're back and we're going. The kids are here for the summer and I'm taking them to Europe."

"I just got back."

"I know. I keep up with you in the papers."

"Ah, yes, the papers," he said, eyes downcast.

In May, I had read that Sterling had retired as the chairman of Flagship Banks, a position he had held since 1964. "Sterling had been thinking about this for some time," the bank's president was quoted as saying, indicating the intention had predated Dennis' murder. Sterling could not be reached for comment. The president thought he was "traveling in Europe."

"I'll see you when I get back," I told him.

"Yes, the house'll be done and it'll be like old times."

"Almost."

"Yes, almost."

I touched his arm as he left and smiled, letting him know in a small way that I was sharing his suffering, the torture of his loss.

At least the jury had spared Sterling the agony of endless appeals holding up execution. It had saved the state money because, in actuality, studies have shown that keeping a man locked up for life is cheaper than going through the appeal-laden process. Perhaps, in Bible-belt St. Petersburg, the jury had followed the New Testament injunctions against killing, the plea for forgiveness. Perhaps they knew Camus's famous argument that no murder's deed can compare with the evil of capital punishment, "the most premeditated of murders." But it would seem that with immediate death, the debt would have been paid. It would be an equivalizer, an eye for an eye. The desire for revenge is the ugliest emotion in the human psyche, but it often collapses into something almost poignant, the longing to find a shred of conscience in people whose moral capacity is grotesquely diminished. Why did they do this? they ask, and they pore over criminal records and family histories hunting for answers, for any trace of that sympathetic faculty by which one person can know and even suffer another's pain. Murder becomes a measure of one's own moral capacity. Many find themselves wanting. Their innocence had been stripped away, their values and beliefs had been badly gouged, if not wrecked. In Sterling's case, a lifetime spent securing social position had been destroyed. More importantly, perhaps, evil was not apart from him anymore, only occurring to other people. It had stolen into his home, seeped deep into his heart. He had to live with the vengeful impulse to return death for death, and, conversely, had to find the resolve to hold himself back. In extremes of emotion, nothing is black and-white. In this area of a multitude of grays, Sterling wandered. One moment, clamoring for the executioner, the next for forgiveness. His anguish had become, for me, personal. It was, in a strange way, family. I shared with Sterling the understanding of how difficult it was to admit one desired a member of one's own sex. We both had fought it for years, had dated women, found the experience wanting, had returned to men. And we both had found love.

We had become wounded people, struggling to go on. For some, picking up the burden of catastrophe is more than they can endure. They retreat into a shell or, ultimately, commit suicide. Others are able to find that delicate balance between the yearning to remember and the need to forget. For some, it helps to ritualize connections with the murdered person. For Sterling it was travelling, visiting places he had enjoyed with Dennis. For me, it was in the company of whores.

3

It was the time of day I enjoy the most, when it seems to be hanging on for the last moment. The last rays of the sun illuminated the western sky. It was yellow-blue pink. The birds appeared at their most graceful, fluttering darkly against a pale sky. I wanted to believe it wouldn't get dark, that the moment would last forever. The kids had gone home, back to school, and, after a hectic summer, I was alone again, taking my solitary walks on the beach again. I walked northward, up the beach and, as I passed Sterling and Ed's, two redwood and glass townhouses stuck together, an extravagant duplex, Ed was walking from one to the other. He waved at me, then called me over. Within moments, I was taking a tour of the place, ending up at the bar in Sterling's living room, drinking a martini.

Inside, it was cozy. The small room had an antique golden glow to it on that night, at dusk. Warm, dusty, with Sterling's stereo playing softly. Classical.

"How's he doing?" I asked.

"Oh, better. Much better now that he's moved in here."

"It's a shame that boy is still alive," I said.

"You know, I've never heard him ask for the bastard to die. 'The jury had spoken,' he'd say."

As Ed was finishing his revelation that Sterling had been "dating" a number of handsome young men, the banker returned with one of them in tow, a fellow introduced to me as Chris.

Ed shuffled off to his own side of the duplex. Sterling invited me to dinner. I went home, changed, and met them at the Wine Cellar.

"I've accepted a trusteeship at my alma mater," Sterling said after we were served our drinks. "I'm working on funding scholarships for young attorneys. That and golf and sailing, I'll survive."

Through the various courses, beautifully presented by Otto, Sterling's favorite waiter, I realized that Grace's understanding of what had happened enabled him to go on, to do something with his life, because he needed to do something, if only to fend off the full experience of loss. More than grief, he needed to save himself from his own powerlessness. If murder was a book of lessons in fragility, ephemeral happiness, the irreversible arrow of fate, the hardest lesson of all was that life is not organized around human needs; for everything he could control, there were a million he could not. For a control-freak such as Sterling, it was a hard lesson but he learned it.

Chris, a soft-spoken young man, rarely entered into the conversation. When we left the restaurant, we got into our separate cars and for a moment, seeing the two of them drive off, I envied Sterling for the first time in over a year.

*

"You know," I said to Sterling after dinner at the Lobster Pot, "after comparing lives with you for years I see how I've been losing: all the while I've met a different gauge of boy from yours."

"This is because you have one kind of cry today and another tomorrow. One kind of man today and another kind tomorrow." His hand slid into my crotch.

"So, what kind of man is it today?" I asked.

"A real man."

It had been two weeks since I had watched him drive off with one of a line of cuties willing to sleep with him for a favor.

My curiosity had gotten the better of me. Or perhaps it was the martinis before dinner, the wine at dinner, and the Black Russians afterward. Whatever it was, I permitted him to undress me.

He blew in my ear as he played with my cock. "Hmmm," he said when he pulled back and took a long look at it. "Your cock's like mine." He paused, sliding the foreskin back tight against the shaft, and admiring it further. "Except it's bigger." And then he went down on it. When it was hard, he stood up and he brought his own cock to my lips. I shook my head and told him, "No, just fuck me," and I sprawled on the sofa, flat on my stomach.

After a couple of Black Russians, it seemed I didn't care, my anus became a slit softening to his pressure. His scent was sweaty. Not athletic sweat but intellectual sweat. Roughly, his perpsiring hands where all over my ass, my back, then my chest. He tweaked my nipples and twisted the hair in my armpits. Burying his face in my back, he kissed my skin and tugged at my earlobes, bathing me in his spittle. I bent over further and his entire sex slid into me. "Oh, yeah," he cried. His hands found my balls, then my cock. He pumped my cock furiously but I couldn't come.

As I lost my erection completely, he pressed my body into the cushions and kept at it, his hands firmly planted on my asscheeks. I'm not sure he came; he just, eventually, pulled his cock from me and went to the bathroom. My ears pounded. I heard a whirr in my head like a cowboy whirling a lasso, the hollow rope whipping through air. As he slipped into his bathrobe, he seemed to be speaking with far-seeing clarity but I wasn't listening. I had made a mess of everything. I'd been too easy. I felt violated, like a little erotic trinket, the latest charm dangling from his bracelet. It was not comforting to think that he would have had to have worn a necklace not a bracelet though because he'd been at it so long. Woozy, a little high, I hurried home.

The sky was faintly dotted with stars. The moon was barely a sliver. My feet sunk into the wet sand. The birds had found beds for the night. Soon I would be in my own bed.

Dawn came streaking across the sky and into my room, exposing itself to me. I huddled under the blanket, examining my body with my hands. My ass ached but I had no visible scars. I touched myself and grew hard just thinking about what happened. After all, sex is sex.

I flung open the window and the cool air cleansed my lungs. Seeing a fat tabby sitting on the seawall, complacently preening itself, seeing the world through squinted eyes, all satisfied, I thought of Sterling.

*

A week later, Sterling had a party, "Sunday at the beach," he said. There was a mob of people, "a prestigious circle of friends," I was assured, but only one appealed to me: Scott, a dark-haired collegiate type with beautiful teeth. Before Sterling introduced us, he warned me that the boy was having trouble with his lover and had come to the party alone. He also revealed that he had taken an interest in the boy's dilemma and that interest had led to several assignations on his couch. "He's a good lay," Sterling assured me.

Scott and I sat drinking at the round metal table on the lanai and got acquainted. Suddenly, he asked for a ride home. I told him I had not driven, since I lived only three houses away, but I would be glad to take him home. We escaped through the screen door and walked southward, without saying goodbye to our host. We slipped out of our loafers and, as the waves crashed and rolled under our feet, I put my arm around around his shoulder and he hugged me tightly to his youthful body. When we arrived at my house, he smiled boyishly with a tenderness that invited me to kiss him.

In my bedroom, he was hungry for it and without even getting completely undressed I gave it to him, on his back so he could watch me. He didn't touch me, just jacked himself off as I screwed him. It was quick, a matter of moments rather than minutes. And then I drove him to his apartment and wished him luck with his lover.

Days passed. Sterling didn't call. Finally, I called him. Scott was the subject. I got the idea: I wasn't to bother what Sterling thought was his property. I apologized but was confused. Sterling had so many, what was one, more or less? I was saddened by my own naivete. I hadn't read the signs. I hadn't paid my respects. To see only with the eyes is blindness.

*

It was unbearably humid and boiling.

I walked up the beach and a handsome young man clad only in a tight bikini was securing the lines on Sterling's catamaran. I remembered him from the bars in Tampa but couldn't recall his name.

"Hi, John," he said familiarly. "I just moved in."

"Small world," I mumbled, still trying to place him. "Ed around?"

"Ed? Are you kidding? He's probably at Baxter's by now."

I remembered that on most days Ed started drinking at noon, hitting several straight bars on his way to Tampa and Baxter's for the cocktail hour. To everyone's amazement, he always returned home safely.

"Joe still talks about you," the young man said.

"How is Joe?" Suddenly, it came back to me. I remembered. Joe, a pretty young blond, had separated with his lover and was living with this young man, who I now remembered was named Kenny, when I met him.

"Back with his lover," Kenny smiled.

"I'm glad to hear that." It seemed I was always a stepping stone for a boy to return to his lover. But, still, they talk about me. Queer.

After Kenny fixed me a screwdriver, Sterling arrived and it seemed like old times. The reasons for our falling out seemed to vanish as Sterling rejoiced in flaunting his new live-in lover. The invitation to dinner came and I accepted. We went to the Lobster Pot and Kenny was attentive to his new partner, listening as Sterling outlined a scheme whereby Kenny could take over the clientele of the office supply company he was working for and start his own business. Sterling agreed to supply the capital and buy a condo in Tampa. "Ah, yes," he sighed, "we'll have the beach house and the apartment in town, just like the folks did back fifty years ago."

Being with them and seeing their blissful existence put me in a horny state. Later that night, I went to the Old Plantation, a favorite hangout for collegiates. The college boys I had met there were notorious losers. Good-looking, sharply dressed, athletic, but worried about getting into a course, writing a paper, passing an exam, adjusting. Preoccupied with problems: school, part-time job, parents, bills. Yet they were at the peak of their beauty. I was drawn to them but repelled by them at the same time.

At first I mistook Jimmy for another collegiate. He could of been, but he'd dropped out of high school. I noticed someone I knew had engaged him in conversation for a long time and I asked him to intervene and introduce us. When he did, I reached out to shake Jimmy's hand and knocked his drink out of his hand instead. Booze flew onto his trousers. He ducked into the john to repair himself and when he returned, I had a new drink and an apology ready. He accepted both. After several minutes, he agreed to go home with me.

Intoxicated with the youthfulness of my companion, I didn't need anything more to drink when we arrived at the condo but I poured one anyway. Jimmy lit up a joint. I left the drink sitting on the bar untouched and, as Jimmy got high, I got high on the magnificence of his body. It was of the type I prefer, thin, yet nicely sculpted, with minimal body hair. When I finally got around to slipping his cock from its resting place in his jeans, he was hard and eager to be sucked. I could have sucked the thin, yet ample cock all night long. But Jimmy had other ideas. He wanted to get fucked. Dazzled, I took him on the living room floor, then eventually we got to the bedroom where I discovered another of Jimmy's proclivities, he also loved to fuck. It was a match made in heaven, I felt, and I orgasmed a second time as he slammed into me.

The next day, I drove Jimmy back to Tampa and left him at a friend's, but not before making a date for later in the week. A dinner date. If I didn't have to pay him, the least I could do was feed him.

*

Seeing Jimmy occasionally hardly quenched my appetite for sex. In fact, it increased it. I continued to call Brett. Ronnie had in fact moved to St. Petersburg but was still only lukewarm to the idea of a three-way. I suggested that perhaps I could pay them to pose for a photo layout. "Start out simple, just in bikinis, and then see what develops," I proposed to Brett. I decided a photo of Ronnie was better than nothing. Several days later, Brett called me back. Ronnie had agreed.

They came to the condo and we had drinks. As Ronnie raved about the place and became flirtatious, Brett began to grow uneasy. He suggested we get on with the photography.

They stripped to their bikini underwear and got onto the bed. Brett lead the way, whispering into Ronnie's ear as he carressed his lighty furred body. I snapped away as I watched them go down on each other. I marvelled at Ronnie's succulent cock, a good nine inches cut, tapering to a thick base, and zoomed in on it as it slipped in and out of Brett's eager mouth. Having had enough of the 69-ing, Brett, always horny, mounted his lover and began fucking him in the missionary position. I was able to get several close-ups of the entry and then put the camera down. My erection was straining my shorts and I could take no more. When Brett saw me stroking myself he said, "Hey, bring that big meat over here."

I stood with my legs pressed against the bed as Brett sucked me while he continued to fuck his lover. Before long, Brett decided he wanted me in him while he was in Ronnie and he pressed himself tight against his lover. I mounted them and slid my cock deep into Brett's tight ass. Sensing Ronnie's delight at this turn of events, Brett decided we should switch places. It was the opening I had been waiting for, in more ways than one. Since Brett had paved the way, my cock slid into Ronnie down to the base without stopping. Brett watched me as I plowed into his lover and took several photos of us, then mounted me. It was the first time I had experienced being fucked while fucking. I came quickly and pulled away from them so that Brett could finish in his lover. Once Brett had come, we took turns at Ronnie's cock until he came.

When they left, I gave them each a $50 tip. It was more than worth it and I had the photos besides.

*

Jimmy posed for my camera as well, but he wouldn't go nude. It was just as well, I reasoned because he had revealed that he had been in the bar with a fake ID. He was really only 17.

"Seventeen going on thirty," I grumbled. I had been amazed at the youth's drug intake. I was no stranger to drugs. During the years of my marriage, I had sought escape not only with alcohol but with cocaine and marijuana as well.

I found that drugs became an intrinsic part of the ritual. "Strictly for recreational purposes," I would say to Jimmy. I found having it available encouraged youths to enjoy my company and besides, it heightened my orgasm to an incredible degree.

Taking my lead from Sterling, I sought to create something to bind Jimmy to me. I gave the boy a job delivering the real estate magazines. This meant he had to come to St. Petersburg twice a week. It was a perfect set-up.

Then one afternoon, Jimmy had been on his way to see me when Kenny was also coming from Tampa on the Howard Franklin Bridge, on his way to Sterling's. Kenny had cruised the boy and they pulled their cars off the freeway at Park Street and, parking at a remote end of the Gayfer's department store parking lot, in the middle of the day, Kenny blew my little friend to orgasm. When he told Kenny where he was headed, Kenny figured out he was coming to see me. Kenny made him promise not to tell me. Jimmy didn't, for several days.

What a mockery, I thought. Kenny's living with Sterling yet he's hustling every pretty young thing he can find, including mine. Maybe things weren't so blissful for Sterling after all, but whatever fun he was having he deserved it.

4

Florida is not its best in the summer. With each day a carbon copy of the last, temperatures hovering in the 90's, it's too uncomfortable to leave the house during the day and claustrophobia sets in. One lives for the nights, for a pleasant dinner with friends, then a trip to the parks, the baths or the bars. Fearful of the parks and bored by the baths, I made a circuit of the bars, usually ending up at my favorite in the late '70s, the Kikki in downtown Tampa. It had the lack of pretension, the sleazy ambiance that always makes me feel at home. When it was finally condemned in the name of urban renewal, the bartender Floyd and his following moved to the Carousel Club on West Platt, where amid chaos and ugliness, there always seemed to be a modicum of beauty. On a steamy night in August 1984, I was following my usual practice of taking in the entirety of it and, within that, disregarding the things that disgusted me and concentrating on the things that seemed to grow more lovely with every drink. Suddenly, at the opposite end of the bar, I saw a new face, a fine face, one that inspired me to rise and take a closer look. I stood behind him and drank in the sight of the young lean, beautifully tanned torso and, when he turned to see who was staring at him, the sly smile. He wore no shirt and I admired the highly developed pectorals. The jeans were filthy and he showed no basket but his face was divine, his dishwater-blond hair falling over it because of an unflattering cut. Considering the totality of it, I knew with a bit of scrubbing, a bit of polish, this could be a diamond.

At first, he was paying unusual attention to the balding, 50-ish man sitting at the bar to his left. I observed the interplay for a while until finally the man got up to go to the john. My desire for the boy was so great that I threw caution completely to the wind and approached him. "Whatever he's paying, I'll double it."

The boy blinked, shook his head incredulously, then smiled. "Okay." Saying nothing more, he reached up and yanked his t-shirt from a rafter above the bar and began moving towards the exit.

As we approached my Mercedes roadster, he chuckled, "Oh, yeah."

"I like it," I said, unlocking my door and hitting the button to open his.

As he slid into the leather bucket seat, he asked, "Where do you live?"

"At the beach," I replied.

"All right," he said emphatically, then introduced himself as "Tracy."

During the 45 minute ride to the beach, he laid his history on me: he was from Texas, had only been in town a short time, had a job at Intertel fixing phone lines and his car had broken down so he had no way to get there. I vowed if I had anything to do with it, he wouldn't have to return to that job.

After a drink at my bar, we retreated to the bedroom and I went to relieve myself. When I returned to the bedroom, he was sitting on the edge of the bed nude. He wrapped his arms around my torso and hugged me, then proceeded to devour my cock. In my heightened state of sexual hunger, I came very quickly, but not without appreciating the quality of his efforts. He seemed to have no desire for me to reciprocate so I joined him under the covers and he fell asleep in my arms. The next morning, he repeated the process, this time jacking off to climax as he blew me. At the height of our passion, I asked him to stay a few days. This involved picking up his things, which were, to use his phrase, "stored" at a man's apartment in Tampa. He told me he lied about the car, he didn't own one, and had lost his job at Intertel. He reminded me of Jean Genet's line, "For a time I lived by theft, but prostitution was better suited to my indolence."

We went to the man's apartment and I witnessed my young lover's ability to open a door by sliding a credit card between the lock and the jam. I knew then I would never be safe from him. Still, he was quite methodical about taking only those things that he said were his and left a note for the man. On the way home, we stopped at a department store and I bought him a few new items of wardrobe, then got his hair cut and highlighted. That night, dressed for dinner, he was absolutely stunning. We celebrated our good fortune with a bottle of champagne. When we returned home, he hurriedly undressed me and began blowing me. When I was hard, he undressed himself, laid face down on the bed and moved his hips seductively, offering up the prize he had not shared with me to that point. I kissed the ass cheeks, then invaded the space between them, first with my tongue, then with fingers coated with lube. Before long, I was charging my swollen flesh deep into his anus and he was bucking to meet every stroke. I wanted it to continue long into the evening but I came quickly, so excited was I at finding such a perfect sexual match. I crushed him with my spent body and he kissed me lasciviously on the face and lips.

The next night, after a late supper, we lay beside each other on the chaise longue on the deck, a salty gulf breeze blowing. I entered him gently and soon his cum was gleaming in the moonlight, splattered against his thigh. Palm tree shadows skittering across my tanned skin, he let me finish inside of him and I went crazy with it. Later, he said he wanted to watch a movie on TV so I went to bed. I switched off the light and the moon was like a lamp outside, illuminating the ripples of the Gulf. I closed my eyes and fell asleep at once, like the falling of a shutter in a camera which ends a time exposure. I dreamt and it was a nightmare of images. When Tracy opened the door, I woke with a start. "I'm sorry," he said, cuddling next to me.

"I'm not," I said, rolling over on top of him. He held me as I moved into position between his legs and rubbed my cock against his. I kissed him violently on the mouth and he squirmed under the pressure.

In a few moments, he reached for the grease from the nightstand. I got on my knees as he applied it to himself, lifting his legs to the ceiling. I entered him slowly and he wrapped his legs around me. Kissing him all the while, I came quickly. We lay there in each others arms and I fell asleep again. I slept peacefully and, if I dreamt, I didn't remember it the next morning.

Around noon, Tracy got up and as he was coming down the stairs, still nude, I sat at the table eating a swiss cheese sandwich on pale crusty bread, slathered with mayo. I felt like Isak Dinesen, who only ate white food. The beautiful blond boy dropped to the cushion of one of the bar stools, just staring at me, a look in his eyes that was at once hopeful and desperate. I smiled, almost as if saying to myself: Take it easy. This too shall pass. But I knew it wouldn't pass quickly, not this time.

It had been two days of bliss. The monotony, the ennui of the summer had been erased in a single, decisive stroke. I knew what I was doing.

As he approached me, I held out my arms. He kissed me as he

lowered himself into my lap. In a matter of moments, he was on his knees between my legs, fellating me with an eagerness that shocked me. I closed my eyes, sighed deeply and prayed that this one not pass quickly.

In order to keep Tracy, I knew I had to invent something for him to do. He was enamored of my computer so I took over the fulfillment operations of the real estate magazine. Like everything else he took up, he became immediately proficient at coding the subscriptions and processing the labels. A routine developed. In the morning, he would work at the computer, then take my second car, the Corvette, to the bank and post office. Our lunch consisted of wine, sandwiches and sex, usually him simply blowing me but sometimes a full blown fuck, depending on his whim. Then he would run on the beach and go swimming in the Gulf while I worked. Dinner was a fancy affair at a fine restraurant. I loved to watch him eat, his appetite was enormous. Afterward, we'd bar hop, see a movie, go shopping or just go home. The affection seemed to flow out of him: He could never ride with me without holding my hand; I could never stop spending money on him.

Evening always ended with his payment to me, namely the fuck, usually with him on his stomach, moaning in ecstasy with my every stroke. As the summer turned into fall, we flew off to Key West for Fantasy Fest, California for Thanksgiving, and New York for Christmas shopping. It seemed I had found the tonic for my boredom in the person of a loving 20-year-old.

But having Tracy with me presented a problem because several months before I met him, both Kevin and Jimmy had taken permanent lovers and, to fill the void, I established a business relationship with Ronnie. After our initial three-way photo session, Ronnie would occasionally call seeking funds. It seemed he was forever broke. I agreed to sex for $50 but questioned what would happen if Brett found out. "What he doesn't know don't hurt him," was always Ronnie's comeback. Eventually the two called it quits as a couple and Ronnie moved back to Sarasota and it happened that it wasn't just $50 he needed, it was a car. I bought him one, telling him he could work off the payments. He understood completely.

Once a week, I would leave early for my drive to Sarasota, ostensibly to see my parents for dinner and, late in the afternoon, stop at the Tropical Palms Motel, renting room Number 7-A. The woman who owned the place gave me a "day" rate, $20 cash, knowing I'd only use it for an hour or so. In the summer, I would call ahead and ask her to turn the window air conditioner on so the room would be cool when I got there. It was worth the five dollar tip. I'd get to the motel early, have a drink, snort some coke and wait for Ronnie to come and make his car payment.

After Ronnie and I talked, we did a few lines of coke, then I would make the first move, stroking his thigh, which was usually naked since he invariably wore clingy nylon running shorts. I would work my fingers up under the filmy fabric and into his crotch. When he became aroused, we would lift ourselves from the bed and strip naked. Then he would lie down on his back and I would shove a pillow under his ass. Sliding between his legs, I would suck his cock, usually for about five minutes. While Brett had a stubby, ordinary cock, Ronnie's was a true sucking dick and I would have been happy to worship it for hours, but when I felt Ronnie could stand it no more, I scrambled onto my knees, applied lube to my fingers and prepared his anus for my assault. I hoisted his legs over my shoulders and took his firm, lightly hairy buns into my hands. As I slowly entered him, he began to masturbate. It usually took less than two minutes for him to come and then I lowered myself onto his chest and, holding him in my arms, I finished. I enjoyed this part the most because I kissed him full on the mouth, sometimes three or four times, then lay in his arms briefly. I felt a oneness with him that I liked to think went beyond sex-for-hire. It was the only time Ronnie actually touched me physically. I had stoically accepted the fact that I was a convenience to him, a hands-off, second hand user of what he had so abundantly to offer: sex. But, occasionally, there would be a glimmer of something more. "I love you but I'm not in love with you," he told me once. "I appreciate everything you've done for me."

On those rare occasions when Ronnie would drive up to see me rather than the other way around, he would mention that he'd either seen Brett at the bar or was going to stop and see him while he was in town. Afterward, Brett would call me and recount every breathless detail of their encounter. "He may've just been with you, but he had plenty left."

I told him I was glad to hear that. "Nothing worse than a limp Ronnie."

"Haha! That'll be the day!"

In a way, it excited me to think that I had prepared Ronnie for his assignation with Brett, confident that while I had been the active one in our encounter, Ronnie would have had to play the aggressor with Brett. "It wasn't like that in the beginning," Ronnie told me once, "but that's what it became. Yeah, it was really boring."

It seemed the worst thing in the world for Ronnie was to be bored. I sometimes fantasized what it would be like to have him around all the time but the reality of it was I would have been a basket case just trying to deal with his boredom as well as my own. No, I reasoned, it was better this way, once a week, "slam bang, thank you, sir." And, as it turned out, I outlasted all of Ronnie's lovers, with the exception of Brett, of course, who was, after all, his first and only true love.

After Tracy moved in, my needs were fulfilled and I begged off the weekly ritual with Ronnie, but only for a couple of months. I began to miss his beautiful cock. I justified duplicity by telling myself that I had made a deal with Ronnie long before I met Tracy and a deal was a deal. During the first few weeks of our relationship, Tracy understood my need to go to my parents alone but in order to see Ronnie, I switched the occasion to a late lunch instead of dinner. I would return to the beach in the late afternoon, still fresh from the sex with Ronnie and Tracy would be all over me, missing me, wanting me. For the first time, I had to refuse him, postpone the event until after dinner. He agreed, but, even though he never said anything, I knew if it had been me I would have been curious about it.

One day I was on my way to Sarasota to meet Ronnie when the car phone rang.

"Please come," Tracy cried. He had been to the bank and on the way home he had run a light.

When I arrived at the intersection where the accident occurred, I found the Corvette was totalled but he was not harmed. "It's a miracle," I said when we were in my car following the tow-truck.

He was numb. His pride was hurt. He had hurt me. "I'm so sorry," he kept saying over and over.

"But you're all right, that's what matters."

"But the car."

"Really, you've done me a favor. I couldn't afford it anyway. Now the lease is paid off."

But our routine was broken. Tracy lost his license for six months.

My young lover was deeply depressed. He moped around the condo for days. One day, I returned from the bank to find him gone. Minutes dragged into hours. Finally, he showed, stoned out of his mind. He sat at the bar while I fixed drinks. Before I had a chance to vent my frustration with him, he fell backward, narrowly missing a glass topped table. I put him to bed.

The next morning, he was still passed out when there was a knock on the door. It was Brett. I had begged off every call he had made to me since Tracy moved in but now he couldn't be denied. My anger with Tracy was such that I wanted to attack someone, something, and Brett provided the perfect outlet. But before I let things go too far, I wanted to show off my prize. We went quietly to the bedroom and I opened the door. Seeing Tracy was still out cold, I let Brett have a peek. When we returned to the living room, he said, "God, he's gorgeous. You'll have to have me over sometime for a three-way."

"Tracy's not that kind. Strange as it may sound, he's very jealous of me."

Brett groped me. "Yeah, I know why."

We went to the garage and I locked the door behind me. As I leaned back on the hood of the Mercedes and began massaging my hard-on, Brett dropped his shorts and backed over me. His hand steadying my erection, he lowered himself onto it, then pushed. He jacked off as he bounced up and down in my lap. We came simultaneously, but I was still in the mood to harm. I turned him around and made him lie across the hood while I continued to blast my flesh into him.

Later that afternoon, Tracy finally awakened. Part of me wanted to listen, the other part couldn't afford the hassle. He had become a hassle.

Eager to make amends, he wanted sex. He caressed my arm, my thigh. As always, I bloomed under his magic touch and, as he eagerly took my cock in his mouth, I knew I was beginning to think too much.

He lay face down across my knees and I played for a time with his bubble butt. I stroked it, pinched it all over, rubbed my hands up and down the division, then pulled the cheeks apart. I put my lips there and slathered the area with my saliva. He was always clean. I never feared touching any part of him. I reached under him and played with his erection as I worked my tongue into his anus.

When he was close to coming, I worked my fingers in and rolled him over. I mounted him and slid my erection into him. Holding his cock tightly, I began to fuck him in earnest; heaving his bottom up to meet my plunges, he came more intensely than I had ever remembered. I followed suit, and, after a final wriggle of my cock in his ass, we lay in each other's arms, breathing heavily. I decided to try to work things out.

But, as the days went by, his afternoon disappearances grew more frequent and prolonged. Occasionally he would return home after running on the beach and mention he'd met a girl and they had talked, but I reacted so negatively to such information that he stopped providing it. When he didn't show until after dinner, I would be furious with him and we would fight, only to make up and have sex, but I realized he had begun to feel trapped. I could sense he was psyching himself into enjoying the sex, pretending that it mattered. Early on, he had maintained he was basically straight, showing a peculiar lack of interest in passive sucking or active fucking. Those things, he led me to believe, he did with girls. I began to sense just having a place to stay became a sorry excuse for his sticking around. It had become a difficult, complex relationship of dependence and attachment, one that often arises between victim and victimizer, abuser and abused. We each had our own idiosyncratic moral vision and it became a thing of knots and complications, often sending me into despair but without somehow ever becoming truly hopeless. With each agrument, it seemed it was an appalling revisiting of the past upon the present. Finally, I suggested we both seek psychiatric help. Tracy agreed but went only once, to take the test and to have a short chat with the doctor. A week later, the doctor confronted me.

"If you stay in this relationship, eventually one of you will be harmed. Terribly harmed, perhaps physically, indeed mentally." In a few moments, he told me everything I knew about my lover. I was amazed that a test and a simple chat could reveal so much about someone. "Oh, there's no mystery to it," the doctor said. "We study sociopaths like him all the time."

I wanted an answer to the question that might give focus to my dilemma: why? But this was the very answer the experts couldn't provide.

"We have few definitive answers," he said. "These people have had troubles from their earliest days. We have studied heredity, looking for a genetic explanation and there has been some evidence that it plays a role."

"Yet Tracy's parents aren't criminals. His father works for the phone company in Texas."

The doctor shrugged, as if the answer was beyond reason. "He may be lying to you. These people learn to become good liars, effective manipulators, as you've seen by his taking you on sexually, effectively learning to assert control over his world. But no matter how much in control they think they are, these people are completely unable to sustain meaningful relationships with anyone. If you know what's good for you, you'll end this."

Tracy was strangely silent when I returned from my visit to the doctor. He had told me he would not return. To him, it was so much "idiosyncratic bullshit." He seemed to sense from my quiet demeanor that I was deeply troubled. He did what he always did in these moments, cajole me into sex, knowing that at the height of orgasm, all is forgiven. I fucked him and he was happy. We went to Tampa to dinner. I had too much wine and, mixed with the coke I had done earlier, I became unreasonable. We argued about the psychiatrist. I wanted him to see him again. He refused. He left the table and called a cab. I followed him. I knew he would go to the Carousel, to return to the place where we had met, to remind me of what a treasure I had found there amid the sleaze. As he was paying the cab driver, I parked the Mercedes and ran to him. Under the influence of drugs or booze or both, my wayward intelligence gutters like a candle. I grabbed at him, tearing his shirt. He swung and connected with my eye. I saw black and fell to the ground on the street in front of the bar, blood spurting from my eye.

The bouncer witnessed the scene and came to my rescue, whisking me to the hospital where an eye surgeon happened to be on duty. After stitching my eye, the officials asked me to stay overnight. When I refused, they ordered me a cab and I had the driver take me to where I had parked the Mercedes. The bar had closed; the lot was empty. I paid the driver $40 to lead me to the beach. On the way home, I recalled the trauma connnected with my father's beatings. Fear. Pain. Hurt. Embarrassment. Degradation. Humiliation. Anger. Resentment. Powerlessness. Helplessness. Revenge. When he'd been drinking, I knew to keep my distance. The worst time was Friday nights, when he would watch boxing. The slugfests would put him in such a state that once they were over, he would seek me out, berate me for being such a sissy and throttle me as I lay helpless in my bed. If Mother had not intervened, I'm sure I would have been killed.

One of the consequences of corporal punishment is that it sets the stage for the child to try out the behavior he has experienced.

In my case, I nearly killed several of my pets. When I tried this, I was scolded and often spanked. Very confusing. So I learned that I needed to grow bigger before I had the right to be violent. I learned that Dad's rules don't have to be consistent. I learned to mistrust Dad. Dad's love was painful. I looked forward to growing up so I could be just like Dad. Mean. Tough. Big. And, maybe, just maybe, I would be big enough to kill him.

As I grew older, I sought out people I could dominate so if they disobeyed, I could discipline them. Power coursed through my body as I would lash out at the girl I dated in college and who eventually became my wife. My violence worked on her. I had earned my privilege of power. The cycle of violence was complete except for one thing, I didn't need to kill my father. I saw he was slowly killing himself with drink. And my wife couldn't take it. Most of the time she spent locked in our bedroom.

But Tracy was not so easily disposed of. My violence did not work on him. He fought back and his rage was greater than mine.

When I arrived at the beach, Tracy had packed his things and the two suitcases were sitting by the front door. He sat on one of the bar stools.

"I'm sorry," he said.

"So am I." It could have been much worse, I realized. It was as much my fault as his. More really. If I hadn't been drinking, hadn't been doing coke...but, still, it had been boiling up for weeks.

"I'll call a cab," he said, reaching for the phone.

I let him make the call. He could always tell the cab driver he'd called in error.

"I wish you wouldn't go - " I muttered, finally, as I lay down on the couch in the living room with a sigh.

"Does it hurt?" he asked, standing over me nervously.

"No, it's numb. But I'm sure it'll hurt tomorrow and then when they take the stitches out in a week or so. But what hurts more than anything is what I've done. What I've done to us."

"It was me. I haven't been right since the accident. I thought you'd take me back to Tampa right then but you didn't."

"No. I couldn't. I love you. I love you but we can't live together."

"I know. I've been all messed up. I really want to date girls."

"Perhaps this was just something you had to try out. Now you have to put it behind you. And it won't worry you anymore."

I rented a car for him for two weeks and gave him enough money to rent a room and keep himself together until he found work. He called every day and finally I agreed to see him. For lunch.

He didn't bother to knock, just walked in. I was opening a bottle of wine and when I looked up my anger with him, with myself returned. He was so beautiful I wanted to smother him with kisses but I stood where I was, waiting for him.

"Hi," he said sheepishly, sliding onto one of the bar stools.

"Hi." As I poured the wine, a chill descended upon me. I handed him his glass and he sipped it.

"Tastes good," he said, half-smiling.

I came around the bar and sat next to him. He took my hand and squeezed it. I shook my hand free, like a young boy confronted with an overardent admirer.

He shrugged his shoulders and brought both hands to his glass of wine. He said he'd gotten a job at a gas station in Tampa and he was dating the owner's daughter, who was only 17.

"Nice pussy?"

"Shit, I haven't got that far yet."

"That's right. Take it easy. When they're that young they need to be broken in slowly."

My denial of his power was coming at a cost of sentimentality. I remembered what my psychiatrist said, that such repression is unhealthy. Sooner or later the hate turns up. In my case, it was the fine line between love and hate. I could only hate something I loved so much. I wanted to cry but instead I smiled and kept listening as he chattered on.

We sat at the bar and ate chicken salad sandwiches and then I cleared the dishes away. When I returned to the dining room, he was still sitting on the bar stool but now he was nude. "I've missed you," he said, stretching his arms wide, "soooo much!"

I stepped close to him, letting his arms envelop me, press me tightly against his smooth, hard body. We kissed. It was a harder, more urgent kiss than any I had remembered with him.

His hand groped me. Feeling my swelling erection, he whispered, "Yeah, you missed me, too."

The removal of my shirt and shorts was swift and he was on his knees, sliding my prick between his lips, down his throat. Before long, he was on his back on the carpet, his legs spread wide, and I was between them, entering him. As I lowered myself on top of him fully, his arms held me again and we kissed. It was as if nothing had changed. Yet everything had changed. As I climaxed, I thought about offering him a hundred a week just to visit me on Fridays for lunch, but by the time I had withdrawn my prick and was lifting myself from the floor, I came to my senses. He seemed to sense I was remorseful. As he pulled on his shorts, he said, "It's not right, is it?"

"No, I'm sorry. This will have to be the end. I can't go through this. Neither can you. I love you more than you'll ever know but it's just no good."

"No, it's me. I'm no good," he muttered and raced out the door.

I slipped into my shorts and ran after him but by the time I reached the driveway, he had driven away. Three days later, I found the little rental car in the drive, the keys in an envelope on the front seat. There was no note of explanation.

5

With Tracy gone, I called Jack and told him I was in the market for some fresh faces. Then I plunged headlong into a new project: re-decorating the condo. I called John Wolf and asked him to start buying some things for the bedrooms. It was a project that went on all summer and long into the fall. When it was finished, I told John I wanted to fete him with a party at the condo but, having made plans to go to my parents for Christmas and then end up in Fort Lauderdale for New Year's Eve, I told John it would have to be in January. He agreed.

And then, five days after Christmas 1985, John Wolf went cruising. It was not something he did very often; he was known to be a quiet man who socialized with a small circle of close friends, but the holidays had gotten him down. John set out in search of a little companionship on cool winter's evening and he headed for the Pier near downtown and drove north to the end of North Shore Park, an area known to have the most homosexual activity in the city. I had travelled through the area a few times and it seemed it didn't matter what time of day it was, the men would be there, often spending ceaseless hours driving and driving, parking and waiting, then driving some more, only to park and wait and wait some more. They risked so much, I thought. Police make about 50 arrests a year at the park on various charges, soliciting for prostitution, soliciting for a lewd act, or simple battery.

On that fateful night, John drove through the park several times in his 1981 Cadillac Seville, owned by his employer of ten years, Joanne James Interiors. Shortly after midnight, he finally settled on a trick, a short, swarthy young man. He took him back to his home on West Flamingo Way. They had a couple of drinks, then the trick followed John into the bathroom. There, John gave his studly visitor a blow job. After they both had come, they left the bathroom and then something went terribly wrong.

It had been the boy's intent all along to rob his trick, Wolf suddenly discovered.

The boy was not content with the money John handed him. The boy demanded more. Suddenly, it seemed the kid couldn't help himself, he started to fight; it seemed all of his stored-up aggressiveness found a vent.

The more he beat at Wolf's head with his fists, the more he wanted to go on. All of the years of putting up with faggots and what they wanted to do to him crested in those moments.

But suddenly he stopped. He tied up the decorator and began to look about for things he could steal. He walked back into the bedroom and saw his bloody victim.

Again, a mixture of fear and hate seized him and he took the metal hand grenade casing he often carried for protection and gouged first at one eye and then the other.

An emotional avalanche continued; he tore one of John's earlobes loose. Then, in a hopeless rage, he ripped both eyeballs out of their sockets, then rushed to the bathroom and flushed them down the toilet. After washing his hands, he left the water running.

The prostitute filled the Cadillac with Wolf's stereo, videocassette recorder, and jewelry.

Then he went back into the bedroom, grabbed a tape recorder and forced his victim to tape a message that he was a homosexual and had propositioned him. He took some photographs of his victim with an Instamatic camera he found. He tried to flush the tape recorder down the toilet, but kept the tape. Then he drove the Cadillac to his home, where he unloaded this booty. After driving the car to Fourth Avenue at 11th Street, he stuffed a sleeve he tore from one of his victim's jackets in the car's open gas spout and lit it.

At 3:45 a.m., Joanne James was called and told her car was destroyed. She panicked for the welfare of her employee, John Wolf.

Five minutes later, a call was received at police headquarters. An unidentified man informed police of the burning vehicle and also that they should check on the welfare of a person at Wolf's address. John was rushed into the neuro-intensive care unit at Bayfront Medical Center. It was thought at the time that perhaps John's attacker, whoever he was, had saved him by calling police in time.

A few days later, detectives were able to question John for short periods of time and put together a composite drawing of several suspects which they showed to the proprietors and customers at the lowlife gay bars in town, The Stuffed Pepper and The Club, but they really had no leads.

On January 7, Sheriff Gerry Coleman announced in a press release that Wolf "may have had AIDS" and that the person who attacked him may have been exposed. This was to answer rumors that several deputies working on the case had been quarantined. "This was not intended to lure Wolf's attacker out of hiding," Coleman said, "but sometimes you get spillover."

Whatever the intent, it seemed to work because less than a week later, 23-year-old Charles Ross Stob turned himself in. The Sheriff said Stob told detectives he went to the police because he wanted to straighten out his life. He was concerned about his health. When he heard that Wolf might have AIDS, he said his reaction was "Oh my God, all my girlfriends will die."

Stob was charged with aggravated battery, robbery, arson and auto theft. His bail was set at $100,000 and he was put in an isolation cell. Police records indicated he had a long history of criminal activity dating back to a charge of hitting a man in the face with a bottle and robbing him in the parking lot of a Tampa bar in July of 1982. The charge was later dropped because the man failed to come forward. In May 1983 Stob was sentenced to three years in prison for grand theft (he stole two guitars in Tampa) and a probation violation. He was on probation for stealing a video camera from Calvary Temple Church in Hillsborough County. He served 27 months of the sentence and was released August 30. David Skipper, a spokesman for the Department of Corrections, said Stob was "apparently a management problem" while incarcerated and was accused of fighting, disorderly conduct and unarmed and verbal assaults. He was involved in at least eight fights with guards or inmates and reprimanded 12 times in one year for "hostile" and "rebellious" behavior. Two of the incidents involving Stob may have been sexually related. On September 26, 1983, he hit another inmate with a two-foot level after they got into a fight. He later told officials that the fight started because the other inmate "grabbed him in the wrong place." On May 1, 1985, Stob got into another fight with an inmate who claimed Stob threatened him repeatedly with violence if the young man didn't participate in sex. The inmate said he sharpened his toothbrush to protect himself from Stob's attacks. Because of this pattern of bad behavior, he was twice transferred to different prisons.

While incarcerated, Stob admitted, "I had a $800-a-day habit." He agreed to attend a drug-treatment program while in prison.

Stob also admitted that he and his younger brother were abandoned by their father when he was about 5 years old. He said he hadn't seen his younger brother since they were placed in different foster homes. He claimed to have lived in 28 foster homes before he was adopted, at the age of 9, by J. L. Stob, who owns a medical supply company in Indiana. Much of Stob's life was spent in Edwardsburg, Michigan, a town of 1,135 near the Indiana/Michigan border. He ran away from home several times and stole the family car when he was 14. "I pretty much put them through hell," Stob said of his parents.

Once, after running away from home and being caught, Stob told police he would rather spend the night in jail than go home. "He seemed to think if he spent a night in jail he'd be a big man in school," a policeman remembered. "But people just didn't care for him. He was a show-off type - loud, bossy, demanding."

"I don't know anything about it," his mother said. "We really don't hear from him. He's been gone for some time." Actually, Stob arrived in Florida in 1980, taking jobs as a mechanic and a construction worker.

A month before the attack, Stob moved into a two-bedroom, two-bath condo with a girl, Lynette Coley, and her 2-year-old son. "This guy had his end of the apartment, she had her end," Coley's landlord told the press. "When he rented it, Stob's credentials were fine. I heard what happened and, wow, how can you predict that? I'm just the landlord. I don't ask people what their religion, race or creed is."

Coley said that Stob was "like a brother" to her. "A likable guy. I'm still in a daze. He was so nice to me. I just totally trusted him."

A neighbor said Stob was invariably polite. She had seen him playing with the toddler, giving him a ride on his black Kawasaki 550 motorcycle and said she saw him spending a lot of time working on the cycle and on a gray Volkswagen Dasher with dented hood. Police said his occupation was buying and selling cars.

Then came a bombshell that rocked the city's gay community. According to Dr. Richard Levinson, director of the Pinellas County Health Department, there was absolutely no evidence that Wolf had the deadly virus. The media had a field day, accusing the Sheriff of irresponsible conduct, demanding an apology to Wolf and an explanation. "Coleman also furthered public misconceptions and aroused unfounded fear about this deadly new disease," an editorial read. "Announcing that some 20 police officers, medical workers, and reporters who investigated the case may have been exposed to AIDS is a strange way to quell public panic. By raising the possibility that people who worked at the crime scene were exposed to AIDS, Coleman gave credence to the mistaken belief that the disease can be spread easily. There is abundant evidence that the disease cannot be transmitted in casual ways. This is unbecoming conduct for the county's top law enforcement officer."

From his cell, Stob agreed to be interviewed. "It was all God," he said. "Obviously, somebody that would be doing something like this wouldn't have a conscience. If I could give him my eyes, I would. If I hadn't turned myself in, I would have gotten away with it. But the hardest part is over. The hardest part is coming in and facing up."

Stob said that after the attack God entered his life and warned him he was going to die four days before Sheriff Coleman had his press conference. "I had to make a choice between life or death," Stob said. "What God has been trying to tell me through this whole thing was that if I just trust in him, no matter what my life has been like, he will take care of me. I had to make a choice."

In the ten days between the attack and his surrender, Stob said he did "a lot of thinking." He went to church with Coley and it was the first time he'd been in a church in some time. He said, "It was as if the sermon was meant for me."

He made three different anonymous calls to the police department asking about the case, calls which were traced to a phone booth on 34th Street. Finally, at about 1 a.m. on the night he surrendered, Stob couldn't concentrate on television and decided to go to bed. He prayed and asked God for guidance. Later, he got out of bed and looked out the window. A police car drove by and he interpreted that as a sign from on high that he had to give himself up. Yet, he wanted another sign. After dressing, he drove to a nearby store to buy the morning newspaper. He turned around and saw another police car. This, he said, was the second sign. He started driving on Fourth Street toward downtown St. Petersburg, then turned around, still not sure. He turned around a second time and drove to the police station. When he arrived, he sat in his car several minutes listening to the radio, "still thinking about doing it." Then, he said, God told him to turn himself in. He drove to the police department and asked to see the composite drawing of the suspect. The officer on duty immediately contacted Sgt. Martin Alan Hart, who quickly drove to the police station. He and another officer, Sgt. Joseph Jesiolkiewic, questioned Stob. In a sworn deposition, Hart said, "He didn't say the Wolf thing right away, he just said, 'I did it.' I asked, 'Did what?' and he said, 'You know what I'm talking about.' And then he said, 'Well, I'm the one that did everything to Wolf.' That's when I advised him of his rights."

"Now," Stob said, "things are going to work out. After all this is taken care of, I won't ever have to worry about this again."

He told police if they would arrange to have his girlfriend come visit him, he would make sure they would get the stolen property back.

At his initial hearing, Stob told Judge Howard P. Rives that he wanted to quickly dispose of his charges. "Mr. Stob," Rives replied, "the court cannot accept a plea of guilty or not guilty this morning. These are very serious charges and undoubtedly you are going to need the best advice you can have."

Meanwhile, Wolf was telling visitors that he was somewhere else besides a hospital bed. Joanne James said he believed he was in California and talked about completing projects at work. She said he was denying that he was blind. A nurse asked Wolf to count the number of fingers she was holding up. Wolf guessed correctly the first time but was wrong a second time. The bandages around his eyes were replaced by clear plastic inserts that resembled large contact lenses. Several areas of his scalp had been shaved where doctors sewed up the cuts from the beating and he had several stitches around his ear lobe. Doctors had strapped him to a chair and he was eating solid food and taking short walks with nurses.

Upon hearing of Stob's arrest, Wolf's father Louis, 77, a retired Lutheran minister living in Naples, Florida, said: "I'm only glad for the fact that somebody else may be spared. As far as John and his mother and I are concerned, it doesn't mean a thing. The damage is done."

In early March, after hearing from two pyschiatrists, Judge Maynard F. Swanson declared John incompetent. Dr. Pedro J. Lense described Wolf as "depressed, confused and uncommunicative." Dr. H. E. Rubin said that Wolf was "totally helpless." He said that he asked the man several questions during his visits and Wolf responded with "just a few words. He couldn't carry on a conversation." He said the victim possibly suffered from depression and atypical dementia, a condition defined as a "deterioration or loss of intellectual faculties, reasoning power, memory, and will...characterized by confusion, disorientation, apathy, and stupor of varying degrees." The Judge appointed two trustees, Elizabeth Owens, a co-worker at Joanne James and Harvey Beck, a friend for more than 15 years.

On March 12, John was flown to the Neurogical Center in Cortland, New York, in a specially-equipped plane. Doctors evaluated his thinking processes and used physical therapy to work on his coordination. Such services were not covered by insurance and the costs were averaging $500 a day. Wolf's guardians said that he had about $25,000 in cash and another $10,000 in a trust fund. To raise more money, they said they planned to sell his home and two rental houses. The gay community rallied and contributed to a trust fund established in his name.

Eight days later, on March 20, at 11:15 a.m., John Wolf died of his injuries. The trial of Charles Stob was scheduled for October 28.

6

"Sure, you can come over," Jack said a week before Labor Day. "I'd love to see you."

"Sure?"

"Of course."

He had known, officially, for several months that he was HIV positive. But it seemed he knew long before that. The night sweats had started in January. Now he was in the hospital and things were desperate.

"I've turned all my clients over to Charles."

"Charles?"

"Charles of the Ritz, he calls himself. He'll take care of you."

I certainly needed some tender loving care of the sexual kind. Ronnie and Brett finally got back together and moved to parts unknown. Now my main source for both drugs and boys was terminal. Since I had moved to Florida, Jack and I had met a half dozen times and talked endlessly over the phone. He was a difficult and unpredictable sort; you never knew what mood he'd be in. He drank a fifth of Canadian whiskey a day and, when he could find some good quality blow, snorted coke. He might be quiet, sullen, on the defensive, and sealed up tight, or he might be, as he always was on the phone, garrulous and sentimental, ready to let the caller, be it boy or trick, cry on his shoulder, list their misfortunes one by one. Now the greatest misfortune of them all was happening to him.

The intensive care unit was like a concrete cellblock. After a while, the sound of the dozen or so respirators inhaling and exhaling, each at its own pace, became interwoven with the clatter and thump, the footfalls, the sobbing. It was a strange hum of despair. My friend was wasting away, skin dry and chaste, he appeared already mummified.

"Hi, Jack," I said.

He opened his eyes and looked up.

"They tell me you're getting better."

He could not speak because of the tube in his trachea. He simply nodded. I held back the tears. What had he done to deserve this?

Was this, I asked myself, what our search for eros has come down to?

*

The moment I saw Bubba, a pleasant young fellow, I knew if I was going to have sex at all, it should have been before my visit to the hospital. Although the boy was attractive in a streetwise-way, I was in no mood for a frolic in the dark. Sent by Charles with his highest recommendation, the lad tried hard to please but it was no use. I paid him, gave him my business card for some time in the future, and sent him on his way. The next morning, I checked out of the hotel and went home.

When I got the call a few days later from a doctor at the hospital that Jack had finally gone I had been expecting it. The call I didn't expect came a couple of weeks later, on September 19. It was Bubba: "Charles was murdered last night," he said. Calculating he might be seeking asylum, I lied, saying I was on my way out of town, but I begged him to give me the details. It seemed Charles was found in his underwear, beaten several times in the face and stabbed several times. "But it wasn't me," Bubba said. "They suspect me but I've got an alibi. Besides, I know who did it."

The day after the murder, the police found Charles' 1978 beige Lincoln Continental at the airport.

All police had on the suspect was his first name and that he was a border in the house. Charles was in the habit of renting rooms to his workers and one of them, a wavy brown-haired, green-eyed boy named Ronald had become a problem. I remembered that Charles wanted to set me up with Ronald but after my first encounter that weekend with Bubba, I had written the "vacation" off as simply a matter of bad timing.

From Bubba's description, they put together a composite drawing which was released to the media and seeing that, on September 25, a unidentified businessman stepped forward and identified the suspect as Ronald Meola. A murder warrant was issued. Police suspected Ronald might have flown to his parents' house in Canton, Ohio, and they notified Canton police. The dragnet began to close in. At a motel in Canton, a disturbance broke out. A young man, who checked in by himself, began breaking up furniture and barricaded himself inside the room. The motel manager called police but by the time they arrived, the young man had slipped out a back window. A check of the motel's registry revealed that it was Ronald Meola. Two days later, Ronald was in custody in Canton.

He told detectives that he got into an argument with Groves over $7,000 in fees he claimed was due him. Groves made derogatory remarks about Meola's sister and the argument escalated into violence. He claimed that Groves pulled out a knife and he grabbed a frying pan and hit Groves over the head with it, then tied him up in his bed and strangled him to death. In sworn statements, he said he didn't remember stabbing the man.

Given the sleazy aspects of the case, the newspapers had a field day. Police were quoted as saying, "Judging by the number of phone calls, it was a pretty active escort business. Groves claimed to have similar businesses in Orlando and Jacksonville." He didn't have a record but police said they had been receiving complaints about the service, which they described as a homosexual prostitution "ring." In David Magazine, a full page ad boasted that Charles employed 35 men and had escorts available from Key West to Jacksonville. Managing editor Jerry Byers knew Groves only from his visits to the office to buy ads. "Until today, I never even knew his last name. We just knew him as Charles of the Ritz." I cringed at the thought that Jack's worn Rolodex with the dog-eared cards, one of which bore my name and phone number, was now in police custody.

I headed back to Fort Lauderdale, drove west on Broward Boulevard to Plantation, leaving the glitz and glitter of the fabled beaches miles behind me, then hung a left on Martin Luther King Jr. Drive, entering a racially mixed neighborhood. Two houses from the corner on 11th Court sits a rundown little crackerbox of a place, its stucco blotched with mildew, its yard overgrown with crabgrass. It was here that Groves, better known as Charles of the Ritz, met his death in what the media had dubbed the "Frying Pan Murder." Directly across the street, on the corner of 11th Court, sits the Faith Lutheran Church and School. The lawn is neatly trimmed, the building freshly painted. The sign on one wall reads: "God Bless Our Kids."

"Ron was not someone you would forget," one of the many men who slept with the boy told me. "He was very clean cut, but he seemed a bit strange because had a hearing problem and talked out of the side of his mouth. But I couldn't see the evil in him."

"Yes," I said, "it was as if he was trying to work things out and instead of that things just careened out of control. But it's a kind of fury that I could account for. I recognize it for what it is. Boys feel they are crossed. They feel powerless, lose control and attack in a rage."

"Look, he was so young. It was an accident. It wasn't murder, was it?"

I shook my head sadly. "Well, it was and it wasn't."

7

Things kept getting uglier. It didn't seem to matter any more where you found a boy, the street, a bar, through a service. Any of them could kill you. They were turning into monsters. Maybe it was the drugs, the times. Both. Whatever it was, all I wanted to do was hide. But where to go? It seemed my paradise had become a hermetic, over-protected world where crime and murder were still common coin. A world where power, money, the search for prestige, and the desire for success could determine an individual's life or death from one moment to the next.

Finally, I could no longer tolerate the solitude, isolation and silence. I went to the Carousel Club. Who knows, I thought, maybe Tracy would be there. It seemed I was increasingly walking the narrow line between fantasy and reality. Dreaming of what once was, wanting it, expecting it, yet knowing it could never be.

"...But you can't hide under a rug," a man sitting next to me said.

"No, but I'd like to," I lamented. "Luck of the draw. Actually, it could've been me. Any one of these guys, it could have been me."

"But it wasn't. Maybe they got careless. Just don't get careless." He finished his Scotch and prepared to leave. "Shit, man, you can't stop living. You have to go on."

"That used to be so easy," I muttered. "It used to work."

I had begun to think of the late '80s as a blue period. Picasso had his blue period. This was my blue period, a blue period for all of us who knew the richness of the '70s. I decided to write about the past. My fantasies were in the past, perhaps I could even live in the past. Soon I began to be so busy looking backwards I didn't have time to see forwards. But the present kept rising up, grabbing me by the lapels, shaking me into reality...

Charles Stob pleaded guilty.

A week before he was to stand trial, after a summer of false starts, the killer really was going to throw in the sponge.

"It must be God," his attorney, who advised him to stand trial, shrugged. "That's what he's said before."

Stob's decision shocked the community because the defense had been claiming that key evidence against him, a jailhouse confession, might not have been admissible because deputies ignored his request for an attorney during questioning. The guilty plea would also come before court-appointed psychiatrists could evaluate the man to see whether he was even competent to stand trial and before the county medical examiner completed his report regarding the cause of Wolf's death. Medical authorities said that Wolf's wounds had healed before he died. Two neuropathologists came back with different opinions as to the cause of death and the medical examiner was seeking a third opinion before trial. The State Attorney said that between 15 and 20 doctors from around the country had reviewed the case but none could make a definite connection between the beating and the death. "We can't proceed with a homicide charge," he said resignedly.

"Maybe he wasn't actually killed by the assault, but he may as well have been," John's friend Kent Robinson said. "To me, being tied down and tortured is worse than murder. And he died eventually anyway." It was hard to convince anyone that Wolf would be dead if the attack hadn't happened.

On October 21, Charles appeared in court, saying he was taking God's advice and not his lawyer's. Holding hands with a couple he said were his "friends in Christ," Stob faced Judge Catherine Harlan and explained how he needed money one night so he decided to go down to The Pier, pretend to be a prostitute, and rob somebody. "The big thing I got out of it was that God wants the truth. He'll take care of things." Before his conversion, Stob said, he was a dangerous person who dreamed of becoming a Mafia hit man. "I hope the Court, I hope everybody can see that God's rehabilitated me."

Prosecutor Bob Lewis likened Stob's religious conversion to a saying about war: There are no atheists in foxholes. "Mr. Stob finds himself in a foxhole now, but there's no guarantee he won't return to his prior ways."

*

On December 13, 1986, almost a year after John Wolf was brutalized, Charles Stob was sentenced by Judge Harlan to three life terms. "This is a crime that shocked the conscience of the community in a way that it hasn't been shocked in years," the judge said before passing sentence.

"I don't think there's any doubt about my guilt," Stob told the court, "I think a lot of people are wondering whether I'm sincere. I think a lot of the problem is...whether I'm doing this to get off. That ain't why I'm doing it." He said he would rather spend his life in prison than be accused of faking religion for a lighter sentence. "The hurt I've done I can't take away. I know the experience Wolf went through. But nobody in the courtroom can experience what I'm going through because I've got to live with this for as long as I can think. It don't go away, man. You wake up in the morning and it's always there. You did it, even though you've changed. I've got to live with that."

8

Fast-forward to April, 1990.

The stripper I knew simply as Gene was one of those young men whom I have come to regard as supreme trade. He was seductive, his cock was quick to rise and he seemed reasonably amused as you sucked it. It mattered not if he came as long as I did.

And that's what one wants from trade. When the press of business meant time was at a premium, yet the desire for sex overwhelmed me, I could always visit the Gaiety in New York any afternoon and take one of the strippers to the backroom. For fifteen minutes I could adore a beautiful body while I jacked off, then pop, I was satisfied and we both could go on with our lives. It was anonymous yet it wasn't. It filled a mutual need. It was painless. It was convenient.

But in Tampa, you had to take such trade to a hotel or back home; there was no convenient backroom at the Carousel bar. Because it was a 45-minute drive each way to the beach, I opted for the well-known hot sheets motel, the Park, on West Kennedy Boulevard.

I had admired Gene's technique and physique while he danced at the Carousel and stuffed several dollars in his bikini. Later, I bought him a drink and became mesmerized by his deep, penetrating eyes. The tattoo on his left forearm of a knife dripping blood didn't bother me. I invited him back to the motel for $50, plus a tip. By the time we got to the room, I was so hot for him, I could have come just sitting in front of him staring at the bulge of his crotch, but he seemed ready for some action. The curly headed hunk stood at the head of the double bed while I unzipped his jeans and pulled out his beefy, cut cock. It quickly responded to my machinations. I fondled his big balls while I blew it, jacking myself off. I paid him and gave him a twenty dollar tip, then rushed him back to the bar so he could turn another trick. I was always accommodating to those who accommodated me.

A week later, I returned to the bar and Gene was no longer in residence. "You know how they are," the bartender told me. "Here one day, gone the next." Gene, I found out, was from Tennessee and made a circuit of Atlanta, Tampa, and other hot spots, dancing and turning tricks, then moving on.

By mid-May, Gene had moved on all right, all the way to Shelby, North Carolina. It was there that he was arrested for the May 15 murder of Michael Whisnant, a 33-year-old divorced man. The victim was found dead at the Hilton Towers on Courtland Street in Atlanta, handcuffed and shoved under his bed; he had been strangled to death with the cord from the window blind.

A quality control engineer for Copeland Corp., a company that makes air compressors and refrigeration equipment, Michael was attending a convention in Atlanta and had gone to the Armory, which is situated near the popular Backstreet disco on Juniper Street, looking for a little excitement. He met Gene and they went back to his room, No. 2419. After agreeing to pay Gene $75, Michael performed oral sex on the young man. When they were finished, Michael paid Gene only $25. Enraged, Gene lost control and began looking around for things to steal. Michael tried to stop him. Gene overpowered his victim.

The following day, a maid had made up the room, unaware of the body. A security officer, summoned because associates of Michael had missed him at the meetings, looked under the bed and found the body at 9 p.m. He said that it appeared that a briefcase in the room had been broken open. "There was evidence that Whisnant was struggling," a spokesman said. "He had scrapes on his body in several different places. The cord was tied tightly around his neck."

Gene had a 15-year-old girl, identified as Trina Brown, with him at the time of his arrest. She and Gene had gone to Shelby to rob Whisnant's home. A neighbor called police when she saw what she described as prowlers. Shelby police said the girl "could pass for 21," and had run away from her foster home in Zanesville, Ohio, when she was 12. Trina said had lived with Gene in Nashville for over a year. Her mother, Cindy Brown, was in prison in Ohio for aggravated robbery.

"If you people don't think I'm a criminal, just wait until tomorrow," Gene, whose full name was Henry Eugene Hodges, threatened upon his arrest. The next morning, true to his word, he not only confessed to Whisnant's murder, he also told police he was responsible for the strangulation death of Ronnie Bassett, 37, of Nashville, a line worker with the Bell Telephone Co., who was found in the bedroom of his house five days earlier. Shelby police ran a check on their prisoner and discovered that Hodges, 23, had been released from a Tennessee jail in 1988 after serving four years for the kidnapping and robbery of a gay man in Chattanooga.

By the time Nashville police arrived in Shelby, Hodges had confessed that he may have killed four or five other people. This sent police in Atlanta and Nashville scurrying to find unsolved cases with similar patterns. "We'll certainly be looking at all of our cases," said Atlanta police Deputy Chief Eldrin Bell. "We're not going to focus on gay killings but on all homicides that could be associated with this pattern."

Police were checking on a murder which occurred on April 22, 1989, when David Paul Thompson, 29, was found with a knife in his back in his apartment on Peachtree Road in Atlanta. He was last seen at the Cove, a gay bar.

Nashville police quickly came up with another make, a murder dating back to September 4, 1988, a month after Gene was released from prison. In this case, the victim, 30-year-old Vernon Larkin, met Gene in the Jungle, a sleazy Nashville bar, and left with him. Larkin's body was found three days later, bound and gagged, in his living room. Several days later, Larkin's car was found in midtown Atlanta.

Also, on July 12, 1989, Barry McDonald, who was starting a support group for homebound AIDS victims, met his killer at a gay club in Nashville and was later stabbed 30 times. Items were taken from his home. In September, newspaper carrier Ronald E. Vandyck was found in the trunk of his car with several bullet holes in his head. In October, Robert F. Sibert, a college professor in Gallatin, Tennessee, was found shot in the head in his home. His car was later found at a Nashville truck stop. His credit cards had been stolen. "These all fit the pattern, close enough that we're checking them out," Nashville police said. "It appears Hodges picked up homosexuals and there are common elements in most of these cases."

The day after the Whisnant murder, Gene checked in at the King's Motor Inn in a suburb of Atlanta. He was driving a green 1980 Pontiac Skyhawk which had no license plate but a 14-day Tennessee tag taped in the hatchback window. The left corner of the windshield had a softball size crack. In the rear of the car were three laundry baskets filled with clothes, a brown suitcase, a box of Purex detergent, and a one-gallon jug of bleach. "He had his car full of stuff," police said. "It looked like he was moving."

Later that day, Trina arrived driving Whisnant's black 1988 Cougar. A few hours later, the two took off for Shelby in the Cougar, leaving the Skyhawk at the motel.

Over the weekend, gays in both Nashville and Atlanta expressed shock at the sordid turn of events. "It's dangerous for people like me who want to go out at night," a young man at the Bulldog and Co. bar in Atlanta said. Another customer lamented: "There's enough problems gays have to deal with without the idea that if you go home with somebody you're going to end up strangled."

Police theorized Gene had been in and out of Atlanta several times in the weeks before the murder. He had banned by the Gallus Club on Cypress Street, according to Maurice Bullock, a security officer there. "I've been working the midtown bars for five years now and I recognize a lot of the hustlers. I turned Hodges away all the time. It got so he'd see me and turn around. I've seen him get in cars of passing johns on Cypress plenty of times."

Cathy M. Woolard, head of an American Civil Liberties Union advisory panel set up to help gays and Atlanta police better understand each other, said, "People who are closeted tend to use bars and anonymous sexual encounters to keep their secret." She added that they ran the greatest risk of becoming prey to violent partners or homophobes.

"One thing that's changed markedly is the behavior of police toward gay crime victims," Bill Gripp, an Atlanta gay activist said. "It used to be the first question asked was: `What did you do to cause it?' They don't immediately accuse the victim. I'm sure we still have officers with attitude problems, but it's changing."

Gary Kaupman, editor of the gay newspaper, The Southern Voice, said when he was a volunteer at a hot-line six years before he would get a call a month concerning violence against gays. "Now we have cases where people are getting hurt on the average of one a week. When you are victimized because you are gay, that's an intense feeling. It's bad enough to be bashed in the head, but if you're getting bashed by someone who's screaming `Faggot!' the level of personal invasion is pretty deep."

In Nashville, a pet groomer who asked not to be identified said his city was becoming "a little Atlanta. I used to live there. I know." He said he had met a man at the Jungle who tied him up with a coat hanger wire, beat him repeatedly, ransacked his house and threatened to kill him if he called police. No arrest was made.

"I was astonished," Anthony Odems, one of Nashville's premier drag queens, said. Anthony, who is married and has two children, prefers to answer to his stage name, Grace Pleshette. "It's like he had been sitting in my house and on my furniture and could have killed me and my kids!"

Others who knew Gene in Nashville said his outwardly quiet demeanor masked an emotional storm going on inside of him. They said he often would take up with a man who would support him, then leave the man and struggle to make his way in the straight world. One of his former lovers, who asked not to be named, said: "He liked to get drunk and high, and when he started coming down, then something snapped and he felt like he shouldn't be doing this, that this was wrong. He had to be high to be gay.

"In my reasoning, he is gay to a certain extent. He wanted the real money that went with a homosexual relationship, somebody to keep him. But he used to look at people real strange - like he was going to explode."

Hodges made the lower Broadway scene in Nashville when he got out of prison. Eventually he took up with a drag queen, with whom he lived for six months. Then he met Trina Brown, who was 13 at the time. "No matter who he was with, he never stopped hustling," an informant said. "Sometimes his anger erupted and at least one innocent man looking for nothing more than a night of passion died."

Hodges not only hustled, he also stripped, down to a g-string, most often at Victor Victoria's. "He was attracted to men who looked intelligent and had money," a customer of the bar said. "Whenever he danced, he came and danced in front of me and I'd cash a twenty and stick dollars in his jockstrap. He was a good stripper. His wiggle was real cute and he looked into your eyes with a very suggestive look. It was his eyes. Now it's scary." Pedro, the owner of Victor Victoria, said, "That type of individual can't stay in one place too long. You get too well-known. You've got to hit the big cities. What's so bizarre is that in any bar he was in that I know of he was known as a gentleman. You just never know."

Cicely Deanka, a drag queen at Victor Victoria, who often shared the stage with Gene, said Hodges always went with the highest bidder. "He wanted to fight when he got full of dope, Valium, or booze. His eyes turned like that flame," she said, pointing to a fake candle mounted on the bar wall, "bright red. He was like a cold hearted snake. He was a hamburger hustler. He went home and did what he had to do and then he was through." To Deanka, Gene's arrest was "like somebody walked over my grave. I thought, 'Oh, my God, he was in my presence. I'm lucky I wasn't with him when he was in one of his moods."

In a sworn statement, Gene said that when Bassett "touched him like a woman," he began to choke him, then handcuffed him and wrapped duct tape around his neck five times.

"Internalized homophobia is not unique to the straight individual," Jeffrey Laymon of the Metro Atlanta Council of Gay and Lesbian Organizations said. "Many gay individuals don't like the fact that they are gay so they find themselves in destructive behavior patterns. They think they must be wrong somehow in not equating with heterosexuals. They accept the fact they are bad or morally wrong and should not lead productive, normal lives and then set about to fulfill that destruction."

When Trina Brown arrived in Nashville, she confessed to being with Gene when he met Bassett in a Nashville park about midnight on May 14. Bassett invited them to his nearby home. When the two men agreed to have sex, Trina left and waited in the car. When Gene came out, he said "I think I've killed this guy."

Bassett's lover said he was hard-headed, "always right," and was the aggressor in the relationship. The lover, who asked not to identified, said he had eaten dinner with the victim the night of the murder but had refused sex. "I believe he picked up Hodges because we didn't have sex and he was horny."

MacDonald was involved in a 10-year relationship when he encountered Hodges at the Jungle while his lover was on vacation. His brother, Perry, of Woodstock, Ontario, said perhaps the victim's biggest problem was that he was too trusting and too accepting of other people. "He looked after the elderly who were terminally ill. I just don't think you'd find him bed-hopping." Returning from his vacation three days after the murder, MacDonald's lover found him between the sofa and the coffee table.

On August 1, Gene pleaded guilty to Whisnant's murder and was sentenced to life in prison. Wearing a prison uniform, he answered in monosyllables as Judge Edward H. Johnson questioned him. After the sentencing, Gene's attorney said he would soon be extradited to Tennessee to stand trial for the murders there.

In Nashville, Trina Brown pleaded guilty to helping Gene murder Bassett. Prosecutors agreed not to try her as an adult as long as she continued to cooperate and would testify against her former lover "if necessary." She was sent to a residential center on the grounds of the Cumberland Hall Psychiatric Hospital, from which she escaped in the spring of 1991. She was found in Tampa and returned to Cumberland. Authorities revealed it was her second escape in recent weeks.

A few weeks later, Gene was brought to Nashville to stand trial for the murders of Bassett and MacDonald. He said he was willing to confess to at least six murders but he wanted to make a deal. He wanted desperately to avoid the death penalty.

"We're in a Catch-22 situation," Sgt. Robert Moore said. "He knows the jig is up. We cannot guarantee someone won't get the death penalty. From our point of view, we simply want to know the truth about the unsolved murders."

Given a sociopath's penchant for pathological lying, the truth, the whole truth, may never be known, offering no encouragement that we will ever hear the end of this story.

Epilogue

"Do you like livin' alone?" the young hustler asked me.

"Oh, yes. I consider myself a solitary person. I write books and I don't ever really feel lonely. I guess because I've lived in my imagination so long, I'm comfortable there. I don't feel lonely when I'm writing but I feel lonely after I finish a book and don't know what I'm going to do next."

"Did you just finish one?"

"Yes. That's why I went out. I guess I was searching for something. You know how it is."

"Yeah, I meet tricks like that all the time, dudes that are searchin' for somethin', someone. They're not sure what."

He picked up the portrait of Tracy sitting next to the one of my two children and gently rubbed some dust from the frame.

"Yes, I'm searching for another boy like that one," I said.

The hustler's big myopic eyes crinkled, emitting sparks and the bassoon voice purred, "Cute guy. Where's he?"

I suddenly felt dizzy, perhaps even blessed, gazing at the boy before me. He looked enough like Tracy to be his brother.

"We had a falling out and I sent him away. He came back once but I couldn't let him stay. My doctor wouldn't hear of it. You've heard the expression, 'You can't live with him but you can't live without him.'"

The boy nodded and put the portrait back on the bureau.

The room was dark and I promptly made it darker, drawing heavy curtains over the windows, as if to secure our encounter against prying eyes.

He settled onto the bed and lit a cigarette. I sat on the edge of the bed, staring at his reflection in the mirror, pitching forward and resting my arms on my knees. A single weak bulb illuminated his drawn face amid a puff of smoke from his Marlboro.

It was late and his eyes were like seawater beneath layers of white ice. A connoisseur of character, sniffing out pretension and falseness, vanity and fraud with the pertinacity of a police dog, I knew, despite the eyes, I had nothing to fear from his boy. I leaned back on the bed, between his outstretched legs. "Why don't you make yourself more comfortable," I advised, tugging his worn tennis shoes from his feet.

Earlier that night, I found myself back at Vinoy Park again. I had stayed away for weeks but it's always a lost cause. There is something in me that simply must search, keep on searching until I find something. Most of the time, I will leave the bar or the street or the park content that there are still boys to be bought, buyers buying.
But now my prohibition was that I wouldn't pick him up unless I could beat him up.
And on this night there was this boy, my type, fragile-looking, blond, perfect buns, walking southward, out of the park. I slowed the car. He turned and smiled. I stopped.
"Lookin' for somethin'?" he asked, his smile beguiling.
"Could be," I teased.

As he snuffed out his cigarette, I moved up on the bed, next to him and soon he settled into the crook of my arm. I kissed the top of his head. He looked up into my face. Suddenly his face was so youthful, so innocent, so trusting, I choked. He reminded me not of Tracy but of a 16-year-old my friend Jack, wishing to cheer me up, had sent me shortly after Tracy left. I had found the youth very attractive but, after drinks and dinner, when he had undressed and was laying on the bed expecting me to have my way with him, I shivered. I couldn't do it. There were no rough edges. There didn't appear to be a chip on his shoulder waiting to be knocked off. I knew he was hardly a virgin. Jack, although he hadn't sent the boy out on any calls, had slept with him and wanted to share him with me, as he did all of the newcomers that came to him. The boy went down on me but I couldn't keep it up. I told him I was too drunk to do anything and turned out the light. The next day I made arrangements for him to fly back to where he had come from.
I kissed this new boy and murmured, "Just let me hold you." I suddenly felt like a demonic presence in this youngster's life.
"I'm afraid I won't be able to do anything."
"Okay, but I still want my money."
"You'll get it. But I'm worried. You sound so desperate."
"Man, a couple of the guys at the park made me give 'em all my money last night. They said I had to pay or I couldn't work there."

"Does that go on a lot?"

"No. It's just the AIDS guys."

"The AIDS guys?"

"Yeah, a couple of 'em have it and they threaten you with it, they say if you don't pay them they'll fuck you and you'll be done for."

"God." The disease, I realized, had become the ultimate serial killer.

"God had nothin' to do with it, man."

"How old are you anyway?"

"Sixteen. That's why I can't get a job. This is all I can do. At least it's warm here. It was cold in Detroit."

"I'm from Cleveland. I know how cold cold can be."

He sat on the edge of the bed and pulled on his tennis shoes. "Will you drive me back to the park?"

"Sure. But I'd rather drive you to the bus station and buy you a ticket back to Detroit."

"That wouldn't do any good. My mom's still with her boyfriend. He tried to kill me the night I left. I can't go back."

"Just back to the park."

"Yeah, just take me back to the park."

*

As we passed the Vinoy Hotel, he saw them.

"There's the AIDS guys, waiting for me," he cried. "Don't drop me here, take me to the Pier."

I looked at the boys as we passed them; they looked just like any other hustlers. And I realized that was the whole point: You never know.

Afterword

I came away from writing this book with the overwhelming affirmation that the anarchic force of the pursuit of eros continues to sweep the world, as strong as ever, if not stronger. No one is immune and it can often lead us into the company of the desperate, a land where very excessive emotions are the rule, emotions that could be triggered by a mere trifle, a word, a gesture, an inflection. In a moment of emotional short-circuit, violence can occur. Sometimes, as we have seen, that violence begets death.

"What's it like to spend days pondering murder?" my editor asked me.

"Well, some mystery writers have said it lets them live out fantasies they've had all their lives. I never had such fantasies. Not me, I'm strictly vanilla."

"Yeah," he chuckled, "vanilla with butterscotch sauce."

"Sauced, mostly. No, it's a lot of work for me to try to figure these things out. It's a puzzle, endlessly fascinating."

"There seems to always have been a fascination about murder."

"No, it's not necessarily a fascination with murder, it's a fascination with power. And with justice. And justice is never served."

To those drawn to compulsive sex, the power game is a lifetime pattern. Violence is part of the power. You see people close up and in trouble; you don't have to wait to see what's motivating them because they're in serious conflict, in a violent situation. Psychiatrists tell us practically anybody could be a murderer, that's what's so scary about it. But it's the why that always interests me. But sometimes I had to put the stories away, so painful it was to think about these boys and how they affected the life of people I knew.

But I was able to carry on because I felt great empathy with these boys and their johns. I understood what it meant to be an outsider. I had the peculiar loneliness of a child with artistic longings, haunted by the feelings of being different than other boys. Eventually, when I retired to write full-time, I turned my infatuation with nefarious sex into a cottage industry and before long it seemed the erotic stories oozed off the pages. But of all my books, this was the hardest to write because it was the closest to home.

Having gone to Florida, the Sunshine State, in my quasi-retirement, I expected paradise. Instead, I soon learned what a terrible place Florida is. In many respects it is an oasis of culture and intellect. It has the longest coastline of any state, with some of the most beautiful beaches in the world. And, perhaps because of these attractions, it also has an abundance of exposed skin, flaunted sex. Oceans of sex. Sex that is, for the most part, untouchable. The frustration can drive men mad. They are afraid to touch anything. As sex educator Steve Brown asserted, "People suffer more from touch deprivation than sexual dysfunction." Men naturally seek outlets to cure this deprivation. But Florida is a state where practically everything is illegal or immoral, populated by millions of seeming sexual illiterates. Therefore, whatever one wants to do becomes more attractive than it would necessarily appear to be if everything was free. This breeds crime.

Starting at the bottom, literally, is Miami. In 1940, J. Edgar Hoover characterized it as "a mecca for criminals, gangsters, racketeers and federal fugitives from justice during the winter season because of the facility of concealing true identification and because of the wide open manner in which illegal enterprises are operated." Dade County still tops the state's crime statistics. The gambling, prostitution and lewd dancing Hoover decried have been replaced by murder, rape, robbery, and drug trafficking as the crimes that most plague law enforcement officers. And these days, crime doesn't come just for the season; it hangs around all year.

It hangs around in every city in the state and much of it is committed by juveniles. According to the latest statistics available, delinquents under 18 were charged with more violent crimes in Florida at a rate of 45% above the national average.

"The explosion of insidious drugs among our youth has resulted in more violent, repeat juvenile offenders than ever before," lamented HRS Secretary Gregory Coler.

"When I first started as a prosecutor," Danny Dawson of Orlando said, "kids committed crimes to kill time on a slow night. Now we see kids living on their own, supporting themselves with crime."

The experts base their knowledge on bare statistics; the reality of it is even more harrowing. Gay people don't report crimes against them, even murder, for fear of harassment. And gay men are easy prey to juvenile criminals. In order to feed their drug habits, the young seek out gays. This is not child abuse. We're talking about seduction, of one by another. Consenting adults is the term most often used. However, when is a child considered an adult? When does a boy become a man? Early on, in sex, boys become aggressive, leading, not being led.

So there are no victims and victimizers. But often, as we have seen, something goes wrong. Evil is the bad elevated to the status of the inexplicable.

Bad we can forgive, evil we cannot understand and can never forgive. Good and evil exist in everybody. It's when evil crosses the line and commits itself and hardens its heart, then it becomes merciless, relentless. Evil is charismatic. It has to do with power and conquest and dominance. Evil has a perverse fascination that good somehow lacks. Evil is entertaining. Good has a way of boring people.

But who shall bear the stain of responsibility here? Men go with other men, often much younger than themselves, expecting a high, not death. But drugs act like Visigoths on the brain, destroying the civilization there, including the most powerful of human instincts, love. Love turns to hate, hate to death.

And who shares the blame? The dealer who sold the drugs? The kingpins who brought it in? The peasants who grow it? The kids who buy it and use it? The johns who supply the money for them to buy it? No, I blame the society that makes it necessary for men to be put in the position of having to seek sex in such a sordid manner. I would decriminalize prostitution, to end the street sweeps and humiliations associated with illegality. One night I had the occasion to meet a young man named Mark who when asked what he did for a living replied, "I'm in the meat department at the Carousel Club (a gay bar in Tampa)." He didn't feel he was a hustler. He felt he was providing a needed service, and my experience with him was delightful, worth the $50 he asked. He was totally comfortable in what he called his "bisexuality" and gave terrific head. Countless experiences like that, many related in this book, have taught me that prostitution can really be regarded as an opportunity for young men to be strong, foster their individuality, take pride in their sexuality, whatever it might be, bartering for a better life.

Granted there are those who say that to be a prostitute means repeatedly submitting oneself to the sexual demands of strangers whom they would not otherwise choose, necessitating that the mind be alienated from the body. I would disagree with that, having had many a young man say to me, "I don't do this," or that, or the other thing. They are free to choose and many have chosen not to go with me at all. And legalization would make them all the more free. It would jeopardize those who are just available for sex and reward those who are good at it. Some have seen my unappealing qualities as a challenge to their talents as a sex provider and I have justly rewarded them. One of my favorite lays, the late porn star Casey Donovan, star of "Boys in the Sand," told me: "My attitude is: to give, if not the best, at least the nicest sexual experience the client has ever had." One of Casey's most endearing qualities was his honesty. He loved New York and rarely went to LA. He regularly ran an ad in The Advocate, offering his services. His price was competitive, not exalted because of his "star" status, and he was one of the most popular hustlers of all time. "I only wish I'd done it ten years earlier, at the height of the 'Boys' thing! I could've bought four guest houses in Key West instead of just one." He succeeded because really cared about his clients. He always liked older men so that part didn't bother him. Ten years after I fell in lust with him after seeing "Boys in the Sand," I finally met him and he impressed me more as a friend than a sex object. I got so wrapped up asking questions about his various film escapades, I lost interest in taking him to bed. But he was, after all, a hustler, and he wanted me to have my money's worth, so he quickly got me back in the mood. He was the genuine article, a hypersexed golden boy who took advantage of his opportunities.

Don't get me wrong, decriminalization is not a panacea for the crimes written about here. Sociopaths would still exist. They would still seek to vent their rage on the unsuspecting. Even the most charming and enticingly wrapped package may turn out to be a time bomb waiting to explode. Consider this a warning: in this very dangerous world, use your sixth sense.

Update

This book was intended to be an "alternative" work, meant to destroy the books next to it on the shelf. Many stores both here and abroad refused to carry it, fearing Helms and his ilk. But radical messages are increasing in appeal and the first edition of the book quickly sold out. This was pleasing to me but even more gratifying was the response from readers world-wide. A man in Ohio, for instance, wrote to say he had nightmares after reading about what happened to John Wolf. I didn't intend to disrupt anyone's sleep, just make readers aware of the chances we take when we seek the comfort of strangers.

Perhaps the rant is the most appropriate literary form of our time. My rantings and ravings in this book are based on no other criteria than my queer and virulent perception of the real and other peoples' denial of reality. I ask you to consider them hypotheses and test them for yourself.

This second edition enables me to update you on the last case in this book, the story of the seductive stripper I knew simply as "Gene."

While he was awaiting trial for his various murders, Henry Eugene Hodges gave several interviews to TV reporters and admitted killing at least eight men who picked him up for sex. He told his audience he had no remorse for his acts.

In late 1991, in Georgia, he received a life sentence for strangling 33-year-old Michael Whisnant, of North Carolina, to death while they were both visiting Atlanta. In one of his interviews, Gene characterized the murder as "an impulsive decision to kill another homosexual" as he and his 15-year-old girlfriend Tina Brown were on their way through Atlanta to Florida.

By early 1992, Hodges was back in Tennessee to stand trial for his admitted murder and robbery of Ronald Bassett, 37, on May 14, 1990, when they met in Centennial Park and Bassett took him to his nearby apartment for sex.

During this trial, Hodges' attorney Donald Dawson attempted to prove that Gene's troubled childhood, combined with his tangled relationship with Tina, whom he described as a jealous girlfriend, lessened the blame he should carry.

Dawson said that by the time Hodges met Tina in the spring of 1989, he was already "traumatized" and "dysfunctional," as a result of a childhood rape he had never reported. Hodges' father, a truck driver, remained married to another woman throughout his 18-year relationship with Hodges' mother, who struggled to raise her five sons with little help from their two fathers. His mother testified that Hodges began sniffing glue and gasoline, running away from home and joining older boys in delinquent acts. He was hospitalized several times for drug abuse and, at 17, was sent to prison for armed robbery and attempted kidnapping.

By the time he was released on parole in 1988, Hodges had developed into quite a hunk. He lifted weights while he was doing time and found that he could make easy money stripping in gay bars. This led to his tricking with customers and then to his working the streets in Nashville.

Hodges told Dr. Barry Nurcombe, a professor of child psychiatry at Vanderbilt University, that he was not sexually attracted to the men who picked him up but he felt uncomfortable around women. Tina Brown, then 14, was the first girl who had ever showed any interest in him and he was as jealous of her as she was of him, thinking that if he worked a "normal" job during the day, she would cheat on him with other men. Brown testified that she was strongly opposed to Hodges' working as a prostitute and she sometimes taunted him by calling him a "faggot."

Early in 1990, Hodges was devastated when Brown told his sister-in-law about his homosexual activities. The girl went so far as to say that she wanted any man who touched Hodges to be killed. His girlfriend's snitching led Gene's confrontation with his older brother, a construction worker, who was providing Hodges and Brown a place to stay. The doctor theorized this argument prompted Hodges' need to prove his masculinity and "he went out and robbed and killed the first homosexual he was able to pick up." Tina testified that she followed Gene to Bassett's apartment after Hodges had met him in the park. When Gene let her in the apartment, he had already handcuffed Bassett in his bedroom and was looting the place. She said that before they left the apartment, she stood at the bedroom door and listened as Hodges forced Bassett to give him his bank teller card code and then slowly strangled him to death. When Hodges told her the deed was done, she went into the bedroom and told the corpse how much she hated him. Nurcombe felt Hodges' murder of Bassett was somehow a "re-enactment" of Hodges' own alleged rape by a male stranger when he was only 11 years old.

But prosecutors characterized all of Nurcombe's testimony as "psycho babble." They described Hodges as an anti-social man in full control of his faculties who killed for both the money and the thrill of it, contending that he robbed and killed gay men to finance his scheme to become a drug dealer in Florida. As for the slow strangulation, prosecutors claimed Gene was fascinated "to watch someone die." They also had serious doubts that Hodges was ever actually molested as a youth.

The jury deliberated for less than two hours before sentencing Hodges to death.

When the verdict was announced, Gene simply smiled.

Tina Brown told reporters she still loved Gene and wanted to marry him some day.

District Attorney General Tom Thurman said, "I think clearly the proof is there. The jury obviously rejected the 'post-traumatic stress' defense."

To the end, Bassett's parents denied their son was a homosexual and were offended by defense attorneys' attempts to lay some of the blame on him. The mother said it was hard for her to maintain her silence during the trial: "We could not defend our son in any way, and that was the toughest thing." She said she would have liked to have told the jury "what a nice person my son was." Bassett, a divorcee, had worked at South Central Bell since 1973, and, his mother said he "helped everybody. Anybody who asked him for a place to stay, he'd say, 'Sure.' That's probably why he was killed."

Bassett's father, Paul, a Memphis shoe distributor, had the last word. As he left the courtroom after the judge ordered the execution, he said that Henry Eugene Hodges "got what he deserved."

ABOUT THE AUTHOR

The author with video star Adam Hart in 1994.

John Patrick is a prolific, prize-winning author of fiction and non-fiction. One of his short stories, "The Well," was honored by PEN American Center as one of the best of 1987. The author's acclaimed romans a´ clef, including "Angel: The Complete Quintet" and "Billy & David: A Deadly Minuet," have now been collected into a single volume. His novels as well as his non-fiction works, including "Tarnished Angels" and "The Best of the Superstars" series, continue to gain him new fans every day. Mr. Patrick is currently at work on the anthologies "Dangerous Boys" and "Runaways/Kid Stuff."

A divorced father of two, the author is a longtime member of the American Booksellers Association, the Florida Publishers' Association, American Civil Liberties Union, and the Adult Video Association. He resides in Florida.